SHARP SPEAR
CRYSTAL MIRROR

SHARP SPEAR CREATED MIRROR

SHARP SPEAR
CRYSTAL MIRROR

Martial Arts in Women's Lives

Stephanie T. Hoppe

Park Street Press
Rochester, Vermont

To the women who went before me and those who will come after

Park Street Press
One Park Street
Rochester, Vermont 05767
www.gotoit.com

Library of Congress Cataloging-in-Publication Data
Hoppe, Stephanie T.
    Sharp spear, crystal mirror : martial arts in women's lives / Stephanie T. Hoppe.
        p.   cm.
    ISBN 0-89281-662-7 (pbk. : alk. paper)
    1. Self-defense for women. 2. Martial arts. 3. Women martial artists. I. Title.
GV1111.5.H66 1998   97-49302
796.8'082—dc21   CIP

Printed and bound in Canada

10 9 8 7 6 5 4 3 2 1

Frontispiece: Kendoists Malyne Chiu (left) and Alyne Hazard sparring on a Northern California beach, ca. 1993. *(Photo: Tom McGinley)*
The chapter opening graphic is based on a photograph by Steve Price of Miyako Tanaka and Malyne Chiu sparring with naginata (Venice Beach, Calif., ca. 1982)
All photographs by Stephanie T. Hoppe unless otherwise credited

Text design and layout by Kristin Camp
This book was typeset in Life with Stone Sans as the display typeface

Park Street Press is a division of Inner Traditions International

Distributed to the book trade in Canada by Publishers Group West (PGW), Toronto
Distributed to the book trade in the United Kingdom by Deep Books, London
Distributed to the book trade in Australia by Gemcraft Books, Burwood
Distributed to the book trade in New Zealand by Tandem Press, Auckland
Distributed to the book trade in South Africa by Alternative Books, Ferndale

CONTENTS

Acknowledgments

A book like this exists only through the participation of those who appear in its pages. I am grateful to all the women I interviewed for the generosity and enthusiasm with which they encouraged me in this project and for the way they shared their lives, thoughts, and teaching. They have enriched my life well beyond this book. Many others who do not appear in the book—and may not even know the impact they had on me—also contributed to the book, and I thank them as well.

I owe particular thanks for introductions, suggestions, and support to Theresa Corrigan, Michelle Dwyer, and Gayle Fillman. Gayle also supplied the title for the book, which is derived from a Shinto purification chant, or *misogi,* taught to her by Shinichi Suzuki Sensei. Theresa tirelessly read, reread, and commented on drafts. She, as well as Michelle Dwyer, Coleen Gragen, Bruce Hopkins, Saskia Kleinert, David Novogrodsky, and Karen Sherr, provided food and shelter during my travels for this book and participated in many helpful discussions about what I was doing.

For assistance with the Japanese language and other things Japanese, as well as much good companionship, I thank Machiko Shimada. For help with Chinese translations, I am indebted to Ron Epstein. Roger Franklin spent many hours in his darkroom magically manufacturing clear prints from whatever I supplied in the way of old snapshots and poorly exposed negatives. Margaret Emerson drew the yin–yang figure of intertwined fish (chapter 7), a welcome representation in the book of the close friendship that has developed from our joint practice and talk about T'ai Chi Ch'uan. If Margy had not just written her own book answering all the questions I would have asked her, I hope she would have consented to have been interviewed here.

The knowledge, skill, dedication, and love of many teachers—including all the women who appear in the book—have shaped my understanding of martial arts and expanded my idea of my own abilities. I thank especially, in chronological order of the important lessons they taught me at critical points as my work on the book unfolded, Janet Seaforth, Gayle Fillman, Michelle Dwyer, Nam Singh, Jeanne Wetzel Adams, Jane Golden, Wen Mei Yu, Margaret Emerson, Carl Carlson, Sam Edwards, Arthur Goodridge, Willem de Thouars, and Wasentha Young. I am grateful also to my T'ai Chi sisters and other training partners in Ukiah, especially Judy Albert, Steve Buck, and Mark Gordon.

I am also grateful to the people at Inner Traditions International who believed in this book and worked to make it a reality, especially Jon Graham, Rowan Jacobsen, Christine Sumner, and Kristin Camp. Emily Bower, herself a martial artist, wielded her copyediting pencil with grace and precision.

Always and above all, I thank Frank Broadhead, first reader, training partner, and beloved companion in every endeavor.

Hefting the Spear
That Has Been Offered to Me

In 1988, at the age of forty, I began the study of T'ai Chi Ch'uan. For more than ten years I had lived with chronic back pain, caused, doctors told me, by a degenerated disk in my spine. Distrusting the surgery they recommended, I looked for alternative treatments. A chiropractor helped me considerably. She was also the one who suggested regular physical exercise, such as swimming or bicycling. Over the years I took up—and grew bored with—jogging, swimming, race walking, and several varieties of yoga. Then a friend suggested T'ai Chi Ch'uan. A teacher was available in the town where I lived, and I signed up.

T'ai Chi Ch'uan turned out to be completely different from anything I had ever done before. My back pain disappeared within weeks—due, I believe, to my learning to stand and move with the strong bones of my hips and legs properly aligned to take the weight of my body and leave my spine and upper body loose and relaxed. But once I was free of pain my interest in T'ai Chi Ch'uan only grew. From the start my daily training was no chore but a treat I looked forward to.

As time passed I noticed that the calm, open, relaxed manner of holding myself that was necessary to execute the movements seemed to spill over into other parts of my life. I felt myself more fully inhabiting my body just working at my desk or walking about. My breath and balance improved, as did my stamina and mental focus. I danced more gracefully and enjoyed it more. One day I realized much of my fear of heights, crowds, and public speaking had dissipated. I found in myself a new

1

clarity about what things matter to me and a growing ability to keep from being distracted from them. I took on public responsibilities in my community that I would have shrunk from a few years earlier. Of course T'ai Chi Ch'uan was not the only influence in my life, but each change I observed seemed to be associated with an increase in the ability to be fully, physically present in the body and mentally in the moment.

So far so good. But other changes were not so welcome. Fiction writing had formed the core of my daily schedule and self-identity for nearly a decade. But my fictional imaginings paled before the immediacy and physicality of my new physical practice. I had avoided reading and writing and even talking about T'ai Chi Ch'uan, lest in capturing the surface of my experience in words I might be cut off from searching depths where words become unreliable. Now I found I could scarcely read or write at all.

I also came up against the realization that T'ai Chi Ch'uan is a martial art. Many people had told me so, but I assumed they spoke metaphorically or with reference to origins of which the practice had long since been sanitized. And T'ai Chi Ch'uan *is* often taught as a moving meditation and health exercise. This was my own teacher's emphasis, although she also showed us fighting applications of the moves and introduced us to sparring. Then one day while I was watching a movie on TV, a fight sequence came on the screen. Ordinarily I tuned such things out, but for once I actually looked at what was going on and was startled to discover that I could follow the interaction. I could discern, too, that parts of the fight were staged with complete disregard for what would happen in reality. I could do better, I almost said aloud. I stopped myself in dismay.

I had always thought of myself as nonviolent—without, perhaps, closely examining what I meant.

It distressed me to think that the capacities and skills I was acquiring might be very immediately grounded in and designed for fighting. Would I have to take up fighting to further explore and develop my newfound abilities?

At this point, I turned to books to explore the recorded history and philosophy of T'ai Chi Ch'uan, but the information that I gleaned, although often interesting, did not relate directly to my experience or address my concerns. And all of the books were written by men. My practice was bringing me into areas of identity and being that are deeply affected by gender in U.S. society, and I realized I needed to know what *women* could tell me. I soon found that books by or about women in any of the martial arts are few indeed and those I found offered only tantalizing glimpses in brief essays, profiles of pioneering women, or narrowly focused descriptions of technique. I knew by then that throughout history many women have pursued—and excelled in—martial arts, but if I wanted to read a book that explored women's experience in depth, apparently I would have to write it myself. I had fifteen years' experience as a writer, but as a practitioner of T'ai Chi Ch'uan I was very much a beginner, and I did not in the least consider myself a martial artist. I did, however, feel the passionate interest that sustains the writing of a book, and so I began.

I decided early on that the largest part of the book should be interviews. I believed it would be important that the women I talked to speak for themselves, in their own voices, with the particular words and turns of phrase they chose. The experience of martial arts, being so much in the body and in the moment, extends far deeper and wider than can be captured by the intellect or in words. Such experience might still be shared, I reasoned, if I recorded the patterns and subtle shifts of speech that reflect individual history and character as underpinning to the words themselves. The art I knew most about, T'ai Chi Ch'uan, is often spoken of as the origin of most of the other arts and in itself, of course, encompasses a vast history and experience that it would take many books to cover. Yet I was curious to also look beyond T'ai Chi Ch'uan to what different perspectives other martial arts might foster and how women who studied them might illuminate the significance of fighting arts for women in general.

People told me I must travel all over the United States and perhaps abroad to seek out women who excelled in the different arts—I must talk to the women who were the best, the stars. Clearly I lacked the expertise to judge such accomplishments; nor did I have the interest. For one thing, I wanted to explore some of the stages of development as well as the effects of a lifetime in martial arts. And although many of the women I talked to have national, even international, stature as practitioners and teachers of martial arts, what I came to find most interesting and most relevant to my own life and practice in all of the women was their persistence, dedication, and commitment to training—how these qualities arose and how they played out over the years and decades. What sort of people were these women? Why did they begin training? What motivated them to persist? What meaning did their practice have for them? What did *they* feel they had achieved?

In T'ai Chi Ch'uan and other martial arts derived from China both men and women teachers are called *sifu,* which is generally translated as "teacher–father." (I'm told that only one of the two Chinese characters commonly used for sifu refers to "father," the other being gender neutral, but my teacher and some other women prefer *simu,* for "teacher–mother.") In Japanese, I was soon to learn, the equivalent term is *sensei,* meaning "one who goes before." In that one word I found my purpose encapsulated: to discover from women who had gone before me what might lie ahead for me. The first step also lay clear before me: to interview my first teacher of T'ai Chi Ch'uan, the woman who is my simu, Janet Seaforth.

As it turned out, when I finished this and each subsequent interview, my next step opened in front of me. Each interview raised as well as answered questions, and as my interests developed and shifted, always someone told me about a woman whose experience was precisely what I was then ready to inquire into. I was happy to find that we have gone well beyond the pioneering generation of women in martial arts, for I found enough women living or visiting within easy reach of my home in Northern California to fill many volumes. That many of the women I met already knew each other or had worked together adds a dimension of community to the book that underscores a value important to all women in the martial arts.

CHAPTER 1

Taking Responsibility for Ourselves

Sometimes only three or four of us show up, but other times as many as a dozen gather on Sunday mornings in a certain grove of tall pines and Douglas fir trees in a city park in the small town of Ukiah in the mountains of Northern California. All women, we range in age from early thirties to sixties. We are varied in our backgrounds, families, and work lives, among us lawyers, therapists, artists, mothers and other caregivers, bodyworkers, carpenters, and teachers. We begin with talk, a mix of personal news and politics, which we continue even after Janet Seaforth, our simu, calls us to form a circle. But as she talks us through warm-ups and stretches we fall silent, giving ourselves over to her voice and coming into a deeper synchrony with each other. When Janet feels we are ready, she assigns us places and softly speaks a ritual phrase of beginning. As one we raise our hands in front of us, right hand fisted in a warrior's gesture, left hand open like a book—the scholar's palm. Covering the fist with the open palm, we bow to the north, direction of Earth, of darkness, of the unknown. In silence we breathe, in, out. This opening breath encapsulates the entire form, Janet has told us: The end goal of all our practice is to stand silent and motionless, fully present in whatever the situation may be, ready to accomplish anything we need to do as smoothly and effortlessly as the breath moving in and out of our bodies.

As we proceed with the form Janet has taught us, our movements uncoil as softly, evenly, and inexorably as our breath. Each movement, rooted in the feet, rises through the legs, is distributed by the waist, and becomes manifest in the arms, hands, and fingers. We place a foot, then slowly transfer all our weight to that foot, picking up the other foot only when it is devoid of weight. In this way of moving our weight remains low to the ground and stable, modulated through our center of gravity; it is called the *tan t'ien* in Chinese, meaning "cinnabar field," an alchemical reference to the region of energy storage in the lower belly, just below the navel, corresponding to the second chakra. If we move correctly, at each increment of change we remain balanced, our options always open to move in a different direction. Brushing the left knee with the back of the left hand, we slowly shift forward onto the left foot and unwind the left hand in a smooth spiral. This movement is called Grasp Sparrow's Tail. Curving our right foot to the shape of a blade, we sweep it forward. Arms unfold, one up, one down, and we lift the left knee into the space we open between our arms: Golden Pheasant Rises on One Leg. We pivot to the left, facing south, and spread our arms wide: Reeling Silk. One by one, the one hundred and eight movements of the Dragon Tiger Mountain form of T'ai Chi Ch'uan unfold.

Most of Janet's classes are for women only, reflecting her belief that women need the context and support of a community of other women to freely and fully explore and develop our capacities. The timing and location of class on Sundays in a public park is not accidental—Janet means for us to proclaim by our presence that our activity has both public and spiritual meaning. In her teaching she emphasizes the esoteric and spiritual aspects of T'ai Chi Ch'uan. She relates the movements in the form to the compass directions of geography and the alignment of the larger cosmos and encourages each of us to claim T'ai Chi Ch'uan for our own, fitting it to our limbs and our lives to shape a practice that serves our needs.

I first interviewed Janet in January 1991, before I ever thought of writing this book. The Persian Gulf War was raging, heightening the urgency of my questions about how she weaves together all the different strands of her life that enter into—and come out of—her practice and teaching of T'ai Chi Ch'uan. I remember how dark and cold it was that winter day, a storm moving in from the ocean. We sat at a small table in the warm refuge of Janet's cabin, which started out as a freight container. Janet has lived in that cabin since the late 1970s, initially without electricity or running water, homesteading twenty acres of Mendocino hill country: working at ceramic sculpture and raising fruit, vegetables, rabbits, goats, and a daughter. In my mind's eye I see her reach across the width of the cabin without moving from her chair to take the kettle off the woodstove that was warming us. A small, slender woman in her forties, she looks resilient, her hands strong from years of working at her potter's wheel and on the land. She poured the water for tea and looked up at me with her large hazel eyes, which are set a little aslant, catlike.

JANET SEAFORTH

T'ai Chi Ch'uan

I gave T'ai Chi to myself for my thirtieth birthday, but actually I had seen it a few years before. It came about through forming the Sonoma Women's Center, in Sonoma, California—in 1974

I think it was. We had this new consciousness and we wanted to understand what women were. We wanted to create a place for women with child care and good meals where we could lounge around and talk about our wonderful ideas and our creativity. What it turned out to be was people would come over to the house on Sundays and everybody would bring something and I'd make a big pot of stew. Eventually someone gave us the front room of their house, so we had an office, but for a year or so it was just open house on Sundays, where any woman could come. We'd sit around and philosophize—and get drunk and stoned. Or dance all night.

A woman called us, whose name was Samantha, and she told us about this gang of bikers in the county that had raped numerous women. She would tell us about the atrocities that had happened to these women, and I thought she was crazy. I didn't believe her. I didn't want to believe her. I was like the typical woman, who when a woman turns to you and tells you about her abuse, you don't believe her. That's the first reaction. It was in those days, anyway.

But we checked it out, and sure enough, these guys had done just gross, horrible things. They'd get the women drunk or slip them drugs and put them in some room and the men would just go in one at a time or a bunch of them at a time and rape them. For days. They had taken pictures of the atrocious acts they'd done to these women and had blackmailed the women. The women would come out total basket cases. Sometimes they would be dumped naked in the ditch on the way out of town. Some of them might have been killed, was what Samantha said.

These guys had gotten off time and time again, because they were very middle class, part of the community. One of them had been our postman. That was what was so mind blowing, that they looked real straight during the week, and on the weekends they'd turn into monsters. Just having a good time! But several of the women had filed charges. They'd been blackmailed, they were afraid for their lives, but they finally got the courage to press charges, and some of the these men might actually come to trial.

There hadn't been a rape conviction for something like twenty years in Sonoma County. Women were getting raped all the time, but it was invisible. We marched in front of the district attorney's office with the women from the Sonoma Women's Center and demanded that this be called rape and that these men be charged with rape and not some little misdemeanor kind of thing. The D.A. didn't want to. It had never been done. Channel 7 was there from San Francisco because we made such a fuss.

And the guys were charged and tried?

Yes. And then we went there for the trial, too, to help support the women. We got three of the five guys convicted. Maybe they went to jail for a year. It opened my eyes to realize that if rape was going to be stopped, women were going to have to stop it. And that we were going to have to learn how to protect ourselves to do that, because men were not going to protect us. You cannot depend on men to protect you from rapists. It just hasn't worked.

So I knew I was going to have to learn some kind of self-defense. But I'd always been the good Christian girl. Growing up in a fundamentalist Christian house, I was taught to turn the other cheek and not want to ever hurt anybody. The idea of fighting is abhorrent to me. I hated Karate, that kind of self-defense work.

Then at the Women's Country Festival in 1974,

up here in Mendocino County at the Woodlands, I saw these women doing this T'ai Chi form together. I was transfixed. It was so beautiful. It was love at first sight—"What are they doing? What kind of dance is that?" They said, "That's also a martial art," and I said, "That's the one for me!" It took me two years to find a teacher. I didn't start T'ai Chi until 1976. My mother died in January, I started T'ai Chi in June, and we bought this land in July, so that was an incredible year for me. It was almost like my mother's death gave me the freedom to be able to explore other things. She was such a good Christian that even T'ai Chi I think would have been a disturbance for her. Oriental studies—too far afield for her. Too frightening.

The other thing that got me into T'ai Chi was that when I was sculpting, I would work for hours and hours and become crippled with being in one place. I would be so immersed in my work that I wouldn't realize I hadn't moved my body. I could hardly get up when I finally went to get up. I knew I needed some kind of exercise, so T'ai Chi was great for that too. But at the end of my working day I would be so exhausted, I would think, "I've got to go to T'ai Chi class and I just don't know how I am going to make it. I'm just dragging around. I can't do this." But then, when I would go, I would have all this renewed energy. It was terrific.

Not only did T'ai Chi help my body, but I realized it helped my mind. I was going through a lot of identity crisis kinds of things when I first started doing T'ai Chi—along with realizing the oppression of women, which was devastating for me. I didn't want to believe that. I didn't want to believe I was oppressed. I hated it! I absolutely hated it!

Hated having to deal with it, you mean? To face the fact of it?

All of it! I had made up my nice little storybook world. I had believed men would take care of me. Most of my friends had been men. I didn't like women that much. I got along much better with the men. They never oppressed *me.* They always liked me. I was one of those! I didn't see that I had ever been sexually oppressed. Now, looking back, I realize, of course I was. But at that time it was, "This is my choice. I love to wear these little high heels and this little short skirt." And freeze my legs off in these little sparkly nylons or whatever, right? My identity was shattered when I couldn't work my marriage. I didn't know who I was. I became invisible. And maybe that was a time that I needed to go through too. It was like a cocoon time in my life when I needed to withdraw and—and become another person. Because the old one didn't work.

So all through those years I was going through a big identity crisis and very depressed about it. Because I didn't want to go through what it took. It was too much work! But when I would go do T'ai Chi, it would give me faith, it would give me hope—even if it was just the oxygen going to my brain and helping me expand and think more clearly. Because when you sit in one place, your circulation doesn't work as well, and you do tend to get depressed. So when you get out and move, it opens up your brain a little better, and you can sometimes make those connections that are just not quite there unless you have that extra impetus of the oxygen creating the right chemistry.

I transferred a lot of my energies. I used to love to dance, and a lot of it was sexual ploy. Again, it's what we're trained to be as women. Your position is in relation to the man and your most powerful weapon is how attractive you are. That's the most important thing to most women even now—let's build up the body, not to be healthy but so we can be attractive! *[Laughs]* So we can be important. So we can be somebody. So we can have position and power. It ruins your sexuality. Your real sexuality gets totally perverted. It's so sad. You miss out on really knowing your own real energy and being appropriate and honest with it. I transferred that into T'ai Chi, which helps me use that energy for myself. Feeding myself. Nurturing myself. It's not sexual, it's spiritual. That was a real transformation. The identity changes I've gone through have made me understand that transformation does exist. When I learned that I could change what had been a false sexual power into a healthy thing for myself, that was great, that was really great!

So on all levels I realized T'ai Chi was great for me. Physically, spiritually, mentally—everything. I wanted more and more of it. I got involved with the temple and kind of followed my sifu around. I felt like a puppy dog, following him around. Nam Singh was beautiful to watch. Incredibly graceful. He went about his general day-to-day with such beauty and grace. I wanted to be like him. I wanted my life to be like that. I've always been a little high-strung and rush-around-and-get-it-done. He got it done, but it was in a very easy, continuous, T'ai Chi type way. I hung out with him as much as I could. Whether it was to carry his bags or whatever I needed to do to be able to be with him. I did several retreats with him where he was the teacher and I would be his assistant.

It was another world that Nam Singh showed me. We came up to the City of Ten Thousand Buddhas in Talmage, here in Mendocino County, when the big Kuan Yin was dedicated. That sea of people, that huge statue—that was an incredible experience. And going into Chinatown in San Francisco to the temples there—totally another world. Nam Singh introduced me to Kuan Yin, who is the goddess of fearless compassion. It was really nice to have a woman deity in my life. I have always had Jesus Christ, you know, as the savior, so it was nice to have a complement to that and have a feminine energy in there. It was very personal and appealed to my womanliness, that woman part of me that I could never share in the Christian church.

So even though it terrified me, because I was, again, raised with this Christian mother, I had to accept it as, "This is what works." You know? That's kind of a standard for my life: Does it work? And if it works, then I have to appreciate it.

Fairly early on you also started teaching T'ai Chi?

We moved onto the land here, but I continued to go down to Sonoma and take T'ai Chi lessons two days a week with my sifu and stay at the temple. I would take the Wednesday night class and the Thursday morning class and then I would come home here. I would be gone twenty-four hours from the farm, but I would get two T'ai Chi classes and also some extra studies around the temple with my sifu. I did that for about a year. In 1978—the Year of the Horse—I had my T'ai Chi graduation, and so from then I could teach.

I did my student teaching with my sifu. He had us teach. Even before I knew the form, he would have us teach what we knew. And it worked. It was another level of learning and, I guess, an important way to learn. We learn on so many different levels. I was glad that my teacher had enough confidence to do it that way. Some teachers won't let you do that. It's one of those guarded secrets. We're so busy guarding our creativity or guarding these secrets, whether it's art or T'ai Chi or whatever—I think it's a real shame. So much gets lost.

Janet Seaforth demonstrating Snake Creeps Down from Dragon Tiger Mountain T'ai Chi (Philo, Calif., June 1995).

Nam Singh never really gave me permission to go out and teach the public. I think I had been teaching the family for about a year or so, and I said, "I'm going to start teaching, I'm going to let other people in the class now." He said, "Are you asking me or telling me?" *[Laughs]* I said, "Well, I guess I'm telling you." He said, "Okay, then."

It helps for me to have a class that I have to go to because I'm the teacher. It keeps my form sharp. And it's a nice camaraderie. I like to study with other people. I find that I especially like to study with women, because they don't take over. When you study with men—even when we had our peace groups, if I wasn't real careful, I felt like the men did take over, even when they tried not to. They can hardly keep from it.

So I enjoy especially my women's classes. I feel there's a real equality there and a real sharing, a real interest in sharing our knowledge with each other. Students discover things about T'ai Chi that I hadn't thought about. By their discoveries they feed me, and then I can pass it on to somebody else. It's one of those inclusive kinds of things that I find really enriching. And I love to do T'ai Chi in a group.

And teaching is something I *can* do. If you find that you have a certain skill in an area, use your talents! Share it! I never want to get to the point where I think I know it all—mine's the best, and it's all mine, and you can't have it. To me it's,

Janet Seaforth demonstrating Pressing Heaven, Pressing Earth (Philo, Calif., June 1995).

And did the T'ai Chi satisfy your need for self-defense? How did it fit as a martial art with your ideas of violence and nonviolence?

My sister just approached me yesterday—we have these discussions about war all the time now—"Janet, when would you use violence?" I said, "When they're coming onto my property." And she said, "Don't you think that's kind of hypocritical, where you're going to help yourself, but you're not going to help your neighbor?" In some cases I probably would help my neighbor too. I was part of the nonviolent antinuclear protests at Diablo Canyon and Livermore, where we sat in the middle of the street and if the cops had clubbed us, we were not going to fight back. It was real Gandhian nonviolence. So I have participated in that form of protest.

You do what you need to do to get your objective dealt with, and you do it with as much integrity and as much peace and love as possible—the core has got to be righteous. I believe it's like tuning in to the true feminine quality. During the rape trial, when I was dealing with possibly having to hurt one of those guys, I went through an immense amount of emotions around it.

let's take it, let's use it, let's share it. I want to experience as much as I can with you of things that are along my path. If they're along my path and they're along your path, let's share paths! It's a joy, it's an incredible joy for me to share with someone—because it's validating for both of us.

By saying possibly hurt one of these guys, you mean you were being personally threat-

ened by the rapists and expected to have to physically defend yourself?

Yes. I had to send my daughter away, I was so afraid. One of the guys used to be our postman, and his daughter was in Bridget's class at school. It was too close to home! I didn't feel safe. These guys and their friends would drive by our house really slowly and stare at us and flip us the bird. They could have done something to us—these guys could be crazy! We kept a loaded gun by the door, which was partly why I didn't want Bridget in the house. I sent Bridget off to her father, which was scary too, because I was admitting that I didn't have a safe home. He could have given me some grief over it, but we worked things out.

My feeling toward these guys when it came down to a gut level was like I was an angry mother, that I needed to shake them into waking up to what proper behavior was about. It was like Jesus when he went into the temple with the whip and cleaned out the money changers. Sometimes, I feel, you have to use violence to wake people up to what's right. I don't mean to come off real self-righteous, but that's how I felt with these guys. It's like they were not trained, they were defective, and if you could just shock them into a wake-up, maybe they had something left there to save. And sometimes I think that there's nothing that you can save in these guys, that you've got to put them away for life. Sometimes it's too terrible. They probably will never get enough conscience to act right.

It comes from this mother, feminine space often. When I really get down there, that's usually where it's coming from. I'm so angry, but it's like they need to be taught, they need to be shown the way to be loving, to be appropriate to their life. Act right and appreciate your life and appreciate what's around you!

I feel we have to do whatever we do until we realize what works and what doesn't work. It's like with the sexual freedom—"Oh, isn't this fun? We can sleep with anybody and are we having fun yet?" *[Laughs]* It wasn't really fun. It wasn't really freedom! Then you get into that whole thing of what discipline is, a structure that actually gives you *more* freedom. I think that's the core there. When these guys are acting out, pushing their weight around—whether it's nationally or personally or whatever, it comes down to, what works? We can beat Iraq to a pulp and yet who really lives there? It's the people, and they are eventually going to win, because they are part of the Earth there, and that's the bottom line. The same is true with what works with energy. I still believe somewhere that love does conquer hatred, because as Dorothy Parker says, hatred's filling but not very nourishing.

Does T'ai Chi give you a means of dealing with these questions?

T'ai Chi is a martial art because the *ch'uan,* the fist, is there, that fist of self-containment that says, I take responsibility for myself. I take responsibility for this body. I honor this body. This is my temple. I'm not going to let it be violated. If invaded, you learn how to protect yourself in the best way that you can. *[Laughs]* Which is usually swiftly and accurately—and then get out of there. So you're eliminating the negative energy. You deflect it or you dissolve it. Whatever. And mostly the best action is no action. Don't confront negative energy—don't go head on with anything. Let it go by. Mostly, negative energy burns itself out.

That makes me think of the movements in the form that are twisting and spiraling, so we're not giving up our space, but adjusting it.

Yes. They talk about deflecting a thousand pounds with four ounces of energy. A thousand pounds can be coming at you, but if you turn slightly and give it just four ounces of deflection you can deflect a thousand pounds. That's true T'ai Chi. It just doesn't deal with the negative energy. It lets it go. But it is that ch'uan respect for your whole body and taking responsibility for your body. And women—so many times we've been taught, you've got to have a man to protect you. Whether it's your big brother or your dad and then it's your husband or whatever. It's so ingrained in us that someone else is going to take care of us, we don't believe we can take care of ourselves. T'ai Chi is really great because it says, you are going to take care of yourself. That's who is going to take care of you. Because we do anyway. It's kind of a rude awakening sometimes when we realize, who's really taking care of us? We are!

I think T'ai Chi and other martial arts create a sense of self-worth on a very, very deep level that a lot of us have given up. Or were never raised with. We're diminished all our life. I think it's important for us to reclaim our power and take responsibility for ourselves. And we can! There's no guarantee you're not going to get raped or killed, but there's no guarantee of that anyway. So the least you can do is fight back and have your life. Do not give up your life for anybody!

In your classes you often say there are three aspects to T'ai Chi: the spiritual and meditative aspect, the health or exercise aspect,

and the self-defense. They're such different categories in Western thought—How do you see them coming together?

Because you do T'ai Chi slowly, because you move in circles, it's very relaxing. That's good for your internal systems—it slows everything down, your nervous system slows down so it's better able to handle all the little messages it's getting from all your organs and whatnot. And when you're breathing deeply, and all your organs are coming into balance with each other, into harmony with each other, that slowness also creates a meditative aspect, so that a peaceful energy can come about. So the physical, health aspect is definitely associated with the meditative aspect—that's one of the finest qualities of the health aspect, that it is done in a meditative way.

Meditation is good for your health, especially when it's done in movement. One of the reasons T'ai Chi was created was because the meditators were dying young because they were sitting so much. T'ai Chi was a moving meditation that would not only be for spiritual enhancement but would also include the body with this relaxed moving in circles, moving in harmony with nature. Moving in imitation of nature too. White Crane Stands on One Leg, Snake Creeps Down, Sparrow Spreads Its Wings—you've got those animal forms in there, that quality of being in harmony, of becoming that animal, that natural phenomenon.

In that sense, it all flows together, because meditation of course then brings the spirit in and good health is associated with that. And the martial aspect—like I said before, it's about taking responsibility for yourself. You take responsibility for your health. You take responsibility for your spirit. If we're creating the place for your spirit to be cultivated, you have to prepare that place, and then the spirit can come talk to you or whatever.

And it changes. You may start off learning T'ai Chi for martial arts. Maybe you've had a rape in your past and you need to feel you can protect yourself, so the main thing you want to learn is how to kill somebody. But you may end up really loving the meditation. Or vice versa. Some people say, "I just want something to meditate with, relax with." And all of a sudden they find out, "Wow! I can protect myself too!"

I was thinking about how I go through the day. First the goats—when you milk in the morning, it's a nice transition place to get into another flow. You can have a lot of tension going on, you can be mad or sad or crying or whatever, and it neutralizes when you go out to milk, because the goats have their own energy. It's almost like the ocean—they absorb whatever energy you happen to be in. They don't negate it, they totally validate it, but it's put in kind of a neutral place. You get in there and you start milking and you realize the world goes on and the daily events go on and it's okay. It levels everything out. You can recreate a new feeling for yourself and go out and get the rest of your work done. It's the same thing that T'ai Chi does for you. It gives you that meditative space to change your mind, to change your energy.

Then I usually do a little studying, if I can, if I have the time. Whatever I'm reading or studying. Write in my daybook, write in my journal. And then either go to my studio, to my own sculptural studio down the hill in my neighbor's basement, or I'm also taking classes one day a week at Mendocino College. I'm taking a *raku* class and a ceramics class there—I'm going through that ceramics program. Working with my hands, with clay, has been a wonderful, wonderful part of my life. It was probably the first thing that diverted me from that normal, average path. I was studying to be a psychologist and then got into nursing. I was going to be a psychiatric nurse. But I didn't

like the system that I saw. I realized I couldn't do it. I didn't have the capacity to jump through the hoops that the professional world wanted me to jump through. I was too much of a—oh, my ideas were too different from the norm.

I was twenty-four when Sue came along and said, "Why don't you be a potter? You could throw forms for me to sculpt." She taught me about clay, and I took right to it. I was amazed that we could make a living from work that we loved to do. We could do it at home. We didn't have to go out into the "workforce." I was always taught that you have to go to school and you have to get your degree and you have to go out into the workforce. Was there any other alternative? Maybe to get married and be a kept woman. Sue believed in making a living at her work. It wasn't a grand living, but it was a wonderful lifestyle. We would go on walks and gather leaves or rocks, or take our notebooks and draw the mountains or a tree or a creek. And then bring that home and translate that into clay.

You talk about your sculpture having a philosophical and spiritual context—

You mean as energy generators? I think good art enhances your life. You can get a lot of violence in art, there are a lot of violent paintings that are popular, but what are they creating? When you look at them, you sense that violence. Which is good sometimes. We need to be awakened sometimes and quickened. Or our consciousness needs to be raised. Art is wonderful for that. That's what it's for! But I think it's also important to create an energy in your home that is going to bring peace to that home. So I want to create a face or an energy there that can do that every time you look at it—that permeates its surrounding as an energy generator. That's something that Sue taught me

Janet Seaforth with one of her goats (Philo, Calif., Spring 1991).

I could let the good spirit and contentment flow and produce something that was lovely instead of something that's full of fear. It's all that same kind of energy, from the womb, from the tan t'ien, the low, emotional subconscious. You have to dive into that subconscious to bring up the creativity into your everyday, conscious self. It's something that comes out that's beyond yourself. Probably with every artist it's kind of surprising what comes through—because it does come *through* you. It's more than just your consciousness.

also. And that you have to spend enough time with your work to create the energy that you want to create.

So that was something that you had in mind before you ever started T'ai Chi?

Yeah, what you cultivate is what you're going to get. Just like a garden. If I started worrying about getting the rent paid, for instance—if we weren't selling enough and I started getting scared, all of a sudden, I'd make all these little pinched faces. Sue would say, "You've got to stop worrying, Janet! You're getting a little pinched here!" You had to, what she called, create a sense of leisure for that creativity to happen in, for that good spirit to happen in. You had to put worries aside.

Which was another reason why T'ai Chi was so good for doing the sculpture work—I could transform negative energy into a neutral place and then from that take it into my creative place, where

Meanwhile you're working in several different places, spending a lot of time traveling and commuting. . . .

Again, you make do with what you've got and try to make whatever you're doing work for you in the best possible, peaceful way. It's like doing your T'ai Chi. You go with the flow and try to make it as relaxed as possible so you can get the most out of it. I enjoy my ride over the hill. The mountain is beautiful. It gives me that meditative time. I can use that. But what I'd really love is just to be home. I would love to get up in the morning, do my T'ai Chi, have my tea, do my studies, and go to my studio on my own land. Dig my own clay. Work in my own garden. I think my life will be a lot better when I get my studio here. I'm looking forward to that.

I also go to Cloverdale one day a week, when I take care of a ninety-year-old woman, Florence. That gives me a chance to tune in to longevity, to appreciate that we are just—we are so temporal.

We are temporary. This body goes. We can do things along the way to keep longevity, to keep our dexterity—T'ai Chi is certainly good for keeping life in your body as long as your body holds out—but eventually it all goes. It's interesting to see that and to see that it doesn't matter how decrepit your body gets; the spirit's always there and it can always be developed. There's always learning that goes on, if older people are at all willing to be open, which most of them are, I've found. I like working with elderly people. They may seem closed at first, but if you sit down with them a little bit and be real, they open up, and you can see that they're still learning, they're still growing, they're still taking things in. That development, spiritual development, conscious development, just keeps going.

That was reassuring to me. Work with Florence has been good for me, for my own personal development. All the things that I do feed me. They feed my development and my consciousness and my own belief in humanity. How to be *here.* Trying to find my own way of how to be here and learn from everything as I go. Keeping what works and letting go of what doesn't work. Trying to keep my integrity that way. Trying to keep my wholeness and to treat every day like that. Not to step out of it. And to include everything, knowing that we're all one. You know, *[laughs]* Bush and Saddam Hussein. I mean, it's *all* one.

It's hard to tell them apart!

Those two, for sure. We may be on opposite sides, but we're all one humanity. And to have compassion for all of them. I may not agree. My job as a conscious woman is to fight oppression. But I also know that we're all one, and I must have compassion for all of it. And that's what helps me get

"Amazon Urn" by Janet Seaforth (porcelain, 7 inches high), 1989.

through it. Otherwise I'd be so angry, I'd be, well, insane. You don't have to agree with your oppressor, but you have to know that we're all in one system. It's all one world.

You have to be aware of how you are participating. That you matter. That every one of us matters. And the impact that we have. Every choice that we make. In fact, that's why I named my studios Choice Studios. Because of the power of our choices. Every choice we make makes our character, influences other people, affects other people. To take responsibility for that—I think that's what integrity really is.

The freedom that I've gotten through T'ai Chi is more than I ever thought I'd have. It—it's a thrill. To be able to really have your life. When you've been raised to give it up. I feel fortunate. My life is good. I was talking at the college yesterday to a couple of the students there about making a living with your work, which mostly I do. I have this one little job taking care of Florence, but mostly I make a living with my work and certainly have made a living at my work, when I was with Sue, for years and years. We never got rich. We were always at the poverty level, but we also managed to buy our own land. I live in this little, simple cabin with just my cold running water and my outhouse; I live simply, but I feel I'm wealthy in the way that I get to do what I want to do. Having this land, beautiful land, and on the beautiful Earth. With clean air and good water. That feels very wealthy to me.

It's a real difference in values. The values that I grew up with were, Do you have a nice car? Do you have nice clothes? All those American standard values. Do you have this nice house, a regular code house—one that meets the building codes? Sometimes I feel like a failure because I'm not fitting up to that old image of what I should have by the time I'm forty. But then I realize what I do have and how lucky I've been to be able to do what I wanted to do almost all my life. Most of my adult life I have been able to make the choices that I wanted to make that benefit me, with the other consciousness of benefiting everyone as well. Because that's really what benefits me. I think we have to come from abundance. Rejecting an issue doesn't make things better. People get it in their heads that, "Oh, we can't take that on." It's not true. We have to take on everything that comes along. We have to tell the truth every point of the way.

But there's also a problem I've seen in many women, who are so tightly scheduled, working so hard on so many different issues, that they get back into that original trap of sacrificing themselves to their husbands and children. They're losing their sense of themselves in giving themselves completely to all these issues.

I can relate to that! Because we're operating in a crisis most of the time. That's true. You have to be responsible for the choices that you make. It's knowing your center and knowing what's the most effective thing to do. You don't get it by overextending. You're going to wear yourself out. Rita and I were talking at T'ai Chi this morning about how we could only watch or listen to the news about the Persian Gulf War for very short periods of time now, just enough to kind of keep track of what's going on. Because it's too devastating otherwise. It rips our energy off.

I have to turn it off. I have to go do my T'ai Chi. I have to go do something that nourishes me. I'll get so depressed that I can't act. I need to know myself well enough to know how to keep my energy, how to use my energy effectively. You know, in martial arts you survey your field, you find what's the best place that you can insert your attack, and you put your energy there and don't let yourself get dispersed.

CHAPTER 2

The Oneness of All Things

Again and again in our talks Janet Seaforth and I came up against the Persian Gulf War—men once more fighting, and women and children as well as men once more suffering and dying. The war ended, at least for most Americans, but my continuing practice of T'ai Chi Ch'uan kept alive for me my ambivalence about fighting. The more I learned about the art, the more clearly I saw how the fighting applications are inherent in the movements. Yet my practice felt, above all, nurturing. Whatever else there might be to T'ai Chi Ch'uan, I told myself, this slow, solitary practice sufficed for me. But I wondered if such things could be so easily separated. Later I was to learn the Aikido term *irimi*, the notion of dealing with an attack or difficulty by directly and fully entering into it. At the time it seemed that the only direction left open to me was to explore more deeply the situation of women with regard to violence.

Chilling statistics are readily available. Men attacking women is documented as the most common crime worldwide[1]—and we must keep in mind that most attacks on women are by fathers, husbands, boyfriends, or other men we know, attacks that often go unreported. Women have learned through hard experience that in every country police and judges rarely take action against men who rape or batter women they are related to, and reporting such behavior often gains the woman further retaliatory

---

1. Naomi Wolf, *The Beauty Myth: How Images of Beauty Are Used Against Women* (New York: William Morrow, 1991), 160.

violence, which, even if reported, will also go un-punished.

In the United States the current escalation of men's violence against women, both in representations in the entertainment media and in actual attacks, evidences the degree to which Americans, like people of other nationalities, view this conduct as ordinary, understandable, and expectable. The number of women in the United States who kill batterers has been going down ever since battered women's shelters began opening in the 1970s; over the same period the number of men stalking and killing wives and girlfriends has steadily increased.[2] Over a ten-year period, thirty thousand U.S. women were murdered by men who had been their partners.[3] Prison terms for men who kill their wives average half as long as for wives who kill their husbands.[4]

In 1992 the U.S. Surgeon General reported that attacks by male partners and family members were the leading cause of injury to U.S. women aged fifteen to forty-four[5]—and these injuries go beyond bruised faces and broken bones. In her recent book, *Next Time She'll Be Dead: Battering and How to Stop It,* the investigative journalist Ann Jones reports, "So many battered women have been infected with HIV by batterers who force them into unprotected sex, in some cases deliberately to prevent their having sex with other men, that the National Centers for Disease Control have identified a direct link between battering and the spread of HIV and AIDS among women."[6]

How can men do the things they do to women? As Janet Seaforth said of herself, so often our first reaction is to refuse to believe that what we see or hear or experience is even happening. And it is beyond bearing to think this is the way the world is. But the implication of doubt is to deny women the dignity of acknowledging the reality of our experience—or to agree that we ourselves have occasioned and are responsible for the criminal acts that men do to us. Of course we are often complicit—our minds and spirits are additional fronts of the war. For finally, what can we call it but war? Whenever I bring myself to face what is occurring I have to admit there is no choice for women between fighting or not fighting, for we have all of us already spent our lives in this war in which the primary battlefields are individual women's bodies and minds.

In class Janet demonstrated the martial applications of the moves we learn in T'ai Chi Ch'uan, how, for example, the graceful extension and lifting of the arms in the movement called Play the Harp constitutes a joint lock whereby one can break an attacker's elbow. Another spiraling twist of the arm and opening of the hand becomes a lethal palm strike if directed at shoving an attacker's nose into his brain. "It only takes eight pounds of pressure," Janet would tell us encouragingly. We were strong, healthy, intelligent women. Many of us had successful careers or businesses or held responsible positions in the community. People who knew us thought of us as competent and capable. Why were we so reluctant to hear the information Janet wanted to tell us? Why were our efforts at kicking or striking a padded target so inept? We loved practicing the form, but none of us wanted to practice sparring or applications with partners.

"We say violence is wrong," the feminist writer and activist Melanie Kaye-Kantrowitz comments

---

2. Ann Jones, *Next Time She'll Be Dead: Battering and How to Stop It* (Boston: Beacon, 1994), 101.

3. Ibid., 42.

4. Women's Action Coalition, *WAC Stats: The Facts about Women* (New York: New Press, 1993), 47.

5. Ibid., 55.

6. Ann Jones, *Next Time She'll Be Dead*, 87.

in an essay entitled, "Women, Violence, and Resistance: Naming It War, 1979–1992." "We say violence won't work—what do we mean, *wrong?* What do we mean, *work?*" She reports one woman's story:

> All of a sudden he got this crazy look in his eye and he said to me, "Now I'm going to kill you." Then I started saying my prayers. I knew there was nothing I could do. He started to hit me—I still wasn't sure if he wanted to rape me at this point—or just kill me. He was hurting me, but hadn't yet gotten me into a strangle-hold because he was still drunk and off balance. Somehow we pushed into the kitchen where I kept looking at this big knife. But I didn't pick it up. Somehow no matter how much I hated him at that moment, I still couldn't imagine putting the knife into his flesh, and then I was afraid he would grab it and stick it into me.[7]

"I couldn't imagine" is a code phrase for "it's wrong," Kaye-Kantrowitz argues; "I was afraid" is something we say when we mean "it won't work." "Sticking the knife into his flesh is unimaginable, too horrible. This horror, this failure of imagination might have cost her life. Her life against his, and she chooses his."[8]

Worried that her teaching was insufficient with regard to self-defense, Janet urged us to look for additional instruction. As an added inducement she said this training would also improve our soli-

tary practice of T'ai Chi Ch'uan. Obediently I signed up for a course in self-defense for women offered by Gayle Fillman at her local Aikido dojo. I arrived at the dojo to find some thirty other women, ranging in age from adolescence to perhaps fifty. Gayle welcomed us with a short, matter-of-fact description of what she would cover during the four weekly class sessions. A stocky blonde woman in her mid-forties, dressed in a white *gi* jacket and a black *hakama*—the traditional Japanese floor-length skirtlike garment worn in some martial arts—Gayle has a fifth-degree black belt in Aikido. She teaches Aikido, gymnastics, self-defense for women and children, and nonviolent intervention techniques to individuals and groups ranging from security teams to battered women and children. She also paints, juggles, and plays the *shakuhachi* and the piano.

We began with a discussion of why we had come to the class. What situations had we encountered or feared? What actions had we taken, and how they had worked or not worked? We started to add up how many situations we had been in in which men had behaved unacceptably and how often we had silently endured or actively excused threats and affronts because they were so ordinary, because it wasn't worth making a fuss that anyway most likely would rebound on us. We talked about our reluctance to trust the instincts that warned us against particular men or situations, and the inhibitions we felt against behavior that might draw attention to ourselves or cause embarrassment to ourselves or others. Wryly we noted how such attitudes on our part could keep us from taking timely action to cut off a dangerous situation before it ever started.

Gayle demonstrated—and then drilled us in—techniques for dealing with the physical tactics men commonly use against women. There are only so many things a man can do with two arms and

---

7. Melanie Kaye-Kantrowitz, *The Issue Is Power: Essays on Women, Jews, Violence, and Resistance* (San Francisco: Aunt Lute Foundation, 1992), 19.
8. Ibid.

two legs. Say he grips your arm with two hands—he's occupied both his hands and you still have all the rest of your body at your disposal. There is always something you can do, Gayle said, although the options may not be attractive or desirable or necessarily effective.

We practiced escaping from each other and from Gayle's advanced Aikido students. I found these encounters with different bodies intriguing. More than once I forgot my philosophical dilemma in the immediacy of figuring out the physical logistics of what I could do. As Janet had promised, much of what I learned did feed into my practice of T'ai Chi Ch'uan. My execution of movements in T'ai Chi Ch'uan improved in balance and solidity, and I felt a new sense of competence in myself. At the same time the very earnestness and supportiveness of my fellow students and Gayle and her Aikido students increased my awareness of the unspeakable reality that necessitated the lessons I was learning: that simply because I am a woman I may be attacked by men. My philosophical questions took an increasingly personal turn. Emotionally draining as it was to go to class, however, after the first session I never considered not going. Ignorance was no longer an option for me. I had to go on. And even as my practice of the physical skills I was learning seemed to increase my awareness of the need for them, they also gave me concrete means for dealing with that reality.

At the final session Gayle outfitted one of her black belt Aikido students with a motorcycle helmet, shoulder pads, and protective gear, encasing his entire body so we could practice defending ourselves against a live person. He was to taunt and assault us, and we would try out the skills we had learned in the course. As I watched my classmates undertake this test, I felt a rush of emotion that I could not at first identify. Then I realized it was pride. So small and slight these women looked in comparison to this enormously padded man, but how gallantly they bore themselves, how bravely they fought back when he attacked. What strength these women had, not just physically, but in some deeper, spiritual sense. Seeing that possibility of strength and power in them kindled something in me as well.

My turn came. I felt nervous but willing—even curious to discover what I would do. Gayle helped me don boxing gloves and helmet and shin guards. I walked across the floor toward the "mugger." He whispered something under his breath, words I couldn't quite make out, a hateful tone of voice I don't even know how I know, whispers that filled me with guilt and self-disgust for having called them forth. I shrank back, near tears, wanting only to escape, away, anywhere, wishing I could die or had never been born. But even as I felt these too-familiar feelings, I realized I had options. My quailing solidified into resolve. The "mugger" grabbed my arm and my resolve exploded in action. I hardly knew what I did—I was astounded to see how much I could do. He fell back. Gayle and the other women surrounded me in a brief flurry of praise and encouragement. They took away the helmet and gear I wore and went to put it on the next woman.

Susan, an Aikido student who is also a therapist, stayed beside me. "Walk around the room with me," she urged. "Keep moving. How do you feel? Tell me." I felt dazed, but because Susan insisted, I spoke. My voice sounded far away, and nothing I said made sense to me. More clearly than the dojo and the women I had been working with these past four weeks, I saw an event that occurred when I was ten or eleven years old. I lay in my bed in the dark in the room I shared with my sister, the lights out although it was early and all the rest of the family were still up. I had been ill with the flu or some childhood ailment such as measles. I felt achy and irritable, unable to read or occupy myself. I remember the murmur of voices from the kitchen and my brother passing back and forth in my room, which he had to cross to reach his own bedroom, a closed-in porch at the rear of the house. He seemed unnecessarily noisy, flicking lights off and on, tossing things about. I told him to be more quiet but he ignored me. I called out to my parents to control him and was told to stop whining. Again my brother crossed the room, openly taunting me this time. I flew from my bed into his room and lit into him shrieking and punching.

Our father was there in an instant, cuffing me aside, drowning our cries with his angry shouts. I think I accepted at the time that I was wrong to attack my younger, smaller brother, no matter what the aggravation. I still don't see my father's anger as misplaced or excessive. Thirty-five years have passed. Why did this memory surface in association with an exercise intended to encourage me to fight back if I am attacked? What was going on?

Heightening my personal distress at that time was the shocking immediacy with which already, during that brief course in women's self-defense, the violence of men in the larger political and economic realm had closed in on us. The course had coincided with preparations for the Redwood Summer demonstrations against corporate destruction of northern coastal forests. Judi Bari and several other organizers of the demonstrations signed up for the course, as they had been physically threatened by timber company supporters. Judi had been run off the road by a man driving a logging truck, and she and her two young daughters only narrowly escaped injury. Judi was in that circle the first night the class met, but the next week she was absent, and it was in class that I learned she had been bombed in her car earlier that day and lay in a San Francisco Bay Area hospital, not expected to live.

Judi did live. Despite an irreparably shattered pelvis and spine she can even walk, although she is in constant pain. Five years later the bombing remains officially unsolved, and the police seem to be making no effort to solve it. Judi's investigations in connection with her lawsuit against local and federal law enforcement agencies are turning up links between them and the timber industry. In the year before the bombing the FBI conducted a "bomb school" on corporate timberland in Northern California at which the participants constructed bombs of the sophisticated type used in the attack on Judi. From other information it seems likely that one or more FBI agents, with or without authorization from the higher-ups in the agency, made and placed the bomb.

Impossible, many people say. Or at least exaggerated. So we come around again to refusing to believe a woman's story of her abuse. As the activist and writer Robin Morgan writes with regard to feminism, "The androcentric power structure managed to go directly from ridicule through defensiveness to boredom . . . without passing through comprehension. Backlash, yes. Repression, certainly. Co-optation, where and when possible. Understanding, no. First the idea was too new, when actually it was ancient. Then the idea was old hat, when it had hardly begun to make its mark."[9]

Clearly, with this brief course in self-defense I had taken but the first step in a long process. I had only begun to learn all I might need to know to ensure my safety. Vast changes in the economic, social, physical, and spiritual makeup of the United States will be required for all women to live in

---

9. Robin Morgan, *The Demon Lover: On the Sexuality of Terrorism* (New York & London: Norton, 1989), 53.

this society in physical safety and with dignity. But how do we get there? And how do we live in the interim? These questions loomed large for me as I started work on this book. Who better to ask them of, I thought, than Gayle herself?

She agreed to meet me for lunch and to talk about her life in martial arts and the perspective it has given her.

GAYLE FILLMAN

Aikido

I had a rough childhood—a lot of violence. I was locked up in the cellar or closets for days at a time. I was able to save myself by leaving my body—I would curl up in a corner and daydream. For a while I was considered slightly autistic. I couldn't talk, and then when I did, I stuttered because I was so nervous and couldn't think of the words.

One time I was traded for a car, because that was the only way my mother could save me and my sister. My grandfather found us and came and picked us up. I remember that very distinctly, him showing up. My mother left after that, and I didn't see her until my sister got married and I went and found her. Through these hardships I did develop my creativity, as sometimes you do through hard physical competition, and I became quite an artist. But I still have a lot of fears.

When I was in high school, my stepmother had some difficulties, and my sister and I ended up not living in the house—we stayed with friends and worked our way through school. I did okay in high school. I was good at art and pretty good at sports. I enjoyed movement. I got along with people. But I always felt low self-worth. I graduated in 1966 at the age of nineteen, which is very late, but I had to work my way through. I found a job for myself, working at a bank. I wasn't real happy working at the bank, but it was good to have a job. I lived near Henderson Center in Eureka, California, and I was able to buy a little red Volkswagen.

There was this Union 76 station in Henderson Center where I went to get gas, and there was this Hawaiian boy there. He was very young and skinny and scrawny, but there was something special about him. He had a light around him. It's like when you see a flower that's really healthy. It looks different. Or a tree that's healthy—it's beautiful to an artist. Something you want to paint. I got to know him, and we made a date to go out. We went out for hamburgers and ran out of gas, and it took us a couple hours to walk back to get gas. He was very accepting, very secure about who he was. On that walk to the gas station and back, all the things that he talked about were so much Aikido—although I didn't know it then. That was the greatest walk of my life. It changed my life.

He invited me to the Aikido dojo. His father, Richard Kahoalii, Sr., was the sensei; I can remember watching how beautiful it was. They were diving over each other and throwing each other, and I said, "I could never do this."

But you did sports? Physical activities? This seemed different?

It seemed overwhelming. People flying off. Diving over three bodies. I said, "That's nuts! That's scary!" *[Laughs]* I was five-foot-seven, long blonde hair, very thin. I must have weighed 125, 130 pounds. There were no other women there. I had all the fear and reluctance people talk about, "This is too hard, this is too scary, this isn't for me." But I began training in August 1966. We started in on exercises and breathing, and everything started to improve for me. I was redeveloping parts of my brain where I didn't get all the necessary movement and crawling in as a baby and I connected to more motor skills. They brought in Richard Sr.'s wife, the sensei's wife, to be my partner. She and I trained together. Of course I was always real nervous, because it was my friend Richard's mother. But it got me in the dojo. She was very kind to train with me. The training was scary and hard, and I was treated badly by some of the male students, but I kept coming back. I worked hard and I became good at it.

Although I was an athlete, I wasn't coordinated, and I want you to know that I didn't control my breathing. When I'd go to bed at night, my stepfather used to come in, and if we made a move, he'd put the pillow over our head or torture us in some way or beat us or whatever. We always were very still and like we were asleep, but sometimes our eyes would blink, so then we would have this happen. So I have always been frightened about breathing. When I'd run around the track in high school or do something really exhilarating—even now sometimes I panic. You know, when you get to that certain point with the in breath, you panic a little bit and then it's really hard to breathe.

I could never really excel in sports because of my breathing, and when I got into Aikido, I can remember at first lying down, I was so exhausted, and crawling off the mat. But it did get better. Eventually I quit the bank and went to the junior college. It was Aikido that made it possible for me to go to college, to feel good enough about myself to go. I struggled in some of my classes, especially with the reading, and I was never really able to tell people about it. I had learned that it wasn't very acceptable, you know, if you're going to be there, do it or don't do it. It's not like you can whine or complain or ask for special help.

My sensei also trained me to teach. I was so proud when he asked me to teach my first class. I can remember making this wonderful lesson plan. I had taken all these physical education classes in college. I had learned how to make the most excellent lesson plan. What equipment you need, how many students you're teaching, the facility you need, exactly what you're going to do, and how long it's going to take. Your goals and criteria. Perfect. I spent a lot of time, because Aikido is very meaningful, and it was a special honor for me.

When I went there he said, "What did you plan to teach for this evening?"

Not knowing it was a trick question, I said, "I made this lesson plan," and I presented it to him. He wadded it up and threw it away.

He said, "This isn't the way we teach in Aikido. You need to watch your students and feel their needs, because things will change from the lesson plan." And so I began teaching in front of him. If I announced something, he'd say, "What about this?" and "Have you done that?" He was very kind and helpful, and I learned to be a good teacher.

He'd train with me after, and we'd go out for pizza or noodles—Chinese noodles—and talk about Aikido and philosophy and all that. I learned a lot through him passing on the information through storytelling and discussion.

So you had more than the physical training on the mat? You had a lot of exposure to history and theory and philosophy?

Right. And when Tohei Sensei (Koichi Tohei) came to visit—I think it was in 1969 that he first came, and he came several times after that. He had been sent from Japan by the founder of Aikido to teach in Hawaii and later in California. I was able to spend time with him and my sensei's family. I was twenty-one by then, and I would go to dances with Tohei Sensei and be his escort. He was a very kind man and always very gracious, very proper. And I was able to be in those discussions outside the dojo about his healing work and all that kind of thing, and see him breathe and dance, and see how he transferred his Aikido into his life. That again made another impression upon me, his dancing with *ki* and talking about ki in daily life constantly while we were together—*ki* is Japanese for energy or spirit, and it's part of the name Aikido. Tohei Sensei had a tremendous amount of ki and healing power. I had had a car accident when I was in high school, and I couldn't bend my finger real well. He did *kiatsu*—his method of using ki for healing—on my finger and healed it.

I graduated and began working in Willits, here in Mendocino County, teaching physical education and art. I taught Aikido in my physical education classes—and swimming, and all the different things that a PE teacher does, but I used Aikido in coaching my girls.

Then I took a leave of absence and went off to San Francisco to the Academy of Fine Arts. I worked on advertising design, thinking I needed to do more art. But I soon realized that I wanted to be in the country. You know, the real thing about Aikido is realizing your oneness and realizing your oneness as being close to nature. Being close to nature my whole life—I ran on the beach every day when I lived in Samoa, outside Eureka. I was close to the trees—once I was treed by wild dogs. Just being out by myself in the woods, I was able to explore a lot of the beauty of this. So here I am riding a bus from Oakland to San Francisco, walking through the Financial District. I made it a challenge to get people to smile and say "Hi" and do the country thing. And finally I broke the ice. The same walk, the same people riding the same bus finally would say, "Good morning." But I decided I needed to come home. And there's kind of a story about that.

There was this teacher at the academy whose wife was dying of cancer. He made TV commercials in Los Angeles. I went out one night with a bunch of people, doing something in San Francisco, when I had a commercial due in the morning, and I put the design upside down on the sheet of paper. Advertising design and commercial TV and all that is very, very competitive, and people are very short and very unconcerned with who in the hell you are. This guy had his little cigar, and he let you have it. Everybody was totally afraid of him. I watched people get raked through the coals. It was scary—it was down there in the city, I was trying to see if I could take my art someplace, and this was the place where you make money with art.

It was my turn, and I realized that I'd put my work upside down on the paper, but it was too late. We were doing this critique, and when he came to mine, he lit into me like he lit into everybody else, in the worst way, and then he stops and looks at you to see what kind of person you are standing there when he's done. Most of the people are nothing. They're six feet under by then. Crumpled. Can't do anything. But I stood there. I looked at him and smiled.

That was a real lesson of Aikido in everyday life and resolution of conflict. My presentation was the only thing that was going to save my grade. "It doesn't matter to me whether this commercial is inside out, upside down, or whatever," I said, "because it's so good, the idea and the concept are so good. I tried to put it on this paper. I was so excited—I realize, it's upside down. And I don't care." I went on and presented the commercial, and because I didn't fall apart under pressure, he respected me and gave me an *A*. The commercial *was* good. But he came over to me later and said, "What is it that you do after class?" I didn't give much emphasis to Aikido. I said, "I was a PE teacher in Willits, and I also taught art, and I'm on leave of absence. I'm trying to explore more the art end, because I enjoy it. I'm trying to make money. I think that it's important to make money."

I came back the next week, and he said, "I mean, really, what do you do? There's something about you. Why are you here?" I said, "Don't you think I should be here? Don't you think I'm good enough?" He said, "You're more than good enough. But why waste your time? My wife is dying. I didn't spend that precious time with her and now it's too late. I know now I should have done things differently and I can tell that you're the difference I should have been looking for."

I said, "But you're famous. You've done all these commercials, you've made all this money, you're rich. Everyone respects you and you have your name on everything." "But I'm not happy," he said. "What is it that you really want to do in life? What are your hobbies?" I said, "I like Aikido and art. I like being in nature." And then, before I ever heard it from Joseph Campbell, I heard "living your bliss" in that statement from him. If you do what you love, the money will follow. So he, in fact, affected my life. I decided that I didn't need

to make a lot of money. I came back and I started the dojo in Ukiah.

Now, that's a very interesting concept, the dojo in Ukiah, because it has always run on trust. I never have made a great deal of money, but strange things have happened, and the money always comes. It doesn't always come on the same level or schedule—and that's been a hard thing, how to have it happen on the right time frame with all the other financial data. The dojo, the gymnastics—I also teach gymnastics to children—and the Aikido have grown and blossomed. I've just been a facilitator of that. It's always been a real happy place for me. No matter what happens in my life, when I go in there and I shut the door, it's like another world. It's a safe place. I feel the energy, and the concept of that, and so around that I've been—I am—a very rich person. If I retired tomorrow, I would still do what I'm doing today. I wouldn't change.

So when this advertising teacher asked you if you were happy, was it that he noticed how centered you were? Or would you really have described yourself at that time as being happy?

I was happy. I was involved heavily in Aikido. I was teaching Aikido at the University of California at Berkeley, and I was very happy to do that and happy with seeing people light up. Seeing women light up when they can defend themselves. Seeing children light up when they can do other things. That made me very happy. But I was still trying to make money, going to school for art. Which is a rotten thing to do. This guy recognized my happiness and my centeredness—the same aura that I'd recognized in my friend Richard—and called me on it. I went up in the woods—whenever I need to think, I get away from people, go into the woods or near water, sit there and breathe, and then it comes to me what should happen next. And so I decided to come back to Ukiah.

You were saying about your childhood that you had access to nature, to the beach and so on. Those were things that were in your disposition before you started Aikido. Did Aikido add something different?

I think the hardships in my life brought me close to nature in a similar mode to Aikido, and then doing Aikido refined it and made the appreciation happen and made me understand myself better and understand the value, the positive value of everything that had happened to me.

We're born of ki—that's the Japanese word. In Chinese, it's *ch'i,* which means energy, or spirit. There's ki in everything, all living and nonliving things. That's what ki is. I think that everyone finds strength from nature, from their own existence. Everyone has a meaning on the planet, and has ki, but they don't realize it. When you take up a martial art, or *budo,* you begin to explore that.

Budo means martial art in Japanese. *Bu* has two characters, it has "stop" and a spear character, and of course, *do* is "the way," like *tao* in Chinese. It came from that. So budo is the way of stopping the spear, the way of realizing peace. That's the nonfighting concept of Aikido. *Dojo* means "the place to study the way."

The meaning of Aikido is beautiful to me: *Ai* is for harmony and harmonizing, and *ki* is this divine energy that we talked about—spirit, or energy. So *Aikido* is the way of harmonizing, becoming one with the universe, and loving and respecting all things. I tried to analyze some of these Aikido movements with exercise physiology and kinesiology, and some of them, you can get to a certain place in understanding them, but then you've got to go with ki to make sense of it.

Ki is in everything that you do, every way that you move. It's like I'm one with that tree over there. I feel good about that. *[Laughs]* I'm one with that car over there. When I train—I'm doing all kinds of trainings, with Model Mugging, with Aikido, with other martial arts—but I bring it all together into the Aikido concept, and then I nurture it out. Even the gymnastics. I coach in a way that people may find funny. I have many champions, but I coach with Aikido. When they go out there, I don't want them doing it for me because I'm their coach; I want them to do it for them. If that's of value to their lives, then they can do it.

Do you have your gymnastics students taking Aikido also?

Some of them. I use the principles. I don't really explain it. They do it, and then later they understand it. That's how it happened with me.

That seems to be happening with me in T'ai Chi. Which is something new to me, because I've always been so much in my head with everything that I do. In T'ai Chi, I don't seem to really understand anything until I feel it.

Well, exactly. Why talk about it when no one's going to understand it? You've got to be able to feel it and do it in some way, with art or with PE, with some kind of physical form. I have a gym-

Gayle Fillman (left) demonstrating a kokyunage, *or "wind" or "energy" throw, at Ukiah Aikido (Ukiah, Calif., January 1996).*

you, you may have me running faster than I ran before. Maybe someday I'll run faster than you, but that's not my concept. It's just to run faster and faster than I did before.

[At the far end of the restaurant patio, a small child trips on the curb and bursts into tears.]

I don't trip so much any more. I used to trip and fall all the time.

I know—I still trip. But now I catch myself. I was very clumsy learning about my body, I hadn't really explored my body, and so I'd bump something. My sensei said, "When you're doing really well at Aikido, you'll bump something, but you'll catch it before it hits the ground." *[Laughs]* And someday maybe we'll train to the extent that we won't bump into anything at all. There are times when I get going, I get into my clumsy mode, but then I catch whatever I bump. And there are times I catch things now, and I don't even know how I did it. It's subconscious. Something's falling, and I'll catch it. It can be something I'm not even aware of.

nastics team now that was coached by someone else. I'm trying to give them the right concept in life and get a balance in their competition. I don't believe in competition against someone else. I don't think that it's okay to win at all odds. To me, competition is to do better than *you* did before. If you were in a race and you ran faster than me, you win the medal. But if I'm right behind

Perhaps it's what you were saying about the oneness with all things—that you are

connected to everything on a very literal level?

Aikido's taken me into areas that I never would have explored. I see things sometimes before they happen. I remember one time at the lake, I was in my sailboat out there, and there were these three men going out in a boat, an old guy, and a young guy, and a middle guy. They flipped their boat over, and the old guy was drowning. He said, "Help, help, my heart!" There were all these people around, and I thought there would be some guys who would jump in with their enormous strength and go help these people.

Then I realized this is my task in life—one of my tasks in life. You know, I could sit here all day and tell you about different things that have happened to me. But anyway, I grabbed some rope. I had one life preserver and some life jackets. I threw the life preserver over to the kid and said, "Kick your way to the boat and hold on to the boat." And then I jumped into the water to go to the guy that was in the most trouble. As I swam by, I threw a life jacket to the middle guy. And then I swam over to the third guy and went under and pulled him part way into the boat, because he had a bad heart and was really going down. And I was able to do that in a very few seconds.

Well, then I had them all holding onto their boat. I swam to the front of the boat and I said, "I want you to hang on, I'm going to pull you to the shore." Meanwhile the old guy was going, "My heart! My heart!" I was worried about him hanging on. I said to the kid, "Move over, see if you can move over closer to your grandfather and hold on." I grabbed a rope tied to the bow. And there were all these guys with boats, and I was going, "Hey, get a boat out here," but everybody was just standing there.

But it was that the time had gone by much slower for me and much faster for everybody else. Finally, as I was swimming in to shore, I was about ten feet offshore, this guy came by with a boat and said, "Here, let me give you a hand." And god, I was getting really tired, but I could have made it to shore. Then when we got to shore, they said, "Look, you're a girl, I don't know whether to hug you or buy you a beer." That was kind of a downer on the whole thing. I said, "You don't have to do either. I'm just very glad that I was here." So that was the end of that. I never did see them again.

But there's this place where you can get into the time of things, and it just slows down. Attacks are like that. Life is like that. I'm always operating on a different mode. *[Laughs]* But when an emergency happens, I go right in there and I have lots of time. I drop into this place, this dimensional place that you can drop into. It's this fine place. The oneness feeling of your body doing technique—it's like being both gentle and strong at the same time.

You can have these massive men attacking you with all their strength, and your technique is as light as a feather. When you throw them there's all this power—it's this gentle power that's so wonderful. You're doing your breathing, you're doing all that meditation, you pull into a single point, your one-point, your center, or *hara,* or tan t'ien. When you touch this person, you lead the mind—you lead the ki, the ki of the person. You're one with that person.

That's what T'ai Chi is too, in terms of Push Hands—that partner exercise—or stopping somebody. You have this oneness with the universe that you're moving with, and it's absolutely stunning, you know? I've been doing this art for twenty-eight years, going on twenty-nine years this summer, and I'm stunned. And I'm so excited.

My training has been a lot from my students. I've been lucky to be the teacher because I have

Gayle Fillman throwing two of her black belt Aikido students with a kokyunage at Ukiah Aikido (Ukiah, Calif., January 1996).

ROGER FRANKLIN

so many teachers. They only have me—and each other. I have all of them. One of the concepts of that is when you begin instructing and giving back, your students are a mirror, or a reflection, of your demonstration. And of your meaning. And of your energy. And so you have this immediate example in front of you of exactly what you're doing. If you're humble and gracious enough to give to your students and want enough for them, then you will see even more. The more you give, the more you get in return.

When you start Aikido, there are many levels, right? You get this rank and that rank and the other rank and all that. That shouldn't be why you train. You should train because of the ultimate enjoyment from training and your exploration of all the areas. Most people quit when they get their first-degree black belt, what we call *shodan*. They quit because in America everyone says that when you're a black belt you're an expert. Well, you're not. The real concept is that it's your commitment to beginning. When you get to shodan, or first-degree black belt, it shows your commitment to learning, and at that point you begin. A lot of people come and go through the martial arts. But I think that it touches them and makes them look at life.

I wanted to ask you about women particularly.

Men can fight with each other, because they have that strength, and so it takes them a long time to learn the concepts of T'ai Chi and Aikido. Women don't have that strength in themselves to overcome. When grabbed by a strong male, there's only one way that they can move, and that's the Aikido way—which is the right way. Not going against the force, but going with it. Mentally it is easier for men than for women, because women have been taught all these concepts that men are stronger and that women can't move. They have to break those concepts, but once they do, it just pours out. I'm extremely impressed with the women that have dedicated themselves in the dojo and continue to train in the dojo.

How do you see getting through that initial step of women thinking that they can't do this?

Usually women find Aikido quite beautiful, but most of them are dedicated to their husbands and cooking dinner and putting the kids to bed, and so we don't have as many women. And here in the country, I have a tendency to have more men. There are more women in the Bay Area and cities. But I have hundreds and hundreds and hundreds of women that take self-defense. In that class I try to give them immediate tools to use to defend themselves and to empower themselves. For that I am completely impressed with Model Mugging. It's violent, because if someone attacks you, you just go into this mode, and you're able to defend yourself. It's very, very realistic. And it works.

I still am very, very dedicated to the Aikido approach, and I can use Aikido in Model Mugging, but I believe that if something is happening to you, you need to win so that you can go on with your life. You meet a mugger, and you need to beat him up—you need to win. And I think that a lot of women need to *know* they can win. On the other hand, I think that it's real, real important to take awareness and prevention as well, because I think that most of the time, ninety-nine—you know, I can't give a solid statistic on it—but you're going to talk your way out or maneuver your way out in some way if you can be aware that there is difficulty at hand.

An important point about Aikido that has made a big, big, *big* difference in my life, and makes a big difference in the lives of people who take Aikido from me, is the concept of safe distance, or *ma-ai*. *Ai* is harmony, like I said before. *Ma* is the space of intention. When I began Aikido, I believed my body was right here where I could touch and what I could see, and that was my body. But then I was soon to learn that if I waited for a snap punch to come to my body, it hurt a lot. And that it was the intent that matters. *Ma* is the space of intention.

We have a dojo cat, a three-legged cat. She got run over and it broke her shoulder. Everybody had said, "Oh, that's such an ugly cat. And she's so wild, she looks so mean." But then we saw her in a different light after she got hit by this car. When we finally found her she had all these little babies. We could see she was in pain, and she was feeding her babies and trying to go on in her pain. So we picked her up and took her in for the surgery, which was very, very expensive. Had the leg removed and part of her shoulder. The kids found homes for the kittens and she's now our dojo cat. She turned out to be the most beautiful cat, and she was so ugly. We call her Ma, meaning the space of intention. Like if you *think* you're going to attack me, then you're already attacking me. That's the Aikido way, that's the ma. In Aikido—and in T'ai Chi, wouldn't you say?—we try to control the mind.

When I work with women, I explore this with them. Sitting this close, our bodies are actually touching. We're touching. We're very intimate. You know, if people could understand that, it's a very, very strong thing. If you were mad at me and I came in very close, you're going to push, and *boom* we're going to have a battle. If you're angry and you want me to listen to you and I stand back, you're going to go, "Wait, listen, listen," and try and pull me in. But if we're here at this neutral place where our bodies are touching, our outer bodies, the warmth of our bodies, our sharing in this energy, like the rays of the sun, and we honor that, we're in a safe distance, and you feel comfortable and I feel comfortable and we can make

this discussion and ask for permission to be closer. We could resist attack. If we practice that concept, we'll have much more kindness, we'll have more respect for each other. But if we're not respecting each other, and we're not giving space, and we're not honoring those areas, conflict comes of that. Physical battle comes of that.

I suppose to be able to gauge the other person's intention, you have to see them as a real person, just to see what they are?

You have to see them as yourself.

You have to respect them and admit them before you can figure out, early enough to do something about it, if they're trying to kill you?

Exactly. This space is called ma, the intent space. It's like a pitcher and a batter. The pitcher pitches the ball. Before it gets to the batter, that thought of where he's going to pitch the ball, that's ma. That's the space. I believe that when we teach women prevention we're making that kind of place.

But for some situations or some women you see Model Mugging as more effective than Aikido?

It's quicker. You can learn some survival skills in a short course, whereas Aikido takes a long time. For women who don't have the time or interest, or for young women going away to college or a job, or those who because of their history as victims can't bear to be touched, perhaps even by another woman, Model Mugging can prepare them to go out in the world and feel safe from rape and harassment. It can restore a woman's confidence to explore life, which she may have lost through the fears that often oppress women.

There are some men, but mostly women, who have a hard time coming in to the dojo and bowing in and working with a man because they may have been raped or sexually abused in some way. You're not going to get around those problems where people have been abused. They're going to bring that into the class. So we have a class in our dojo—and some dojos do have that—we have an introductory Aikido class for women.

I am proud to have the class and I'm proud to work with women and that they'll come and feel safe enough to allow that with me. There are a lot of women who wouldn't normally take Aikido if they didn't have this entry-level class. But I feel that people need to move on from the women's class. I feel a strong imbalance by having women constantly with just women. I encourage the women to get involved in the coed class. Some of them don't want to move on to do that. It's hard for them. I'm always searching and thinking of new ways to encourage them. We're not looking in there at who we're going to have a family with or who we're going to do our life with, but instead we're people in there harmonizing in terms of our spiritual growth and our physical growth and our mental growth, having class together, and working at balancing male and female within each individual.

Overall in all the martial arts, it seems that in mixed classes of men and women, women are in the minority and don't have as many role models of skilled or advanced students who are women, because there just aren't as many.

I think we're slowly changing that. We talk about it. We instill that we're in this space, doing this martial art, and everybody needs to work together and help with the areas that need help. If that means there's only one woman and she needs to feel more comfortable, then everybody has to help her feel more comfortable. If that means there's a weak man in class, then the stronger man has to help. And if the stronger man is using more strength than he needs to, then everybody needs to help him. We all have things that we have to work on to learn whatever we're learning, whether it's Aikido or T'ai Chi or whatever process that we're learning. We need to make this safe space where we're not involved with sex and we're not involved with weakness or strongness or whether someone's perfectly made or not perfectly made. Or who's judging that. To grow spiritually we have to reach back to finish a circle. It's only a half circle to go up. You've got to go down and up the other side and keep going. As you understand, you can help others, and as you help others, they can become better at the art, and that helps you have somebody to train with.

If you get to class and you're a black belt and there are no brown belts or no other black belts, well, that's like being a woman in an all-men's class. Or a man in an all-women's class. You're now a black belt in an all white belt, green belt, or whatever class. So what do you do? Do you throw them all like they're all black belts? No, you can't do that, you're going to hurt everybody. You have to balance with what is. That's what class is about. And when you're attacked on the street, you have to balance with what is. You can't go faster than the attack. You can't assume anything. You've got to be in harmony with what is happening to change it so that you don't become involved in a physical altercation.

You can change the energy if you can feel that energy, but if you don't allow yourself to feel that energy you're never going to change it. If we take feeling out, then we have people running around having to use physical strength, because they didn't feel. We have to have feeling, we have to have this process in a safe place, and we have to understand that we need to work together. Some people become frustrated. Some people take longer to learn that process. As a sensei, I have to maneuver people in the class and watch for their safety. Not just because they're female—because of all the difficulties and imbalances that may occur.

O-Sensei—Morihei Ueshiba, the founder of Aikido, who we call O-Sensei—wanted men and women to work together. He felt strongly about the concept of having the weak work with the strong and the strong work with the weak—not necessarily meaning that women are the weak.

But it seems, from what I've read, American women who've gone to Japan to study Aikido were mostly put in women's classes, where the training wasn't as serious.

Yes. I'm going to be careful that my women's classes don't become this way. I don't want it to become a separate class. I'm into helping people that have had problems come through to a place to go on. Even those women who have gone on into the other class like being in the women's class. They come regularly to it and then go to other classes as well. O-Sensei wanted to integrate men and women, but it is one of the mysteries of our culture—we're so involved in the cultural significance of male and female that it's very hard for us to allow ourselves to have this place that I'm talking about. Our dojo is one place where it's happening. I'm sorry it's not happening in Japan, because it was O-Sensei's intent that men and women train together, but even in his time, I hear from discussions and talking to other people, the minute that he left, the men wanted to go train with men, and the women wanted—basically wanted to train, but I think they ended up training with each other.

Many dojos have problems like you were talking about, of women feeling uncomfortable, and men feeling uncomfortable or dominating, and roles coming up in the dojo. Until people realize that we need to take steps to evolve that process, it won't evolve. That's one of my purposes in my training and my teaching, to evolve that process, so that men and women alike can train.

I think Aikido is a lifetime training. When we're young, we may need to throw each other around and get real physical, like cubs playing with each other roughly, but eventually we all become old and frail, and Aikido is good for everyone. Eventually those people even that had the harshness of training in their youth in Japan will say, "We need to train with everyone." Once they get to a certain place and they're more spiritually evolved, they'll say, "We need to train with everyone." Because there's such a lesson in this balance of sexual and other differences and in openness to letting go and going into the safe place.

O-Sensei was one man, developing an art for world peace. I didn't always understand that, but I really believe that there's only one way the planet will change, and that's that each individual has to realize their oneness and value the planet and value each other. And that comes from the training.

It's amazing to me how mystical the martial arts become at some point. You get to this place, which is totally accidental, in terms of your training and teaching and giving and sweating and just dedicating yourself, and then something mystical happens. Some door opens up to a dimension, and if I speak of that, it just sounds like I'm nuts, but I'm telling you this door opens into this dimension where learning takes place. Like O-Sensei said, learn all the techniques and then throw them away and let it happen. Just let it happen and go with nature.

You know, there's a certain reality and then there's the real reality. Most of our life, our economic structure and what we do, is a myth. The whole democratic process is a myth. What's keeping it together is belief in the myth. The value we give it is what creates the process. I don't see Aikido as a myth. I see Aikido as more than a martial art. I see it as a functional reality. I see it as a way, the Way that is, the Way of existence, the Way of loving. And I'm not talking about religion, I'm talking about being. When people think about money, when they think about society, they think that's real. I say that's a myth. And when I talk about Aikido and spirituality, they confuse it with religion and they say that's a myth. But *that's* reality! *[Laughs]* It's puzzling.

CHAPTER 3

A Question Larger Than Resolving Conflict

Gayle Fillman spoke of her dojo in Ukiah being a world apart, a safe place where people could work together for spiritual, mental, and physical growth. Yet people bring all that they are, for good and ill, to this study—and so they should, Gayle believes. Ultimately, for Gayle, the practice of Aikido is not apart from the world but a way of more fully engaging with it, a method for achieving peace on a world-wide scale through the countless possibilities of actual individuals and events. She told me Aikido originated in the work and vision of a single man, Morihei Ueshiba. Born in Japan in 1883, the descendant of samurai, he grew up in a time of ferment in the martial arts in Asian countries when the introduction of guns had rendered unarmed combat obsolete. Many people were seeking new goals and purposes for traditional fighting disciplines. After studying with several of the foremost fighters of his day, in 1919 Ueshiba joined a pacifist religion whose leader, Onisaburo, advocated nonviolent resistance and universal disarmament. As Onisaburo's assistant, Ueshiba continued his martial studies and teaching, developing the spiritual and martial art that he named Aikido and worked on until his death in 1969.

As I understand it, Aikido draws partly on the principle I know from T'ai Chi Ch'uan of using the force of an attack to nullify it, and during a visit to China in 1924, Ueshiba is said to have studied T'ai Chi Ch'uan. Correctly applied, four ounces can deflect a thousand pounds, the Chinese classics of T'ai Chi Ch'uan say. In Aikido this observation is developed into an explicit philosophy: One should seek not just to deflect attack but to harmonize it—spiritually and physically. To enter into an attack, blend with it, and transform it. Gayle described for me how this works on a practical level: "If we block an attack, we're blocking the physical body, and secondarily we're blocking the mind. But if we blend with that attack and we very softly help it come through, the mind says, 'Oh, this is very gentle.' And it does not reject it, and the next thing you know that person is on the ground."

Morihei Ueshiba cultivated excellence in combat skills and withstood the many challengers who came to test his abilities. But he intended for the intensity, focus, and discipline of effective fighting to be channeled toward a higher purpose—"the restoration of harmony, the preservation of peace, and the nurturing of all beings."[1] "Words and letters can never adequately describe Aikido," he also said. "Its meaning is revealed only to those who are enlightened through hard training."[2] Here he refers perhaps to a process that is not so much mystical or mysterious as experiential—Aikido exists in the doing of it. This doing may occur in any arena—in a street attack, on the practice mat, in everyday activities of ordinary life.

When I discovered that an aikidoist who lived in a nearby town had worked for four years as a volunteer in a women's prison, I thought, here was surely a situation that would illuminate the practice of Aikido and its role in the world. Kathy Park is a sculptor and bodyworker with a second-degree black belt and sixteen years' experience in Aikido as well as training in Karate. When I called

HENRY WOOLBERT

Kathy Park in her sculpture studio (Jaroso, Colo., February 1996).

her, it turned out that she was winding up her prison work as part of an impending move out of the state, but she agreed to talk to me about what her experience had been. We met at her home in Healdsburg, California, where she took me to sit in her backyard, a bluff top with a magnificent view of a long sweep of the Russian River curving toward us. As we settled into lawn chairs overlooking the river and Kathy poured tea, a Siamese cat emerged from the tall grass.

"That's Santo," Kathy said. "He came from the prison. There used to be lots of cats. The prison doctor supported the cat club, an inmates' club, by writing a memo detailing the benefits of rela-

1. Quoted in John Stevens, *Aikido: The Way of Harmony* (Boston & London: Shambhala, 1985), 23.
2. Ibid., 21.

SHARP SPEAR, CRYSTAL MIRROR

tionships with pets—the physical comfort, the touching, the healing, an object to love, and so on. For a while that memo worked wonders. The cats were vaccinated and neutered, they were given feeding stations and little 'cat hotels' to sleep in. Santo was in one of the last litters from a black cat named Mama. The population was stabilized at ten or so. But some of the women took to sneaking the cats inside their housing units at night. A cat sprayed, or so I heard, and the warden put his foot down. All the cats were taken out. Now you might see one or two. They can get in through the wire fence, and the women do still manage to feed them."

Santo sniffed at my fingers and allowed me to scratch around his ears. Presently he wandered off, obviously at home in his new surroundings, and I looked up at Kathy. In her early forties, lean and wiry, she lounged in her chair with the easy grace I was to find in many women martial artists. I gestured at the young cat, now intent on a blade of grass. "You brought him out of the prison," I said, "How did it come about that you were in there? What exactly were you doing?"

KATHY PARK

Aikido

I was introduced to a woman who trained at the same Aikido dojo as I did. I probably trained with her—that's often the case, where you know someone on the mat, but you don't really know who they are, what their shingle is, or anything like that. Our teacher, Richard Heckler at Aikido of Tamalpais in Mill Valley, introduced her as Tracy Thompson, the doctor who was in charge of eight, nine hundred women out at FCI Dublin—the Federal Correctional Institution, Dublin, which is the only West Coast federal prison for women. Dr. Thompson had been urged by several long-term inmates, women who've been in prison for up to fifteen years already, and some of whom are looking at sentences that go deep into the next century, to find volunteers to work in the prison. Living in the Bay Area and having a chance to listen to radio stations like KPFA and so on, they'd realized that the Bay Area is full of alternative health practitioners in particular, and a lot of people who are social activists and call themselves liberal progressives, and, "Why aren't they out here in the prison being volunteers?" *[Laughs]*

One particular woman who was lobbying Dr. Thompson—Tracy—for alternative health practitioners is an atheist, and she was getting kind of tired of the standard, heavily Christian flavored, dogmatic-type volunteer—"Bless their hearts!" You know, I've met a lot of them, I'm glad they're in there, and they do walk their talk, I can say that. But I sympathize with this inmate, I'll call her Maria, because it can get kind of slow. She had an interest in learning more self-help, self-massage, stress management, personal growth—that field of things. Tracy asked Richard and he threw it in my direction. I went, "Help? Sure. That'd be an adventure. I'll go out to a prison and run a couple groups. Volunteer twice. No problem."

That was in the spring of 1990. It took us all summer to get the paperwork done, because I wrote in my résumé that I'm a black belt in Aikido and apparently that alarmed the prison officials.

So right away we got our first lesson in how not to play that up, how to reassure them that that's not what was going to be in the curriculum, it's just, "Oh, by the way . . ." We've learned a lot about diplomacy, strategy, and how not to antagonize those we have to work with. I thought I was just going to go in there twice, and I ended up creating a whole program, writing two grants, getting myself funded for a couple years. Here it is 1994, and I'm still involved in it! I got smitten by this group of women.

They were long-term inmates, women who were looking at at least ten years and who had been down—you're going to learn some prison slang here—had been down for five, ten years already. These were seasoned women, these were veterans. They were leaders. They'd had enough time to get it that they'd better make something of their lives.

When I think of what women generally go to jail for, I think of prostitution, small-scale drug and property crimes—trying to make a living in a world in which you have to wonder if women are even supposed to be able to support ourselves and our children. But perhaps it makes a difference that this is a federal prison?

FCI Dublin, at the time we started, was what's called administrative security, which means all levels of security, from minimum up to maximum, all mixed together. We had in the population I'd say mostly women who were in on some kind of drug-trafficking crime, but also some heavy crimes, maybe murder or attempted murder. I'll get to the political prisoners in a minute, because they're pretty key. Another huge cut of the women are in

on conspiracy, and that can overlap the drug question. Again, I don't have a legal background, but my understanding is that the conspiracy law, passed during the Reagan and Bush years, expands the net of people involved with a crime to include, in this case, the women. Maybe their involvement was they slept with the guy who did the crime. Maybe that's it. To hear the women speak about it, that's the impression you get, that basically they're in there because of a bad choice in partners. Or amplified on that, yes, they knew what he was going to do, but there's no way they were going to blow the whistle on it, because he was holding the threat of some kind of violence over them—"You talk about this, bitch, and I'll smack you one." And look at our society—women aren't trained to stand up against that kind of pressure. My god! It's a rare women who has the resources, the support community to do that.

I knew none of this, Stephanie. I was a good liberal, and I thought, "Oh, this'll be good for me." And I got my butt kicked, in terms of waking up. Especially the political prisoners. That's their term for themselves—the United States would never use that term. "We don't have political prisoners!" But that's what they call themselves. Especially there is a group from Puerto Rico, who are the Puerto Rican Independentistas, who are fighting for the independence of Puerto Rico, and I guess took that fight to the level of armed struggle—back in the seventies, when a lot of groups were looking at pursuing the revolution and entertaining those ideas. They probably were involved in bombs or something—I don't know.

The prison staff thinks of them as terrorists and maybe that's what they did, but knowing them, I'm not comfortable with that term. I see that they seriously walk their talk. They have a worldview, a political worldview, that's a bit of a stretch for me, but I see their point in terms of U.S. imperialism and all this—but I don't want to get into that. I think a lot of them wouldn't be comfortable now with that rhetoric or with the level of violence that their particular group was using at the time. You can argue about their methods maybe, but here they are, doing time for living a highly principled life and fighting for a noble cause. Also they're doing time because they refused to snitch other people off—more prison slang—and that's highly principled to me too. And they're under a lot of pressure. I mean, after twelve years, you'd start to think about, "Well, if I just say one name, I might get five years knocked off." So. Very highly, highly principled women. Very courageous women. Very strong. Very clear. And women who—all of the women I worked with in the Long-Term Stress Group, really—have and had an ability to look at the whole picture and care for the whole picture. They had a sense of backing up and being able to see the dynamics. They weren't just caught in their own stew. They had some sense of community, some sense of, "Yeah, I have it bad, but you should see these other people who have it even worse than I do in prison." There's a sense of extending their vision and their care and their compassion beyond themselves. Which is very impressive to me.

What is it exactly that you do? How does it involve—or not involve—your Aikido training?

I worked with that particular group of fifteen or so women for about a year. I introduced them to a variety of disciplines and skills such as meditation, yoga, conflict resolution, listening without judgment, communicating more clearly. And I introduced expressive arts—journaling, drawing, singing, making music, dance, circle foot rubs. Aikido came into play with the conflict resolution and stress management. I introduced the ideas of grounding, centering, 360-degree awareness, moving from the center, getting "off the line" (out of the way) redirecting the energy of an attack—whether it's verbal, physical, emotional, psychic—and staying neutral, calm, relaxed, balanced, and ready to move in any direction. We also did a lot about how to mind your own business, energetically speaking, how to refine control of where your attention goes, and have more choices as to states of mind, reactions, solutions to conflict, and that sort of thing. This proved especially helpful to the women in dealing with difficult inmates and staff. The women reported that they experienced less hassle and conflict simply by managing their own energy more skillfully and consciously.

It went well. The women anecdotally reported so much benefit and progress and better sense of health and well-being just across the board, and on the medical records it showed up too. A lot of them stopped using—or abusing—medication for chronic pain. They stopped medicating themselves to deal with their problems. They started to learn how to deal with their problems in a different way. In 1992 Tracy won an award from the Bureau of Prisons as best clinical director, which speaks of the relative health of the prison population. The circle of that started to spread. It became natural and obvious that the next step was to expand the program into a full day. My time commitment at that point was just two hours a week, coming in and sitting with this group or doing whatever we did.

So I designed a whole new program, and I wrote a grant—two grants—to fund it, and I implemented the program before I knew I was going to get the funding, I was so dead sure about it. And then, sure enough, both these grants came in. One was enough money to make it a part-time job for myself for a year, and the other one was much smaller, kind of kitty money, for art supplies and postage and the myriad things that we didn't realize would come up. I expanded the program to a meditation group, a creativity class, two stress management groups, individual bodywork consultations—because I do bodywork also—and bringing in lots of outside volunteers.

Somewhere in there is when Tracy and I brought in Wendy Palmer, another person you might want to talk to. She's taking over the directorship now that I'm leaving. She came in as a guest teacher with her particular brand of Aikido in disguise. I've trained with her individually and in her off-the-mat Aikido work. She's called it a number of different things—Aikido as a clairsentient practice, or the development of the intuitive body, or conflict resolution and boundaries. It's basically using Aikido movement and Aikido principles as a form and as a discipline to actively work with your own energy and as a centering, grounding practice so that you start to develop all of that as a reference point for those situations in which you tend to go off, tend to lose your balance. That's a form that I'm comfortable working with too, although I have such a strong thing with the expressive arts— that's the other big component that I brought in, the whole creativity, arts and crafts component.

Between the two of us, with me handling more the expressive part and Wendy handling a little more the discipline part, it really was, I think— *is*—a well-rounded program. Even before Wendy started, we brought in other volunteers, lots of guests, and bit off a couple of huge projects. We had a whole day of women's spirituality, a mini-camp, where we utilized the Women's Alliance, a group down in Oakland that I was involved with for a short time, that's involved with women's spiri-

tuality. That was a whole beautiful day of different workshops and coming together around this idea of women's spirituality. Also I got involved with creating a council on racism, and out of that we had a two-day multicultural festival. Those were the two major big events. I'm kind of skipping ahead in the years now. This past year, 1993 and 1994, we've scaled back quite a bit. The efforts to get more funding have been fruitless, so we're back to basically just getting paid mileage. We're back to being volunteers. The program had a real curve to it in terms of ambition and stuff that we actually pulled off. I'd say the heyday of it was 1992, and since then it's been trimmed back. But it's gone deeper too.

Is that just the general government money situation or is it the prison administration?

We've never had any government money. Our granting has all been private. It's totally free as far as the government's concerned. I don't have that much experience with creating organizations and watching them evolve, but I would guess that there's a magic honeymoon time and then there's a reality time. I know that my sense of "I can do anything" started to wear thin, especially when I realized that I was spending really a lot of time doing the prison work and not very much time with myself and my own creativity. My dreams started to show me that I was just throwing bones, you know, out in the backyard into my art. I know myself well enough to know that I often serve as a catalyst, and so I had to come to grips with—kind of throw myself forward so that I could imagine looking back at it in hindsight, kind of time traveling there—that it was my job to start this, and not my job to continue. And I had to make that all right. I still have to make that all right, because it's hard. And I'm going to be really missed.

And you know them, and they're there until 2015, or whatever.

Yeah. I wanted nothing less than to transform the whole community—which I can kind of laugh at now. It was big, what I wanted, what I saw, but also, that's how big things happen, it's when people have big visions. And it was remarkable what happened. I feel good about handing it off to Wendy.

You also hinted at the prison administration. At a certain point we ambitiously decided to include working with prison staff. Which I don't know if I'll look at that as a mistake or not. It changed our stance. It forced us to identify less with the women, more into a middle path. My joke about it was, "Okay, it's blown my mind that I would fall in love with these, these prisoners, but now you want me to fall in love with the staff? Oh, god." Because I guess that's where I am still stuck at somewhat of a stereotype mind. A lot of them *look* like stereotypes to me. A lot of the prison guards and staff are just walking around in their own prisons. Ugly prisons. In their bodies, the way they form their bodies, the hardness in their eyes, the flintiness around their hearts. When I try really hard, I can see the pain in back of that, but, god, their defense is to be assholes, to really develop their asshole. And they're good at it. It's hard to see through that and go, "I bet you this little boy was beaten by his father." And it's probably true. But meanwhile, that's their defense.

Tracy is very sensitive to any criticism or weird comment from the staff—she has to be if she wants her job to survive and the program to survive. Pagan, satanic, witches, you know, the hot buttons of the conservative right. Or anything about lesbians. So we toned our more adventurous programming way down. We still are concerned about weird, negative comments about the bodywork, or about Karina's voice class—that's Karina Epperlein. She might be another interesting person for you to speak to. She teaches T'ai Chi in Berkeley. Her class is anything but toned down. But it's also clear how valuable this work is, so we're going ahead with it, eyes open and alert. Of course the women complain that the program has changed, it's not like it used to be. They're right. The honeymoon becomes reality. But we're still there every week!

From the women's perspective, how do you see the program working?

I think one of the best things that we have given the women is a sense of how to not escalate a conflict. Here we are in a prison, and the roles are set in cement. There's such a heavy expectation about how the guards—or as the women call them, the police—are going to relate, and there's such a heavy expectation about how the inmates are going to relate back. For the women to have any breathing space around that, or even more essential than that, to see that it's a dynamic that two parties create—that's the definition of a dynamic, *dy,* right? "Two." It's not a *monamic.* It takes two to tango. For them to get that they had that tiny little pivot point of power in changing the dynamic I think has been the most major gift.

For them to get that, we had to point out to them on an energetic level what they were doing. Even when the cover story is "I'm not doing anything," we had to show them that the words don't mean anything if the body and the energy below is "C'mon, sucker!" We had to strip down some of the levels into that it's not just about words, that there's body language and there's energy language. Especially the energy language. To teach them to mind their own business energetically—how to pull their energy in, how to collect themselves, so that they're really minding their own business and not energetically out there cruising and looking for a fight. Because a lot of them were in the strong habit of doing that and didn't know it. I think it took someone like Wendy or myself, having trained a lot in that, in the Aikido format, especially with Wendy's work, to get a sense for that and be able to point that out to the women. I don't know where they would have gotten that from any other source. And I think that it's been absolutely transformative to a lot of the women.

They would speak about getting on a particular guard or a particular associate warden's shit list. It's like, there's your enemy. There's your enemy walking by. So every time you walk past them, in the cafeteria—not the cafeteria, food services, or whatever it's called, you know, to get your tray of food—every time you pass them in the compound, you can expect that there's going to be a hostile interchange. What we had to point out to them was that they had a part, that the fact that they expected to have a hostile interchange started to set it up right there, in a way. That they were starting to gear for it. That even them harboring, "So-and-so is evil, I hate her, grrh-grrh-grrh-grrh," harboring those thoughts and feeding those thoughts constantly, daily, supporting that kind of thinking, one to the other . . . I mean, keeping an enemy alive is a way to ensure that you will set up that conflict!

This was tough for them. They would come back at us, "But you don't understand! These people are really awful!" And we'd go, "I'm sure they are! I'm sure they are! But you've got to see that you're keeping yourself stuck in this too." We tried things. We would say, "In your mind, wrap a black belt around one. This is your worthy adversary. This is your worthy opponent. This is your training partner. This person—let's just say that this person exists on Earth to teach you about your energy and about how you lose your center in their company. Let's turn it on its head so you can start to begin to thank them for the lessons that they're giving you."

The women would look at us like we were from Mars! [Laughs] But it would start to sink in. It would. We would get reports back like, "I walked by so-and-so the other day, and I minded my own business, and I breathed, and I did all the centering practices, and I felt my feet, and I went interior"—whatever the particular practices they were working with at the time. They'd say, "It worked! She didn't bother me. He didn't say anything."

I think that the notion of irimi has been helpful to the women too. Going toward something. First recognizing that you're avoiding something, and then seeing if you can turn it on its head and go toward it. Even if that's, "I hate the associate warden," turning it on its head and going, "I respect you." [Laughs] Or whatever! You know, somehow saying something true, but that goes forward rather than negating.

I take it you can't actually teach a martial art. How explicitly can you use Aikido?

Officially this is just moving meditation.

But you do physical training and even some partner exercises?

To some extent, but nothing that you could walk by and sort of take a snapshot in your mind and go, "Hmm, that looks martial." So, no, we wouldn't be able to work with, "Now this person punches and now you take them down and fall." But Wendy's taught them how to roll, I've taught them how to roll, the two-step, some of the blending practices, stuff like that. But if we involved a grab, we have to be really careful around that. It stretched us to figure out different metaphors, different ways to work the metaphor, or physicalize the metaphor.

Did you find alternatives that worked just as well, or do you think it would have worked better if you could have just taught them straight Aikido?

Probably both are true. I think it's important as Aikido teachers, or as teachers of holistic health or whatever, that you are able to teach somebody in high heels and that you also are able to teach somebody handicapped or someone in prison with those kind of rules and regulations. It's important to have a huge repertoire to get it across. So I don't regret that at all. And at the same time—oh god, I think everyone should be training in Aikido! Absolutely! Straightforward, with the mats and the gi and the whole thing, it'd be great! For staff and inmates alike.

Now, staff do get some Aikido training, but my suspicion is that they just get sort of the lockdown, wristlock, police-hold-type Aikido. You can bastardize Aikido like any other martial art. You know, already, with Steven Seagal and that whole thing, Hollywood has tried to bastardize Aikido, which just breaks my heart. I hate to see

that. But we live in this country; that's what happens in this country. And in fact, where Tracy was first introduced to Aikido was at an obligatory prison-staff training. She learned *ikkyo* and *nikkyo,* and I don't know, some of the more police-style Aikido. She was inspired to go ahead and train and then she realized, "Oh, it's a whole other world! This is far out."

I think it would be great on all levels, as a discipline, as a way to develop a great relationship with your body. A lot of the women who come into prison, their bodies go to pot. Or that's how they defend themselves, just bloat and eat. I see it from doing a lot of bodywork. It's typical to put on thirty, forty pounds and just eat your way through it. That's a good defense. Numb out. Put a thick layer around you, physically and energetically, and feel rotten about yourself. Some of them have come through that. Some of them are on the track every day, or lifting weights every day, or sitting in meditation every day. But it's rare. Hopefully, we support those people.

In the four years I've been there, I've seen people come in and out of it. I've seen some backslides. Some violence against each other. Or somehow putting themselves in the line of fire, energetically. Women can be really nasty to each other too. One of the women that we worked with was attacked in line waiting for the microwave by another woman who came at her with a utility knife, a razor blade. The woman who was cut raised her arms in defense—she had some wits about her and didn't attack back. But she was cut. And since then, it's been hard for her, as you can imagine. I mean, right through the cheek to the mouth. It's been really hard for her to deal with that, being scarred up like that, but also, "Why? What was it?" I think she—well, you know, I won't ever know, but I think there's a layer yet deeper that she needs to look at that has to do with her somehow getting herself energetically in the line of fire. That there *was* something she was doing that set her up for that. I think right now she would say, "No, I wasn't doing anything," and I—I don't quite believe that.

Where she started from was being a tremendously psychic woman, powerful woman. She's from Chile, she's in for drugs, and I don't know exactly what she did. I imagine she carried, she was a mule. Has had some training in some of the Latin American occult religions, Santeria, I'm not sure exactly what to call them. It seemed to be a mixture of religion, but also maybe black magic, maybe psychic powers. I had to chase her out of my dreams several times. "Out! Stay home! We're coming to you. You can trust that. Get out of my life." Very interesting.

She has made progress. That whole idea of minding your own business and collecting your energy and not assigning yourself the task of fixing other people on a spiritual level, which is really an arrogant thing to do—she's stopped doing a lot of that, and as a result, she's had a much easier time. She has fewer enemies. She has to notice that. Well, she swears up and down that this prison is absolutely the perfect place for her to be, that the reason why she's in prison is so that she met me and met Wendy and met Tracy and went through these experiences. She sees it as school and that it's essential to her life. And there are a few women—only a couple who'll go that far, but quite a few who will go almost that far. And then a huge amount of them that will say, "Oh, this is really helpful; this is making my stay here doable." But they won't go as far as to say karmically speaking maybe that's why, you know, I'm *supposed* to be here. I mean, that's quite something to say that.

That would be hard!

It would be hard for me too.

But—karmically speaking—do you have ideas why *you* are in there?

Well, in no particular order here, just off the top of my head, I definitely, I think, went in there to get my butt kicked, in terms of waking up to another reality, to the fact that there are a lot of women, who really are a lot like you and me, who are in prison. And who are largely forgotten about. And some of whom I don't think did anything wrong. Even though it's been painful to find out about a lot of stuff that I know about now, I'm very grateful. It's shocked the complacent part of me that tends to be happy with just paying lip service to certain problems, and it's made me kind of get in there a little bit more, a little bit more engaged. That's been great.

I've been searching for a community of women just for personal support, a community of peers. At a certain point I wasn't even sure if it was supposed to be women, but it seems likely that it would be. I didn't think I would find it in the prison, but that's really the circle that I've been sitting in. It's been in prison. Those women have been my peers and my support and have mirrored back to me stuff that I just—it blows my mind, what they know about me. We're doing a lot of talking about leaving, because that's what's coming up, and we're looking back a lot at what happened over four years of working with each other. One woman who's been in the Long-Term Stress Group since the beginning said, "You know, Kathy, there was a time when you were working out here in the program when it was obvious to us that you were more in prison than we were. In terms of how you were carrying the burdens, your particular burdens. That you were suffering much more than we." This is a woman who has been down thirteen years and is looking at 2000-something—2014?—to get out. She's telling me? That I'm in prison? It really stunned me. Because it was true. There was a way I was carrying the burden of being the administrative force behind this whole thing and being the codirector—there's a way that I carry things—*a* way, not the only way—but I can carry things as though they press me down.

So how ironic, how ironic that I would go to the prison to learn how to carry my load more lightly. Isn't that amazing? I'm just starting to articulate that one, Stephanie. I don't really know it yet, but I'm just struck with how ironic that is.

And part of that was—again, I have to use prison terminology here a little bit—last spring was the critical point for us—Henry, my husband, is involved with the program too. We were on the rocks. None of the grants were coming through. I was having terrible dreams about my artwork. I was dreaming about starving horses out in the field. I'd forgotten about them, I didn't know if their feet were all bound up in barbed wire, I hadn't watered them in weeks, I hadn't fed them, and I started to go toward that pasture to go take care of them and then I'd forget! Ohhhh! This recurring dream—awful. And I know who those horses are, I know who they are. And things getting sticky within the program staff. At one crisis point Henry and I sat down, and we said to each other, "I want to know when my release date is. I am not a lifer."

We had to make that decision. "I am not in this for life. I want to know when my release date is." That really changed some things. We realized that freedom on some core level is something you give yourself. And *they* know that. They don't have

"*Metta: Goddess of Lovingkindness*" by Kathy Park (Lignum vitae wood, 21 inches high), 1996.

the kind of freedom we have out here, but they have a kind of freedom that we don't have. How does that make sense?

Anyway, since I've made the decision to leave and to move to Colorado, move toward my art, I've felt a lot more free in my being. And they are totally supporting me. "Go!" Isn't that wonderful? What support! Maybe they're identifying, maybe they're riding with it. I think it's a big enough swell so there's plenty of room for everyone to ride on it, because it feels bigger than me too. But it feels—the prison experience feels core to whatever feels liberated in me. I don't know how to say it better than that. They're related. They're intertwined. *[Takes a deep breath]* So I feel like I have my art back, I have my energy back, I have my vision back. I have my horses back. I have more of a sense of why I am here on the planet, and somehow they helped give me that. So that's huge. That's a huge karmic thing.

A couple more things come to mind. One is bringing my outside contemporary, peer, friends into the prison and watching them get their butts kicked. *[Laughs]* I enjoyed that!

So there's a little bit of prison guard in you too?

Oh, I'm sure. In all of us. But that's not the only thing that happens. They also fall in love and they also get real inspired. And they bring back a whole level of appreciation for the freedom in their own lives. Those are all things, just going there, anyone would get in the first take. The women in prison are such appreciative students, they're so hungry, they're so grateful. They're the best students in the world. Especially, you know, contrast that with some of my bodywork friends in Marin County—"Oh, there's a workshop on this, naw, I don't think I'll go, I don't really feel like it." That's not what you'd run into in the prison! There it's, "Oh, someone's coming in to teach us? Oh-h-h-h, god!" And they would all be there! No jaded thing, nothing cynical, just, "Thank you! Thank you for driving all the way out here. Thank you!"

I needed to be around that—maybe that's more of kicking my butt, kicking *my* cynical, jaded butt—to bring more appreciation into my own life. But to watch that happen to my friends, to share it with them—I think it's important. Especially some of my friends who have not really developed

their political acumen. I guess I think it's important that they do. Whether they pursue it or not, I want them to know. And also, in bodywork, and in the Aikido world too, it tends to be a closed society. And it's a luxury. I mean, look at who affords it. It's important that it get spread into other communities, communities of color, communities that aren't exposed to this kind of stuff. It's important for us to expose ourselves to them and their flavor on it, and it's important, I think, vice versa, for the women in prison. That was a lot of my motivation with bringing in all the women from the Women's Alliance, bringing in all the people for the multicultural festival. That kind of mutual exposure. And weaving in the personal growth movement with some social action here. Because it pisses me off that it's so separate and that politics and spirituality tend to be different camps. So I enjoyed that feeling of being a weaver. Of having a vision, having a big vision, and then having it come about. It's a great thing. And also having it be such a huge collaboration. All of this is new ground for me, all of it. I got in way over my head, and I think I did well with it, actually. And now I'm learning how to let go of a program. That's been hard too. "They're not doing it the way I would do it!" *[Laughs]* That's right!

How does this prison experience fit with your Aikido practice?

I've gone in and out of Aikido, I would have to say. Last May I went for my *nidan*—second-degree black belt—after twelve years of ambivalence about it. I trained up until about June, when we went to Colorado for the summer, and I've been back to the dojo maybe twice. Aside from teaching my own class, I haven't trained. And I seriously doubt if I will pick up formal training in my move. For a lot of reasons. It'll be a drive, it'll be a schlepp. Also, it's not what my body wants to do.

So that's another huge change. It's not completely unfamiliar, because I've taken long hiatuses from Aikido before, and they've been important and enriching, and actually it's been very integrating at times, to be off the mat. There's a lot of stuff about Aikido and the Aikido community that I feel very questioning about right now.

I question the hierarchical structure for all the standard feminist reasons. Teacher can become power abusive. Student can become powerless and abused. I've seen it happen. I've felt both in myself. I think it's important to undercut that in as many creative ways as possible.

I question the politics—actually, I don't. I've stopped relating to the politics. At last. What used to surprise, shock, and upset me—that people who practice harmony with the energy of the universe could still hold toxic grudges against each other, not communicate, sabotage, or betray one another—is now not so surprising. Corruption can happen to anyone. I guess I've grown up and let go a bit here. I've stopped needing my teachers to be perfect and then hating them when they're not. But I also have stopped looking for community in the Aikido community. I've been disappointed too many times. And community has come to me in different faces, different places.

Lately I've been seeing how much my disappointment with anything says more about me than the thing itself. If I accept the thing exactly as it is, how can I be disappointed? It's only when I want it to be different that I set myself up for disappointment. So if I let the Aikido community be exactly what they are, then I am no longer wanting them to be different or more or better. I am also unhooked from my disappointment and free to look elsewhere, or create what I want anew.

I'm not sure what's come from the prison and what's just come. Something about reclaiming myself as a creative being and the freedom in that has been real core in this last year. I think that that comes somewhat from liberating myself from my own prison, deciding to leave the actual prison and move toward my creativity, wherever that's going to take me. And also realizing, okay, form and discipline—they're all right. They do good. They have a place. But I don't want to keep developing that right now. That's not what's up for me right now. What is up for me is not so much gaining more control, it's more loosening control. I see that a lot of the women in prison are not at that place. They're in that, "I want more control." That's kind of what Wendy addresses, and there are fewer women that want to work with me and some of the other juicier, expressive people who come in. Most of the women are wanting to get a grip on their anger. They're wanting more control and more discipline.

It's more formless for me. It's more, "What's the energy? What's needed? What can we do creatively, collaboratively, to work with whatever it is that's up?" I've gotten a lot of practice in the prison working that way, and that has definitely informed how I teach Aikido here. And vice versa. It's also informed how I approach my life.

Life's not about control. It's about being present. In some kind of agile, movable way. So that when the universe gives you its little whisper of information or the fish flops out of the river you see it and somehow that informs you. That's where the information is to do whatever it is. The next painting. The next sculpture. The next move. The next thing to say. Maybe it *is* about discipline and form, because you have to be present. You have to have some kind of stability, some kind of reference point to be here. But maybe I feel like I've got that, or enough of it. For me that's not the edge. Being silly and outrageous would be more the edge, more of what I'm interested in doing. And encouraging. Joy.

One great example. *[Laughs]* It's a great story. My fortieth birthday party was at the prison, and it was a surprise party. At the time we were meeting in the chapel, and Tracy delayed me going in—I couldn't figure out why, she was very evasive—but I realized as soon as I walked in, because they had it all spread out with all this contraband food that they had cooked and a computer-generated banner that said "Happy Birthday, Kathy." Two different cakes they'd paid for through the black market. They'd paid the cooks to create these two cakes. They had guacamole. They had M&M–peanut–raisin kind of gorp. And they had these enchiladas. They had chicken enchiladas and cheese enchiladas.

They started serving out all this food, and I got fascinated with the enchiladas, which were quite good. "How did you cook these?" "Oh, we just cooked them." "But *how* did you cook them—do you have kitchens in your units?" "Oh no, Kathy!" "Do you have microwaves in your units? How did you do this?" They were all laughing hysterically at this point. Finally, Maria was serving, and I said, "Maria, tell me, how did you do this? How did you make this?" She says, "I ironed them." I went, "You *what?*" "I ironed them. We iron it. That's how we cook here, we iron stuff." Can you believe this? "All right, Maria, tell me how you do this!"

She said, "Okay, I'll give you the recipe." There is a commissary there, so they can buy food. You buy Dorito corn chips, canned chicken, package of cheese, jar of salsa. You acquire guacamole or get someone to bring some avocado and garlic and cilantro back from the kitchen. There's an elaborate black market, of course.

A whole world is recreated.

Of course! *[Laughing]* So you take out half of the Doritos, and the rest you leave in the bag and you pack them down a little bit and then you start layering whatever it is, all your inner ingredients. And then you take the other Doritos, pat them down on top and close the bag carefully and place that bag between two damp towels and iron for a long time.

It must take quite a while!

And it was excellent! So that blew my mind. Finally we got to the cakes, and they lit the candles, and they were those weird candles.

Oh, that don't go out—

What happened is it made the smoke alarm go off. In the middle of all this hilarity the smoke alarm goes off and we realize the guards are going to come running. So all the food is tucked underneath people's coats and underneath chairs and behind books. In a matter of seconds the place is cleared and we all trundle out—this is the part of the story about hilarity and joy and how powerful it is—we're all standing outside and the guards come in. "Ummm-hmmmm." With their walkie-talkies. "What's going on here?" Their faces completely pissed off—"How dare you!" And we just—we were circled out in the courtyard, and the women would look at me, and I was just laughing my head off, and I was looking at Tracy, who was laughing her head off, and in the midst of that trying to talk to the guards. I don't know what she was saying—"Oh, it was just a birthday party!" And she's looking at the women, who are all laughing. We kept each other laughing until finally the last guard left, and he's walking through all of these laughing women, and you can see *[she sets her face in imitation of the guards' steely expressions, and then lets one corner of her mouth twitch]* this smile—escaping from his prison—from his prisoned face! It's just so powerful!

That's the direction I would like to go in my life. If I'm going to continue with Aikido—or mutate it in the direction I need to go—it's got to bring a lot of joy and fun. Maybe that's more toward the dance of it, maybe that's more toward making sound. I don't know. It's got to go that way, or else I need another form that does incorporate more dance, that's got that kind of contact and that kind of thrill of intimate contact. And maybe some falls too—I love the falls. But I think its pivot point wouldn't be around the same question, How do we resolve conflict peacefully? I think it would be, How do we work with contact creatively?

We did a thing in the prison the other day where one woman said, "What would it be like to spend a whole month, and every sentence that you said was in the present tense?" She said, "That would blow my mind!" So we went around the circle a few times, and that was the only requirement, that you say something that was true in the present tense. It was amazing.

So—to make contact with the present moment, to make contact with your own body. In all of its levels. To make contact with another person. To make contact with the truth. All that stuff we're afraid to do. And it seems to me, if that's what you address, if you can backtrack it to where it's still just a seed, then the conflict, the violence, never grows.

CHAPTER 4

Balance Doesn't Always Mean Being Cool, Gathered, Contained

A few weeks after talking to Kathy Park, I met with Karina Epperlein, a performance artist and teacher of breath, voice, and theater as well as T'ai Chi Ch'uan, who also volunteers at the Federal Correctional Institution, Dublin. A small, fine-boned woman recently turned forty, Karina is German by birth but now lives in the San Francisco Bay Area. The day we talked she wore bright-colored clothes and dangling earrings and ear cuffs, which glittered and softly chimed when she moved about the room as she spoke. She was not so much restless, I thought, as engaging her whole being in talking. When she alighted on a couch, she sat very erect and alert, bringing all her body and being to sitting. She put me in mind of the carvings on Indian temples of many-armed figures that always appear to stand forth, fully rounded, from their background. She herself said, "When I do something, I do it fully. I get very focused." She laughed and added, "For some people it's too much!"

Our talk ranged over all the questions I had brought to the making of this book, answers—and new questions—arising from Karina's descriptions of the interconnections she sees between her practice of T'ai Chi Ch'uan, her theater work, volunteering in the prison, and the documentary film she has been inspired to make about several inmates.

KARINA EPPERLEIN

T'ai Chi Ch'uan

Originally, in Germany, I was a dancer. Dance was an artistic expression with an energy form, and that was more than sports to me, though sports I liked too. I was interested in the life of the body and the energy, not just the body as a mechanical instrument. I liked all the earthy, down-on-the-ground kind of dance—classical dance made no sense to me, because it left out gravity.

But even with the dance I had, I kept missing something. So even before I left Germany, I was interested in T'ai Chi and it had come toward me. People had said, "This might be something you really want to do." I took a few classes, but I knew that I wasn't able to really commit myself to it. When I heard that I was going to be coming here—to the San Francisco Bay Area—with a theater company, I also heard that this is a great place for T'ai Chi, and I knew I wanted to do that. I sensed that there was more to it than people moving slowly in a certain choreography, even though that in itself is entrancing. The stories I heard evoked magic and mystery, and there seemed to be a promise that one could reach with one's own body and energy into the realms of philosophy and the spiritual.

This was in 1982, when I was twenty-eight. I looked at different teachers and decided on the Inner Research Institute, Martin Inn's school. This is the form of Cheng Man-ch'ing, the short form, thirty-seven movements. It was a totally right choice for me. I liked the way Martin taught, the way he approached T'ai Chi, the way he looked when he did the form, and how he passed it on to us as Westerners—because most of us were Westerners. He demonstrated the form clearly and encouraged questions and even philosophical discussion. It was a good balance of the mystical and the practice.

And he integrated a lot of Chinese medicine.

I remember in my first class already I was getting these surges of energy which were so powerful they would transport me. I couldn't practice by myself for the first half-year, to my embarrassment—I never wanted to say that I wasn't able to practice by myself! I was frightened. I thought I would explode, with fire. It was just too powerful! And yet I liked it so much!

After a year of regular classes three times a week I wanted to know more, and I asked Martin how I could deepen my experience of T'ai Chi. This idea of ch'i, energy—I wanted to research that. Martin suggested that I learn to teach. I was reluctant. I had taught dance and wanted to get away from teaching.

Did he say what teaching would do for you?

He did not—here he was a very typical mysterious T'ai Chi master—"If you want to get into this, you should teach." I wanted to hear, "Read this book and read that book," but he said none of this. He said, "Teach." It was mysterious to me. I let it sit a couple months, then I said, Yes, okay. It was more my trust of him than understanding where the teaching would lead me.

He trained three of us, two men and me, as assistants. It was a very fortunate period for us, because he spent a lot of time with us, tutoring us and teaching us. It was hard training—three to five hours a day. We learned Push Hands; we learned the sword form; we learned the fighting with the sword form, the T'ai Chi style fighting; we learned *ta-lu,* which is the Push Hands that moves in a choreographed form. We also assisted in the classes, which meant correcting, hands-on correcting. That is still substantial in my teaching—hands-on correction is very important. I learned that from Martin, and that was a real gift.

Then he gave me a workshop to lead—a group of people I had to teach the first third of the form in a few days. I was able to do that—though in class I forgot a few of the names of the moves. I was able to cover up, and I didn't embarrass myself in front of everybody, but I felt humbled, because I saw how difficult teaching is, how difficult it is to be inside *and* outside at the same time. After that Martin gave me my own class within his school, and I would also teach for him when he was gone, big classes, sometimes. I felt very honored, because he believed in me and expressed it to me and helped me.

Then he said, "You're ready to do your own school. Do it." I felt very much thrown out of the nest, but it turned out well. I rented a studio and remodeled it myself. I called it the Blue House. I opened my school and had quite a lot of students. I ran this for four years and it developed into a wonderful community. I had some very faithful students who stayed over time and one assistant, a woman who would assist me and teach when I was gone. It was very enriching—and empowering, because I saw that I could find my own way of teaching and make my own kind of school and fit my own style and rules.

I realized as a woman I approach it differently. It's much less competitive, the way I set up my school. I didn't want any competitiveness within the class or between the students. I thought that wouldn't further what T'ai Chi has to offer on relaxing and softening. I was interested in the inner world of the students. I broke some of that traditional wall between teacher and student. That's a difficult balance, because you also can't just be buddies with your students. You need some structure as you teach.

And this felt different from teaching dance? You were saying you didn't like that.

Yes. Quite different. Because the T'ai Chi—it's one simple form, and the rest is really about tuning in, into your own body, into the energy, and then into other people. For me the T'ai Chi has always been something mysterious and sacred. It's not a means of making money but rather a holy activity. I know I don't know enough about it. I want to understand it. I want to penetrate deeper. For me it's been a tool for that.

And did you also learn more about your own T'ai Chi through teaching?

Oh, yes! By then I totally realized—this was maybe my fourth year of T'ai Chi—that teaching was an incredible teacher to me. If my students looked a certain way and kept making the same mistakes, that would teach me what *I* was maybe not doing quite right. They're like a mirror reflecting me.

I was very into being as clear as possible about explaining the form and it was—how do I say?—a success experience for me when the students would get a movement easily. Which was something I had gotten from Martin—if I'm very clear, then my students will get it easily. I kept searching for more clarity within my body, so that when I would demonstrate, I would be able to show all the little details and the inner changes, making them as visible as possible.

And you were also continuing your theater work? How did that fit with your T'ai Chi?

Another reason why I wanted this big studio in the Blue House was to do my theater work, my own training, my own research in acting and physical theater work. I was able to do performances—original theater pieces I developed in collaboration with other artists. We put some wonderful little pieces on, where even the critics of the *San Francisco Chronicle* and others came. It launched my career as a solo theater artist. The T'ai Chi and the theater kept nourishing each other. From the very physical kind of theater I was doing, I would sometimes bring some of the looser exercises or more improvisational ideas into my teaching in the T'ai Chi. T'ai Chi was a big part of my physical training, the approach of grounding, the way of working with gravity, the way of working from the center, coming from the center, be it a movement, be it a character, or the voice. That has affected and informed my theater work up to this day.

I was interested in seeing where does T'ai Chi link with our psyche, our emotions. That was for me a big problem—that the emotions were left out of T'ai Chi. All that was said was, "Calm the emotions. You should not get excited. You should not be angry." You should not feel this and that. You just are balanced. And I realized, but I'm not! I can try, and what it felt like was squelching. I saw that part of my spirit sometimes was squelched because I tried so hard in my practice to be in this balanced state. It meant that my energies weren't flowing freely, because I couldn't acknowledge that I was angry, that I was unbalanced. The theater pieces I developed were sustained by an emotional power, a raw energy power, and that was a link where I started working with emotions in T'ai Chi and with what was going on

PAMELA GERARD

Karina Epperlein in her solo theater piece i.e. Deutschland *(San Francisco, 1993).*

with me personally—how I could use T'ai Chi to open myself and let flow and release instead of holding and contracting. It has taken me quite a while to find where they all link: theater, T'ai Chi, emotions. Balance! It doesn't mean that you have to be always in this cool, gathered, contained place, but that you also acknowledge all the other places, all the other voices. The places where you are out of balance, the places where you are weak, the voices who want to scream or those who want to be lazy. I also started my own therapy, Jungian at first, with lots of dream work.

I had to work with myself. I would go to other

T'ai Chi classes, either traditional or more New Age, and I wouldn't find what I was looking for. I wanted to go to this difficult place where it is *experienced* in the body—whatever I find out, I have to understand it in the body and not just as an idea.

I was told that the first ten years in T'ai Chi are sort of the beginning, and then with ten years, I would feel there's a certain solid ground. I was looking toward that, wondering whether that would happen, and I must say, it has been true. Now it's thirteen years, and around the ten years, after that, there is something there, which has become so much part of my body and being that there is a solid ground, a depth one gets just of sheer perseverance, I think, of having stuck with it and done it year after year. And I also must say the T'ai Chi has improved and strengthened my health tremendously.

Thirteen years. It's been quite a journey. It meant for me constant creative work: Where does this T'ai Chi fit in my life? How much can I integrate it as a Westerner, as a woman, as an artist? How can it feed all that? How is it connected to that? And in the last five years, the use of voice and sound.

That seems very interesting to me! There's so much emphasis on breathing in T'ai Chi, but T'ai Chi practice is almost always in silence. Voice seems like the next extension—almost a natural enlargement.

I became more and more interested in, Where does this all come from? How can we work with emotions? What is a good tool for it? The breath comes first. It carries our soul. Just through breathing, so many emotions get very easily activated. Breathing with awareness can bring healing. In my ex-perimenting with the breath I'd see that there's a relationship between ch'i—the life force—breath, and our feelings and inner life. This made me explore how to work through emotions like pain and anger, how to release, how to transcend, how to let go. How to let it wash through.

I work with voice, sounds, and the breath in the warm-ups so people get this feeling of the breath rushing through and cleansing the body. Also I work with the resonances—so that you really feel the vibration, in the chest, which is fairly easy for people, in the head, or in the belly, which is difficult, but that's ultimately where you want to feel it, the energy in the belly, the tan t'ien, the center. That's where it all begins. I experimented with myself, and then I integrated it into my teaching.

At the same time I started working with teachers from the Roy Hart Theatre, which is based in the south of France. There's a group of teachers who work all over the world, and they have this center for voice and theater work. They approach the human voice as a tool with very wide range, using screaming and sighing and crying and all kinds of animal sounds. Using the emotional muscles—in this teaching the voice is called "the muscle of the soul." Some of that work I had done before in my Grotowski-influenced theater training, working very physically with the voice in the body, different parts, the hip, the belly, the chest, throat, and head. It was very profound for me to get this kind of voice training and then to see how T'ai Chi fit right in—there were so many parallels. I would coteach workshops with these voice teachers or just teach them the plain T'ai Chi. That taught *me* a lot. They are already so open in their bodies, because they're people who have worked for twenty years with voice, and a lot of physical, subtle work too. Many have now integrated T'ai Chi into their work.

What is it they find in the T'ai Chi that was missing from what they had before?

They found extremely helpful the grounding, to know about your axis, the vertical alignment where the body can start to relax because it places itself naturally, one bone over the other, and underneath is the ground supporting us. To feel it in your body—not just have an idea but to really embody that and to ground down. Because they see the voice as very physical, so that when you sing or speak you do it from here—the lower belly, the tan t'ien—not here—the chest [stands up to demonstrate]. Opera singers will say, "Yes, you have to support it from below," but they will often stand with locked knees and they—they push it up. Well, my idea was, you sink, you sit basically—the T'ai Chi stance—and then you relax and you let it come up from down here [she gestures to the tan t'ien].

They found that really great, the stance, the relaxing down, the opening the body so when everything's soft it can resonate. The practice of awareness. That was what I looked for in my theater too—how can you act with a depth and an authentic place where you're not just pretending? It has to be physically as well as in the mental state.

My T'ai Chi teaching has become very—very inner over the years. Allowing people to see what happens inside and having them reflect it back out. We talk. More experiential talk—not so much philosophizing but, "What goes on? What do you feel?" What often comes up is that people don't like their bodies. Or they start to feel pain and they don't like it. We talk about it—big themes are acceptance, gentleness, and acceptance. Patience. These are the traditional old virtues, right? Part of my German heritage I used to reject as a teenager—"All this old bullshit! I don't like the old wisdoms, all this discipline and patience." [Laughs]

It's been great fun for me to come back to traditional wisdom through T'ai Chi and understand it through my body and—and see the wisdom afresh and anew and not as this stale word or concept. Especially me as a rebellious person, to find myself back to these old values of perseverance and patience! Through the T'ai Chi I can believe it and fully say, yes, that is important, that makes sense. The older I get, the more I think there is a truth to it which helps one to stay morally grounded, ethically grounded.

Do you think that comes too from having this clear physical sense of oneself? That you need that first?

I think it is helpful to be in one's body, to know intimately one's body, because one appreciates life with that, understands life and nature, and then moral and ethical decisions can arise out of that very naturally. They're not just a rigid rule which somebody told you but make sense from one's own respect for life and death.

I want to touch briefly—because it is a difficult area actually to touch with words, I find—on the spiritual aspect. It's almost something I've kept secret to myself, because I find as soon as I go out into the words, there're words there which have been used a lot and have been misused. Like the word god. But I'm going to just use god, because for me it means spirit, eternal life, and the T'ai Chi, in its very simple, grounded, profoundness of doing daily practice, which is about becoming aware, becoming centered, and has become a spiritual practice in connecting me to god, to life, through the inner world.

I use T'ai Chi like a meditation, always have, and that has intensified. Maybe simply by getting older—with most people when they get older the spiritual life gets more intense. I guess the sitting meditation is not as appealing and not as powerful for me because I don't have as much energy running in my body. With the T'ai Chi, I'm able to be on this Earth, connected to the ground, connected to Earth, aware of it, grateful to the Earth that it holds me up, and at the same time connected to the spirit, which would be heaven. That image of my feet connecting with Earth and the top of my head connecting with the heavens is very powerful for me.

The stillness of standing meditation is important, I think. That opens up the worlds inside and the voices inside. Letting the thoughts pass by, letting the emotions wash through and breathing and staying simple—all of these things can happen easily in the standing meditation. It becomes a prayer for me. It becomes a way to reach out to god, to life, by reaching in. It's a way of healing myself. Sometimes I send prayers out asking for help. I use it for all kinds of communications with the higher power, the higher self. There're many words for that, and I'm reluctant to use them, because I don't belong to any religion really, and it's a quite individual process. But I've been very grateful to have this structure for it.

I also am really aware as an artist what the T'ai Chi gives me through the ritual and through this time of slowing down and being still and being aware—my intuition is right there for me, my creativity is right there for me, because it's very nurtured. If I want to know something, how to make changes in my life, or when I need to find a decision, after just going into a standing meditation and grounding down I come out with some kind of answer, or clearness, better understanding.

How does your prison work fit in with this? You don't actually teach T'ai Chi in the prison?

No, we can't teach martial arts. I teach a weekly two-hour class called Finding Our Voices. We explore the body as resonator and as musical instrument. We play and work with breath, sound, song, movement, and writing to learn to listen to ourselves—freely, spontaneously, and from the center.

I use the T'ai Chi stance—in all my voice work, the T'ai Chi stance is the essential thing. And the women learn about the axis, learn about sinking energy—how to not push up, how to just sit. They love all of that, and it empowers them to have a stance and to know you can have that connection below and know you can be big and strong. There are so many pressures on women to not just sit down and be big but rather to be up and thin and brittle, you know? These are interesting things to learn for women. The women in prison catch on very quickly. I have seen them open up, learn to trust me and one another, and find within themselves capacities for artistic expression as well as resources of strength and self-esteem they never knew they had. Half of the women in my group have been able to go off medication like antidepressants. With their ch'i flowing, their health improves. With releasing anger, fear, anxieties, they get along better with each other. Prison life is very, very tough, designed for daily humiliation. The immense overcrowding—three women in a cell built for one—constant noise, constant observation, systematic infantilization.

It's a horrible system, especially hard on the women. Eighty percent are mothers, cut off from children and family, and they are the caregivers, the men absent in most cases—and often the men are the ones who got them in prison in the first place. They truly are victims of societal chaos. It is a life where you're stripped of everything, to the point where you're almost stripped of yourself. But the good part—if there could be a good part to it—is you can compare it to a cloister almost. What we voluntarily want in a retreat or in a cloister is to strip ourselves of extraneous stuff so we can get to the essence. That is forced on them—prison is not voluntary or nice! But it can be a turning point. At the same time some women feel protected and happy to be away from the streets. Sometimes I feel this total paradox. I can't understand it all, I have to just try to hold it.

What do you see the women gaining from your teaching?

I think most basically what I bring to them is probably my person and what I embody. My composure teaches them very much. How I hold myself. How I move. When somebody else comes into the room, how do I handle this? We have lots of emergency situations. How do I handle them? Am I in my center? Am I true and authentic? Am I really listening and interested in their well-being? Those are important teachings for them, and they observe you on that level. Very much. So I personally saw this incredible value if you come just as a human being. The old T'ai Chi teachings go on about that too—if you embody it, then you teach it. I'm starting to see that happen in my life.

When the women tell me stories, I listen. I affirm them, I say it is hard. That's a lot what they want—they have almost no space where somebody would say, "Yes, this *is* very hard. The way you have to live is horrible, and it's hard, and I hear you. I hear you." And just let it sit for what it is. In the circle I hold the pain for them so they can

learn to hold pain, their own pain, not just run from it. And then later I say, "But it's all about you really. You might get angry about this person, but it still is about you." I'm very careful about how I bring that in. I might bring it in with a personal example, how challenging it is for myself, and how I failed to do that myself, maybe. They are in a very powerless place. The only thing they can do is try to take care of themselves and not get hurt. That means that they have to be flexible and be in their center and protect themselves without lashing out, because lashing out is always going to hurt you if you're in a disadvantaged place— or any place really!

So maybe the relevance of T'ai Chi here is what it gives *you* rather than anything you teach them about it directly?

It helps me to go in there, to move in and out. You have to be very grounded. If you're not, you're going to get scared, you're going to be whacked around by the system, the prisoners will try to pull you left and right in their neediness. If you don't know how to be a center, you can be taken apart. You have to be really down to earth. It just happened that I had the right tools. I dropped in there and I had great fun with my first class. Since then we've become—I'm becoming friends with them and they with me. They see what we're trying to do. They understand it. They value it. They are very grateful that somebody like us exists. That's been a great gift to feel that. I struggle more with that in the so-called normal world on the outside.

But not all the prisoners want to come to our program. There's a lot who look down on it or even give it bad names. Some say my class is diabolic because we do screaming. And because it's addressing women's issues, it's been labeled as satanism and—what was it?—goddess worship. It's not just the authorities and church officials who label it that, but some of the prisoners.

From what Kathy said, it sounded like conditions at the prison are becoming increasingly restrictive. Do you feel that pressure? Do things seem to be changing?

We are definitely moving into a repressive stage—inside and outside the prison. The work of volunteers is often unwanted and made more difficult by the authorities. Programs are being cut, anything that "coddles" prisoners. In my opinion the prison experience is very crippling, with little or no chance for healing or transformation. It costs huge amounts of money, more than a college education, and then we release damaged and broken people after much too long sentences. It's a mess.

I feel, though, that my work with the women, and now also going into the prison to film the women—this unusual work, which is very subversive work—is protected and guarded. "The angels are with us," the women often say. The warden has not been bothering me like he has been recently doing to Kathy, really intimidating her. It's been bad, and for her quite a struggle with how to deal with that.

He only came once to my class, and I went right up to him, and he kind of backed away. You know, this is when I try all my martial arts things out. I saw him come, I walked away from my circle, toward him so that he couldn't get to the circle. "What do you want?" "Why are you here?" One of my other strategies is I try to talk to him outside of the group. I go to his office and ask for something or tell him something. I feel that he's

in some odd way maybe halfway afraid of the kind of work I do and halfway intrigued or fascinated. So he doesn't want to know about it, he doesn't want to make a big fuss and throw me out. If he really knew what I'm doing, I think he would not allow me in there, and I think he wisely underestimates me in some sense—which is great, and I play it at that level.

I wonder if this difference in your experience and Kathy's is something of the difference between T'ai Chi and Aikido? She talks about trying to blend with what they're doing and watch what her energy is, trying to keep it peaceful, where you're being much more up-front martial about it, claiming your space.

It is true, I—I was consciously thinking, we've got a federal prison, which is based on military strategy. I was aware that if I want to make that film, I need to deal with them. I can't just ignore them, and I can't blend with them, because then I'm on their turf. I felt like I had to come right at them. I was seeing the Push Hands. In Push Hands you learn to go right at it—not *hard*—soft! But you have to touch so that you know what's going on. I need to go right at the warden, even go close to him, because otherwise I don't know enough about him.

And maybe that has worked. Oddly enough, at the time I started, my whole preoccupation was fascism and the Holocaust—the solo theater piece about German history and culture, *i.e. Deutschland,* that I was working on then. It brings me back there! How fascism works very subtly—it's based on intimidation and fear—and how you buckle down eventually. When I ask the women what is the struggle to survive in prison, some of

Karina Epperlein (left) leading a class at the Federal Correctional Institution (Dublin, Calif., July 1993).

them say explicitly the biggest struggle is "to not become like them."

There have been many books written about prison situations, with writers using that for a metaphor as well as for a story in itself. I feel it's an odd but maybe important thing to have this prison appear in my life through Kathy and you and Wendy Palmer just as I start on this book.

Prison is a very powerful archetype and metaphor. Even before going to the prison I often thought about the prisons we have, individually and as a society, the invisible ones we carry. I think always of that rib cage of ours—that's where we feel the most unfree often—with our heart, with our emotions, with the breath, with the giving out, the let-

ting out, and the letting in, the receiving. Prison is an externalization of our own prisons in body and mind. My desire to break out and have a flow between the outside world and world inside prison, that bridging of inside–outside, is a theme of my work throughout the years.

The process of making this documentary about the women in prison has been a rich experience for me, on all the levels of organizing, working with the prison authorities, and seeing how just a little bit of hope can change something in a human being. How we all need perseverance. How we all need love and support. The women supported me at this dead point where I almost gave up on our theater performance and on the film. "I'm not getting anywhere, I'm ready to throw in the towel." "It will happen," they said. "Don't worry, we'll make it." They worked hard. They pulled a lot of strings for me, and they took good care of me. Without them I could not have achieved it, because I was getting quite exhausted, banging my head against closed doors.

It felt like I'd gotten myself into something which is too much, biting too big a piece off. So then I had to open myself to the support of other people, the women especially. And then when the performance the women in my class put on for the prison volunteers and the other inmates came out so great, and I saw how much it gave them, I felt probably the most fulfilled I've ever felt with having done some art. The power, the transformative power of art, the magic, was so alive at that moment—if you have never believed in art and its power, that moment, everybody did. Those moments—you don't get them too often!

◆ ◆ ◆

The performance Karina mentioned was a forty-five-minute collection of original songs, dance, and poetry four women in Karina's class put on in the prison auditorium. Actually there were two separate performances, one for inmates and one for volunteers, because the prison officials would not allow the two audiences to mingle. Karina filmed one performance for the documentary she was making about these women, and I later saw excerpts at a performance Karina herself put on in a Berkeley, California, theater to showcase her work in progress on the film and raise funds to complete it. This performance, called *Pouring Love into Bones,* included video clips from the prison as well as dance and voice pieces by Karina and her collaborator Gwen Jones, a composer and musician who works with ancient and indigenous instruments, many of which Gwen has built herself.

In one song in the prison performance the four women inmates compared prison life to living in a bathroom with strangers. Standing in line in the Berkeley theater rest room after watching the video

clip, a dozen women from the Berkeley audience and I looked around and saw each other and the two-stall institutional rest room in a new light. "I'll have my bed here," one woman said to her companion. "Your bed can go over there. But how are we going to fit all these other people?" "Bunk beds," her friend answered. A third woman added, "There would be one toilet only, and no walls around it. That would free up more space." We gazed around at the dingy white walls, exposed sagging pipes, the single small wire-mesh window with frosted glass that you couldn't see through, each of us trying to imagine what it would be like to be locked in this room, the whole group of us, overnight, all week, thirty years.

"So it became real!" Karina exclaimed when I told her about the incident. "Not just this cell on a TV screen—I've seen that so many times. It doesn't scare me till I imagine what it is really like sitting on the toilet, for example, and being exposed to everybody else in the room. I won't be able to shoot much of how the women actually live, but I'm starting to see that it is like reading a book—when you can't see things they sometimes become more powerful."

This was also very much Karina's method in her own dance and voice pieces that she interwove with the prison film excerpts. Many of the pieces felt to me more like rituals than performance as it is generally understood, in that Karina and Gwen did not so much portray as reenact the situation of the women in prison—and people imprisoned in other ways. I was put in mind of the religious element I think of as underlying ancient Greek drama: the mysterious power that we feel moving within us when we participate in or even witness activities we perceive with more than our conscious mind.

Karina's comments in her interview about breath and sound and their centrality to her T'ai

Chi Ch'uan and her artistic work took on substance for me in the variety and power of the sounds Karina and Gwen obtained from their instruments, including their voices. The sounds they made filled the room, so that humming, roaring, crying, laughing, strumming, and melody seemed to pour out of the walls and ceiling or well up from the floor to surround the audience in a new and fascinating and very tangibly physical environment. There was a physicality too in the slipperiness of distinguishing the sources of the sounds in Gwen's voice or Karina's, this horn or that stringed instrument. These ambiguities underscored the impression given by the video clips of the women in prison that all of us, audience and performers, are in the most basic respects indistinguishable—except that some of us are in prison, which is totally other and different.

When I visited Karina after the performance, she seemed pleased by my observations. She had wanted to engage the power of ritual, she said, and to make the whole performance into a prayer. "It didn't actually come out quite the way I envisioned," she added and described some of the changes she had made over the three nights *Pouring Love into Bones* played. I admired her ability to use live performances to revise her work. "I've been bold about that," she agreed. "I feel that it has to be good enough so that you can show it to people, but I also want to experiment. I have a vision, but it's still so vague that I need to see it manifest in steps. Developing my theater pieces, I keep doing them and changing them and making them better and more distilled. I've been lucky that it's never been really a disaster."

"But it's not just luck, is it?" I asked. "Isn't it also discipline and training and other qualities in yourself that you bring to both the theater work and your T'ai Chi? We've mostly talked about what we learn from martial arts, but surely each of us

Karina Epperlein playing cello in a performance (San Francisco, 1993).

also brings something to it."

"That's true," Karina said. "I always say you get as much out of the T'ai Chi as you put in. Somebody—probably my teacher—told me that, and that struck me as true, very true. When I do something, I do it fully. I commit myself. I engage my whole body and soul and my spirit. I bring that to the T'ai Chi, to the theater, to the prison work. I'm seeing now that I'm doing it with the film, the same way."

Karina completed her one-hour documentary film *Voices from Inside* in January 1996 and it is now in distribution.

CHAPTER 5

Something in the Movements Was Like Coming Home

People speak of martial arts being hard or soft, external or internal. In hard or external styles the emphasis is on conditioning the muscles and training for specific techniques of kicking, punching, and blocking. Karate and Tae Kwon Do are often held up as prototypical hard styles. In soft or internal styles practitioners seek to develop internal energy, the life force or life energy called *ch'i* in Chinese and *ki* in Japanese. T'ai Chi Ch'uan and Aikido are generally considered soft, internal styles. In reality probably all styles are a mix of external and internal, and none is wholly without aspects of the other.

The external qualities of muscle and technique are easy enough to see and understand, though long training may be required for skillful execution. Internal qualities are subtler and more elusive. The distinction is *not* one of body and mind: Mental and spiritual discipline is required for hard as well as soft styles, and internal energy is by no means wholly mental or spiritual but very firmly grounded in bodily being. Modern Japanese and Chinese researchers report they have measured the flow of ch'i, or ki, through the meridian system of acupuncture points on the body.[1] According to the Asian view that mind and body are not dual but inseparably one, accessing and developing one's ch'i, or ki, opens an avenue for simultaneously culti-

---

1. Yuasa Yasuo, *The Body, Self-Cultivation, and Ki-Energy* (Albany: State University of New York Press, 1993), xii, xxiv, 69–96.

vating bodily health, spiritual clarity, and an ethical practice of responsibility for one's behavior in human society and the world at large.

For me this integrated perspective opens a new understanding and appreciation for why things are the way they are and how they can be dealt with skillfully and appropriately. As an example far more dramatic than anything that has happened in my life, I think of how Kathy Park and Karina Epperlein used physical exercises that were metaphorical applications of their martial arts to enable the prison inmates they worked with to develop increased self-awareness, self-control, and bodily health.

A lot of what is claimed as internal power is no more than wishful thinking, however. In the case of Kathy and Karina it seems to me that their grounding in the physical training of their arts, together with a notable degree of maturity, spiritual honesty, and intellectual rigor, enabled them to clearly identify the boundary between metaphor and make believe and give their students true coin. When I talked to Wendy Palmer, a fourth-degree black belt with twenty-five years' experience in Aikido, who has also studied Buddhism, meditation, and yoga, I was curious to explore further in her martial arts practice and teaching what is the physical ground of these internal energies and psychological metaphors.

I met Wendy just as she had taken over the directorship of the Prison Integrated Health Program at the Federal Correctional Institution, Dublin, from Kathy Park and added a second full day each week to her time at the prison. She would volunteer a third day as well, she told me, except that with a mortgage to pay and a child to feed, she can't afford it. We arranged to talk over a late dinner one night after she finished teaching Aikido at the dojo she and two partners founded in 1976 in Mill Val-

ley, California. She invited me to watch the evening's classes and indeed to participate in the beginner's class and try out Aikido for myself.

I arrived a little before five and climbed the rattling metal stairs at the back of an industrial-looking building to the loft where the dojo is located. Through iron-sashed windows the densely wooded slopes of the hills that surround the town could be glimpsed between tall redwood trees. Even with the clatter and bustle of students arriving, greeting each other, and preparing for class, the dojo had the feel of a place apart from everyday life. Wendy, a wiry, athletic-looking woman in her fifties with short, thickly curling graying hair, greeted me warmly. Before turning me over to an assistant to sign a release of responsibility for injuries, she gave me a quick etiquette instruction: Bow to the *shomen*—the photograph of Morihei Ueshiba, the founder of Aikido, flanked by vases of tall gladioli at the front of the room—before stepping on or off the padded practice mat, which covered the entire floor space except for an aisle from the entrance to the reception desk and the changing rooms. For the rest, Wendy said, observe the other students.

Class started with the students kneeling in *seiza* in a line at the edge of the mat and bowing. Then followed warm-up exercises, some very like the circles and stretches my simu, Janet Seaforth, uses for T'ai Chi Ch'uan. Others, based on Aikido techniques, were new to me, and as I struggled to translate right and left from Wendy's opposite example facing us, a student appeared at my side to illustrate the movements more slowly so I could follow.

Before I could thank him, Wendy clapped her hands and everyone lined up again in seiza at the edge of the mat. She called on a student to help her demonstrate the technique we were to practice:

munetsuki kotegaeshi (literally, "strike to the middle of the body and wrist twist throw"). Half a dozen times, from different directions and angles, the student attacked and Wendy threw him, pausing now and then to point out details and warn of common faults to avoid. She and the student bowed to each other, and everyone paired up with a partner to practice. The several newcomers, including me, Wendy took aside to learn the back roll in which the technique ended. This too she broke down into digestible pieces, and rather to my surprise I quickly found myself working up to at least a semblance of the desired move.

Clap. With another student as attacker—called *uke,* or "receiver," for in Aikido training it is always the attacker who receives the effect of the technique and is thrown—Wendy demonstrated refinements of the technique. Then she instructed us to practice further with new partners. A tall man in the long, skirtlike hakama of an Aikido black belt bowed in front of me, offering himself as partner. He patiently worked through the technique with me, alternating left and right sides and attack and defense. In my turn as uke, I aimed a punch at my partner's middle. "You shrink back," he observed. Yes, I thought—hasn't it always been my first line of defense to abandon my body, avoid participating. I called on the calmness and centering of my solo practice of T'ai Chi Ch'uan, which I had found available to me in such stressful occasions as reading at book signings and speaking at public meetings.

"Expand," my partner suggested. "Follow through. Relax. Sink." Hands here, feet here, weight here. I began to feel the pattern with my body and move more easily, with less thought. I punched. He grasped the wrist of my striking arm, pivoted to stand beside me facing the same direction, and then pulled me around in a circle to face

him, more by the momentum of my punch than by tugging on my wrist. He drew my hand up, curling it back toward my forearm. To escape the painful hold I dropped to my back knee, rolled onto my back on the mat, and rolled forward again to spring to my feet.

Switch hands. Switch roles. Now I was *nage,* or "thrower," and my partner was uke. Switch partners. Another black belt, a red-haired woman smaller than me, bowed in front of me. She was softer in her movements and more flowing, which drew me into executing the technique more smoothly but at the same time made it more difficult for me to distinguish the details of what she did. Her turn came to attack. "Put one foot out or the other," she instructed me. "That determines the side of the attack. *You* initiate the attack." "Oh!" I exclaimed. I hadn't realized that the nage—who of course ultimately prevails—is not merely the innocent recipient of attack but rather makes the determining move that opens the exchange.

No time to think about this now! Punch. Pivot. Grab. Twist. Fall. Again. And again. Once more Wendy clapped her hands. This time class was over. We lined up in seiza and sat in silence for several minutes, just breathing. Wendy made several announcements. There was to be a fundraiser that weekend for an aikidoist in Sacramento whose neck was broken in a freak accident colliding with someone as she did a back roll. The accident rendered her a quadriplegic, but now, a few months later, she had recovered some sensation in her arms. Probably such accidents happen no more frequently during Aikido practice than while walking down a street, but I felt sobered. This was not a game, although I did have fun, I thought as I followed the others in a concluding series of bows, ending with acknowledging the particular persons I trained with during the class. As the class scattered, I realized that I had not learned my partners' names and likely would not recognize them in street clothes. Yet I thought I would know them again by their presence and the feel of their energy.

Even before the beginners' class ended, more advanced students gathered around the edges of the mat, stretching and warming up. Most of them wore the hakama of Aikido black belts or the brown belts that denote the highest rank below black. Watching them practice I realized that the evening's training had unrolled one layer of my outsider's eye. In the sweeping gestures and whirling rolls and falls that on other occasions had seemed to me purely mysterious—although always entrancing—I started to make out patterns and logic, skills one could decipher and learn. Through it all, Wendy glided, her spare figure very erect but supple as she demonstrated, corrected, encouraged. Wherever she went among the twenty or thirty constantly moving students, who were similarly dressed and mostly larger, I could pick her out. There was a clarity about her movement and being, as if the light were more focused around her, or as she herself later put it, the field of her energy was more coherently organized.

After class Wendy and I walked through the dusk to a nearby restaurant and I told her a little about my background, my previous books, and how I came to this book through my practice of T'ai Chi Ch'uan. At once, she inquired whether I do the T'ai Chi Ch'uan partner training of Push Hands. She commented on the importance of the relationship one finds only with partners.

"I'm getting there, I guess," I answered ruefully. "Perhaps I need more time of solitary practice to become comfortable with myself before I start partner work. I do like weapons," I added, for I had recently begun studying sword, a solo form like the open hands set.

Wendy approved. "In Aikido we have the wooden sword, *bokken,* and the *jo,* the stick. I always encourage women especially to study weapons. To be able to control the tip, you need to have a strong base, and you also get used to expanding your field. It's a wonderful way to develop your ki and to expand your sense of self and your base. Plus there's a lot of fun and beauty to it."

As we talked, it struck me that these interviews were a kind of introduction to partner practice for me. Hungry though I was after exercising, I felt myself keyed up for more than an ordinary meal when we reached the restaurant.

WENDY PALMER

Aikido

I was a hippie in the sixties and lived that kind of simple life. We didn't even have telephones—you'd think about someone and then they'd appear. Some friends of mine were going to an Aikido class and they said, "You should come check it out." I'd always been interested in sports, and I liked the martial arts—I did a little Judo in college, because it was available. I went, and it was one of those things that I just saw and I knew immediately— my being, my spirit, went, "Oh, yes, right. This is what we'll do now." I told people, "This is it. I'll do this for the rest of my life."

Everybody laughed at me, but that's the way it felt. It felt deep, and it felt familiar, even though I had never seen it before. There was something in the movements that was like coming home. I totally loved it. Of course, practicing was a whole other thing! But I had this feeling that I would do this for a long time.

How old were you? What year was this?

What was I?—twenty-four, twenty-five, something like that. I believe it was 1971. In the beginning it was a small class, twice a week, in the Unitarian Church in San Francisco. The mats were kept up on the podium, and we used to have to go upstairs and throw them off the podium onto the chapel floor. We bowed in to these chairs that were stacked in the corner. My teacher at the time never brought a picture of O-Sensei, so I trained for six months and never saw O-Sensei. I just loved these moves that we were doing. If I had to, I would hitchhike into the city, just to be part of it.

Then I went through this period where I would cry all the way to the dojo, in the dressing room, through the class, and all the way home because I was so frustrated. I had run into myself—which is inevitable in training. I'd be sniveling on the mat, and people would say, "You sure you want to do this?" I'd say, "Yes," sobbing. It was because the implication of Aikido is that the attacker's not outside of you, it's within, which I totally agreed with, but bruises were appearing on my arm, and it felt like, "I didn't put these bruises on my arm." My teacher kept saying, "Get it together with yourself." I realized the implication was that in fact I was orchestrating all my pain and discomfort, but I couldn't do anything about it yet.

This was how far into your training?

A few months, probably about six months. I still have periods of ups and downs, but that was just so dramatic for me, to come up against myself and not have any way out. I kept saying to my teacher, "He did this." And my teacher would look at me and say, "If you had it together, it wouldn't have been a problem." He was a bit tough. I'm more mothering about it than he was. But he was right, and I got the point. That radical place got better—it's one of those things, like even with this knee injury I have now, you get so far into something and you think it'll be different, but then you can't really remember the point where it started to turn around. It's almost like a magician's trick that the universe does, a sleight of hand. It did shift, but for quite a while it would get a little better and I'd get real excited, and then I'd run into myself again.

People talk about having sudden illuminations in which difficulties come clear. But I wonder, in something like this, where you're working through your body, whether inevitably it comes in stages without your always noticing as you sort of catch up with your body, or you catch up with your mind?

There're definitely the sudden illuminations. There have been nights when I did amazing things. I remember one time I was training with George Leonard, my partner, who's six-four and very big. It was very much toward the beginning and I was pretty spaced out. I did this simple throw, and George flew across the room and landed in the stacked chairs in the corner, and everybody in the whole place just stopped. I looked at my hand and

Wendy Palmer (left) demonstrating tenshinage, *or "Heaven and Earth" throw, at the Santa Cruz Summer Aikido Retreat (July 15, 1995).*

I looked at George, and it was like, Wow! Some wild ninja thing from the fifteenth century! George climbed out of the chairs—he wasn't hurt, thank god!

There're always moments, certainly for me there were, and other people record them in the martial arts, when you suddenly do something and it's brilliant—and you can't repeat it. Or maybe even for a night you're more on. You understand it deeply and it's there. I've had beautiful moments when I've touched all the places that people talk about and all the descriptions in all the writings— I'll touch it, but then I won't be able to sustain it. Over the years, slowly there's a sustaining value that is building, that is deeper. I can hold places now that when I first started I could only touch. It's like jazz—I play jazz too—as soon as you achieve that level, then the next level opens up, so you always feel as much of a beginner, but you're actually progressing.

Jazz and martial arts are similar to me in that they have endless possibilities and varieties and you need a strong working base to be able to let it open up as much as you can, still keeping the working base in mind. I've been in the martial arts for twenty-five years now, and you know, even the first year that I heard some of these amazing concepts, like soft is strong, I loved it. And then a year later, it was like, "Oh!" And then five years later it was like, "Oh-h-h!" And ten years later, it was like, *"Ahhhhh!"* and then fifteen years later—every few years I feel a geological experience of the insights. It keeps getting deeper and deeper, the tremendous possibility of discovering the feeling that goes on inside these amazing ideas and concepts.

It sounds like from the start Aikido was taking up a major portion of your time and your life. Or were you also pursuing a career and raising children or whatever else?

I was raising children and trying to pursue a musical career—I was in a band. And I was holding down a job as a waitress. In the beginning the Aikido was only two classes a week, but I'd go home and with my friends who were studying, we'd do it in the park and we'd do it in the kitchen and we'd do it in the house. A year or two after we started, my teacher opened a dojo and that became a big school with three sensei—later I got my black belt there. Even though I was working and raising children I was always thinking about Aikido, and all my spare time I was practicing with my friends—it was very much an obsession.

In twenty-five years, the longest I've ever taken off from it was once for six weeks when I went to Hawaii. I was an addicted windsurfer, and I sailed the waves in Hawaii for six weeks. What it felt like was Aikido. When I got back it was so funny— "Oh, an arm to grab instead of booms." Because I had been holding the boom from my windsurfer for six weeks, and it was a similar feeling. The forces are the same. The wind is this gigantic force and you have to finesse it and you have to relax. But it felt so good to grab an arm!

My experience with Aikido is like being in a relationship. There've been times I've been really frustrated with the art and with myself, times I've been really romantic about it. I was involved in Capoeira, which is a Brazilian martial art, for about five years, and my joke was that I was married to Aikido and having an affair on the side with Capoeira. I was still doing Aikido, but I was rushing off to Capoeira class too. Windsurfing was the same way. But Aikido has been my longest, most enduring relationship. It's my marriage, no question about it.

I gather you've also had injuries from Aikido—you mentioned your knee. My T'ai Chi teachers always said that if we hurt ourselves, it meant we were doing something wrong and we should figure out how to do it right. Of course just stretching and exercising can feel painful at times. But I've heard people who do other arts talk differently about injuries, almost as if it belittles the power of the art to think one would *not* **be hurt by it. I wonder what your feeling is?**

If the techniques were done perfectly by everybody, no one would get hurt—the techniques are designed not to hurt, but there's a lot of stress on the joints, a lot of torque and pressure, and we're not all very accurate all the time. So I would say the likelihood of getting injured is pretty great. I've had ongoing thises and thats, as well as the knee injury. We joke about it. I always say everyone has been hurt and probably will get hurt again, and if being hurt is going to stop you every time, then you're not going to do very much in this life.

I guess I was thinking not so much of accidental, catastrophic sorts of injuries, but the kinds of stress injuries that you kind of have to work at.

I've had tendinitis. Part of it is learning how to heal it up and keep training—or not—but keep training is the way I've always done it. You can do it, but it takes mindfulness. You have to tape it and then you have to tell people, "Don't throw me on this side," or "Don't throw me hard," and it's a pain, but you learn how to take care of yourself. Bodies can heal. Part of it is learning how to work with the energy so it can heal itself. People get into sort of whining, "God, make it better," "I want it to be better," "Some Western doctor make it better," instead of taking the responsibility for getting an injury like that, a stress injury that means we have to stop and learn.

Injuries are always saying, pay attention. Always. People like me, I'm so stubborn, I need a two-by-four over the head. I don't get those little gentle pats. My friend said, "At least you're not a brick-wall type." And it's true, I'm not a brick-wall type, I'm a two-by-four type. Part of me has accepted that I'm not going to get the first tweaks or twinges, that it's going to take tendinitis for me to go, "Okay," and change. That's my personality. Some people will get it on the tweak. I don't have any judgment that the one's better than the other, I really don't. I think that we have to learn how we are, and for me, it takes something pretty major to slow me down or stop me.

Hardly ever have I seen injuries where someone was just a total asshole and hurt somebody. Usually the person who's training sets up the situation—the training is strong and they get injured. You don't have to train strong. Training strong is an option, always.

I noticed two people in the advanced class tonight, a woman and a man, who were at the end of the mat near where I was sitting—it was a technique where they were being thrown down so they landed on their stomach and then one arm was twisted behind their back. This particular pair was carefully and slowly—almost tenderly—but very deliberately twisting each other's arm. And that person was waiting—you could see from their face that it really did hurt—before slapping their hand on the mat and ending it. I was fascinated watching them. Is it that you need to do that to really learn what you are doing? To discover how far you can go—for both persons? I can see that you don't want to stop the move before you have gotten the person helpless, but this seemed more than that.

It's called a pin, you put the pin on them, then you put the pressure on the pin until the person taps, and tapping means, "You got me." Usually what happens is they're practicing finding where that pressure is. Some people don't tap, they want it to hurt before they tap, and some people tap before it even begins, they just on principle don't want anything to do with it. It's that whole range of personalities, every type is going to be there. On certain nights, certain people, it's like I know I'm hurting them, but they're not tapping, and I'll just not pin them any further.

There's a certain level of training—it was the brown-belt level for me, before my black belt—where I wanted to kind of feel what really worked or what it really was, and there was even some questioning, What is this as a martial art? Once you get your black belt, there's a feeling of okay, now I'm a true beginner, I can settle down and go through this more long-term stuff in the art, but until that time you're building all your techniques and getting your sea legs.

Sometimes the brown belts just before their black-belt tests are just impossible. A lot of people get injured in brown belt. The nicest, sweetest woman in the world will suddenly just be cracking you and yanking you and everything's going. It's this kind of frenzy that happens getting ready for their test, and this personal inquiry, and their energy just kind of goes crazy for a few months. Almost everybody does it. It's a trip to watch. I've seen the blue belts complain about it—"I won't do that!" Then there they are when it comes their turn. They have all these excuses why, and I say, "It's okay, I understand. Just back off or train with each other or something," because they're doing it to me.

It's kind of a self-inquiry about what that is, and everyone in something like Aikido, at some point needs to explore their edge. Where is my pain? What am I willing to take? What's it like to put that pressure on someone else?" It's an exploration, because you want to understand more about all that area instead of just, "No, I always want to be nice and never hurt anybody." In some sense I want to understand, what is this thing with hurting people? How do we get to it and what does it feel like? In some ways it's a valuable area, but it's tricky. It's touchy.

I encourage people to explore what they feel. I say, "Take responsibility. You can get hurt and you can hurt somebody. So if you're going to train like that, try to pick someone who's bigger and stronger than you, so the likelihood of hurting them isn't very strong." They weren't in class tonight, but there're a few young, strong guys that anybody can just train with, and you can go pretty much full out and you'd be hard pressed to hurt them. *[Laughs]*

You keep a few around for everybody else to practice on?

We do, and then sometimes those guys train with each other, and they're scrapping around in the corner and everyone's looking at them. I think it's therapy, they need to fight with each other a little bit, kind of explore that and feel themselves. Feel that testosterone going. Some sensei don't allow it, but I figure it's an area that people may have to understand about themselves, what it feels like to go against someone—because of the whole thing that Aikido is done soft, that's the whole principle. It's like T'ai Chi, you don't fight it. But for some people, one of the ways you know what not fighting is, is by exploring fighting.

Aikido's actually a pretty benevolent circumstance to explore it in. Studying Capoeira for five years made me understand Aikido better than anything I ever did, because Capoeira's partly about fighting. It has the playing *with,* which is a demonstration, but when you play *against,* it's a very mean, competitive art, and people hurt each other. I felt what it was like to be in that space and to be hurt and get pissed off and want to hurt someone back.

That comes up in Aikido, but it's not up front, it's a kind of covert thing that happens and you struggle with it or whatever. Capoeira's just "I want to get your ass." Straight out trying to win. And then when they did, I'd get pissed off, and I'd think, "What is this? Wendy, what are you doing?" It was important for me to see myself do that. It's why I stopped. I didn't like myself because I would get hurt and it would make me mad and I'd want to hurt people back. It made me see how important Aikido is as a philosophy. How it's implied not to do that.

There seems to be a lot of ritual around Aikido, which perhaps contains the activity. T'ai Chi doesn't have that—some teachers provide that, and there are so many different kinds of T'ai Chi—but Aikido really comes with it.

It does. It comes with the setup of bowing and then making that little interaction here and then bowing again. Yeah, very much. And so that's helpful. And there's still a lot of weird stuff that can go on. In the early tradition there was more fighting than there usually is now. When O-Sensei was first having his dojo, I think it was referred to as the hellhole, because the training was so severe and combative. He had taken this totally different approach to martial arts, and he was challenged by other martial artists. There are quite a few traditional guys that will take more of my approach of allowing the exploration of fighting. One of my teachers, Ikeda Sensei, is very liberal with that. You can't fight him—he just does Aikido on you. "You guys want to try to work it out, go ahead," he says. "You'll stop eventually. You'll get hurt or you'll get old."

But not because you'll learn?

Well, some of the women learn quicker. The truth is, most women can't fight a guy who's two hundred pounds. So we can learn real quick. Whereas the guys who are two hundred pounds—you know, they'll quit because I tell them, but it's like inside they go, "Yeah, but—" So that's why I'm trying to give those guys a little more chance to tough it out. "Go ahead." Within reason.

It's more since Aikido's come to America that they're into not fighting. It's sort of that's the Aikido thing, not fighting. But in Japan, some of the training has been so severe that it was never a question.

Have you been to Japan?

No, but I've studied with quite a few Japanese teachers who have come here. Maybe there are some great teachers in Japan that I've missed, but I can't go to Japan and deal with all the stigma of being Western and being a woman and fighting my way through that. I get more respect here now that they come here and they see that there are so many women doing it and that women are having dojos and students—women are getting a lot more respect in the United States than they get in Japan. So in a certain sense you get better training from the Japanese teachers here than you would if you went there.

It's also a little bit more creative here. They say that this is the place where Aikido is going to grow next, because Japan is so much tradition. My joke is that Japanese teachers come here and say, "Stand this way," and the Americans go, "Why?" Nobody ever said "Why?" to those men in their whole life! For fifty years everyone said, "Hai!" "Jump off a cliff." "Hai!" "More quickly." "Hai!" And then here, these men say the most simple thing, and people ask, "Why?" These Japanese *shihan*—master teachers—don't know how to respond to why, but they are learning.

I think it's been good for these guys, because they *are* masters, they are tremendous, and they've never been pushed like this mentally. They've developed themselves very, very much with their ki and their capacity, but because of the nature of the Japanese tradition, people would never have these kinds of conversations. But I'm there picking their brain, asking them, "What do you think about? What's your training? What's your background?" They all at first were taken aback by my forwardness. I figured if they really didn't like it, they'd tell me to stop. And they were going to have to tell me to stop or I was going to keep asking questions.

And out of that started coming some interesting responses. I saw they were having to reach inside themselves and think about what it was that they were actually experiencing. Their training was so deep since childhood, most of them. They grew up with it, and they never had a psychological point of view of what does this mean and how do I do it. They just had always done it—and it had gotten very powerful for them. At first they were shocked at being asked, and slowly started to talk a little bit more about it. It's interesting.

I'm beginning to think that one needs students as well as a teacher. You may outgrow your teachers, but I wonder if you forever need to have students?

I think so! I think it's very important. One of my teachers is very Japanese and doesn't talk very much to his students about their training. I tell them to keep asking him to talk about training levels. Encourage him to be more articulate about what it is he's doing, and he's going to encourage you to develop your bodily practice. We do need each other. Everyone has to grow here.

At some point you yourself started branching out from Aikido—or expanding it or bringing in other ideas. How did that work?

Yeah, how did that work? My first Aikido teacher, Bob Nadeau, had been teaching Aikido principles and calling it Energy Awareness. So I had some ideas from him about working in an informal way. Also, there's a woman named Helen Palmer— who's no relation. She'd done a lot of work with enneagram, intuition, and psychic readings. Helen came over to the dojo one day and watched a class and afterward—Helen's very forthright, very up front—she said to me, "What you're doing is really great. I want you to come over to the East Bay. I'm going to set you up with a class and I want you to teach me what you know. And I want you to study with me, and I'll teach you my stuff." I was willing, so she set up a class with about twelve people, she and her husband and some other people.

She made it clear she didn't want to do formal Aikido, so I started working on just principles with them. We called it intuition work. The prem-ise was that I was what she called clairsentient. There's, you know, clairvoyant, clairaudiant, clairsentient. What I could do is get information through the sensations of my body and that way I could work more skillfully with people, in terms of moving them or affecting them or understanding them energetically. The classes grew. She gave it a name, Aikido as a Clairsentient Practice. Now I call it Conscious Embodiment.

We do partner exercises that have no throws, no falling, but are just a way to study energy in relationship. As soon as you take someone's hand and start moving with them, you're in relationship, and energy—something occurs. Basically I'm trying to abstract the emotional charge. I tell people, think about it as intense—it's not bad, it's not good, just intense. That means there's a certain amount of energy, which means you need a certain amount of ground, a certain amount of breath, and a certain amount of awareness of your field. Then your system can handle a lot of intensity.

But what often happens is we take off on our reactions, we don't ground it. What we're doing in these exercises is finding a way to stimulate that response without it being personal. Most of the people don't even know each other—or that's the ideal—and they're leading each other around and they're doing all the things they would do normally in an intimate relationship, but they're able to look at it as an energy pattern.

I was seeing these things occur in Aikido, but they'd go by like that [snaps her fingers]. And then fall down and get up, fall down and get up. It was too fast to really study it. We take something that might happen in two seconds on the Aikido mat and we'll spend two hours on it. Because while you're going through one of those interactions, like you did in the class tonight, a lot occurs in those several seconds; but in formal Aikido, you can't discuss it, you can't study it, you can't go back and "slo-mo" it, you just have to keep doing it.

So this isn't just an alternative way to do Aikido, it's looking at things that Aikido doesn't get to?

Right. Because Aikido's going too fast. This is studying things that would be surfaced in Aikido—which is a reflection of your life too—or in a personal, emotional relationship, and then slow it way down and study the energetic aspects, the physics of it, taking it without content, and then hopefully we can look back at the content with greater understanding.

I remember once a woman who was a black belt in Aikido was doing this class, and someone—one of the older gentlemen who's studying with me—made a comment that what they were doing was the baby class and Aikido was the real stuff and harder to do. She said, "Oh, this is much harder to do." And he said, "Really? Why?" She said, "In Aikido you get to throw the person, they fall down, and the connection's broken. You can use the form to break the intimacy, but in this work, you're going really slowly and there you are. You can't throw somebody down and step away. Everything you do stays with you. You have to take responsibility. It's much more intimate, it's much more of a study of yourself."

It was interesting to hear her say that she thought it was more challenging to do this work. For me, if I pay attention, I can see more deeply into myself. What Aikido does is it flushes out things I need to look at, but I can't study them that deeply, because everything moves too fast in Aikido. So things that'll surface in Aikido or in my domestic life—when I ask for issues in this class, if people don't come up with them, I bring my own, and I'll say, "Well, this is something that I've been struggling with, so let's choreograph it into a movement, and let's look at all the factors that are going on here, in the energetic part of it."

Some of the people who have been studying with me for a long time say they find that it has been the thing that has made the biggest shift in their lives, in terms of being able to—how can I say it?—more acceptance, more satisfaction in their relationships. Because there is more understanding. They take more responsibility. I talk a lot about tolerating energy running through your system. When difficulties arise, instead of trying to fix them, just be with them really directly and recognize this is painful and it's the truth and I have enough center to just be here in the pain.

My premise is, discipline is freedom. I just wrote a book about this training. The next book I'm writing is on the issue of what is freedom. I want to ask the question, not answer it, but to me one of the strongest elements of it is discipline, that then we have the freedom to choose this or that. Otherwise, we're just swept along. I want to teach people to have enough ground that they can get interested enough to get involved in whatever is—interest being the psychological version of irimi. To me Aikido has this incredible concept in irimi—"to go into whatever it is." It's been very interesting for me all these years: How does that apply to my life? How can I move into life in a way that's soft and open but still moving in, not away? So when something's difficult or painful or confusing, we can be stable enough to be interested in it.

That may be an answer to another question I had—about violence. Not just muggings in

Wendy Palmer (right), in front of the shomen at her dojo, demonstrating a Conscious Embodiment training exercise in which a student faces a wooden sword, learning to manage the emotions evoked, at Aikido of Tamalpais (Mill Valley, Calif., March 1996).

---

the street, but the forcefulness and violence that pervade our society in the way, as a society, we exploit people and exploit the environment. Do you see Aikido as having a role, a social role, in dealing with the violent nature of Western societies?

To me, we have to get centered enough to get interested in what the violence is. That's the root of it. That's my Buddhist background, that it always

stems from within. If I'm centered enough, I can inquire into the nature of it. I see that people are violent because they're in so much pain.

I was feisty when I was young and I had a terrible temper. I saw my propensity for aggression emerging when energy comes up into my system—I don't know that violence is what it was, but definitely aggressive. And just feeling it all starts at home—the whole idea of compost, that you've got to recycle, and you've got to work on your own violence and your own judgment and anger—that's one thing that martial arts can teach. Even the most aggressive martial art teaches you about self-control, and that's a valuable thing for someone—and I'd say particularly women, because they really need to get their energy out more and learn some discipline and self-control and work more directly with discomfort. A lot of violence upon women is drawn in on themselves by women's overreceptivity. The martial arts have a great gift to give in teaching them about that. And hopefully there's a place in the more internal arts to get us to inquire into the nature of our own violence. I think it's an important area for everyone to be interested in rather than judgmental about.

I like that way of formulating it—as a question of interest. That seems like a productive approach.

For me it is, because we have to look at this carefully, and so just making the assumption that it's all bad doesn't help. We have to understand it more. And nobody's really right. You may not have done something, but you may have thought about it. I may have wanted to kill the sonofabitch. If that thought's gone through my mind, and I just didn't have the ability to do it perhaps—

That's not much of an excuse . . .

It's not! To me it's really about helping everybody get themselves together. I say in my work, if you love someone, the greatest gift you can give them is to get yourself together. Everybody needs to get themselves together, and anything we can do to help that, whether it's turn them on to T'ai Chi, Push Hands, Conscious Embodiment, or Aikido—

you know, this culture needs some help! We are not doing really well with whatever we set out to do here.

In your prison work, you are really jumping into one of the most difficult parts of that.

I am, and I'm so into it! Although I didn't realize at first it was going to be a women's prison. Tracy Thompson—she was at the dojo tonight, training; she's the physician at the women's prison where I work—invited me to do a workshop there, and I said, "Sure." So we're driving there, and Tracy starts talking about the women, and I go, "Women?" And she goes, "Yeah, this is a women's prison." And I go, "Oh, no!" Of course, she's more like you, it never occurred to her that I would be more freaked out about going to a women's prison than a men's prison. "Nine hundred women? I'd rather go to a prison with three thousand guys!" We still laugh about that.

But there I was, and about two hours into this workshop I had this funny feeling in my chest and I realized—I was supposed to be there. That this was somehow a part of my destiny, and I might be able to help bring some useful practices to the situation.

So I kept going. Sort of like Aikido, it just got bigger and bigger, and now my vision is to get a holistic health program in every federal prison in the United States. And then possibly go to the state prisons. I'm in the federal system, so that's where I'm working first, and it feels like it's a possibility. The current administration is big on rehabilitation. The problem is the staff that work in prisons don't believe in it; they think prison should just be for punishment. So you have the higher-ups that are supportive of it, but the actual everyday guards and people—it's a dilemma.

And all the statistics—they say in fifty years, if we don't do something, half the United States will be incarcerated. It's the war on drugs, and the conspiracy laws about drugs that are putting all those people in prison. Seventy percent of the women are in for conspiracy. A murderer can get ten years and out in seven—but there's a woman in for conspiracy that has three consecutive life sentences.

Anyway, that's not my business. I'm a teacher, I'm not a politician—the politicians have to work that one out. I'm into teaching in the prison and getting other people to bring meditation, yoga, conflict resolution, which is the version of Aikido that I can bring, because you can't teach martial arts to the women. They can't even do T'ai Chi, not even the slow, healing forms—nothing that looks like martial arts. But the conflict resolution, which is like the Conscious Embodiment classes I was just talking about, I teach them that. They love that, and you can accomplish more with that than with the wrist locks, I'll tell you! [Laughs]

But you do some physical training with them?

In the conflict resolution classes we do centering and grounding. We push on each other. We practice the breathing. We do the two-step movement that we did in the beginning of class tonight. Practice raising energy and grounding it. Occasionally I'll do exercises where they actually hold each other and practice settling, practice centering.

Some of the women have no idea how to take their center. Their whole life has been serving men—and they're in for conspiracy for men in almost every case. The concept that they can in some ways find their own center and make their own choice and not have to be codependent to a man

is amazing to them. It never occurred to them that they could say no to a man.

I try to find ways to help them think about it that aren't going to get them into trouble and make them feel weird, but that they can do without disempowering the guy. Just like with the prison staff—they have to find ways to work with the staff without disempowering them, because it won't work in prison, the staff'll get back. There are ways that you can hold your center without disempowering the other person. That's my experience from Aikido and this other work. I'm trying to show them possibilities about it. But it entails a lot of work. They have to meditate and do concentration exercises and get hold of their mind.

It's my belief that people really need to meditate. You need that time to self-reflect and to really touch back into yourself. It increases your capacity for Aikido—or anything—if you can steady your mind and still your mind a little bit. To me, in Aikido, you can have a perfect form, but if your mind moves, it's like an airplane flap going down, it changes the energy. If a person's very sensitive, they can feel it. If you can keep your mind steady on whatever it is, the centerline or the balance point or whatever, that person cannot resist you. But as soon as your mind flickers onto them or their resistance, then they can push you. I think that one's ability for power really has to do with the ability to still your mind.

I have been meditating for twenty-five years, and I've felt it's only in the past ten years that there's been some of that real ability to take hold of myself at the level that feels valuable. As you get more into Push Hands, Stephanie, I think you'll find it helpful, because part of it is being able to keep your concentration and that real feeling point. If you can do that, you can *feel* when your partner is starting to make a move—because your mind is less distracted.

We started the yoga last fall. We needed a yoga teacher and no one was coming out, and I had a little yoga background, so I said, "Well, I'll do it until we find someone." And I'm totally into it, because it's helped my body so much. I'm even doing it at home.

Then I also do a prerelease class, which is for women who have a year or less to go, and I see eight people individually, half-hour slots. They're usually people that Psych or Dr. Thompson says, "I don't know what to do with you; go see Wendy." Everybody's given up on them and they're about to ship them to Lexington, a large prison in Virginia with medical and psychological services. It has the reputation among the inmates of being a hellhole, and the women don't like to go there. So I'm their last chance.

There's five of them that I see every other week, a regular half-hour slot, because they just said their lives have been so deeply in crisis that they need a little bit more ongoing support. And Psych is overburdened, and often if the person isn't improving, they just give them drugs. Give them Prozac.

That's not how I do it. My understanding of the Buddhist point of view is that they need to complete their cycle. And if you put them on a drug—sometimes you have to, because they're going to kill themselves or someone else—but if not, and you put them on a drug, they just stop where they are and don't get to go all the way through it. So it only serves the counselor, because then the counselor doesn't have to deal with them any more.

To me the trick is just to go through the hell with them, until they can find their way to pull themselves up, out the other side. And most of them will, if you hang with them and you encourage them. There's this spirit of survival in everybody if you can just track that, give it a lot of support. They want to come out the other side. They don't usu-

ally really want to kill themselves or anyone else. Sometimes they just don't know how to—to breathe. There's some I just give breathing exercises. It's amazing what the breathing exercises will do! *[Laughs]* It's so simple, but it's just so great, you know, to follow a practice, a certain order of breath. Your system gets to balance itself.

This all must be pretty wearing on you.

Actually, it's not. Even though I'm working solidly, and I'm seeing people who are in a lot of pain. I don't come away feeling stressed or in pain. I feel I'm there to hold their story and support them. And that's why I'm going ahead so much, taking on the directorship of this now Kathy's leaving—I feel this is what I'm supposed to do. That I can work very hard and not get tired, not get stressed out, seems like a sign: Keep going in that direction. If it was a difficult thing, I wouldn't keep doing it. That's not my style. It just really feels like where I'm supposed to be.

Watching the dignity and integrity with which the women are taking hold of their lives—it's very inspiring. It inspired me to keep developing in my work and wanting to be more free from the whining kind of suffering, the inner, sniveling conflict stuff that I go through. *[Laughs]* I'm definitely improving on that dimension, and a lot of it is because of this situation. So they're great teachers for me, the women, very good teachers.

I'm not much of a future person. I've always been kind of, well, whatever comes, I'll work with it. This thing about the prison, seeing a holistic health program in every prison in the United States, is the first vision I've ever had. I'm a little overwhelmed—I hope it's a good thing whatever does come. I'm sure it'll keep growing.

CHAPTER 6

Defying the Limits
of What the Body Can Do

Breath is basic. Our life span is measured by our first and last breath. Through our breath we sustain both ourselves and the gaseous envelope of our planet that is the medium of our existence. The rhythmic inhale and exhale of the breath of each one of us resonates in the air and drums unceasingly against the bodies of all others. I have read that because oxygen atoms are so small and mobile, and there are so many of them, each breath that we take is nearly certain to include a few atoms of oxygen from any breath anyone has taken over the past several thousand years.[1]

Every breath I took in the weeks of spring weather that followed my evening with Wendy Palmer connected me anew to the nine hundred women in the federal prison at Dublin. Moving barefoot in the soft, young grass under the flowering trees in my yard as I practiced T'ai Chi Ch'uan each afternoon, I felt acutely, and yet could not comprehend, the situation of the women in prison. Restricted in all their movements—when they can go outdoors or to the bathroom, when and what they eat, what work and other activities they do—they live crowded together in spaces too small for their numbers, with never any privacy, and overseen by guards inevitably coarsened by the system they implement and often sadistic in their behavior toward the inmates, who have virtually no recourse. Yet it seemed that in applying the

---

1. David Bodanis, *The Secret House: 24 Hours in the Strange and Unexpected World in Which We Spend Our Nights and Days* (New York: Simon & Schuster, 1988), 125–126.

learning they gained from Kathy Park, Karina Epperlein, and Wendy Palmer, some of these women obtained far greater results than any of us on the outside, for all our freedom, will ever achieve.

Powerlessness and empowerment, incarceration and cultivated self-discipline: They entwine like the light and dark "fish" that follow each other in the yin–yang symbol. The U.S. prison system, in which, I hear constantly, we incarcerate a larger percentage of our population than any other country now that the apartheid government of South Africa has been dissolved, reflects basic characteristics of ourselves as Americans that we ignore at our peril. The situation of these particular women in prison came to seem to me a baseline for my exploration in this book of women's lives, a measure for the experiences of the other women I would meet—a sort of bass note, low and booming, tolling underneath all else.

The desperate situation of imprisonment also reminds me that most martial arts originated in the desperate situations of people with no resources beyond their bare hands to ensure their physical security against overpowering force or weapons. Yet these arts are also linked to empowerment beyond what any material wealth can afford, together with health, joy, and beauty. In Capoeira, a martial art developed by African slaves brought to the Brazilian state of Bahia during the period of European colonization, I found that these contradictions come to the fore.

For slaves, direct confrontation with the owners was foolhardy, but indirectly they found ways to assert some control over the conditions of their lives. Forbidden to possess weapons or engage in any sort of self-defense against their owners, under the guise of celebration and play the slaves practiced techniques developed from African traditions of bare-hands fighting. At the approach of the authorities a Capoeira match in fact became the singing and dancing it appeared to be. The accompanying philosophy is one of indirectness, trickery, and turning the tables; of not being fooled by appearances of friendliness or order; of not trusting people or situations too far; and of being ready always to defend—and assert—oneself. Capoeira masters today talk about the relevance of these attitudes to the modern world, and many of the songs that accompany modern Capoeira games concern the connections between life and the game.

Slavery ended in Brazil in 1888, but Capoeira continued to be illegal and subject to police repression. Nevertheless, the art survived on the streets and among the mostly impoverished groups of people who had always played it. In the 1930s and 1940s, after legalization, Capoeira was systematized and popularized as a national art and sport. Masters raised in the Bahian street traditions opened schools in São Paulo and Rio de Janeiro, where the art was adopted by middle-class university students.

The format of celebration, music, play—and trickery—remain. In a Capoeira match, or game, two persons meet in a ring formed of the remaining players, who serve temporarily as musicians, accompanying the game on tambourines, bells, and drums. Over the whole the *mestre,* or master, presides with a *berimbau,* a single-stringed instrument made from a gourd attached to a long stick. The neck of the berimbau sways and bobs above the players' heads like a tall, ungainly waterbird, and all the while the instrument buzzes and drones in an eerie way, as if to give notice that something out of the ordinary is about to happen. Often enough it does. The music is not mere ornamentation but the heart of the game, shaping the play and the players. With spectacular flying leaps and cartwheels the players are upside down or in midair as much as standing upright. It is a heady mixture of dance, acrobatics, and fighting.

Capoeiristas can play either "together" or "against"—and perhaps more often with a shifting mixture of cooperation and competition. Close play is prized, and in the small space left by the ring of musicians and onlookers, two rapidly moving persons are of necessity accommodating themselves to each other even as they attack and counterattack. Good capoeiristas say they always have enough space to do what needs to be done. They will even claim to have an advantage when backed into a corner—then they undertake their most flamboyant acrobatic movements to underscore the futility of their opponent's apparent success. Sometimes it's a bluff, and sometimes the bluff is successful.

Traditionally a male, even macho, activity, Capoeira remains so in Brazil, especially in Bahia (though of course many African traditions include powerful women warriors). Where women do play in Brazil, it is more often in the academies patronized by the urban middle class outside Bahia than among the people where the art originated. With time, however, ever more women are playing Capoeira in Brazil, and Capoeira is proving popular among women in the United States. One Brazilian master who opened a school in the Mission District of San Francisco expected to attract Latino youths but instead found his classes filled by Anglo women with backgrounds in dance.

Karlon Kepcke, who has studied Capoeira for over ten years in the San Francisco Bay Area and Brazil, is the first U.S. woman to achieve *professor,* or teaching, rank in Capoeira. I talked with her at her home in Richmond, California, a high, narrow, blue stucco house with bright-colored flowers in the front that looked like it might have been transported from Bahia. Karlon herself, a tall, long-limbed woman in her thirties with a curly mass of reddish hair, is engagingly open and friendly and quick to laugh—she told me her Capoeira nickname is Sorriso, or "Smiley." That day she was walking and moving rather gingerly due to a back injury, but as I got to know her better and learned more about Capoeira, I could see how it was the martial art for her and I do not doubt that she proved a formidable player and opponent.

KARLON KEPCKE

Capoeira

I was in my early twenties. I read a blurb in a community college newspaper about this martial art, Capoeira, and I thought, How fascinating! So I started training. I had never thought about training in a martial art, but I was athletic, so I wasn't intimidated by the idea of a physical art form. I loved it the moment I heard the music—and this was a tape, I didn't even hear the music live! The man who was teaching that class was a black belt in Tae Kwon Do. He had maybe three years of Capoeira, and he was a very humble man—just said, "I'm a very beginner at Capoeira, but I can teach you all something because you're here for your first day."

But he taught Capoeira very much like Tae Kwon Do. Or actually, I've never taken Tae Kwon Do—he just didn't teach Capoeira like Brazilians teach it. More like individual moves, not like playing with one another. For months I learned movements, never encountering another person, never escaping, never doing any counterattacks, just movements. With this tape player on. I had no idea what the instruments looked like or anything—and that's a big part of the art. When I met my master, Marcelo Pereira, it was like *now* I'm studying Capoeira! That was in 1984, when he came here and started our school, the Capoeira Institute of the Bay Area, now called Capoeira Mandinga. I've been studying with him ever since.

How intense was your study?

I went to class three, four times a week, and during intensive periods I'd train on my own, so I'd train about five times a week. I learned the music on my own, practicing the rhythms, because there isn't that much time in class to do all of that. Sometimes we'd organize groups, getting together with students to work on music.

The art itself is very freestyle. There's no *kata* that you learn by yourself, where you would just do a series by yourself. You can make something like that up as a training exercise, but there's nothing fixed. There are some *seqüências* that we teach people as learning tools, and those are done two by two. In our school there are three different types. The first one is a beginner's sequence, which exercises attacking and escaping and counterattacking without a lot of movement in between—playing close. The second one is a series of take downs, scissor movements where you take the person down, or sweeps. That isn't a real fixed

sequence. People make them up, but it's good to make up a series of those to work on and get them down, pattern it in your mind and body so that you can do it spontaneously. The last one is throws, where you throw one another. Those are exciting, but I had to overcome an immense amount of fear to do those.

To throw other people or to let yourself be thrown?

Both. Because to throw people, you have to trust yourself, and to be thrown, you have to trust the other person and yourself. Plus as much as Capoeira's acrobatic, and I might look acrobatic in my game, I don't like jumping in the air and not having anything touching the ground. I have not totally gotten comfortable with that.

There's kind of an interesting story. I was learning the throws, sort of by watching other people do them, and I knew it was my next step, but I wasn't engaging, I wasn't doing it. I was scared. Then I had a dream. I was passing a hallway, and the whole hallway was orange, and there was a woman in there all dressed in orange so she was practically invisible. She was fighting—hurting someone.

I went in to help the situation or stop it or something, and she and I ended up fighting. But instead of fighting where you're angry, we were fighting where we were having a really good time. And we were throwing each other—doing these throws! Afterward—I think we had hit one another, so we were, you know, maybe a bloody nose or something, but we just sat down and were so exhausted. But exhilarated and happy. And after that I could do the throws—I still had to learn them, but I was open to learning them. I remember that dream vividly, because it was such a good experience. I never had a dream of fighting with anybody before, and it was also a fight that started off with anger but ended with this exhilarating release of energy.

Was that because it turned into Capoeira, or how do you think that the anger got transformed?

I don't know! I was going to protect somebody or put an end to that, and then she—I know that she came at me to hurt me and instead it got turned around. Maybe because I didn't try to hurt her. I was just trying to stop her. In Capoeira the whole lesson is defusing the energy. The teaching that I have in Capoeira is that when something comes at you, you just move a little bit so that it goes by—then you look for your opportunity. When you see that you can knock them off balance, that's when you sweep them.

The Capoeira I've seen, I got the sense it was like bluffing each other almost. One-upping each other was kind of where the competition seemed to be.

That's a good game when you see people playing like that. It's fun to have a game like that, that's challenging and you're pushing your mental ability and your physical ability. Once you reach a certain level, wear a certain belt, or play a certain type of game, the challenges do get harder. Now I play in the masters' *rodas—roda* is the circle where we play Capoeira—I see there is a different level of competition going on, of challenge. It's more fun, actually. *[Laughs]* It's not that it's scary; it's just a whole

lot more fun. You're ready for a harder game.

I like competitive Capoeira, people pushing each other, but there's another level where it's about domination or something like that that isn't fun—it's out there too, really violent and aggressive Capoeira. You can go to schools where that is okay and they allow it or even, in my opinion, they endorse it, because they promote students who don't know how to control their anger. When I see high-level students that play like that, I realize that this is condoned in this school, that they're not expected to mature beyond that. That's something as a visiting capoeirista, when I go and visit schools, that I look at. How do the advanced people play? How do they play with strangers? There are schools that have very bad reputations.

It depends on the master that's the leader of the school. Certain masters won't tolerate anything that goes beyond a certain line. My teacher's master has a great way of making jokes when he doesn't like what's going on. He'll stop the roda and make a joke. But then if it continues I've heard him say, "I am not going to play berimbau if you guys continue." And the berimbau—that's the bowed instrument—leads the roda, so he's basically saying, you people shape up or this is over.

The game that's played at any given moment in the roda has to do with the music. In Brazil the songs the people sing say a lot about what's going on in the game—they'll pick out something that happened in the game and sing about it.

Did you need to learn Portuguese to do this art?

I learned the language mostly by going to Brazil. I'm not a good student in the way we learn in school, by memorizing. I learn much better by

Karlon Kepcke (center) and Marcelo Pereira at a roda (San Anselmo, Calif., August 1997).

place, it's like deep breathing. For me it was a big revelation when my friend Janet—who's a very musical person—started singing. I could find my voice and sing when she did the solo, and I could sing the call more comfortably. It opened up a whole new thing, and I think it shows the importance of that female role model.

So all the time you studied you had never heard a woman's voice in the solo?

Never! Not until my last trip to Brazil. There were women in my school, but none that sang regularly. We'd sing when we were forced. Then Janet started singing solos, and now I can do it in front of lots of people and it's okay. I taught a workshop at Seven Star Women's Kung Fu Academy up in Seattle. I started the workshop with some songs and everybody sang and it sounded so beautiful! I was like, "Wow, there's not this struggle of pitch and stuff that we go through with men and women trying to sing together." When I sing the solo my master half the time can't respond, because I sing too high, and he can't sing quite low enough to be an octave different. And when he sings sometimes I can't sing in the right key. But when we had all women, everybody just *sang* and it sounded really good.

You mentioned going to Brazil—was that oriented around Capoeira?

And the beach! It just happens that because of my

application. And of course you learn to sing the songs, and then you learn the translations. It's all call and response. Solo sings the lead, and then the chorus sings the response. Some of the songs are—oh, silly! Really silly. And some of them are traditional slave songs almost like the African-American railroad songs, some of those songs about working. There's one about cutting cane and gathering coffee and how the black man needs to fight to survive. It's a pretty song about harvesting but it's also about revolution and liberation.

It was always easy for me to go to class and learn the physical, but I had to work at home on the music. It was hard for me when I had to sing the leads—terrifying! I had all the music, passed all the tests, and then I was lucky Marcelo graduated me without singing the lead. But I made it my goal, so within a few months I learned it.

Finding your voice if you're a woman singing with all men is hard! Your voice comes from way in here, a certain part of you that—it's a very deep work—I manage an import business—that it's easiest for me to go at Carnaval time, which is fortunate and unfortunate. If I was a crazy, wild partier, it would be my ideal. But I tend to go, "What's going on here?" I get confused by Catholicism. This whole thing of Lent, you know, party like crazy and then give everything up.

My first trip, when I went for five months, I spent a lot of time with my teacher's teacher, Mestre Saussuna. It was a great experience. It's a little hard at that school—it's what I call a boys' club. It just will take one or two women to venture into the high ranks there to change it, but it would be a very brave one or two women. As an outsider I can go there and be very comfortable. I think they would be accepting of Brazilian women too; I just don't think that the teacher really knows what it takes to be supportive of women or how to train women.

And it's not even that I could tell somebody how to do that. You know what I mean? It's a school that's always been very male, and young male too. I think a person in their thirties may have a hard time at that school—although I'm in my thirties and I go. I guess the reason why I can go there and get a lot out of it and feel very comfortable is that I'm a visitor—I'm not dependent on it being my school.

My friend Janet went to Brazil this past year and at events she saw women with T-shirts saying Grupo Feminino, acknowledging that possibly the women need some solidarity, that you just can't come up through the ranks with the guys, and that that needs to be acknowledged and maybe even have some organization around it to bring women into the art. Because classically it's not a women's art in Brazil.

I think of Brazil as being a fairly sex-segregated culture—but so are a lot of the Asian cultures, and most of them have a tradition of warrior women.

I never heard any folklore or stories of women in Capoeira, but recently someone showed me an interview with one of the old masters, who's now dead. He listed people he called great capoeiristas of the past, people who were dead when he was talking. I guess they would have been playing Capoeira in the early years of this century. He included two women—their Capoeira names were Fogareira, which means "Fireball," and Maria Homem, "Maria Man." But I don't know anything else about them.

For women to play Capoeira in Brazil they have to overcome a whole lot of social conditioning—they're still working on it. The economy there doesn't permit women to break out of traditional roles very easily. When you're there, it's hard to comprehend how anybody survives. The minimum wage is *so* low. I don't know how they maintain equilibrium at all. In 1985, on my first trip to Brazil, I would say that there were quite a few women playing in Rio de Janeiro. Outside of there, I didn't see that many women playing. My second time back, I felt similarly. This last time—well, there were many more women who had started training, but when you get into the higher levels, you feel like you're in a boys' club, no matter what. Now there are two really good women that are teaching in the United States who are Brazilian women, one in New York and one in San Francisco. They're some of the first that have gone that far and are teaching.

One thing I can say for being a woman in Capoeira is it's an art created by small people. A lot of it is about escaping inside the movement and making yourself really small and then getting big.

So that would actually give women an advantage?

I think so—and it's an art based on trickery instead of force. They have a word, *malícia,* which literally means "malice," but in Capoeira it's a very honorable trait, so it's hard to talk about that word in relation to English, because it carries really negative connotations in English. In Capoeira, it's a very renowned quality. Also *mandinga.* That's another hard word to translate. It can mean "to disguise" or "to trick." They have songs about it, about being tricky and skillful and a master of illusions. That's where playing Capoeira goes beyond force—it's mental and physical.

My favorite Capoeira is where people are using all those skills and trickiness and the beauty and the acrobatics and are still never vulnerable and are still trying to get each other. Of course, if somebody's just blatantly out to get you, if you start doing acrobatics, you are vulnerable. You have to be careful in those situations.

And when they meet in the roda, can the aggressive, brute-strength people overpower the trickery? I'm wondering how—well, because that's the T'ai Chi principle, that you should be able to finesse your way through an attack, and if someone uses brute strength, you should be able to use that against them. I always wonder how well that works in practice—and this seems an example of that situation.

I think the capoeirista who's focusing on the trickiness will change their game when confronted with somebody who's being really direct, but the person usually can't overpower them, because their skill and speed are still there. The minute somebody plays that direct kind of game with me, I see they're out to get me and I simplify my game a little. I don't leave as many openings. And the game becomes almost boring. If they can trick me into staying open, then they'll have many more opportunities. It's much harder to escape when the person uses their trickery and uses all their style and grace *and* is still playing a competitive game, because you don't know when it's going to come. One minute they're dancing with you, the next minute you're on the floor. When I'm playing with somebody and we're both trying to do our most beautiful moves, most beautiful escapes, *and* not be vulnerable *and* try to get one another, it's so much more satisfying.

An aikidoist I talked to told me she also studied Capoeira for several years—she really liked it, although it didn't displace Aikido for her—but she said she finally stopped because she didn't like what she saw coming out in herself as she played Capoeira, the aggressiveness she saw in herself. Talking to her, I felt she found a container in the ritual and philosophy of Aikido that wasn't there for her in Capoeira.

The roda—the circle—is the container, but Capoeira is about improvising within that, and it's up to the individual to learn how to deal with it. The way that I teach people is to never act from that adrenalin rush that you get if somebody does hit you or sweep you or something, but to stay calm, breathe deeply, keep playing your game, and try to find that center again. To act from that adrenalin rush will throw you really off balance.

I've seen people get into these cat-and-dog fights, hitting one another, boom-boom-boom, you know, trying to punch and hit. I think that is horrible to see. "Ugly! Yuck! Get it under control!" If that comes out in our classes we usually put a lid on it. I think the thing about the aggression is that the roda is a place that just about anything can happen. It is up to the masters in charge to control it, but sometimes it only gets put under control after something has erupted. Because it's also encouraged to—to fight. We're not totally peaceful. There's a thin line between losing your self-control and playing a really intense game.

When some people are playing really intense, they might even be doing a bit of kicking at one another and battering the body—which I avoid at all costs! I don't want to be hit, so I don't do it. But sometimes people do that and they're having fun. It's when the energy shifts that it becomes ugly, if you know what I mean. I'm sure I've found myself having fun and doing that.

You go through a stage of that along the way?

Yeah, jamming people and stuff like that, and I could probably still do that and have fun. I don't like to be kicked, so I don't do that to other people. But I don't mind taking people down, sweeping people and knocking them down. The main thing if somebody hits you and you get pissed off and you start being really aggressive, they're going to close down their game, and you're never going to be able to take them down. So if somebody gets me and I want to get them back, I just stay calm, and they think, "Oh, Karlon's playing her usual game, and she's always a sweetie," and then I'll sweep them.

You have to have good control of your emotions to do that. You do get to see all sides of yourself. A beginner told me he was afraid to come to class because of what he might learn next about himself. He was realizing that he's physically dyslexic. He goes, "On paper, I'm not at all. I'm a geometry teacher." He couldn't understand right from left in following someone he was facing—it was very charming to see that it really frightened him to have this part of his brain that didn't quite function right or something—"right" in whatever terms right is. I was born dyslexic, so I'm like, "No problem!" But mine was more on paper. Physically I probably am too, but when you learn a physical art form, you learn perception and translation into your body in such a different way that I can never imagine going back now to really knowing what it is to be a beginner in that way.

After this student told me that, I always teach with my back to him, so then he can completely copy, and it's not this facing and trying to figure it out. So it was good that he told me that, because now I know that that's what he needs as a student. I think he's discovering all kinds of other things about himself too, which is nice. That's what it's about, really, is discovery.

And are there also ethical or religious or spiritual teachings in all this?

Some schools and some masters who are more involved with religion on a personal level will bring more of that into their work. My teacher, not at all. What I find is that a lot of people who are looking for that are not very satisfied with how it's communicated in Capoeira. To me it's right there in the art form itself, and as you live it and experience it, it becomes more full and more rich.

As the masters talk you sense what the philosophy is. I feel strongly that I have the philosophy of our school and of my teacher. It's communicated in the game, in what is emphasized and what's encouraged in the game itself. How we encourage the students to play and what we ask of them.

When you go to Bahia you feel the roots of how Capoeira is in all the—at least in all the men. The young boys all know how to do kicks and play a little, like boys play baseball here. You don't sense that in São Paulo, in the big city. There people go to the academies to learn Capoeira. And that's where my teacher comes from. He put a lot of emphasis on transmitting the cultural information, but these were things that he was taught. Earlier masters grew up in Bahia. Then Capoeira went from being this art that everybody knew and was happening in the streets to being in a more formal context. Then it spread from Bahia to Rio and São Paulo. As it moves out of Brazil, of course there might be controversy over how people are receiving the art or how it's being transmitted, but controversy is not bad usually—usually it creates some kind of dynamic that pulls things into balance or opens things up more. In general what I hear from masters who come to teach workshops is that they think the level of Capoeira here in the United States is good.

Karlon Kepcke doing a voltando na ponte *in the Capoeira roda with other members of the Capoeria Institute of the Bay Area at the San Francisco Ethnic Dance Festival, 1990.*

ROBERT BRYANT

What about in your own life? Has Capoeira made changes in you?

That's hard to answer, because I've been training for a long time—more than ten years—and subtle changes have just kind of gone on. It's sort of like how you see a seed grow and it—it just grows. I definitely see it in my approach to being physically aware in my body. I remember noticing when I had gotten some proficiency at training that I was walking the streets asking myself, "Do I have my reflexes? Am I prepared to defend myself?" That never crossed my mind until I had trained those reflexes some.

Right now, with this back injury I have, I feel very vulnerable. I feel like I'm at half capacity—so how could I walk the streets? Even though it's not even dangerous—I mean, it *is* dangerous in a lot of ways, but in a lot of places and situations it's not. When you know what it takes to be on balance and centered and approach an aggressive situation and you know that you're hurt—it's hard. It makes me empathize with older people or people that have a physical difficulty. Every time I get injured I tend to see those people and see what courage it takes just to be in the street.

I do remember that transition to becoming fully aware that I had some skills to defend myself. There's been a real shift in that consciousness. Even just how you walk and look around. This is simple self-defense stuff, but when you train for a long time, it's in your cells—this is *in* the body and that feels fabulous!

I've been in situations with masters in the roda where they are pushing me really, really hard, and it feels like they have three legs and they're all coming at my face at once. I'm glad to be challenged like that, but I don't know how it translates into a street situation, where there can be weapons or multiple attackers and there are no rules.

Do you feel more competent to deal with a street situation?

Oh, definitely, definitely. One time before I had any training, I was in a situation of somebody trying to break into a building that I was in alone. I scared him so bad he was shaking, and he jumped off a window ledge in a situation I would never think anyone would want to just jump off. I was scared the minute he got off the window. I continued to work in that building at night, mostly alone, and I was scared for years!

And now you wouldn't be?

Oh, I bet I would be. But I feel like I have a zillion more resources right now if I was going to be approached, and knowing that is just wonderful. In Capoeira, with all the trickery, you're always dealing with unknown situations. Although I think if I needed to know how to absolutely defend myself or immobilize somebody, I'd learn Jujutsu. You know, it's just breaking joints, just really brutal. I don't feel confident that I know how to immobilize people, but in terms of feeling really good and present in my body and knowing that I can dodge a lot and find a way to escape a situation, I feel confident in my training. Also I know I have the ability to stay centered and not panic.

I took a workshop with Lloyda French about fighting in pairs. It was focused around women, lesbian women—hate crimes. We paired up and I was working with this woman who's a Tae Kwon Do artist. We talked about our assets as fighters and then we had five people attack us. And in a split second I was out of there and they were attacking her! They didn't even see me! So I thought, this is my asset, when anybody's with me, just tell them to hang on to my shirttail, and we'll be out of there.

Part of the training was also, when that attack was over, to talk about how it worked and how it didn't work. We talked about how my partner was ready to stand there and just keep fighting, where I had a good eye for finding the way out. I was, "Okay, we'll get this person out of my way and I'm gone." So we started doing that. She would hang on to me and we'd get out. And then we had them chasing us, but sometimes if you're backed in a corner or you're in a situation where you just gotta get some space to deal with maybe one person at a time, it seemed like it could be useful. It was funny to see that my impulse was not to stand there and fight at all! I'm outta here. Whooom! Which is very Capoeira—a main principle of the art is escaping.

There're all kinds of ways to get out of the game and get out honorably. Even masters will say, "If somebody's getting on my nerves or being really violent—if their whole intention is to hurt me—just shake their hand and leave." One master was talking about this: "Some guy will ask me to play, and he's a really violent or aggressive person, and I'll go, 'No, no, my back hurts,' or something. And then later I'll play, and the guy'll go, 'Well, your back hurt.' And I'll go, 'Yeah, it stopped hurting!'"

I didn't get into the martial art because I felt I needed self-defense in my life. It was more that I was in a place where I was open to trying things. And what I found through training was, yeah, I feel I can defend myself, but that feels like just a by-product. What I felt more is that there was a part of me that used to hide the feminine side of myself, and through training, I feel like the feminine could come right out on the surface, because I know how to protect her. That was the transformation for me—to express my femininity much more. Because my upbringing is that you're vulnerable if you're female.

Some people might think that's contradictory—the stereotype seems to be that martial arts turn women into brute malelike people.

I don't think that's true at all. I think whatever your true nature is, it comes out more. Through the challenges it comes out in the body and you get to know your true nature more. If your true nature might be more androgynous—more whatever—whoever you are can come out much more because you explore it more, and you explore it on a physical level, which unlocks a deep emotional level. That's different from exploring who you are mentally. I believe that we contain who we are on a cellular level, which is a physical level, much more than we contain it in our concepts of who we are. Physical art forms can help us explore a lot of unconscious material.

So that is what I felt is the biggest transformation for me—not all this fighting, but more how you can move in the world and be more of who you are and know that. Through these challenges, it just comes out in the body. It's important to find the right art form to be able to express the different parts of your personality. Capoeira feels right for me because it's very free and freeing.

What about your back injury? I've had an ongoing conversation with several aikidoists who say injuries are inherent in Aikido. It goes so fast, you have to commit your body without having time to consider everything you're doing. You can't expect *not* to get injured. So everybody is always walking around with bottles of liniment. But in both T'ai Chi and Aikido there's the idea of ch'i, or ki, and the healing powers of that. I wonder to what extent the injuries or the healing are a part of Capoeira?

Injuries are a part of Capoeira!

Is your back injury from Capoeira?

Yeah, I think so. It's not to say that the one movement that hurt it caused the injury, because it was a movement that I do all the time. I think there was something out of alignment previously. One thing I can say about Capoeira is there are tons of movements that you do, and that I've done, that are totally bizarre, really hard to do, and I don't think that I've ever hurt myself in those situations. I've hurt myself sometimes doing things that are very simple that I've done a lot of times.

I personally believe injuries don't just happen—there's some lesson in the injury, something to be explored. That's a hard one too. You know, then you think, if I just get it intellectually, it'll go away, but there's a whole way of being open for healing that has to happen too.

There is not a lot of talk about healing principles or properties in Capoeira. There isn't talk about ch'i or channeling human energy or working on that level. A lot of the Capoeira that I practice—there are more simple versions of Capoeira, schools that teach a more militaristic style—but I feel like the school I come from is very much about defying the limits of what the body can do. And pushing beyond that. That's one of the things that I like about it, that's very liberating, but it can be hard on the body.

When I was a beginner I remember some guy saying, "Capoeira's really hard on your joints!" And I thought, "What's he mean?" I didn't get it. Now, a few years later, I have wrist wraps and ankle wraps and use them all the time for protection. Because if you're really committing yourself to some of the acrobatic movements, you're landing hard, you're diving onto your arms really hard.

And you don't do this on mats?

No. At different times we've had opportunities to use mats, but other than that, it's just in a park or on a wood floor. In Brazil I think it's usually concrete floors. They do this stuff on concrete! And they love it. *[Laughs]* It's truly a tropical art. I've never hurt myself in Brazil. It helps to have the hot air and the humidity. It keeps the muscles supple.

A lot of capoeiristas say they never hurt themselves until they left Brazil—"Until I came to the United States." Of course they also got older in the process, so maybe that's part of it. But you know, I can also understand that. I've never hurt myself in Brazil. And these guys push it to the limit. The art is constantly changing. The Capoeira that's being played today is nothing like the Capoeira that the Africans originally developed. Nothing at all. And every year it's different. You go back to Brazil and there's this new thing or new movement or new way of playing that people are doing.

Everyone's encouraged to develop movements and try new things. And then everybody cops everybody else's. There's no holding on to it. You do it and you're putting it out there and people can figure it out. The same with the songs—they're transmitted across the continent by word of mouth, and there's nothing rigid like, "We don't sing those songs at this school," or anything like that. Because the art form doesn't have anything set, there's not any one way to express yourself within the art, so it feels very open. *[She paces, looking uncomfortable.]*

Are you doing okay?

Yeah, I'm kind of achy, but if I walk a little bit—I wish there was more about the healing aspect! I think capoeiristas do accept a certain amount of injury. I'm glad to hear that it happens in other arts—that they have this attitude that it just happens and it's out of our control. Because we get together and woe about our wounds sometimes.

That is refreshing to hear that about the Aikido! *[Laughs]* Actually, I did think people probably got injured, except probably not in the same ways. In Capoeira, flipping your legs backward and forward, you get shoulder, sometimes neck injuries. I've had more problems with ankles and calves and my back than anything. That's probably because I'm not willing to jump in the air. All fours off the ground and land on my hands! I'm still overcoming that fear.

For a long time now Capoeira has been the central thing in my life. I remember when I made that transition. I was also a visual artist, and I used to try to spend time doing the visual arts and doing Capoeira, and it got to the point where I was never thinking about my artwork, I was only thinking about Capoeira. That was where my creative energy was at. I decided that I wasn't going to fight that any more, and I just devoted myself to Capoeira. I've been pretty dedicated. And it's been great to have something like that in my life that I love so much and that fills all the gaps and the needs for creativity—that's been really great. Now,

being injured and not being able to train—and I'm not teaching either—I'm going through a lot of transitions with the art.

Do you think perhaps that's *why* you got this injury? Marking—or masking—some bigger transition?

Yeah. It's good for me to get some space from the art and decide what relationship I want to have with it in my life now. I'm trying to not get emotionally frustrated with the fact that I can't train now, but realize that there's a time for everything; there's a time for healing and a time for training. It does get a bit scary sometimes when I feel I might never be able to do the art form again. I don't believe that that's true, but I believe that if I don't time things correctly, I could hurt myself in a way that I might never be able to do it. Or at least not in the way that I would like to do the art form.

I'm trying to stay balanced with that anxiety. If I give in to that too much, I give over my power to heal. So the attempt is to try and stay balanced with what's going on and see things as a transition and change rather than get frustrated. And just realize that a lot of things are changing and that if I don't know the outcome of all those changes it doesn't mean that there won't be a good outcome. I have to have faith that there will be a good outcome.

CHAPTER 7

You Just Have to
Do It and Do It and Do It

All the Asian martial arts, it seems, have roots in China. Fu Hsi, a legendary ruler of
six thousand years ago, is credited with inventing many of the basics of Chinese
culture; he also established a system of exercises, described as thirteen animal postures, on the basis of notions of circularity and transformation that lie at the heart of
Chinese cosmogony and martial arts. Fu Hsi's exercises were health oriented, a "Grand
Dance for the enhancement of the limbs and the curing of the diseases of the people."[1]

Some sources state that Fu Hsi's teacher was a woman. This is a tantalizing mor-
sel of information for those who argue that martial arts are a late and narrow application of knowledge developed in prehistoric matriarchal times about accessing and
developing the inner resources and energies of the body. That Fu Hsi's exercises were
animal postures is also intriguing. The names of modern Chinese health and martial
exercises also often refer to animals—in the form of T'ai Chi Ch'uan I practice we
have, for example, the movements Snake Creeps Down, Stork Cools Her Wings, and
Horse Whips Her Tail. In some cases similarities to animal movement camouflage
fighting applications from the uninitiated. One can also speculate that such refer-
ences, and the movements themselves, survive from rituals and shamanistic practices

---

1. Huang, Wen-Shan, *Fundamentals of Tai Chi Ch'uan,* 2nd ed. (Hong Kong: South Sky Book
Company, 1974), 53.

akin to those that have been used in many cultures to awaken and develop inner, intuitive qualities, for which animals are often noted—qualities deeper than thought, speech, or the physical body.

Perhaps the very origin of martial arts, and certainly a repeated theme in Chinese history, is the integration of physical development, whether for fighting or other purposes, with spiritual, philosophical, and religious knowledge. Records two thousand years old refer to Taoist exercises that seem to have consisted of a series of postures intended to develop breath and ch'i to obtain spiritual enlightenment and physical invulnerability or immortality. Taoist adepts—many of whom were women—often practiced fighting arts as well.

Many famed Taoist and Buddhist temples have been known for martial arts training as well as religious studies. In the sixth century, following the introduction of Buddhism from India to China, the Indian Buddhist monk Ta-Mo reportedly spent a number of years at the Shaolin Temple in Honan province. Observing that the monks' sedentary lifestyle, revolving around seated meditation, impaired their health and consequently their spiritual progress, he taught them breathing and stretching exercises from the Indian yogic tradition, which by then was already well developed. Combining the internal energy from yoga with preexisting indigenous fighting arts gave rise to a wide range of fighting systems still known as Shaolin boxing or Kung Fu. The Shaolin Temple remains today a center of martial arts and Buddhist learning. I have seen photographs of the ancient buildings perched on rocky crags and of the stone floor of the training hall, where pits are worn several inches deep from centuries of students bringing their feet down in the same exercise in the same spot on the floor.

T'ai Chi Ch'uan is sometimes traced to a Tao-ist warrior monk, Chang San-feng, who lived during the Sung dynasty (960–1279) and is said to have been inspired by a dream or vision or actual observation of an encounter between a bird and a snake. Attacked by a bird, sometimes identified as a magpie, other times a crane or heron, the snake fought successfully with deft, economical movements of its supple, spiraling coils. The essence of this discovery seems to have been a new synthesis of physical training with spiritual traditions emphasizing seeing what is and moving in accord with one's own nature and the reality around one.

More mundane historical accounts credit the scholar-knight Chen Wang-ting with founding the earliest system of martial arts that can truly be termed T'ai Chi Ch'uan, in the Wen district of Honan province in the 1660s. In writing about his system, Chen noted the circular movement and openness to change that characterize T'ai Chi Ch'uan today.[2] Chen's descendants have maintained his practice through twenty generations to the present day. For most of this time the knowledge was kept within the family, but in the nineteenth century a Chen master broke with traditions of secrecy and taught outsiders. From this, master's students derive the modern Yang and Wu family styles of T'ai Chi Ch'uan commonly practiced in the United States today. The Dragon Tiger Mountain form that Janet Seaforth taught me is an offshoot of the Yang style. But all T'ai Chi Ch'uan is based on the same principles, with variations of the same fundamental postures and techniques.

The *ch'uan* in T'ai Chi Ch'uan, meaning "fist," or "system of self-defense," is what identifies it as

---

2. Gu Liuxin, *Chen Style Taijiquan* (Hong Kong: Hai Feng Publishing & Beijing: Zhaohua Publishing, 1984), 2.

Chinese cosmogony. In the beginning was the void, which was empty but contained the potential for everything. This potential eventually manifested as a difference. The existence of difference caused movement, which is cyclical, waxing and waning within the limits of its nature. This movement created change, transformation, and the "ten thousand things," or infinite variety of living beings. That change itself is the only constant provides the theoretical basis for T'ai Chi Ch'uan: An attack will proceed to an extreme and then collapse; by accurately perceiving and timing one's response to take advantage of this inevitable change, one can overcome the most powerful opponent with slight effort. (Drawing by Margaret Emerson)

a fighting art. The term *t'ai chi* itself is a Chinese name for what Westerners often call the yin–yang symbol—the interlocking dark and light "fish," each containing a central spot of the other and continually waxing, waning, and transforming into the other. *T'ai,* I'm told, literally means "big"; *chi* refers to "extremes," or "polar ends." T'ai Chi Ch'uan can thus be thought of as an approach that encompasses all that lies between the extremes or ends of experience—that is to say, all there is, and then some.

I have most often seen *t'ai chi* translated as "the supreme ultimate," a term that I have always found stultifying, although it does contain something of the idea of "everything and then some." "The grand terminus," another common English rendering, can be understood as a wheel, returning us to the circular, cyclical yin–yang symbol.

Note that *chi,* as in *t'ai chi,* and *ch'i,* or the life energy, are different words, represented by different characters in Chinese and pronounced differently. The apostrophe indicates an aspirated consonant—thus *ch'i* is pronounced more or less as it looks in English without the apostrophe, but *chi* has a softer sound, more like a soft "g" or "j" in English. And in fact confusing the terms does not really lead us astray. Ch'i, or life energy, is basic to the practice of T'ai Chi Ch'uan—together with posture, breath, flexibility, adaptability, and concentration. As none of these are martial qualities per se, but rather capacities that are useful in any endeavor, the commonly heard shorthand "T'ai Chi" without "Ch'uan" also accurately reflects the notion that this is a study preparing one for a far wider range of activities than physical combat alone.

In its broadest applications T'ai Chi Ch'uan shades into Ch'i Kung, a term that means "skill with ch'i, or life energy," and includes a range of health and breathing exercises one can learn and practice on one's own, as well as healing techniques employed by highly trained and specialized medical practitioners. Some Ch'i Kung includes martial moves, but its primary purpose is for cultivating and circulating ch'i in a general way.

Jane Golden is a practitioner and teacher of T'ai Chi Ch'uan with a background of traditional study of the art, having learned the classical Yang-family style of T'ai Chi Ch'uan from a Chinese-born master whose grandfather studied with a member of the Yang family. Jane has also studied with several Ch'i Kung masters, exploring the continuity between T'ai Chi Ch'uan and Ch'i Kung.

I spent a pleasant Sunday with Jane in Santa Rosa, California, where she teaches. Her early morning class in Ch'i Kung started with a slow breathing exercise in a sitting posture. Jane then led the group through increasingly complex movements of our heads, shoulders, arms, and torso. By the end of the subsequent standing exercises I felt my entire body had been gently but thoroughly energized.

A T'ai Chi Ch'uan class followed. Sunday morning is a time slot Jane reserves for beginning students, although in all her classes she works with students at every level; for a fixed monthly fee, students may attend as many of her four weekly classes as they wish. That day we concentrated on the half-dozen opening moves of the form, working on details of the posture for each move and the shifting of weight in the transitions between moves. Jane would demonstrate several moves at the front of the class and then go around the room correcting us as we repeated the sequence. A small, brown-haired woman around forty, she has a presence that reminded me of what Wendy Palmer referred to as an organized field of energy. Jane's gaze is what I noticed most: very direct, her eyes bright and clear.

I was gratified to find that my own teacher's emphasis on the basic principles of T'ai Chi Ch'uan had given me sufficient foundation—and a firm enough sense of balance—to enable me to follow Jane and her students through the unfamiliar moves of this different form. Although the time I spent with Jane was short, her instruction took remarkable hold in me, giving me new perspectives and insights that I have since incorporated in my practice. When I learned more about her, I realized mine was not an unusual response to her teaching.

JANE GOLDEN

T'ai Chi Ch'uan

My interest in T'ai Chi came about by accident. In 1974, when I was twenty, I lived in Los Angeles. A woman—her name was Susan Burke—was starting a class on Venice Beach. My roommate was on the list of names Susan had, but I answered the phone when she called—my roommate wasn't home. I'd never even heard of T'ai Chi. I had no interest in martial arts. I had been practicing yoga since I was thirteen or fourteen, and I was hiking and body surfing and dancing—I wasn't looking for another type of physical activity to get involved in. But she was very enthusiastic, and I went to see what it was about.

She didn't demonstrate T'ai Chi at the first class, so I still didn't know what it was. She had us take a basic T'ai Chi stance—front foot forward and the back foot turned out at an angle between 45 and 90 degrees—and shift the weight back and forth keeping the hips facing forward. And I couldn't do it! It was such a basic thing, so to the core of everything. I could see it instantly—the center. And I couldn't do it. So I was intrigued. For several classes all we did was work on the base—feet and legs and hips. I think in the third class she finally demonstrated a little bit of the T'ai Chi slow set, and I was mesmerized. But I was already hooked before I even saw that.

Just the learning process was incredible to me. From my yoga practice, I had developed a sense of body awareness and spirituality and mind focus. T'ai Chi has postures, like yoga, but they're connected in a sequence with flowing, continuous movement. Within the first year T'ai Chi corrected all the postural problems I had. It was like night and day how much my body changed. I was also very inspired by my teachers. I started with Susan—she had classes twice a week—and quickly started going also twice a week to her teacher, Marshall Ho'o.

Marshall Ho'o was in his fifties and in very poor health when he started studying T'ai Chi. It saved his life basically, and he did a tremendous amount in this country for getting the word out about T'ai Chi. He had access to a lot of people because he was a professor at the university. He traveled across the United States in the 1960s promoting T'ai Chi, and he was responsible for bringing some of the early people from China over here.

He was president of an organization called the National T'ai Chi Ch'uan Association, which I joined. They offered classes in T'ai Chi and they had a program where after you were training for a year or more, if you were inclined, you took a test to be certified as a junior instructor. It was part of the program so I went along with it. It was kind of a funny thing. I had rebelled against school, I couldn't get out fast enough, but here I was in a T'ai Chi class, in front of these judges. There was a written exam, and then you were called up to demonstrate some part of the form. I got to do the kicks, lucky me!

These are kicks that are in different parts of the form? Or there's one particular section with a lot of kicks?

The slow set is composed of three sections totaling one hundred and eight movements, and the movements get progressively more complicated.

Jane Golden performing a move from the Yang-style T'ai Chi Ch'uan double fan form she designed (Occidental Calif., Winter 1995).

At the end of the second section there are eight kicks—that's the kicks section. You're never really holding a posture when you're doing the sequence, but you're moving very slowly and coordinating the timing of where the arms and the legs are, and you end up standing on one leg for a long period of time. Especially the first two kicks, because they're not just straight kicks with your heel. They're called separation kicks. You have to open up your hip joint and separate your leg to the diagonal. And when you're in a group of people watching you and you're nervous—it's a very hard part of the set to execute well!

But I went through the test and I got certified as an assistant teacher. Then when Marshall Ho'o was near retirement, I came across a demonstration of Tung Kai Ying's Academy of T'ai Chi Ch'uan in Venice, California, where I was living. I was impressed. Master Tung taught classes six days a week and twice on Tuesdays. I showed up on a Monday, and then I showed up on Tuesday morning, and then again on Tuesday night. I can't say literally, but pretty much, I never missed a class. And Master Tung responded very well to my dedication. He gave me a lot of attention. The great thing for me was I already knew the set. Marshall Ho'o had studied with the Tung family, and there were only slight variations in the set, which had occurred through subsequent generations. For me it was great to have had so much input from Marshall Ho'o with all the theory and all the philosophy—learning the form with someone who really communicated it well—and then to have concentrated time with Master Tung, with no more talking about it, but years of just doing it and doing it and doing it, with a lot of corrections.

I studied with Master Tung four, almost five years, and then I decided I couldn't live in LA any more and I moved north. I had taught in Master Tung's classes almost from the beginning, and he encouraged me to start a class of my own so that I would have people to practice with. So I did, once a week at the community center in Occidental, here in Sonoma County. I had a job—I was working here and there to support myself—and I was going to LA periodically. Probably every two months I would go down for a week.

Within the first year Master Tung started

coming up to Palo Alto to teach, and then also to San Francisco. I used to go every Saturday to San Francisco to see him, and at my job one week they said to me, "You've got to work on Saturdays, we need you." I said, "I can't." So they fired me. I had a pretty good number of students by then and instead of getting another job, I decided to expand my T'ai Chi classes, go to Santa Rosa—a bigger town—and put my energy there. And that's what I've done ever since. I have a large student body here in Sonoma County and around the country. A lot of my students who have studied with me for years have moved away. I've encouraged them to teach and spread the form, and then they bring me in to do workshops, so I travel a lot.

In class this morning you were thorough about showing the martial applications in the moves, and you mentioned you've studied and teach sword and fan and other weapons, as well as Push Hands and sparring exercises. What do you see as the roles of sparring, fighting, and self-defense in T'ai Chi practice?

I'm trained in the weapons and in the martial applications of the form, but I am not into competition. To me, the beauty of T'ai Chi is its noncompetitiveness. Even as a martial art, it's not competitive.

My way of approaching the self-defense aspect of T'ai Chi is that the calmness, the centering, the awareness, and the intuition develop your self-defense, not your mastery of strikes and punches. The form teaches all these concepts, so it's through the practice of form that you learn the self-defense, physically and conceptually. And through cooperative practice with your fellow play-

ers in Push Hands.

I might be able to knock down people in my class, but it has a lot to do with the fact that I'm the teacher. As soon as we start to push hands, they already think I'm better than they are. If I go out in the real world and somebody jumps me in the street, I don't have that advantage, and I may or may not be successful if I'm relying on my practical application of skills. But if I rely on my intuition, my centering, and my instinct, that's where I'm going to have the best chance of being successful in taking care of myself in a situation. And of course avoiding the trouble you see across the street instead of thinking, "Hey, I've been doing this for twenty years, I know how to fight. I don't have to be afraid of anything."

Once when I was a young student, maybe just a year or so after I started practicing T'ai Chi, I was in a nightclub and somebody approached me from behind and grabbed me—not to fight, but in a very inappropriate manner. I didn't know who it was, I didn't know what they wanted. I was not thinking. My body did a T'ai Chi move, and I succeeded in getting rid of that person.

Now, had their intention been more serious and in a different situation—I can't tell you what might have happened. I have never had to use my T'ai Chi in a fight, but I have used it more than once in a situation like the one in the nightclub. I'm a pretty small person physically, but I've been able to keep people from handling me in ways I don't want them to because I have control over it. If I'm in Push Hands with somebody who's really skilled and I'm thinking about what I'm doing, my skill level doesn't always show up. But if I'm in a situation where I'm guided by my instincts rather than thoughts, it's right there. There's no question.

But I don't spend a lot of time looking at how

T'ai Chi has worked as a self-defense in my life. I look more at how much it's served for my self-development, physically, mentally, and spiritually. My life works well. I live in a very beautiful place, I have loving friends, and I receive a lot of respect. If anybody asked me, "What would you ideally live like?" the answer would be, "The way I live now." I'm emotionally stable, mentally stable, and physically healthy. Spiritually high. All of these things are a direct result of my T'ai Chi practice. I get to do my art for my life's work, and I think it's because of what I've learned from my practice of T'ai Chi.

My interest now in my teaching of T'ai Chi is helping my students with their physical development. When a new student comes into class so out of their body and with so many health problems, and a year later they're a different person physically, that's where I get my reward. It happens not only to my students but also to myself. I'm getting better as I age, not worse. My body's getting more physically conditioned. I'm learning more about myself.

Is this where the Ch'i Kung that you also teach fits in?

I've always practiced Ch'i Kung through my T'ai Chi—picking out individual postures and using those postures as Ch'i Kung exercises, and different combinations of different postures. T'ai Chi *is* Ch'i Kung. Ch'i Kung is a broad term—it means "work with ch'i"—and T'ai Chi is work with ch'i. The Ch'i Kung I'm beginning to teach now is for healing, but it's also for developing internal power—spiritual as well as physical. These things about Ch'i Kung are very interesting to me. Now that I've had five or six serious years of Ch'i Kung

study, all kinds of lights are going on. I'm realizing how the systems are connected.

A woman I studied Ch'i Kung with had an interesting perspective—she said T'ai Chi, in fact all the martial arts, came from Ch'i Kung. Ch'i Kung is the oldest. She said that originally with Ch'i Kung, people were letting the ch'i move the body rather than directing the ch'i with the mind. When the ch'i is aroused, it will move your body, and if you follow the movements—and this is how she teaches—you will have your own form. If you follow the ch'i, it will move you into the forms. This is how the martial arts were developed.

I believe her. And to me it follows that in the story about Chang San-feng discovering T'ai Chi, what he witnessed with the bird and the snake when he was meditating was a lesson that came down through nature and came from inside. These monks did study martial arts, and they had to fight to protect the monastery from brigands, but the lesson about T'ai Chi is that Chang San-feng wasn't fighting, he wasn't defending himself—he was meditating. I think that the origin of T'ai Chi was not in martial art—it was spiritual.

It's the energy that's first?

Yes, and the application is secondary. T'ai Chi is an internal art, but with T'ai Chi the outside leads to the inside. The way I teach, and the way I've been trained, the shape and the structure and the foundation have the purpose of lining up your body and opening your channels so that you can get to the inside. Ch'i Kung on the other hand starts from the inside and leads you to the outside. That's my personal definition, from my experience, and it's why I think T'ai Chi and Ch'i Kung should be inseparable as a practice.

You know, I was—I am—a very serious practitioner. I haven't taken any time off since I started. I've put in a lot of hours and a lot of dedicated practice—but for the first ten years of my training in T'ai Chi, I was not moving internally at all. Maybe a little bit. But not really. Not until I started practicing Ch'i Kung seriously did I really wake up the inside. But because I had had all this training and my body was conditioned, I probably got it faster.

That's my personal experience. Now I see that incorporating Ch'i Kung into my classes has helped my students reach levels in six months that took me *years*. I think it's because of the way I've taught them and how I've incorporated different focuses. I had to figure it out myself. I had hands-on input, but only at my teacher's discretion, not at mine. Once I hit a certain level I was left to do it on my own. Everything I know, Master Tung taught me, but my understanding sometimes has come from other places.

Several women have mentioned that they feel they have figured things out to give their students that it took them much longer to get from their male teachers. It's not only that women are going through something of a struggle, but they are producing things that are really working.

I agree with that. Maybe that's just the basic nature of female and male—not that a man couldn't have female energy. There's that nurturing, caring quality about women. Women's hearts are really in seeing somebody develop, where men tend to favor the students who get it a little bit easier. They find it more suitable to them where they don't have to carry somebody along. If a person walks into my class and sees somebody stumbling all over the place, they might think, "That's not a very good student." But that person could be my best student! The one who's made the most progress. [*Laughs*] The guy that comes in who's twenty years old and has been playing sports all his life and can sit down in lower posture—yeah, I'm proud of that person too. But I don't necessarily regard him, or her, as my best student.

I have a pretty good balance of men and women in my class. I don't really have the problem where men don't want to be in my class because I'm a woman. I'm sure it has happened, but not too much. I think it's because of the quality of my training and the traditional nature of the T'ai Chi school I hooked up with—we're not just dancing in there.

But I have seen a lot of, "Yeah, look at her form, she knows the form. She's nice to watch. Her weapons sets are proficient. She's flexible, it's beautiful, but she can't knock me down. She's no good." There are a lot of guys who think, "So what if the form is pretty, big deal. If it doesn't have function, then it's no good." Their view of function, in my opinion, is very limited.

This occurred at a workshop I just attended. The teacher had different people demonstrating their Push Hands. It reminded me of those videotapes you see of the competitions. They were duking it out, you know? Getting harder and harder and harder. I heard someone say, "Let Jane—I want to see Jane!" So they called me out on the floor. One of my students was with me, who's an exceptional student, really good, and I said, "Come on," and she said, "You're not going to push me, are you?" And I said, "No, let's just do what we do."

No one had seen anything like it. It was great that the group was so open—even the men were really open to it. At first I was thinking, "They're going to be laughing at us." And I didn't really care, I just didn't want to put myself in that situation. But people didn't laugh. And there was another surprise for me. In the course of the next few days every guy there wanted to push hands with me. It was very different from what they were used to doing—shoving each other and brute strength. They'd push with me and their reaction was, "I wish I had this." "Well, there's only one way you're going to get it. Stop shoving and follow." I think women get the form faster than men, but women have a more difficult time learning how to discharge energy.

I have that problem. I freeze and flinch—

My teacher helped me out a lot when I was a young student. I can remember a class where I was working with a peer of mine on pushing and discharging energy, and I said, "I'm going to get it this time." We were trying and trying and trying, and neither one of us was getting it, and we called Master Tung over and said, "Master, how come I can't push her?" He looked at me and he said, "Because you don't want to." *[Laughs]* He said, "You like her! She's your friend. You have to want to push her down on the floor—you've got to want to do it."

It was a hundred percent right on. I teach Push Hands now, and I love it. I love to do it. I love to teach it. I think everybody should do it. A lot of people in my class hate it. I don't make them do it if they don't want to, although I try to help them get over the hump. But I also say, "You do not have to push somebody down. Push Hands has a lot of different aspects to it. There are valuable lessons to learn from it for your slow set."

Can you explain how that works?

Push Hands is what it's most commonly called, but Join Hands is another name for it, and from my perspective it's more appropriately named Join Hands. That describes what it is.

When you're doing the solo sets, the open hand sets, and the weapon sets, you're cultivating and redirecting ch'i in your own body and your focus is on your own body. Of course, when you do the set as a martial art training, even the slow set, you do visualize a partner or an opponent so that you're doing the applications, but you're still working primarily with your own energy. In Join Hands you literally join hands with somebody. You make physical contact, and the reference changes, because you give yourself up and you focus on the other person. You learn to be sensitive to their energy so that you can detect it.

The theory behind T'ai Chi is the person who moves first loses. It's a defensive martial art. You initially practice yielding, or receiving. You join hands and you're making circles with your upper body while your lower body is remaining rooted and when the other person's moving forward, you're following that person, moving back and taking in the energy, and then you're turning it and redirecting it back on them. One of the first things is letting them come in so that you can yield and redirect. Then you want to learn how *not* to let the person come in, because if you let the person in, you're creating an opportunity for them to be able to apply a move to you. So you practice your Ward Off rather than your yielding.

There'll come the point where I can't get in and you can't get in, so it doesn't go any further. Rather than trying to muscle it or be stronger than you, which might not work—and it's against the principle—what I would do is create an opportunity for you to be able to try to get to my center and then I would use a different principle to not let you do that. I also have to become very good at *fa ching*, or discharging energy. Once I let you in and redirect your energy, I've got to get the power behind it so that I can send you away, or however you want to phrase it.

Every person that you push hands with is different. There are no two people who feel the same. Consequently, each time you have a different partner, you change and you develop something in yourself. If you practice with one person for a long time, you might get pretty good, but then when you go to another person, the things that work on the one person might not work on another person, and then there's a whole new door that opens up and a whole new perspective that you have to have. For Push Hands training, the best way is just to do it, and do it with as many people as you can.

And there are different approaches to all of this, just like with slow set. Some schools will teach you one posture and you can't move out of that posture until you can do it well. At other schools— this is the way I teach—we'll teach you the set, a rough version, and then you refine it, rather than making you refine it one posture at a time. You can approach Push Hands the same way, in the sense that you can take a technique from the form and practice the technique over and over again, or you can practice the principles of yielding and following and sticking and you'll end up in the forms.

You'll suddenly discover that what you're doing is using the forms?

Right! They're the same ultimately. It's just a different approach.

And how about weapons—what do you see as their role?

A weapon is an extension of your energy. It gives you another dimension, an extension of your mind. And it's more precise. The intention is different. With the open hand forms, when you're applying with your hands, you don't have the sharp edge and you don't have the point. The intention, the extension, and the weight of the weapon help you develop strength and waist turning. You may do Four Corners like this in slow set *[illustrates],* but when you've got a knife or a sword in your hand, you're doing it like this *[illustrates a longer sweep and reach].* You get more physically conditioned with the weapons because of this extension, and of course the weight.

A weapon adds another mental dimension as well. I think that the weapons help you get more internal, because to connect everything up and extend it out that far, you've really got to discover more of what's going on inside. And then when you go back into your slow set, because you don't have the weight and you don't have to extend as far, you actually improve your form.

Slow set is my true love. Everything else would be expendable as long as I could do slow set. That's what I fell in love with, and to me the weapons only helped my slow set. I never really got fascinated with the weapon aspect of T'ai Chi until one day I got a fan in my hands. Then I said, "This is a weapon!" *[Laughs]* I wish I had brought it today, because you'd probably really like it too. It's practical. You can't walk around with a knife, you can't walk around with a sword, and you could even get arrested for carrying them if you have real ones. But a fan—

This has steel ribs that are sharp at the tips? It's a weapon fan?

It's not sharp, but it's metal and it's heavy. But most people wouldn't even know. I was coming back from Hawaii and I had mine in my carry-on luggage. The person at the X-ray machine saw a long, metallic, oddly shaped object in my bag and said, "Okay, you got to open up your bag." I said, "I know what it is, it's my fan." I pulled it out, and they said, "Oh, your fan! Okay."

It was just automatically what you would think if you're not familiar with martial arts. But the fan weighs a lot. It's very heavy. It's like a club. The form is beautiful. You do all these fancy things with the fan open, but in practical application, you don't use an open fan, except maybe to feint. If you needed to defend yourself in a situation and you had a fan with you, you would use the butt end—now I'll answer your question about weapons that I couldn't answer before! The fan gave me a new level of confidence. *[Laughs]* Really, it's unbelievable to me. And it was such a joy!

It was fun for me to recognize that feeling of a weapon in my hand. I had been through this whole system of Master Tung's, and I pretty much learned all the sets that he teaches. I'd been practicing them for years and teaching them for years, and then all of a sudden, there's a new thing, that didn't come from him, but it's Yang style, it's the same system of T'ai Chi. I got to start a brand-new form again without having to completely change my whole style and the whole system of T'ai Chi. Plus I liked the whole idea of the set, because it's balanced—it's feminine and it's masculine both, very strongly—and beautiful, and it's got sound effects, from snapping the fan open and shut, and you do a lot of dramatic postures in it.

With the swords and the knives—and we practice with a nine-foot staff as well, and two sticks that are maybe thirty-three inches long—when you hold them, you're extending your energy into the weapon. You're not holding the weapon in your hand and using it. But with the fan, you *are* holding it in your hand and using it. With the sword, you don't change your grip. It always feels the same in your hand. Maybe there are a few places where it changes a little bit, because your energy inside changes. With the fan, you're still connected and you're still using your internal energy, but you're changing the grip all the time, so you're relating to the fan as separate from your body. I don't relate to the sword as separate—my arm extends out there. With the fan I've got a weapon in my hand! And I know how to use it! And it's only just over a foot long, so it's very practical. You can take it anywhere you want, and no one would ever suspect.

Is there a traditional order for studying the different open hands sets and weapons? Do they develop from one to another?

Master Tung teaches a progression. You start out with slow set, fast set, then a Tung family set that his grandfather created, which is a combination of slow and fast movements. The first weapon is the knife, which is actually a broadsword.

That's the same as a saber? A curved single-edged sword?

Yes, broadsword and saber are the same thing. We have two broadsword sets in our school. The first set is pretty simple and straightforward. The second set is much more elaborate. The next weapon we learn is double sticks, then the double-edged straight sword, and then the lance. All along you learn applications and different types of sparring where you practice the applications with partners. We have a hard set too. It's another slow set, but it's done with spread fingers, spread palms, and you never release the tension. A slow, slow set. It's a killer. It really builds strength. That's probably last. The Tung school is very complete. It takes a long time to get through everything!

Given all that and your teaching, do you find yourself short of time for your own practice?

If I wasn't making my living teaching, that would be the case, but in actuality I spend a lot of time on my own practice. I found a way right from the beginning to incorporate my practice all the time. If you just think about the principles, you're practicing—sitting here with me, you're practicing. Or when you brush your teeth. It's mindfulness that's the practice, and that you can practice all the time, whenever you get up out of a chair or walk across the room or talk to somebody. I've spent a lot of time practicing—as much as I can keep my focus, and that gets better and better and better.

My routine is not so much that I get up every morning and do a slow set and then five fast sets and then family set and then sword and then knife—it's more that I'm always doing something. If I'm home and I have a couple of hours, I practice what I feel like I want to practice that day. I'm not a very regimented person. In my training I was more formal, but it probably had to do with the fact that when I was learning I would practice what

it was I was learning. Now that I have the whole picture, I go with what I feel I want to practice at a particular time. Once you learn T'ai Chi, you just have to do it and do it and do it and do it. My classes give me the opportunity to do it over and over again with everybody.

But you have this roomful of people that you're responsible for?

I'm responsible to teach them, and I spend a certain amount of time doing that, and then they need to just practice it. At that point I don't really think about them any more, because they can watch me. If I'm thinking about them, they're not going to get as much from watching me as if I'm really doing it myself. I'm giving myself more and more space all the time to do that. It used to be I was so responsible that my energy could only go out to my students. I'm getting much better now at incorporating my own practice into my classes, without neglecting the students. It's similar to what I got from my teacher. I would just stand next to him and I would . . . absorb. He transmits his energy while he's doing T'ai Chi, and that goes into you if you're receptive.

In class this morning I was more verbal than usual. That depends on my mood, and who's in the class, and the mood of the class. A lot of times I don't say a word. Instead I'll go and stand next to students and do the form, trying to transmit my energy into their body. I now have a way that I can project my energy out of me so they can feel—

So the next stage beyond weapons is working with students!

That's right! *[Laughs]* It's good training for me, and I'm getting tremendous results. I've been doing it for several years now, and I've had people, especially at the camps I teach, tell me, "When you stood next to me and did that, I could *feel* it." I've had students from other teachers attend my camps, and they've told me, "My teacher taught me how to do it, but you taught me how to feel it." This is something that I'm developing in my own practice for my own sake, but also in my teaching.

I had the best of both worlds. I got to be a student and a teacher simultaneously for many years. I could always go right back to my teacher for input, and I could also take what I learned from my teacher and put it out. Since I don't see him so often any more, I no longer have that security that I can just go right to him to make sure I'm on the right track, and I also lost the role of student to a great degree. A few years ago I was really having a hard time with this.

It got out of balance. Although I had enough practice time, I didn't have enough student time. Then a friend of mine who does a lot of graphics and photography offered to help me with a new brochure. He came up to take pictures. I kept wanting to do a certain posture with the fan, but he said, "I don't like that posture. It looks crouched down. Photographically, it looks better to see your posture and your energy up and open."

After he left I was thinking about the move that I had wanted him to photograph that he said was too crouched—and all of a sudden, I changed entirely how I did it. I didn't stand up higher, but I opened up in the application, and it felt like that was the way it should be done! He's only been doing T'ai Chi for six months and he taught me! All of a sudden I had the best correction of my life, and where did it come from? It's coming from everywhere now. It's okay not to be in line, look-

ing at the teacher and being dependent upon him for all my learning.

I always knew it has to come from me, but I was like, "Well, *how*?" Now I'm getting lessons from places that I would never have been open to before because I thought, "I have to get this from *my* teacher in *that* classroom." I clung to this for so long, thinking I'm going to be lost without it. And I was at first, but I made it over that hump.

Do you think teaching other people does something too?

Absolutely! Without my students I would not be where I am in my own practice. Not even close. When you have to get it across to somebody else, you really have to understand it. And I spend so much time watching that I can actually see—I'm amazed sometimes at what I can see. I can sort of see inside people's bodies. Somebody'll come into my class, a total stranger, and from the first movement, I know their life story. I don't know the details, I couldn't tell you specifics, but I could tell you what kind of a life and what kind of a personality and what kind of an attitude this person has. I know a lot about somebody the minute they walk in the door and stand there.

This intuition comes from teaching. From watching, day in and day out, thousands of people coming in and out of the door, over and over and over again, and seeing the things that everybody does and the things that only certain people do. It's a little sideline for me—I get a lot of entertainment from my teaching. And it made me realize that my life shows up in my body too.

With teaching you go through the same things that you go through as a practitioner. At first it's, "Oh, my god! I'll never be able to do this." And

Jane Golden demonstrating the double fan form she designed (Occidental, Calif., Winter 1995).

COY BROWN

You get to a plateau, and then you've got to start on the bottom of the next level. It's not that you've regressed—it's that you're now at the bottom again of the next level. This is one of the hard things about teaching, because a lot of times I get to a new level and the whole thing falls apart—and I have to come to class and teach! Maybe from the outside it doesn't fall apart, but from the inside it's, "God, I don't know how to do this!" You start questioning everything you've ever taught, never mind everything you've ever done, and it's a hard thing to get through.

But you do. You get through, and then you realize that you did teach the right thing for that time and now you understand something else and maybe you still will teach it that way. Like I said in class today, "If you're a beginner and you don't know what I'm talking about, don't worry about it, I'm not talking to you. I'm talking to the people who have been here for ten years." That's one of the things I'm working on in my teaching, and it seems that I'm getting a good reputation for it—I can teach a group of people that span ten years of T'ai Chi practice in the same room and everybody walks away happy, the beginners not overwhelmed and the advanced students not bored.

I learned that way. I went through the cycle over and over and over again. I learned each set

then a few months go by. "Hey, I'm getting pretty good!" And then another month goes by and, "What happened? I used to be able to do this. I can't do it any more."

from beginning to end several times, step by step by step, and each time you go over something like that, you find there's more and more. In T'ai Chi you don't just learn something, drop it, and move on to the next. Every time you move on, it brings you right back to the basics. All the time it goes back.

And is that how you get to the spiritual aspect also—with time and attentiveness and repetition?

When I start the form, standing there in the preparatory position, first I feel my body and then I go inside to experience my spirit. It's alive, and I can feel it. It is difficult to describe. The Chinese call it *shen.* They say you can see it in a person's eyes. And in fact, in Chinese medicine, you determine somebody's health from their shen—not just by looking in their eyes, but from the light that comes out of their eyes—

I've noticed that my eye color has changed since I've been doing T'ai Chi. Years ago, this friend of mine was studying to be a chiropractor. She took a course in iridology at chiropractor school and she looked at my eyes and said I was supposed to have blue eyes and it was because of all the toxins or whatever in my body that they were brown.

And they were quite brown twenty years ago, but now they're almost green. I was just noticing the other day, there's not much brown left. They aren't blue, but they also aren't brown any more.

[Laughs] That's not shen. Shen will affect the physical characteristics of your eyes, but it has more to do with the light that comes out of your eyes. When there's no light, there's no health. The light is the spirit, and without the spirit there's no health. It's inseparable in Chinese medicine. Your spirit has to be alive for you to have good health, and it shows in your eyes. Traditional Chinese doctors look at your eyes not only for the color and the shape or whatever, but for the life force, the shen. That's what I'm talking about when I say spirit. T'ai Chi releases it. Or gives it rise.

I believe that if you never read a book and you were deaf and mute, you could still come to all of this. It's like Zen—it just *is.* If you didn't have a teacher, or if you maybe found somebody to teach you initially and you kept practicing on your own, it may not happen as fast as if you had help, but you'll get there.

If I wanted to be a martial artist, I probably would have gone and studied a lot of different things, but I'm not that interested. Or I wasn't earlier. Now I'm very interested in the martial arts because I know what the essence is under all of them—they're all the same. I respect them all, but I already found my thing. By accident! Purely by accident.

CHAPTER 8

Finding the Fighting Roots

From the beginning of my study of T'ai Chi Ch'uan, in addition to our empty hands form (or slow set), my simu, Janet Seaforth, also had us train with the staff for a few months every year, usually in the spring; the staff, being wood, is associated with the Wood element in the Chinese system of five elements, and spring is the season of the Wood element. We used a wooden or bamboo staff about an inch in diameter—a size to fit easily in one's hand—and six feet long; closet poles served well. All of us were primarily interested in the slow form and the meditative and health aspects of T'ai Chi Ch'uan, but we were intrigued by the reach and sweep of a long weapon and the feeling of power it gave. Janet taught us a short staff form full of whirling leaps and long strikes, and in pairs we practiced patterns of attacks, defenses, and counterattacks—exercises no doubt designed to teach timing, precision, control, and responsiveness. But for the most part we subverted this outcome through taking such care to avoid injuring our partners that we held back our strike until the defender got her staff firmly in position for blocking. Once I was partnered with a bolder woman, a soccer player who occasionally came to our classes. She took Janet's instructions at face value and aimed solid strikes at me, forcing me to scramble to defend against them. I remember the occasion for being out of the ordinary—and because I discovered that I could in fact defend myself from being hit.

Janet also told us stories of her early studies with her sifu, Nam Singh, in Sonoma, California, where Michelle Dwyer was one of her fellow students—a T'ai Chi sister, as

Michelle Dwyer demonstrating the Double Dragon Plum Blossom Sword form with double Chinese swords at her home (Albany, Calif., June 1997).

T'ai Chi Ch'uan Push Hands and weapons, whereas Janet stopped sword practice because of a hip injury and forgot the sword form Sifu Nam Singh had taught them. But sometimes she brought out her wooden practice sword from its sheath of quilted fabric for us to admire.

To me and Janet's other beginning students in our ragged sweats and T-shirts, struggling with stiff muscles and a rudimentary grasp of proper posture and movement, Janet's stories seemed to belong to a mythical otherworld of warrior goddesses and heroines. It became a game among us to make up stories to cap the stories Janet told us. One day as we spun a tall tale of Janet and Michelle in their heyday, Janet said, "Michelle lives in the Bay Area. I could call her up and see if she'll come teach a workshop." Our mouths fell open. We would as soon have thought it possible to call up Athena.

Janet did call, and Michelle did come, a lean, athletic-looking woman in her forties with sharp, alert features, gray hair, and a modest, even rather self-effacing, manner. She must have wondered why we watched her every move with such portentous expectation. Before teaching us something appropriate to our level, she demonstrated for us the Northern Shaolin Kung Fu Double Dragon Plum Blossom Sword. "Double swords are traditionally a woman's weapon," she told us as she unwrapped a silken bundle to reveal a pair of silvery blades with hilts interlocking so one could hold both swords in a single hand. Glancing around to measure the space available, she gripped the swords in her left hand, holding them upright against her body, and bowed to us.

I have since seen Michelle perform Double Dragon Plum Blossom Sword a number of times, usually under better conditions of space and light, arrayed in a costume to match the flashing swords. But that first time shimmers in my memory as a measure of the suppleness, power, and beauty of

Janet put it. Janet remembered Michelle as being quiet and reserved, with a seriousness in her practice and a love for the art that Janet both shared and felt inspired by. In 1978 Janet, Michelle, and several other students were initiated into their teacher's Taoist temple in a three-day ceremony of fasting and meditation. At dawn on the last day, heady from the lack of food, they climbed into the hills and did the form together. It was the Year of the Horse in the Chinese calendar, and as Janet tells the story, it seemed at the time only natural that a herd of wild horses appeared from nowhere and drifted through the formation of students, snuffling and nosing at them, lashing manes and tails. Well schooled by then, the students resolutely continued with the form and waited for the next test.

From the beginning, Janet said, she was more interested in the spiritual aspects and Michelle more interested in the martial practice of T'ai Chi Ch'uan. Michelle went on to study other soft and hard-style Chinese martial arts as well as advanced martial arts movements when turned outward in display. It was not just the sunlight glinting on the metal that made the swords flash that day as Michelle turned and twisted and twirled and thrust and feinted with a sword in either hand—all of us who watched could plainly see the swords come alive and shine from the flow of *her* life in them.

Michelle Dwyer looked so comfortable with a sword in her hand that any lingering question as to the appropriateness of these pursuits for women was obliterated from my mind. In China women have always pursued martial arts, with and without weapons, as indeed have women throughout the world. Even in countries where women are most disempowered today, traditions speak clearly of powerful women fighters and leaders. Michelle told us that the double sword was considered a woman's weapon. I have read that battle skills well beyond ordinary soldiers' practice were standard for women and men of culture in China. Legends speak of heroic, skillful swordswomen championing the poor. During the T'ang dynasty of the eighth and ninth centuries, women commonly surpassed men in certain areas of martial practice, including acrobatics, darts, poisoning, whips, and spears, as well as swords. Men were considered superior in physical strength and in the use of the larger cavalry weapons, such as halberds and maces, but in actual combat, quick, clever women were expected to prevail.[1] Within the clans and families that traditionally kept martial arts secret from outsiders, knowledge and training in fighting skills might be withheld from daughters and sisters, who were intended to marry and spend their lives in another clan—but entrusted to wives and daughters-in-law.

In the Yellow Turban Uprising in the second century B.C.E., Chinese women forcefully asserted their rights. The seventh-century female emperor Wu Zi-tien was known as a brilliant politician and military strategist. About that same time a woman named Mulan took over her father's command and led the army as its acknowledged general for twelve years. Ch'in Liang-yu and Shen Yun-yin, two women of the seventeenth century, also took successful command of armies after their male predecessors (who were also relatives) were killed. Forty all-female combat divisions, each containing twenty-five hundred soldiers, are recorded as fighting in the Taiping Revolution (1851–1864), with a primary aim of obtaining equal rights for women. In the early years of the twentieth century Chinese women again organized themselves into battalions and fought for the republican cause, taking names like the Women's National Army, the Women's Murder Squad, the Women's Military Squad, the Team for Military Drill, and the Amazon Corps of the Dare to Die Soldiers. Later, when women were refused the vote, the National Assembly had to send for (presumably male) troops to protect the (certainly exclusively male) members against an armed siege by women.[2]

All in all, the upshot of that day's workshop in Ukiah was certainly not to demythologize women in general, or Michelle in particular, but rather to deepen our awe. Over the years Michelle has taught me many skills, but I have also learned

---

1. Deng Ming-Dao, *Scholar Warrior: An Introduction to the Tao in Everyday Life* (San Francisco: HarperCollins, 1990), 12–13.

2. For these and other exploits by women, see Janice G. Raymond, *A Passion for Friends: Toward a Philosophy of Female Affection* (Boston: Beacon, 1986), especially 120–121; Robin Morgan, ed., *Sisterhood Is Global: The International Women's Movement Anthology* (Garden City, NY: Anchor Press, 1984), especially 147–148.

much simply from the quality of her being. I see her shining with a subtle, supple, ungraspable, but very real and powerful, energy. I was to learn that for her, this magical shimmer had its origin in disciplined and dedicated effort. For this interview we met several times at her home in Albany, California, moving back and forth between a table in the living room where we sat talking and the backyard where we practiced under a wide-spreading elm.

MICHELLE DWYER

T'ai Chi Ch'uan, Northern Shaolin Kung Fu, and Hsing Yi

When I was in my early twenties, my partner, Bruce, and I went on a vacation to Hawaii. On the beach at dawn we saw a big Samoan man—he must have weighed three hundred pounds—doing this beautiful, flowing exercise in the sand, and I said, "What's that?" Well, from walking around San Francisco's Chinatown, Bruce knew it was T'ai Chi.

We were living in Guerneville, north of the Bay Area, at that time—this was in 1974—and when we came back from that trip to Hawaii, on the laundromat bulletin board was a sign for T'ai Chi classes in the park. The teacher's name was Francesca—she was studying pottery up there for the summer and wanted to give T'ai Chi classes.

Bruce and I had been exploring different spiritual paths. For about three years we studied kundalini yoga, hatha yoga, and Taoist yoga, but our yoga class had stopped, and so I thought I'd try the T'ai Chi. It was in the park. It was summertime. Five or six hippies, people my own age. It was fun. It was a continuation of my spiritual journey from the yoga classes, but it suited my personality better because it was more active, you could do it outside in nature, and it was more social—you mingle with people in classes. It was athletic and spiritual at the same time.

Did you have any interest in it as a martial art?

It wasn't considered a martial art at all in that class. It was an art form and therapeutic and spiritual exercise. Though I don't think Francesca emphasized the spiritual aspect. In fact, except for a few explanations, I can't remember her giving any lectures on anything. It was basically a form class.

One of the things that I think attracted me was I needed some mental therapy and the T'ai Chi gave me that more than the spiritual at the time. You get an incredible feeling of well-being after you practice T'ai Chi, which I'm sure you've experienced, Stephanie. It is something that is hard to put into words, but you feel—well, calm, but full of energy, and also very refreshed. It's like you're getting washed from the inside. It gave me a feeling of purpose and inner strength that I didn't get from the yoga disciplines.

The focus of the mind on something really basic and physical was exactly what I needed. It was an anchor—it anchored my mind to my center and kept me from being imbalanced mentally. It put me on an even keel. I'm not a person who goes to therapists, and I had been at my wits' end of what to do. Within three months of starting

T'ai Chi I felt much better, more in control of myself. Also T'ai Chi really helped my health. I could see how well rounded it was and what a good therapy it was. And you know, this is exactly why I decided to teach—because of what it did for me. After only three years of doing T'ai Chi, I knew I was going to be a teacher. The whole rest of my classes I focused on how to teach it.

Francesca's class only lasted three months. When summer finished and I wanted to keep going, I went down to Chinatown in San Francisco to study with her teacher, Kuo Lien-ying, weekend mornings at dawn in Portsmouth Square. Francesca introduced me and told them I had practiced with her for three months and knew this much of the form. After that I would go on my own—take the bus down there, stay with my sister, and walk at 5:00 A.M. to the park. It was a public square, but they would bring a weapons rack out and a couple flags and stand them up, stake their territory off that way, and different groups would be practicing. I was taught by senior students, but Kuo Lien-ying would circulate. He'd spend a few minutes with everybody and give you posture adjustments and stuff. I remember he smelled strongly of garlic. *[Laughs]* He was already older at that time.

Going down to Chinatown was a great cultural experience, a big adventure. That made it fun, but it was just too much and too far away. I was there about six months, and then I practiced for another six months on my own, and then I drifted away from it. For about a year I didn't do any T'ai Chi, and then I heard about Nam Singh in Santa Rosa. I started going to his classes and really loved his form—and him. He was very exotic, you know. We used to go to class just to see what he would come dressed in.

Then he moved his class to the state university at Cotati, and he said, "My whole group is at the beginning, Michelle, so you can start again." So I started again with that group. Then he moved to Sonoma—getting farther and farther away. I would drive fifty miles to Sonoma, fifty miles back, once a week. And again, "Michelle, start over, because I have a whole new group." Three times I started over. It took me three years to learn the form from him.

After I started over the third time, he started practicing with Master Tung Kai Ying, who taught the classical Yang-style T'ai Chi, and he changed the whole form around—this was after Janet left the class, so the way you learned the form is from before that time. For me it was, "Start over again, Michelle." Learn it the new way. I knew I wanted it. I really pursued it—and I learned it well!

T'ai Chi was really not a martial art with Nam Singh either, unless we bugged him for applications. He was much more into health. After about five years with him, I was getting interested in Push Hands, and he could only take me to the very basic level of Push Hands. I was teaching all his beginner people, so I was learning how to teach—I was getting some good out of it—but I started looking around for another teacher. With Denise, who was my classmate, I came down to the Bay Area for Peter Ralston's class, and Master Chang's class, and you know, shopping around for a teacher.

At Peter Ralston's we saw a picture of Mr. Wong—Jack Man Wong—on the wall and we asked, "Who's this?" Peter Ralston said, "Oh, that was my teacher; he teaches in San Francisco." So we said, "Let's go check him out!" And Denise did, and said, "Michelle, this is the one to try!" So I did, and I really liked it because it was a Chinese teacher, and it was full of Chinese-American men. I thought, it's like a Chinese restaurant—if the Chinese people are eating there, it must be good.

I learned Push Hands from Mr. Wong, but then I was seeing these guys jump around the room like popcorn, you know, bing-bing-bing-bing, with all these exotic weapons and Kung Fu hand sets—it was Northern Shaolin Kung Fu, the low, long, expansive style of Kung Fu—and I said, "I want to learn that stuff too!"

Mr. Wong was really very good to me. I would say, "I want that set. I think that one's pretty," and he would teach it to me. And then I'd say, "I want that one!" And he'd teach it. I'd go three times a week. He'd teach me every single class, so I had to practice—I had to or I could never keep up with the pace.

So although you went there for T'ai Chi Push Hands, you switched to studying Kung Fu?

It seemed like a natural progression. And I'm glad I did it that way. I spent three years of yoga class getting stretchy and five years of T'ai Chi getting strong—getting my knees strong. I was already thirty-one, way too old to start Kung Fu. If I hadn't had those eight years before that, I probably would have had bad knees, injured knees. But I had good preparation. I was at the peak of my physical energy and stamina and strength—and it was a challenge. Kung Fu is the most physically demanding exercise I have ever met. From the low stances to the high leaps—you have to be incredibly stretched and incredibly strong. And incredibly smart, because there's so much material, to memorize it all.

It was also a gender challenge. After I'd been there for several years, this one young man I trained with said, "There's never been a woman in the history of this school who learned all ten Shaolin sets, Michelle." By that time I had learned half of them, the easy half. It became my goal to be the first woman to learn all of the hand sets.

It was also a cultural challenge, because there're very few white men who've learned the whole system in the history of this school. I said, "I'm going to be a white *woman* that learns them all. And then they'll remember me. Even though there's a long history in this school and people coming and going all the time, they'll remember Michelle."

And I did it. I earned those guys' respect. Just by being there and practicing. Not missing a class. New Year's Eve, Christmas Eve, Mother's Day—three times a week. If you miss classes, then they know you're not serious and you don't get taught the next class you show up. You don't get scolded but just don't get taught. It took me a year to figure that out. Although I rarely missed classes, my friends would come back, "Teacher didn't teach me!" "Well, you weren't here last time." I think the only time I missed class was when I was out of town, visiting my parents or traveling.

I beat myself up the mountain, learning those Kung Fu sets. I learned them all—the ten basic ones and four warm-up sets. There're guys who've been in class twenty-five years, and they're still learning new stuff from Mr. Wong. But I learned the fourteen basic Kung Fu sets, the only woman in the history of the school.

How does the Kung Fu compare to the T'ai Chi for you?

Kung Fu is faster and has a few more exotic stances, but basically it's the same stances and the same principles. Our style of T'ai Chi is not so extreme as the Kung Fu, but the body lineup is exactly the same.

Kung Fu is mainly for exercise and good health in Mr. Wong's class. Nobody in class ever sparred—if people were interested, they would go out in the hallway. But it can be a fighting sport and a method of self-defense. The energy that you feel—well, it burns your energy. Your endorphins get going, so you get a very exuberant feeling from practicing Kung Fu. In T'ai Chi, instead of the physical challenge, I feel you get more of a mental challenge, because of the internal aspects—you're focusing on the posture and the tan t'ien and the ch'i flowing.

What I learned from T'ai Chi that helped me with the Kung Fu was concentrating on the principles of posture and centering in every movement and coordinating my breath with my movements. I learned that from T'ai Chi because it's slow. Then when I moved fast, my breath was already coordinated. So T'ai Chi helped my endurance with the Kung Fu. Also I have incredibly better balance and agility in my Kung Fu from the T'ai Chi. What I got from Kung Fu that helped me with my T'ai Chi was extra strength—so I could get lower in my postures—and extra flexibility, and knowledge of applications. I understood what many T'ai Chi moves meant much better, which helped me understand T'ai Chi as a fighting form.

I would say Kung Fu is more basic than T'ai Chi—T'ai Chi is a kind of Kung Fu. That's the way it's taught in the Orient. You learn Kung Fu as a young person and graduate to T'ai Chi as your physical powers diminish and your inner strengths increase. It's a natural progression from Kung Fu to T'ai Chi and then to meditation. My history has been backwards. I studied meditation, then T'ai Chi, then Kung Fu. It suited me.

My teacher, Mr. Wong, actually taught three systems—Kung Fu, T'ai Chi, and Hsing Yi. I decided to practice Hsing Yi because years ago at a PAWMA camp—a women's training camp put on by the Pacific Association of Women Martial Artists—I was in a sparring class and the Hsing Yi girl beat me up bad. I was able to at least hold my own with all the other styles, but with the Hsing Yi girl I could not. Also Hsing Yi has that stutter step, that entering, forward motion. I needed that for my T'ai Chi Push Hands because I couldn't get any power into my push. I could never really uproot anybody, really lift their feet off the ground. So I said, "This is going to help my T'ai Chi."

And also I had learned all the Kung Fu hand sets and all the weapons and all the T'ai Chi, and I still didn't want to leave my teacher. Hsing Yi is an incredible system. I can do my T'ai Chi lazy, I can do my Kung Fu lazy, but I cannot do Hsing Yi lazy, because the power is inherent in the moves. It carries you along, and you can't do the moves without the power. Kung Fu is like a fast burn, T'ai Chi is the very slow warming up, and Hsing Yi is somewhere in between, a slow boil where you constantly use your energy. It's like you're jogging, just trotting along. It's more aerobic than T'ai Chi, but not as exhausting or spend-it-all as the Kung Fu. It's a good balance between hard and soft.

I find it fascinating to watch—those long, forward marching movements, and then the precision and forcefulness of the turns and strikes.

It originated in marching, as exercises for soldiers on the march. It's very practical for fighting and self-defense. And it has animal movements—there are twelve animal movements where you feel the spirit of the animals—so it's fun. But it is a complete system, like the T'ai Chi, that would take twenty years of practicing all the time and studying and exploring, and I—I'm still a baby in that system.

So is Hsing Yi your current emphasis in studying?

Not formally, because I left the class, but I practice. I got filled up to here in forms. I couldn't absorb any more. These last couple of years, I've been trying to digest it all, get it to be mine. So though I haven't had a teacher, I've been incredibly occupied.

Michelle Dwyer with Chinese double-edged sword at FIST martial arts training camp for women (the Netherlands, 1994).

I also didn't learn Mr. Wong's T'ai Chi form. He teaches classical Yang-style T'ai Chi, and through the years I finally said, "I would like to learn your form of T'ai Chi." He didn't want to teach it to me. He said, "One T'ai Chi form is enough. If you do it right, then you don't need another one." I liked that, because he kind of said, "Your form is legitimate."

At that time there were several spots where I really questioned the form. Mr. Wong said, "If you can make it better, you should change it and make it better. This is how the art form stays alive and keeps getting better instead of getting watered down." After he told me that, I was ready to change

it, and then I looked at it deeper, and I decided it was fine the way it was. And in fact, places where I changed it, I'm going back to the way it was originally. If you don't understand something, you have to explore it and change it, and then through your explorations and changes, you maybe understand it better so that you can go back to the original and say, "Okay, now I do understand this move as it was originally."

Later I made other changes. I modified the form because of the practical applications, the fighting. Finding the fighting roots of the form became very important to me from going to the PAWMA camps and hanging out with the women, the fighting women, who are into the self-defense and the fighting and the martial part of their arts, and that's what they're there for, to be good fighters. They're not there for good health; they're there to be strong and powerful and take care of themselves. And here I am, with Janet and other T'ai Chi people, doing this meditative stuff, the soft and internal, and these Karate people would be looking at us like, "This is a martial art? What are you doing here?" You know—New Age Nancys.

So I said, "I know T'ai Chi is for fighting, it started in fighting though now it's for good health first, with fighting down the line there." I wanted to understand every application of every move so that when I did teach a T'ai Chi workshop I could show these tough women that these beautiful, flowing, slow motions can be used for fighting if you put the yang part of it in there instead of just emphasizing the yin. Every move has some yang in it, just like the symbol, right? Nothing is totally black or white. The yielding has some strong in it, and the strong has some soft in it.

Many years of studying Kung Fu and Hsing Yi have helped me understand that our form, the Dragon Tiger Mountain form, has many different styles of martial arts in it. From my studies of other martial arts I go back and do my form and I understand, this is just like a Hsing Yi move that I've been studying. Or these movements are just like Kung Fu moves. It's fascinating to me to do my form—which I love. Our form is fairly rare. Nam Singh doesn't do it any more. Just Janet and I and our students. Nobody else does it. It's going to be the Northern California form. I love that. It's like in China, where every little village had its own style.

I have a vision of T'ai Chi and martial arts becoming part of mainstream culture in Western countries. I think martial arts are a good tool, or path, for learning about yourself, working on your weaknesses, and confronting your fears. If you're strong inside yourself and know yourself, then you can be more accepting of other people and different ways. Everybody else can do whatever they want, and you're fine. This is how I think martial arts can help individuals and the whole culture to become less aggressive—to know and love yourself is a first step to world peace, basically.

Also it's a wonderful bond between generations. I see it especially with my Chinese-American friends now they're starting to teach their children. There was no kids' class at Mr. Wong's Kung Fu school, and they all started having kids and they wanted their kids to do Kung Fu. But Mr. Wong was not going to teach them! So this is what finally brought them to be teachers. They've been twenty-five years in class, not even teaching yet. Waiting for their teacher to retire and pass the lineage on to them. But now they are teaching the next generation. It's wonderful to see these parents and their kids and all their friends' kids have this thing in common.

And at some point in there you also started teaching?

As I said, I knew I wanted to teach when I was in Nam Singh's class, but I didn't have quite enough skills. I studied a couple more years with Mr. Wong and then I asked Nam Singh, "Can I have permission to teach your form?" He wouldn't give me permission. I studied another year and then I asked Mr. Wong. I said, "I want to start teaching, but my old teacher won't give me permission." He said, "I give you permission to teach." I went and told Nam Singh, "I'm going to start teaching now. I got permission from my teacher." And he said, "Oh, okay, you can teach." *[Laughs]*

So I started teaching, and for three years I didn't make any money at all. Just learning how to teach, I went through a lot of students. You know—this works and this doesn't work. Lost that student. Well, that didn't work. I didn't feel that my teachers gave me a very good example for teaching in a progressive way. They never had any drills, just, "Here's the next move!" Never broke it down, feet, the hands.

Mr. Wong's class was anarchy. We came in and did our own warm-ups and he wandered around and spent five minutes with each student and then you practiced the rest of the time. He spent five minutes with everybody in the class, and that's it. I liked that as a student. That was good for my personality. I don't like structure. I do things because I want to, not because the rest of the class is doing fifty push-ups. I'd push myself hard at my own pace. But I pretty much had to design my own style and method of teaching. It took me many years.

Going to the PAWMA camps through the years has helped. I would think, "I like how this teacher teaches, so I'm going to try to remember her methods, the progression of her class, and try to add it to mine." Or "I don't like what this teacher does, so I'll never do that." Just sampling a lot of teachers at the women's camps helped me a lot.

I started making a little money when I got my college jobs—I've been teaching T'ai Chi at Napa Valley College for nine years now and at Holy Names College for eight years. That was something new too, because I had to teach in big groups instead of just wander around like my teachers had. How do I teach groups? Every step is a challenge. But it's been fun, and my students have been patient and encouraging—and appreciative. Whatever I did, they would try hard, and they helped me learn a lot about teaching.

Do you find that teaching changes your own practice?

Before I started teaching I was much more focused on my own inner awareness. Since I started teaching, the focus of my training has become much more external, because I'm giving it out. I haven't focused on the spiritual part, although it's always been very interesting and important to me. I do teach meditation at Holy Names. An hour of our class is meditation, and people enjoy that part. In Napa it's more of an exercise class.

In my own practice I have a left-handed approach—that's a Chinese term. Right-handed approach is the formal, conventional way. I learn these things and then fit them into my lifestyle— instead of creating my lifestyle to fit the meditation, I made the meditation fit my lifestyle, washing dishes or lying down, not sitting in lotus or standing in posture. And I do my Ch'i Kung. But I'm not very organized.

We all know how hard it is to train our bodies, which is our physical discipline, and we also know how hard it is to have our mental discipline, like if you take a math class or learn a language. To train your spirit I think is the most difficult of all the disciplines, because the spirit is so elusive. It's like taming a wild horse, to try to tame the spirit. It's difficult, but it's rewarding. I think if you meditate, those drops of awareness and spiritual growth that you get from just fifteen minutes stay with you for the whole rest of your life. They never leave you.

I think T'ai Chi, with the mind focused on this physical form that you're doing, frees the spirit from wandering thoughts. With the mind focused on the body, your spirit is free to grow and be refreshed. We get this feeling of well-being after our T'ai Chi because from the mind and body being coordinated our spirit is being—well, watered. The spirit is enlivened that way.

So you don't find the spiritual aspect, or at least not so directly, in the harder styles of martial arts that you practice?

No, not in the physical performance of it. Although with the endorphins going, the well-being of the body I'm sure trickles up to the spirit also. But I'm sure—I know!—in the old country, meditation was as much a practice of the external martial arts as punching the bags and everything else. We, I think, lost that a little bit as it has traveled to the West. I'm sure that they spent an hour of meditation for every hour of exercise in the real tradition of all the arts.

Because you couldn't do what you had to do physically—you know, to dodge a samurai sword, you couldn't do it without the meditation part of it. No matter how good a physical athlete you were, if you didn't have the spiritual concentration, you couldn't do what was required of you physically.

I want to get your class into Push Hands more, Stephanie, because you need that to really progress in your T'ai Chi solo form. You learn to be soft and relaxed and balanced in the form, but you need the force from another person that you get with Push Hands to test your level of relaxation and softness. Without that outside force, you can't know if you're really doing it. Dealing with an outside force also makes you sink your energy, the ch'i, which you need for your form.

We talk about it! Janet's taught us some basics. And just about everybody has gone to take self-defense classes from Gayle Fillman. Janet tries to get all of her students to do that, just so we get something that she feels that she's not giving us. I do

some Push Hands now—I'm pretty much convinced there's something there. But I am also reluctant.

Don't like to be touched or get your arms and legs all tangled up with someone else?

I guess it's partly I don't like doing things that close. I'm not used to it and I'm nervous about it. And then I don't know how to do it, you know, and so it makes me feel incompetent. I don't like that either. So I'm just not getting into learning.

It's a fun game, though. It's a sport. It's the sport of T'ai Chi. It's like a tennis match, you know? I toss some energy to you, and you have to deal with it and then toss it back at me, and I have to deal with what you gave me and give it back.

Michelle Dwyer (right) teaching a sparring exercise at a workshop (Ukiah, Calif., June 1994).

ROGER FRANKLIN

I hate tennis.

Oh, well, I do too. What I have found that has helped people past that reluctance to being in somebody's space and touching and really getting close is a two-people T'ai Chi form, which is a form, so it tells you exactly what to do. I've taught that to a lot of my senior ladies. It's foreign to them to get close, to get their arms and legs all tangled up. They didn't want to be touched. But I said, "Come on, this is fun!" One step at a time. And then they loved it. They get up there and they start punching each other and go through the whole form. I would never push hands with them, because they're elderly, and I don't want them to fall. This two-people T'ai Chi form gives them the same understanding of T'ai Chi principles that you can get from Push Hands, but you're not knocking each other over. It's a good way to get used to the proximity of other bodies, and maybe then you can get into Push Hands.

Also there're all these great techniques in it, fighting techniques, or pushing hands techniques, so that when you begin to do your Push Hands, you may be borrowing some of those techniques from the two-people form to actually use. It's a good way for people who have some skepticism about pushing hands to get into it, I think.

◆ ◆ ◆

We went outside, and side by side on the hard-packed earth under the wide limbs of the large black elm, we went through the Dragon Tiger Mountain form in our different styles. I was used to the company of less experienced practitioners—Michelle's presence beside me was much fuller and more alive. Going back into the house through a utility porch, I glimpsed Michelle's staff hanging on the wall with her long, tapered wooden spear tipped with a metal blade, a red tassel tied around the shank. Michelle told me the purpose of the tassel, traditionally made of white horse-hair, was to sop up blood that ran down the blade during combat and prevent the spear from becoming slippery to hold. Now these weapons hung amid brooms and mops on a wall bracket, but I had seen them come alive in Michelle's hands in demonstrations.

In the house, she pulled a dozen or more swords and daggers and other weapons from her closet, plain wooden practice weapons as well as metal weapons sheathed in intricately inlaid scabbards. We sat on the floor, piling the weapons around us as we looked them over one by one.

I've been fascinated by the sword ever since I first saw you doing the double sword set. Why do we like this so much? Is there some basic instinct that attracts us to the flashiness of weapons? Sometimes I wonder if this is something we should resist.

I think the reason that we continue playing with swords after the advent of guns is for health. T'ai Chi gets the lower body, but there's not much for the upper body. Weapons give our upper body a workout so we're in balance and get a complete physical workout.

Also weapons teach you to extend your energy outside your body, to the end of the weapon. For fighting, even empty hands, you don't want to stop at the surface of the body, you want to penetrate through. In massaging, you also don't want to just get the surface, you want to penetrate in. So that extension of your energy is for healing also.

Another reason I think that women are attracted to weapons is, you know, we just have these little skinny arms, and when you have a weapon, it makes you much more powerful. I think that women are attracted to the power of the weapons. I feel much stronger with something in my hand. I've always been attracted to the beauty of weapons—the sword first, T'ai Chi sword. Nam Singh really inspired us. I think we started the sword right after learning the T'ai Chi hand set, and that's what I make my students do. Then when I went to Kung Fu class and saw these guys jumping around with these beautiful weapons, one right after the other, I learned all that. I really loved the weapons, and now I have more weapons in my closet here than I have clothes.

The sword was my favorite for many, many years—until I learned the spear. And I think I'm back to the favorite of the straight sword again. Actually, the broadsword, or saber, is the basic short weapon. The straight sword requires much more precision and finesse. It's what the aristocrats and scholars used, I think because it was an expensive weapon and also because it took a long time to train. The poor people didn't have time to train with it. The saber was the common soldier's weapon, more hacking and hewing. The spirit of the saber is the tiger. A fearless fighter and dangerous opponent.

The staff is the basic of the long weapons. It's power in the arms. It builds up a good foundation and upper-body strength. The form I know from Kung Fu is called the Earth Dragon. That's the spirit of the staff. This year I designed a fighting form with the staff with Coleen Gragen—it's the first form I designed, basically.

You were saying you really fell in love with the spear, for a while anyway. Why was that?

I think just because it's bigger and longer. In the Northern Shaolin system, the spear is the king of weapons. It has the spirit of the dragon. It may appear to be a simple weapon, but like the dragon it's multifaceted, elegant, and demanding. You learn power from the spear, and focus and more precise movement.

I like the long weapons. Just for the range— you fill up a big space! The spear is very beautiful with the tassel out there. Crowds always love it— it's exciting and you have a feeling of power. It takes less time to master. *[Laughs]* You can get pretty good at the spear within a couple years, but you're always struggling for perfection with the sword. *[Takes up another sword]* My wooden sword. And here's a Japanese sword. And a dress sword. A knife. Double sabers—Bruce bought me these for a birthday present. And here's my prize— a real samurai sword. Don't touch the blade, okay? My Dad got this after World War II. I have seven brothers, and he gave it to me. I thought that was pretty good.

◆　◆　◆

She hands me the samurai sword in its sheath, a severe-looking affair of black and gray metal. I pull out the blade a few inches and see the pattern of wavy lines in the blade from the ancient method by which the steel is tempered. The sword feels very cold and heavy in my hands—I find it unsettling and soon put it down. Meanwhile Michelle has found something else.

◆ ◆ ◆

Gee, I didn't even know I had two of these. Here's another one! And some daggers. I have some shooting stars around here somewhere.

And you've learned forms with all of these?

I don't know double saber. I'd like to learn that some day. I should just start practicing. Double saber's like tigers' teeth, they just chop it up! I'd like to learn double dagger someday too. There's a great form—double dagger against the spear. I lust after other forms. I'd like to learn a fan set and I'd like to learn the whip chain. And *kuantao,*

which looks like a ten-foot butter knife. The double sword is my favorite, the Double Dragon Plum Blossom Sword form. And it's the most difficult—probably take another twenty years to get it good.

At this point can you just work on it yourself? Or do you need to go back for further instruction from your teacher?

Just work on it myself—balance and speed and rhythm and good stances. Like we were saying outside, you learn the form and then explore it and perfect it yourself. A teacher can say, "Oh, your hip is a little too high." You can get advice from the outside, but basically once you get the skeleton then you work it and make it come alive for yourself.

CHAPTER 9

I Have a Path, a Spiritual Path

Michelle Dwyer no longer studies martial arts formally in a school, but the ties she maintains with practitioners in different arts constantly bring new influences to her practice. She participates with a lion dancing club in the annual Chinese New Year's parade in San Francisco, also performing lion dances on Saturdays throughout the month of February in the children's rooms of the neighborhood branches of the San Francisco Public Library. She often trades lessons with other martial artists, teaching her specialties in exchange for training in new arts and techniques. At the time I interviewed Michelle she was meeting once a week with another practitioner of T'ai Chi Ch'uan, Wasentha Young. Michelle spoke with great respect of Wasentha's skill at Push Hands; for her part Michelle was teaching Kung Fu spear to Wasentha.

I was intrigued by the range of interests and training practices I was finding just within the single category of Yang-style T'ai Chi Ch'uan. Like Karina Epperlein—but in a very different manner—Wasentha practices Cheng Man-ch'ing's short form, which he derived from the older Yang-style T'ai Chi Ch'uan that Jane Golden practices. Born in China in 1900, Cheng Man-ch'ing was an artist, poet, martial artist, and physician. In the 1930s, a time of great upheaval in China, with civil war exacerbated by the Japanese invasion, Cheng had the task of teaching T'ai Chi Ch'uan to army conscripts, police, students, and a variety of other ordinary citizens very different from the leisured or highly dedicated persons who usually pursued the art. Believing that morals and character, sorely needed in this difficult time—as well as the people's health, which had suffered greatly from widespread hardship—could be nurtured through the practice of T'ai Chi Ch'uan, he simplified and shortened the form from one hundred and eight to thirty-seven moves to get across the principles and essence of the teaching to a broader audience. Later Cheng came to the United States, living in New York and teaching T'ai Chi Ch'uan for a number of years. His U.S. students have made this form probably the most widely practiced of any in the United States. Wasentha's teacher, William C. C. Chen, was one of Cheng's senior students.

When I called Wasentha to ask for an interview, I discovered she was not one to settle in one place for long. Her home base was Berkeley, California, but she was traveling a good deal, partly in connection with an impending move to Michigan. We did eventually connect and arranged that I would attend a Saturday morning class of Ch'i Kung and T'ai Chi Ch'uan and afterward we would talk.

A striking-looking woman in her early forties, with large, dark eyes and strong, shapely bone structure to her face, Wasentha has a calm, relaxed, and relaxing way about her teaching that quickly set me at ease. I particularly liked the Ch'i Kung exercises she has developed from individual movements of the form. Other teachers often use the individual moves as postures for standing meditation; Wasentha emphasized the transitions between the postures. With large, flowing movements, she led us in the turns and transformations that have always most fascinated me about T'ai Chi Ch'uan. Change is an aspect that greatly interests her as well, I was to discover. As I asked about her background of more than twenty-five years in martial arts, she went her own way to answer with sometimes elliptical stories and anecdotes—but she always did answer, winding up with a laugh, alerting me that she was now answering my question.

WASENTHA YOUNG

T'ai Chi Ch'uan

When I was seventeen—this was in New York City in 1969—I had this couple that were mentors, they were like parents to me. In the summertime, when I was working, I would go to meet them at their T'ai Chi class, and we would go shopping and go back to their house and hang out or go out to eat or whatever. I would always get there early because of the timing of when I left my job and when the class started. At a certain point I figured that since I was there, I might as well participate.

They were studying from a guy named Peter—Peter Chen, I think. They studied with him for maybe a year. But his main focus wasn't T'ai Chi—he did other arts—and they decided to study from then Master, now Grand Master, William Chen. So I said, "Oh, well, I'll go there also."

Even though it wasn't really your idea to study T'ai Chi, once you started, something in it appealed to you and kept you going?

Well, for one, my mentors were doing it, so I had a family, so to speak, of people that I could hang out with. I was the youngest, so I was treated like—taken care of. It gave me some sense of belonging. We would all do T'ai Chi and then after T'ai Chi class we would take a long walk downtown into Chinatown and eat and go to a Chinese movie.

I learned the form, I started doing some Push Hands, and then before I knew it, I was in the boxing class—kick boxing really. The way we used our bodies was T'ai Chi, but more the fighting style of T'ai Chi, and with a boxing format. We had gloves, we had shin guards, arm guards, chest protection, head gear, mouth piece—the whole bit. We *boxed.* It was heavy-duty stuff. That's what William Chen's emphasis was. I had fun with that, though it was difficult sometimes—you're getting punched and kicked and you're doing the same. I wound up in the hospital once, and I have a floating kidney from getting struck with an internal kind of strike. But that was the progression, and I kept doing it.

Then I married William Chen's top student, James Turner, and it was twenty-four hours a day of T'ai Chi. James was an impeccable boxer. He was incredible in terms of understanding the timing and the state of mind of T'ai Chi. He could roll in slow motion. It was like if you set something in motion in outer space, and whatever that velocity is, or that thrust is, that will continue through space. There were times when I would push him and he would go into a roll and he'd keep rolling and rolling, effortlessly, and when he would get to the wall, he could roll up part of the wall and he would somehow come down with his feet on the ground and just stand there and look at you.

It was like watching—who's the basketball player who just jumps and keeps going? Michael Jordan—he just keeps going up into space until he gets to the basket, and the camera's not going slow or anything. Or Baryshnikov, where he twirls up in the air, and you would think that he should be down by now, but he might do two or three more twirls before he comes down. It offsets your senses a little bit. It would give me a jar like that when James would do things like that. He just said, "It's a state of mind. T'ai Chi is a state of mind." And his body was stiff! When he crossed his legs, his knees were up by his earlobes. He was tight, muscularly and everything. He wasn't a loose person. He changed his state of mind—I don't know how else to explain it.

James wasn't someone I should have married, and we didn't stay married, but he taught me a tremendous amount and he gave me form corrections. That was my second time going through form corrections. It's part of the process—you have to let go of what you thought you knew to learn something else about that same movement. William Chen didn't like to give corrections. As a matter of fact, he used to sometimes look at us and say, "Excuse me," and he'd go in his office for a little while. I asked him later why he would do that, and he said because it was painful to watch us. It wasn't until years and years and years later, I would say about eighteen years later, that I understood what he meant by, "It was painful." I did something else with that than what he did.

Can you explain how the form corrections worked for you—that process of letting go to learn something new?

How I see it is that you learn a movement, you feel a certain amount of success about having learned that movement. You have an idea of what that movement is and how it goes. Then your teacher or someone points out places in your body that you are tightening or are out of alignment or not enough energy flows through or whatever, and then you have to change that movement, or allow that movement to change. It is essentially the same movement, but your understanding about it deepens.

You have to let go of your idea and see what happens when you do the movement, because otherwise you start making the movement fit, making it be a certain way. When you do that, you do what is called "jade" your form, and once your form is jaded, it's like, "Well, what fun is this any more?" One of the things that a woman named Maggie Newman taught me was that you never say you've got it. When I first started going through the process, I was saying that I thought I knew what I was doing. Or when I got a correction, I would say, "Well, wasn't that what I was doing?" You know the kind of thing—total denial that I could be doing this wrong or that something wasn't happening in it that needed to happen. This idea of being perfect.

But at a certain point, after my second set of corrections, I started getting the hang of the letting go of how I thought it was. Learning how to change. It taught me a great lesson about life—you have an idea, you work through it, and you watch it flow, but you have to be able to let go.

I started to feel different about myself. My focus got better. My tight clothes—that all changed. I became more relaxed, more comfortable in my body. That kept me going with it, seeing that obvious change, though it wasn't until maybe four, five years into it that I started to see the changes. Because of my age—you don't see a whole lot when you're seventeen, eighteen, nineteen. Twenty, then it starts, twenty-one. When you go into the adult world more, you start learning in a different way.

I went through different stages in T'ai Chi. I learned it as a martial art at first. I learned the application of the movements. And then—well, I'm kind of jumping a little bit, but one of the things that I learned is that fighting and self-defense are different. I started to see how I could read energy because of how I trained with the art. I studied with Chögyam Trungpa Rinpoche and learned about meditation. Then I saw how meditation was a part of doing T'ai Chi. And of recent, studying at the acupressure school and learning about the meridians and points, and then learning more and more about Ch'i Kung, I see how all of these things are involved in what it is you are doing when you are doing T'ai Chi.

A lot of people look at T'ai Chi as just being a martial art—how to get power from it, how to store your power, how to root yourself. I see it as a means of people being able to get deeper into themselves. You need to give your body and your mind a chance to touch your core, and then touching your core, you're touching the core of the universe, the energy of the universe. We're all attached in some way or another, but we don't all know how to reach that inner resource and get information. When I teach, I try to transmit that information to people, offering them a vehicle—if not T'ai Chi, just the knowledge that we each individually have to do something for ourselves, to seek that out, whether it's yoga or you want to sit and meditate or whatever.

I can see that that's what the sages did. I see myself as a sage. I see a lot of people who could be called sages, but in the West we don't know that's who we are. Because we're not respected in that way, we're not nourished in that way. I would like to nourish that part of all of us.

And has teaching then become integral to your practice?

My practice is my way of being in touch in myself. Grounding myself. Relaxing. Working with my health. My teaching is integral, I think, to my life, to who I am. I serve, and this is the way I like to serve. I look forward to a healthier people, a more connected people, in touch with themselves, with each other, and with the Earth. I feel that all of those things that people talk about in philosophies and different religions—Taoism, Buddhism, Confucianism, and all of that—people can get to themselves if they relax their feet on the ground, relax the abdominal muscles, open themselves up, let themselves be.

But was it through studying the fighting that you got more insight into the meditative and other aspects of it, do you think? Was the fighting a useful or necessary foundation for you?

The fighting part of it I think gave my body a certain amount of relaxation. To know that the body knows how to use itself, to defend itself, I feel that is something that is good for each human being to know about themselves. So I in no way think that people shouldn't study that aspect of it.

I think people should know how to use their bodies. They should know how to throw a punch, throw a kick, ward off, neutralize force. I think people should know how to do that. I'll teach my students how to throw a punch. I'll let them work out on the bag, the heavy bag, to feel that weight. We'll do freestyle Push Hands to play, but I won't

Wasentha Young (right) pushing hands with Janet Aalfs at PAWMA training camp (Olympia, Wash., August 1995).

say, "Put the boxing gloves on and put up your dukes." I won't teach people to fight with each other. Because I feel like that's sort of working something out on somebody else sometimes.

Somewhere in there, you said, you learned the difference between fighting and self-defense?

William Chen always taught me to push hands with different people, not just people from your style.

There was a martial arts teacher in Boulder, Colorado, when I lived there who I had a connection to through someone else. I called him and he said, "Sure, come on down and push hands." I came down, and he had me working with this student who knew Hsing Yi. Hsing Yi is a harder style than T'ai Chi, and the student just was hammering at me, and I'm going, "Damn! What is going on here?" So I asked him if he did Push Hands, and we started doing that. Well, the teacher came over and said, "You came from William Chen's school. You know how to freestyle spar, so freestyle spar!" He wanted his student to get the opportunity to work his Hsing Yi stuff out on somebody who was doing T'ai Chi, only I didn't know this.

Then to top it off, one of my friends came by and said, "Beat him up, Wasentha!"—just in passing and just as a joke, but *boom!* The student just fluffed right up and got even harder. But I stayed there, and once he got that I wasn't there to challenge him in that way, then things went smoother, he got softer, and we played. But I had a huge black-and-blue mark on my shin because he tried to sweep me, and he had on hard shoes. He didn't sweep me, but I went home feeling like I was a battered woman. And I said, "Damn it, Wasentha, you put yourself there. You said, 'Let me see if I can take this.'" So I beat myself up for a little while.

Then I was out in Denver, at the bus station. It was getting dark, and I was waiting for somebody to come pick me up. When I exited the bus station I saw a man, and he said, "Hello," and I— you know, human to human—said, "Hi!" and walked down the block. Out of my peripheral vision, I saw that he was talking to a friend of his, and they started walking down the block toward where I was waiting. They got within ten feet of me and I saw this bolt of light come off of each one of them. One of their lights went to one side of me and the other one's light went to the other side. When I saw that, I started to step around the outside bolt of light. As I started doing that, they started walking toward me, but I was circling around, so they found themselves kind of trailing me—I was already behind them and walking down the block. They said, "Hey, wait a minute!" And I said, "No!" and just kept walking, and my friend came and picked me up and so on and so forth.

Later I realized that I defended myself without lifting a finger. That's when I realized the difference between self-defense and fighting, and that sprung me off into another level of understanding. When I moved from Boulder, I moved to Santa Fe, New Mexico, and I went into trying to understand more about the transformation of energy— that's even another level, less ego involved, because to transform energy, it's nothing that you do necessarily. What happened was that as I was crossing a street, a car was coming out of a driveway and was going to make a U-turn, but I stepped down off of the center divide as they came out to do this. I was standing there, and they couldn't make their turn. I stepped back up, and I said to the driver, "Pedestrians have the right of way."

He got out of his car—he stopped his car right there, got out, jumped in my face, and said, "You got a problem?" I said, "No, I just said, 'Pedestrians have the right of way.'" He stared at me and got back in his car and drove off. And I said, "What happened?" I mean, he was ready! That's when I started understanding that there's some such thing as transforming the energy around you.

There was a part of me, though, that wanted to knock him out, so I knew that I still have plenty of ego. But I got a glimpse of something a little higher—I say "higher," but it doesn't have to be higher, just something different, that I preferred. But again, I don't say that you shouldn't know how to fight. It's just different levels. All of it was steps I needed to go through. And understand.

When I left New York, I went to Taos, New Mexico, with James. One thing in my relationship while I was still with James, he said he was going to teach me, and I was going to be the one to teach people. For a period of time I was confused as to whether I was doing this because I wanted to or because he said that's what I was going to be doing. He did teach me a tremendous amount during the time that we were together.

After you separated, was there a process that you had to go through to claim the T'ai Chi for yourself apart from him?

Well, it's interesting that I didn't think about it. I just did it. I was assisting him and one of the things that made us separate was when I started talking about teaching my own classes. He took that as me wanting independence and said, "If you want to be independent, be totally independent, not partially independent." And we split up. So I just went ahead and did what I said I was going to do at that point. When I got to Boulder, I started teaching. I got into the Free School in Boulder and taught there. And there was a Sufi group there. The guy who ran the house where people came and did their meditation came to me—he knew I was living in a house with thirteen people—and he said, "If you will teach the people in my house some Ba Kua or Hsing Yi"—which at that time I had been doing—then I could live there. They had a chicken coop that was converted in the back of the house—it was a meditation room, really, but that's where I lived.

In Boulder I received a lot of information about meditation because Naropa Institute is there,

and Trungpa Rinpoche ran that. I got a chance to assist the T'ai Chi teachers that came to that school—all of them were Cheng Man-ch'ing's students. William Chen studied with Cheng Man-ch'ing, but William left the school and went his own way, and he definitely has a different style than Cheng Man-ch'ing had. I learned from William to go my own way. I'm not stuck with one teacher. I'm not stuck with one way of doing this. I might have one form that I do, but I've allowed myself to explore within that form different ideas about what it is that you're doing physically in the form. That has had an effect on how I teach as well, telling people that if you see somebody doing it different, doesn't mean it's wrong. But at that time I had to give up William's style of doing T'ai Chi. It was because I so much wanted to be part of the Cheng Man-ch'ing group in Boulder.

Well, they weren't having any, because there was the conflict—you inherit your teacher's karma sometimes. William Chen left his teacher, so they had an attitude about William Chen. And William Chen was into boxing and—"No, no, no! With T'ai Chi you don't do that!" It sort of translated to me. As much as I tried to become part of that group and give up doing William Chen's thing, they still would not let me into the group. They would say things like, "Let's not talk about that because she's here."

I was let in enough to play with them and to learn from them. I learned a tremendous amount about the form from them. One person told me that Cheng Man-ch'ing told them, "You six make me"—referring to his senior students. I thought to myself, Maggie knows about the intricacy of movement, Tam Gibbs knows about the dynamics of motion, William Chen knows about the application of the form, Ed Young knows about the tao within the form, Ben Lo knows about the rooting within the form. I figured that if I could touch base with each one of them, it would give me more insight as to the holistic idea of it.

And I believe that Cheng Man-ch'ing taught differently at different stages in his life. As I have. In his latter years when he was here, he was older, sicker, and he really barely moved his body. So people have this very relaxed way about doing the form. One thing that I began to understand, starting with Tam Gibbs, but then developed from learning from other teachers who teach Yang style, was there's more dynamics to it than that. So you have a range of people who do the form in this very effortless way and then some people do the form where you can see a lot of the ebb and flow and the filling and emptying of the movement.

When I started exploring with these other people, I relearned the whole form with whoever I was studying with. Each time I would drop whatever I had been doing or whoever I was imitating, so to speak. I would go through corrections and that would get integrated into what I do, so now what I do is a combination of all of them.

And then your next step was learning more about healing? Or was there something in between there?

In between was myself. Primarily learning how to love myself. That came hand in hand with my T'ai Chi. It also seemed to come hand in hand with the area that I lived in. The land itself which I lived on generated a certain type of energy.

In New Mexico I was learning to survive. Things in New Mexico have to learn how to survive. It's drier where I was living, not a real flourishing, growing place. It's more struggle—the only way I think anybody can really flourish in that is if they have some kind of money. I don't know if that's true for everybody, but for myself, it was the case.

I moved to Boulder the first time I left New Mexico. Then I went back and then I moved to Ann Arbor—that's where I started to learn more about how to love myself. In Ann Arbor, even though there's winter, when it gets green, it is *green.* I got so much in touch with my body—and my mind and my spirit. Became more comfortable with me. And all of that I can say too happens with age. I can't tell the difference any more between my T'ai Chi and what's the natural progression of growth. It's all one big thing for me. Melting pot, so to speak. When I got to Ann Arbor, I got in touch with a bodyworker, who I allowed to get deep into my body—and open me up. My T'ai Chi started changing at the same time maintain that openness. My feet were more connected to the ground. I got much more grounded. My movements opened up more. My energy flowed through my body more. My hands would get nice and warm. The internal energy started kicking in there.

My student population changed. It's almost like my student body is my body, like I'm looking at myself in the form of students. When my T'ai Chi developed to a certain level of clarity, and my ability to express the principles in the movements and show people how to find it, then I started having more people coming to me to study. I think that that is related to me loving myself, because in loving myself more, I know myself better. I have a certain amount of clarity within myself, in relationship to myself, and that's attractive. How did I get there? Part of it is because of who I am, yes, but a lot of what I experience is experienced from some form of meditation. For me it's been T'ai Chi. People who want that type of meditation

Wasentha Young (center) demonstrating correct T'ai Chi Ch'uan posture to students at her Peaceful Dragon School of T'ai Chi Ch'uan (Ann Arbor, Mich., Fall 1995).

aspect of how the energy moves in the body, and the healing aspect of it. I would say one of my focuses now is healing. Our own individual healing. To do that, there has to be an element of love. I'm not talking about, "I think I'm great!" I don't mean that kind of love. I mean more of an acceptance. An acceptance of your being and a connection of your being with the Earth and people around you. You don't have to go to other people to get that connection; it starts inside. The thing that's happening for me now is my form is healing me. It's transmitting that energy to other people and my interactions with people have changed as a result.

Do you make a living from teaching T'ai Chi or are you planning to do that with acupressure? Or do you do other work to support yourself that's separate from this?

That's a good question. The one point where I tried to make T'ai Chi—*make* T'ai Chi my living—it was a struggle. I hated it. I found myself trying to jump through hoops to make people happy—

Like you were saying about William Chen not wanting to do corrections? Finding it painful to watch students?

Right—and that brings me to that point. When I was in Ann Arbor, I realized that it's painful to watch other people's tensions because you can feel it in yourself. So I said, "I can go into another room and breathe, or I can get right in there and help them release their tension so that it releases it in me too." That's where the loving of myself came out and affected other people and just bounced back to me again, so to speak.

would like to get it from someone who has a certain amount of clarity about it. If I had low self-esteem I would not be able to transmit the information clearly enough to people. They would get my low self-esteem—that transmission would go along with everything else I taught.

Here in Berkeley I started studying at the acupressure school to learn more of the technical

In terms of making a living from T'ai Chi, I know I can make a living from my T'ai Chi. If I had the time—the money and the time—to do my advertising, do my mailings, create my seminars, and all of that, I could make a living from T'ai Chi. But I'm busy learning other things, so I can't do that right now.

When I was in New York and growing up, I learned something about herbs, and I managed an herbs and spice place called Aphrodisia. When I was in New Mexico, the guy who ran the school I was teaching at was a naturopathic doctor, so on occasion I got to go on herb walks with him. I continued to work on bodies, work on myself physically, friends, family. And herbs—you can see on the shelves over there all those tinctures. When I came here, I wound up getting a job at the San Francisco Herb and Natural Food Company. It kept me in touch with herbs, and I began to look at, What are our nation's problems? What herbs were being ordered? What are people asking for on a wholesale level? We sell tons and tons of senna— senna is a laxative. So America's constipated. *[Laughs]*

I've stayed in touch with all of those things, and going to the acupressure school heightened that. But in the acupressure school, I saw that I just touched on this stuff. There's a vast, big old world out there, in relationship to this information. I don't always want to rub people down. That takes a lot of physical energy, and I'm forty-two now. It was just a source of information for me.

So learning is more what you're interested in rather than acquiring a profession or whatever?

When I first went into the acupressure, I definitely thought about that. There's a part of my ego that grasped that and said, "Oh! and then you have the clientele from your T'ai Chi students, who would want to have bodywork too, and da-da-da." That part of my ego did that. But when I got in there and started seeing all of that information, I went, "I'm not ready to do anything like that. There's so much more for me to understand here!"

But I can lay my hands on people. I work with it. I would rather just do neck, shoulder, back release work, and very rarely, unless I just want the practice or whatever, work on a person's whole body. It'll come around in some way or another. It will be utilized and valued and I may have some monetary flow coming toward me because of the knowledge that I have. I've learned not to rush it. I have a path, a spiritual path. I can see what my future is—there's part of me that sees it right in front of me, what I am to do in this world, how I'm to interact in this world. But I can't rush any of it. A step at a time.

And meanwhile influences keep coming from all different directions?

Right! When you're doing Push Hands, you don't want to always be programmed to do the Roll Back move, because the force might come from another direction and you want to use that arm to do something else. I don't want to fix myself into this way here, because like you said, the information can come from someplace else that doesn't fit that Roll Back arm that way. So I just as much as possible try and stay in tune with the forces, so to speak, the flow of energy, and that's the best I can do.

That has increased over the years. When I was first learning that the form can teach me how to stay open to change—because now the movement doesn't go the way I thought it was supposed to go, it goes a different way—Maggie Newman said to me, "Wasentha, can you take some of your self out of the movement and just let the movement happen, let it flow?" Then when I got to be around twenty-seven or so, people said, "When you get to be about thirty, girl, you're going to start reevaluating your life!" That kind of thing. *[Laughs]* When I got closer to that, I heard that that period is called, in astrological terms, the Saturn Return, and I was ready, willing, able, and excited about it. Because it represented change to me, and I said, "I got the hang of this! I'm going to let myself see myself, and let myself work with myself, and let myself *change*. I'm not going to resist that change."

That's where it started for me. Now I can get a bit of information from someone, feedback about myself, and compared to how I was when I was younger, change very rapidly. Before their eyes I could be a different person—say, "I understand what you're talking about," and be a different person at that moment. That I learned from the form, as the vehicle.

From doing the form and then reflecting on it intellectually or spiritually as well?

If you stay open to connecting your mind, your body, and your spirit, it's not really a *reflecting*—it's all the same. It flows in and out of all of those awarenesses. When I do something with my body, if I learn how to let go of this tension, well, something in the thinking mind releases too. Something in my awareness mind releases. Which then opens me up more to my spiritual being—and then my spiritual being relates back, "Ah-h-h-h." *[Gives a sigh of relief and then laughs]*

When I was studying with all these Cheng Man-ch'ing people, I had a hard attitude that, "*This is the way it's supposed to go.*" Then I was invited to teach at the Aspen Academy of Martial Arts by Marshall Ho'o—I think this was in the early eighties. Late seventies. Somewhere around there. Al Huang was there doing a workshop. I knew people were like, "Al Huang, what does he know about T'ai Chi? He's a dancer. He calls himself a master. How dare he?" I said, "I'll check this dude out, see what the story is here."

He was up there—"Move! Feel your body! Move!" He had people rolling about on the floor and prancing around and carrying on, and I said, "Well, I understand why people give him a hard time!" But then I started doing it and looking at the people in the class, and I said, "Some of these people have never ever moved their body before in their lives. He offers them a way of being able to do this—and I'm having a good time!"

That was something I'd forgotten in my practice—the Joyous Lake. That created a big shift for me in my relationship with myself and my form, and my relationship with me and other people and doing the form. So even though he is like he is, I learned a great lesson from him. And appreciate who he is for that.

In 1990 I studied a little with Yang Zhen Duo. He helped me start to understand the extension of the energy in the body. He was talking about T'ai Chi here in America, and he says, "What's this? These little floppy arms, floppy hands?" *[Laughs, waving wrists and hands limply]*

Certain things that he would say and show us helped me to understand more about the extension of the ch'i in the form—how to let the energy get to the palms and fingertips. Movement stems from the feet, travels through the legs, and is controlled by the waist and it emerges out through the palms and fingertips. Instead of just moving your hand in that direction, you have to allow energy to flow through your body. He had us look at our hands and he said, "I want you to just let your hand be relaxed and look at it. Then slowly begin to open the fingers, straightening the fingers, and when your hand looks like the lightbulb came on, then you know you have your hand in the right place."

It's like a brightness in the palm. When it's like this *[holds out one hand with the fingers loosely curled]*, you can see that the light isn't on, but when you get your hand to be about like this *[fingers open but not stiffly stretched]*, you can see that it's alive. Just that little exercise began to let me reflect on how to get that energy to the fingertips, how to get that energy to extend itself.

With the wide experience you have of teachers, how do you feel about the way these things are transmitted, or translated, not just from teacher to student, but from the mostly Asian cultures of origin to the United States?

I have a story: I went to a conference for writers, Caribbean writers, in Pomona, California, the college there. They had this white male talking about the colors of masking and Carnaval. He was saying that in Trinidad only the fair in color got up on the floats, and people dressed in all these colorful colors as a form of escapism because they can't do that in their everyday kind of thing.

I was looking around and the people who were there were humphing and huffing and twitching, because they were from Trinidad and they'd been to Carnaval—they'd lived it. They're crossing their legs and gritting their teeth and waiting for him to get through. Before that I was outside, and I saw a group of Asian people practicing T'ai Chi. I sat

and watched them and I was thinking, the teacher's not telling them that their knee isn't in line with their toe or that their shoulders aren't relaxed or this or that.

I was really going into this thing about, "How's this teacher teaching these people?" But after a while, I said, "Wasentha, just be quiet in your head and watch." And I did that and I came back and that's when that guy came on. Finally he finished and the hands flew up. This woman jumped up, and she says, "First of all, I want you to look around this room and look at the colors in the room. And look at the colors of my scarf, it's *orange!*" And she flicked it at him, just telling him that he has his nerve presenting this material like this is the way it is. She said, *"Everyone do Carnaval!"* That was great! That was the best part of the whole conference. It was so fiery!

Then somebody got up and started talking about Marcus Garvey, and I said, "Well, this guy here is a little boring," so I went out and I saw the T'ai Chi practicing again, and I heard my mind saying, "They're not telling them to put the knee over the toe! They're not telling them"—you know, from before, and I said, "But what's most important here? *Everyone do T'ai Chi.*" It's not who you study from. It's not how you look. It's just you're doing T'ai Chi!

I see myself as a Westerner, yes, and we have our own perspective, our own way of interpreting the idea. But they have that same type of trip in China too. Different people do it differently. And T'ai Chi is organic. It's growing. We use it slightly differently here for our stress reduction and other things, and we use it somewhat the same too. Now I know that the information is not just my information and it's not just their information—it's information to be given. So I feel okay about how I teach.

There's also the question of how men have dominated the martial arts field, including T'ai Chi—I don't think that the field is inherently related to men, but the way it's been taught for so many years is certainly permeated with male energy. I wonder how that's been for you—in studying with William Chen and James Turner, it sounds like you got a pretty heavy dose of a male version of it. Was that an area where as a woman you had to translate it to fit yourself? You were describing your response to students as opposed to William Chen's going into the other room . . .

I think that's my individual response. There are men out there who do similar things, who can be very soft and gentle—noncombative. But most of the time, when I was approached by men in terms of T'ai Chi, they wanted to challenge me. They wanted to know whether I could beat them up. They wanted to know about what people call the practical aspect, though I don't necessarily think application is the only practical aspect of T'ai Chi. I felt like I had to be able to say, "Yes, I know how to use it." "Yes, I can handle myself with it." "No, it's not just for health and relaxation." It was always that I had to defend T'ai Chi.

Now when somebody says, "Can you kick my ass?" I'll say, "Probably not." *[Laughs]* And then what is there to talk about? I used to be more invested and say things like, "Maybe I might, maybe I can't, but you *would* get hurt." Which only made them want me to prove it to them.

I had one student who was like that, he wanted me to push him, "Show me, show me, show me." He wanted the opportunity to show me that because he's a construction worker and knows how to sling that sledgehammer, he could physically dominate me. But I never pushed him—I never gave him the opportunity to snap into that. I had some other man in the class show him, and then I let him try and push me. So he only felt himself being vulnerable, because he couldn't push me.

Too many men have been indoctrinated into believing that they have to be physically domineering. Hence they try and build the bomb, you know, the one that's going to make people afraid of you. This show of power. But that's not what I think power really is. Mostly with men, I'll let them do their pushing thing, and let them see maybe they can't push me as well as they thought they could.

Is there also an aspect of being African American that makes a difference in any of this?

Me being African American actually has been more of an attribute, because there's an element of intrigue that people have because I am an African American doing this. How did *I* get to do this? Eventually in studying from me they stop seeing me as an African American and just go to the information.

You mentioned wanting to teach in the African-American community—that is something that matters to you?

Yes. *[Pauses]* It's hard to express this. Because to a certain degree I'm removing myself from my own race in talking about this. But the exposure that African Americans have to alternative lifestyles is minimal. And yet I find that alternative lifestyle is an essential part of being an African American. There's so much that we can benefit from, taking a walk in the park, doing yoga, taking T'ai Chi, or whatever, the alternative ways of being—alternative for today—that because of the struggle that so many people of color have in terms of being in this society and being able to survive—they can't do anything but survive. Having to take a little time, pay some money—it's very difficult to be able to set that aside because life for many people is so much taken up by survival. I find the white population has more of an opportunity to be able to take that time and pay that money.

There are plenty of people who have never explored alternative lifestyles, don't even know anything about "alternative lifestyles," and that ignorance is great amongst all races of people. But for me in particular—there may be a way that I see it and that I understand it that I will be able to express to people from my own cultural background, and I would love to share it with people of my own cultural background. It's like that's my family and I naturally seek to uplift my family.

When I go back to Ann Arbor, I may go into the neighborhood, into my own cultural neighborhood, so to speak—although America's my cultural neighborhood—but as an African American, I'll go into my cultural neighborhood, with the people who don't have much money, and volunteer. To give more exposure to some alternative ideas. Reach more people with it. Whatever they want to do from there is up to them, but at least they'll get the exposure and the information. They need to know that it's accessible to them in some way.

As we've talked, I've been struck with the many different teachings you've integrated in your life, and how you found these experiences in different physical, geo-graphical places. And you mentioned having a path, a spiritual path, and the model of the sage. It reminds me of the stories I've read about wandering Chinese Taoists—people who literally and spiritually follow a path that somehow opens for them, traveling and studying and moving on.

My going from place to place is not premeditated—that's how I live my life. A lot of times my moving happened around relationships, but I also find that the relationships were just a catalyst to get me to another place to learn some more things. More than the relationships themselves, the land, the energy from the Earth, and my own evolution brought me to different places. One might look at it and relate it to the wandering Taoist kind of person, but also in my background is Native American. There was a lot of movement within the different nations of Native Americans, in particular the Seminole and the Cherokee, which is what is on my mother's side of the family. We're assuming that it's Taoist because we're talking about T'ai Chi.

And I'm getting kind of tired of wandering around. I'm getting ready to start settling down. I hope that I have put enough of myself in the world where people will come to where I am and study rather than me having to go everywhere. My goal is to have my own studio to teach at when I move back to Ann Arbor next month, so that I could control the atmosphere. At first I thought it was out of my reach financially, but when I went to Ann Arbor recently to put my feelers out, I talked to a few realtors, and I saw that it's feasible.

Next summer I want to have a retreat. I know what it feels like to be able to retreat, to be able to regroup, what it does for my life, the quality of my life. I would like to participate in the world in that way, enhancing people's quality of life in a way that I know how to do. It'll be T'ai Chi, meditation, Ch'i Kung, and acupressure, which is a part of Ch'i Kung—the kind of acupressure where you work on the points yourself. I don't have enough knowledge to teach people about working on other people.

And I plan on going back to school. There're a lot of resources that school has that I can benefit from: bringing me up to date with the times, the language, and the challenges of today. And I can increase my marketing strategies and understanding by being more informed about what's happening—the computer world, fellowships, grants, and things like that. If I'm going to not move around so much, I still need to get my name out into the community. Maybe through my own writing—writing a book, writing articles on T'ai Chi. I think going back to school will help me achieve that. Marketing is something that I do in the "regular" world, and all of that I think is going to enhance my marketing skills for what I want to market rather than other people's things.

You were saying earlier that you didn't like having the pressure on your own practice of making your living from T'ai Chi. Are you still thinking that you don't want to depend on that financially?

Yes, that's right. Just three days a week for now. But I think that it will grow. Everything that I do is moving to that place. I don't need to force it, I just need to be where I'm at and follow my heart. It seems as if things have moved to the point where I'm ready to have a retreat—to see if I have developed my T'ai Chi to that extent. Have I gathered that amount of ch'i, so to speak, to support having something like that happen? We'll see! Stay tuned!

CHAPTER 10

A Martial Art Developed by a Woman for Women

This is a story women told me. Three hundred years ago, during the time of the Manchu invasion of China, a Buddhist nun named Ng Mui lived at the Shaolin Temple, which was known then, as it is now, as a center for martial arts as well as religious studies. The men who had taught Ng Mui praised her skill at martial arts, but she was not satisfied with her practice. She felt that fighting the way the men did failed to fully engage her capabilities. Her martial arts practice was important to her, and she often meditated on this dilemma. One day while meditating in the temple grounds, Ng Mui, like Chang San-feng, saw a bird—in this case a crane—attack a snake. She took note of the slow, fluid movements the snake used to evade the crane—and the final quick, explosive attack with which the snake drove off the bird for good. It struck Ng Mui that the snake's techniques were precisely what she was looking for, and she set herself to develop a fighting system based on the snake's movements.

About that time there was a tofu seller who sold his wares in the market square of a town near the temple. This man had a beautiful daughter named Yim Wing Chun (which I'm told means "eternal spring") who helped him in the market. One day a Manchu general spotted Yim Wing Chun in the market and was much taken with her beauty. He decided she must become his concubine, and he told her his servants would come to her home to fetch her at such and such a time. With an army of occupation at his back the general could expect his demands to be met, but what he proposed was not actually abduction or rape. Concubinage was less than marriage, but it entailed a certain security and status. Socially speaking it might even be something a tofu seller's daughter would aspire to.

But Yim Wing Chun had no desire to be the general's concubine, and anyway she had a fiancé she wished to marry. She went to the Shaolin Temple to ask Ng Mui for advice. After considering the situation Ng Mui advised Yim Wing Chun to ask the general for a year's delay. She could give the pretext of a death in the family, which according to custom meant she could not participate in any sort of celebration, such as would be involved in installing her officially as the general's concubine. Yim Wing Chun went to the general with this request, and he agreed. He also agreed to a second request Yim Wing Chun made, which was that at the end of the year he would meet her in a physical contest, and only if he could overwhelm her would she be required to become his concubine.

Of course, Yim Wing Chun spent the year studying with Ng Mui, and when the time came for her contest with the general, although she was not able to beat him she did withstand him, and the general let her go as he had promised. No doubt he grasped the risks of taking an unwilling woman with her abilities to his bed. And perhaps he feared the example she might set for the other women in his household. Yim Wing Chun married her fiancé and taught him the martial art, which she now named after herself. At Ng Mui's request, the two of them opened a school to teach and spread their knowledge.

Today practitioners of Wing Chun can be found all over the world, but almost all of them are men. In the United States Bruce Lee's name is closely connected to the style. Nowhere can I find any trace recorded of a tradition or lineage of women in the art subsequent to the founder and her student. Many men dispute the details of their story and even the women's existence, but after twenty years in the art, the Wing Chun practitioner Sandy Wong told me she has no doubt that a woman initially developed the art. Proof for her lies in the small, quick movements of the techniques, which she has found uniquely suitable for women's bodies and energy; she has also observed that women learn the art more quickly than men.

Position and timing are what matter in Wing Chun, not strength: "We rely on learned positions to maintain control over the opponent's movements," Sandy said. "The techniques are very precise and depend on movements that aren't natural, so they must be trained thoroughly—mostly at slow speeds to assure accuracy—to become imprinted in the mind. Wing Chun takes many years to perfect, but the principles can be used in practical situations after a few short sessions." She finds that people without previous martial arts experience often learn Wing Chun more easily than someone coming from a different style. The movements are so radically different from those used in other styles, it seems better to have no preconceptions.

I met Sandy when she taught a workshop for women martial artists. I was intrigued by the idea of a martial art developed by a woman and curious to find out for myself what it felt like. Sandy started with showing us the basic fighting position of Wing Chun: a "horse" stance in which the feet are set wide apart but sharply pigeon-toed instead of parallel as in other arts I have observed. This stance brings the knees close together, which felt awkward to me at first but turned out to enable rapid turning from side to side, useful in jockeying for position. Buttocks and pelvis are tucked forward and the head is held high, even to the point of creating a slight backward incline of the body.

Once all the women in the class were in position, Sandy showed us the standard Wing Chun punch: Starting with the elbows drawn in to the centerline of the chest, place the right fist above the bend of the left elbow, shoot it forward along the left forearm, and bring the left fist into position at the crook of the right elbow for the next punch. Each punch, Sandy pointed out, sets up the position for a punch with the other hand. She called this series of punches *chung choi,* which she translated as "following punch," or "chain punching." After only a few minutes' practice we noticed we quickly reached our target with a very solid blow.

Next Sandy showed us a block, *bong sau,* or "wing hand," in which instead of punching as we had just learned, one pivots the elbow upward to bring the strong, bony underside of the forearm into position to block an incoming punch. Now we were ready for partner practice and could experience for ourselves, as we exchanged and blocked these short punches, the close fighting distance of Wing Chun. Sandy, who is herself five feet tall and 127 pounds—a compact but muscular woman—commented, "I feel safest fighting no more than the distance of my forearm's length from the other person. Wing Chun is also called the elevator style," she added. "That's because it's so close in. It's ideal for fighting in elevators. For Wing Chun practitioners, personal boundaries are very small. If someone crosses into your boundary, there is no doubt that that person has threatened your space!" Her voice is soft and low, so one almost misses the sharply pointed asides she frequently inserts in her conversation. In any kind of confrontation I think there would be no mistaking her resolve and ability.

In subsequent sessions Sandy introduced us to a further range of techniques. Serious students learn three sets of one hundred and eight hand movements and kicks, as well as the *mok jong,* or wooden-dummy set, I was later to observe at her school. The dummy is a wooden pillar bristling with dowels on which one practices patterns of arm and leg movements for accuracy. The fixed position of the dummy helps the student learn the correct fighting distance to an opponent and provides practice in dealing with strong, stiff force and the timing of combinations of rapid strikes.

Freestyle practice in Wing Chun is based on *chi sau,* "the sticking hand," which seemed to me like T'ai Chi Ch'uan Push Hands with Wing Chun stance and techniques. As in T'ai Chi Ch'uan, an absence of tension is key to the presence of mind and attentive focus necessary to discern and anticipate the force and direction of an opponent's attack and to execute counterattacks with speed and accuracy.

Sandy traces the modern history of Wing Chun to 1949, when the grand master Yip Man came from China to Hong Kong. Wing Chun was considered unsavory in the 1950s, Sandy said—for the pursuit of street bullies in Hong Kong. Sifu Kenneth Chun, a top student of Leung Seung, was one of Yip Man's most dedicated students and brought to California his knowledge of the style. Sifu Ben Der, Chun's top student, also grew up in Hong Kong, where as a boy he encountered Yip Man; but his primary training was in California. He has been teaching in the San Jose area since the early 1970s, when Sandy became his student. When I visited Sandy in San Jose, I had the opportunity to observe her and other advanced students training at Sifu Ben Der's school, the San Jose Wing Chun Club.

Conveniently for Sandy, classes are held in the backyard, basement, and garage of her home in San Jose's Japantown. Throughout a gloomy

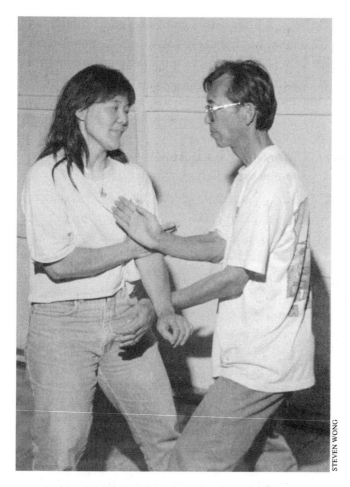

Sandy Wong (left) sparring with her sifu, Ben Der, at the San Jose Wing Chun Club (San Jose, Calif., Spring, 1996).

Saturday of unseasonable off-and-on rain, students came and went with little ceremony, training—or visiting—as suited them. Others dropped by on errands and stayed to visit or train. It was all very low key and casual compared to, say, the Aikido classes I had attended—more like the Kung Fu classes Michelle Dwyer described, with the teacher working with each student in turn on whatever was that student's emphasis at the time. As I wandered about watching the students spar with each other and train with the wooden dummy in the basement, Sifu Ben Der and his students good-naturedly interrupted their practice to answer my questions and demonstrate details of the art—often continuing the discussion among themselves well beyond what I could follow. Later Sandy and I walked to the nearby commercial center of Japantown to eat at a restaurant where her daughter works. Sandy herself works at a produce market in Japantown. Now in her forties, she and her husband, Steve, have been a part of this community for over twenty years and raised their four children here. But she has been training in martial arts even longer.

SANDY WONG

Wing Chun

Growing up in Hawaii, martial arts were just kind of there, at least up until the 1960s. Although there were restrictions—for the Japanese arts, Karate anyway, you had to be at least twelve years old. The Chinese arts were only taught to Chinese. If you were non-Chinese, you couldn't find somebody that would teach you.

We saw a lot of movies—Chinese movies had the one-armed swordsman and Japanese movies had the blind swordsman, Zato-ichi. They even had a movie where the two met. I don't remember who won—it could have been one of those where it was left up in the air. This stuff was always there, and we all wanted to do it.

Kids played martial arts instead of cowboys and Indians or baseball or whatever?

No, we played the same things, but there was that fascination. And people did martial arts—you had uncles and fathers or whatever that did Judo, Kendo. One of my friends in elementary school, her father—who was one-armed—taught Kendo. He was supposed to be one of the baddest guys around. I learned of his reputation in San Jose rather than Hawaii. He was my friend's father—no big deal. We passed through his dojo on the way home from school. Then when I came here it was, "Oh, Mikami Sensei! He'd beat you up with one arm!" *[Laughs]*

When I was in high school and college, I was on the bus a lot, working, going to school. I never liked seeing, in other people or myself, that feeling of being afraid to be by yourself, but I could never be waiting around for somebody to take me or go with me somewhere. I think it was something my mother passed down to me—don't depend on people. To me it came down to taking care of myself. So I started doing Aikido. I guess it was 1966, 1967, around there, the end of high school. I must have been seventeen, eighteen.

I was lucky I was in Hawaii. I had a really good sensei, one of the old guys—Eto Sensei. He was a lot like Sifu Ben, very mellow, very humble, but a very powerful person. Tohei Sensei used to come every year on his annual trip to Hawaii. He would work out in our dojo. He was a powerful, powerful person! When you meet people like that it inspires you; it makes you want to learn more. You see the kind of power that they have and you hope that maybe sometime you can develop. If you meet the right kind of people along the way, it carries you.

Why did you choose Aikido rather than some other art?

I don't really remember. I was a little familiar with it because one of my neighbors taught Aikido. He had a family of four boys. He always had them out in the yard working out, and I used to watch them. I thought it was fascinating. When it got to the point where I wanted to do it, my friend said, "Oh, I'll do it too," so we both started going together. He and I used to fool around a lot—Pink Panther style, you just attack each other out of nowhere—

Leap out of the refrigerator? Is this an Aikido thing? An Aikido sensei I talked to mentioned the Pink Panther being one of her favorite movies.

[Laughs] It helps to keep you in the art, I think, if you have that kind of sense of humor about it. I think why I stopped practicing Aikido when I came to California was—well, first of all, it was hard to find a school locally. But even when I did find one, people were so serious. At that time—this was 1970, 1971—they carried this air of almost arrogance: "We're the heavies, we're doing this nonviolent art." Almost a prima donna attitude. I had a hard time with that.

Were the people in California more remote

from the origins? Had your sensei in Hawaii trained in Japan originally?

I don't know if he trained in Japan. I think he was local born. But he trained in the old school. In the old school, my sensei used to tell me, "Nobody held your hand and walked you through it." You never asked questions. They demonstrated one time, and you got up and practiced. Now everybody wants step by step, reasons why, applications right off the bat. In some ways I can see the method of the old school. In Wing Chun sometimes, even if you explain things, if a person's body hasn't gone through that yet, if they haven't taken that time to actually repetitively do a certain exercise or whatever—it just doesn't translate. They don't get it.

We were pretty insulated in Hawaii. Although there's a lot of ethnic diversity and groups had their cultural differences, as a whole, just to live on the island and survive, people had almost a homogeneous feeling about how they did things. People judged you by your manners, your respect or lack of it, and your teachers. It wasn't uncommon for kids to be walking down the street and if one of them did something wrong, some adult out of nowhere, somebody you never even knew, would reprimand you. You never mouthed off to anybody! It was, "Yes, ma'am!"

So then in the early 1970s, after you finished college, you came here to San Jose and you looked for Aikido and didn't find any—did you start looking for other martial arts or kind of let it go and it snuck up on you?

Kind of that. I was at San Jose State, in the Asian-American Studies Department—where I met

Steve. Nobody there knew what Aikido was, but they said, "We know somebody that teaches Hapkido. Maybe that's similar." I had never heard of Hapkido, so I said, "Okay, let me go check it out." You couldn't have gotten more different! But I decided to try it. And the guy—Lowe Sensei—turned out to be a real good friend of Steve's. He's my kids' godfather. His method of teaching was he didn't charge you unless you missed a class. You paid for every class you missed.

That was rough training! We practiced outside in the dirt, on the ground. We were taking hard falls, and I would get incredible headaches. He learned in Watts from a real Korean master, and that was back in the sixties, so it was really hard style. They've softened the training a lot since then. It was really, really rough training, but it was good.

At San Jose State, through the contacts I made in the Asian-American Studies Department, I met a guy who was learning T'ai Chi. He was one of these natural martial artists—he could use everything he learned. He studied with a guy that he had to ask for a month—the old man in the park, you know, every day—"Will you teach me?" "No." Go back the next day. "Will you teach me?" "No." He did that for one month before the old man would teach him. He had some of the best T'ai Chi I've ever seen. His energy was really good. He started teaching me some T'ai Chi, but one day he said, "My teacher found out I'm teaching you and he told me if I don't stop he'll stop teaching me."

I did a little bit of Kyudo—Japanese archery. I also did some Naginata at State, with Dr. Hazard, Malyne Chiu's father. Malyne's someone you should talk to! He was the only Naginata sensei in Northern California at that time, but their bringing in sensei from Japan to visit was what really captured me—all women. Beautiful women! Naginata in Japan is considered a woman's art.

Men wouldn't touch it, the old traditional men. But Sensei Hazard was—you know, he was cool.

When my first child was maybe three months old, I wanted to start working out again. Some of my friends had started the Wing Chun with Ben and they were over at State, so I went to go check it out. It seemed good, because it was not a lot of movement, so I could take the baby—we were going to arrange it so Steve would come with me and watch the baby while I worked out. But he liked it so much, he started it too. He had been doing Kendo, Hapkido, Northern Sil Lum, but he eventually gave those up and just did Wing Chun. The Wing Chun was really nice. The kid would be crawling around and not get hurt and people would still be working out.

That was in 1974. I think Ben was teaching for about a year before that. That class, the roots of the Wing Chun Club in San Jose, was politically motivated. There was a lot of political tension between mainland Chinese and the Kuomintang from Taiwan, the Nationalists. There was a group on campus called the Chinese Cultural Club. They were mostly students from mainland China or from Hong Kong who were more tied to the mainland than the Nationalists. They had a cultural program one night, and in the middle of it this group of Kuomintang students came in through the back, marched down the aisle, and grabbed the emcee off the stage.

People in the Cultural Club were friends of Ken Chun, Ben's teacher, and Ben. Ken and Ben were in the audience because they were going to do a demonstration. This big old fight broke out, and some of Ken's students who were there jumped right into the fight. Even back then—Ken's my age, so he must have been like maybe twenty-three, really young—but even then, when he saw one of his students about to hit a guy with one of these regular old punches, Ken was on the side going, "Chung choi, chung choi!" Which is the Wing Chun—it means "following punch." We used to call it chain punching. *[Laughs]* He stayed out of the fight, but he was there directing it.

After that, students from the Cultural Club approached him. They wanted to learn self-defense. I don't know who actually started teaching first, but Ben took it over, because Ken wasn't situated in this area. Twenty years, and Ben's kept a real good core group of people.

Once you found the Wing Chun, was that it for you ever after? You stopped studying other arts?

I remember at one point, about two years after I started the Wing Chun, I thought I missed the grappling part, like in Aikido where you roll and you throw people. I knew an Aikido sensei—he did Kendo with Steve and was part of the dojo down the street here—and he said that on the nights he taught, I could go and work out. So I thought, Yeah, I'd like to do that. But it didn't work out because the Wing Chun just kicked in. They would try to do a move on me—and the Wing Chun movements are so subtle, if somebody moved around me from the back, I would automatically drop, but they couldn't see it. They couldn't move me. And I couldn't go with their movement.

There was one incident. *[Laughs]* There was this blue belt guy I was working out with and I was supposed to throw a punch—one of those long, wide punches. I couldn't do it, so I did a Wing Chun punch, and he said, "You can't punch that way." I said, "Sure, I can." He goes, "That's not a punch!" I said, "Yes, it is a punch." He goes, "You can't hurt anybody with that." I said, "Sure, you can."

He shows me his jaw and he goes, "Okay, hit me here." I said, "I don't want to do that! I don't want to hurt you." And he goes, "I'll show you. Come on, hit me here. You're not going to hurt me." I said, "I will hurt you! You don't want me to hit you." So he sticks his hand right next to his jaw, like this, facing out *[she demonstrates]*, and he goes, "I'll put my hand here. Hit my hand." I said, "You don't want me to hit you!" He goes, "No, no, seriously, hit me, hit me." So I hit him. *[Laughs]* His teeth went *crunch.* He kind of blinked and said, "I believe you." What an idiot! The sensei just shook his head and walked away.

That was my first taste of actually seeing that Wing Chun worked, and that's when I realized too that Wing Chun and Aikido basically eventually try to teach the same thing, but Wing Chun gets you there a lot faster. With the sensei in Aikido I knew what they could do, but it took twenty years to get there. In Wing Chun you can use it pretty much in a matter of weeks. You can even teach a quickie self-defense lesson using Wing Chun principles.

Someone at your workshop was talking to me about Wing Chun being pure self-defense without the accoutrements of ch'i, or ki, and philosophy and spirituality—just straight, stripped-down self-defense—and that's what she liked about it. I wondered how you felt about that?

I think you can make it what you want it to be. The background of Wing Chun has been strictly street style—the rogues in Hong Kong, anyway. It is for fighting. It's definitely a fighting style. I think what makes it quick to learn, as far as being useful right away, is because it's taught that way here.

My teacher and his teacher don't deal with the frills and froufrous or whatever.

But I think the more you do it, the more you understand that there's more to it than that. Part of that too is what we were just talking about, where you have to go through the physical part for months or years or whatever it takes before you get that actual understanding of application and you know how something will work. I don't really know how to explain it—it's a good tool for building your stamina, but once that builds, it also tunes you in to developing more of a meditative tool. It's hard to say—the way you develop this is subtle, because you concentrate on the physical a lot, but other things happen on the side.

You saw in the class today how arrogant we get to each other, but a lot of it is in fun. When we work out with people from other schools, you see the humility and respect that our students have for working out with people. They don't just come up and blast them. I see people from other schools try to blast our students, and our students hold back a lot, out of respect for Ben, for the way he teaches us. And he doesn't teach it to us directly. It's this kind of by-product of the way he is.

So it's not something that everybody who studies Wing Chun necessarily gets?

I think you learn it through your teachers. You're lucky if you have a good teacher. A lot of people from other schools are real arrogant. It's kind of an atmosphere that permeates the whole class. In this school people that come in with that kind of arrogance don't last. It's not anything that Ben says or does directly to the person, but the older students will take care of that person in some form or other. People that don't learn leave, not by being forced out, but I guess they feel, "Well, I really have to leave now. I don't like this school."

There was one guy, he came from a rich family in Hong Kong and he showed up a few times but wouldn't pay Ben. It was like, "I'm doing a favor here, having people touch my hands." Nobody liked this guy because he was very arrogant and we knew he wasn't paying Ben. And basically Ben's students, including his own son, who is very, very quiet, very respectful of the older students in the class—everybody was pretty much standing in line to take this guy on.

In our class everybody takes care of Ben. Any troublemakers come in, the first one in line is Steve. If Steve can't deal with it, if he's just too fed up with the guy, he'll come inside and go, "Sandy, you go work out with this guy."

"I'll sic my wife on you!"

Well, guys have a harder time dealing with women. I've found with guys generally you can squeeze them down with words, kind of ridiculing—"Why do you want to do that?" *[Laughs]*

We don't do well in tournaments with people from other styles. I discourage our people from competing with or even working out with people from different styles, because ours is such a close-in style, it's like any little thing they give you, if you respond with any kind of effect, it's a hard blow. They complain, "I'm controlling my punches, how come you're not?"

Or they say, "That can't do anything. You can't hurt me with that." People from other styles are used to distance and just powering it in and they don't believe that anything that close can do any damage. So unless you just lay them out, they don't really understand it, and to me that's just kind of useless. It just becomes rhetoric—either that or somebody gets hurt real bad. Steve separated one guy's shoulder. The guy was coming in strong because he thought he had Steve, and all Steve did was just bring his wrist down, with *no* energy. Or you turn your horse, your stance, say a half-inch. A half-inch turn—that with the movement of just dropping your arm, that'll take out somebody's shoulder. Steve and some of the other guys have worked out, but I really don't like it.

They've started doing Wing Chun tournaments in the past year or two, and even that's a different kind of training. You work for different techniques and to do things differently. Our school is pretty nonaggressive, and you have to learn a certain kind of aggression to do tournaments, because you have such a limited amount of time and you have to work within a limited space. Points count against you if you move out of that space.

I remember the first tournament any of our people entered, one of the guys got disqualified because the person he was fighting was very incompetent—just flailing at him! The guy had no Wing Chun technique, nothing we would consider Wing Chun technique, though he came from a Wing Chun school. Ben and Ken's style of Wing Chun, I think, from what we understand of Wing Chun, is a real true form of the concept of Wing Chun. People doubt a lot of the softness, the ability of smallness in this style, but you look at Ben and there's no doubt. You've seen him. He's very small and very soft. Ken's big and very soft.

I was talking with Ben the other day and he said Ken said we really need to get our Wing Chun out there. We've been pretty much of a closed-door school, but there's so many people out there who want to learn it and they're just being fed a lot of junk. Giving up their money for junk.

What is the situation of women in Wing Chun? Given that it was invented by a woman . . .

I met a T'ai Chi teacher in Hawaii who said the biggest problem with Wing Chun is it was started by a woman and the men took over. He hasn't seen it taught right since.

There seem to be fewer women in Wing Chun than other martial arts. I think a lot of it is it's not out there as much. It's not available. Not much is known about it. Most women don't know that it is a woman's martial art. I think that's mostly it, the lack of information. Because there sure seem to be a lot of women in other styles, Karate styles and Tae Kwon Do and the rest.

Didn't you say you were teaching, or thinking about teaching, a class just for women?

I was thinking about it. Ben was teaching a women's class, but his work schedule was changed, so he switched the regular class to that night and told the women to come to that. A lot of women don't like to come to the general class because it's way more guys and they feel intimidated by that. But the response that Ken has had from doing seminars is that women out there really want it. I don't think I have the temperament to teach. My long-term attention span is about two months. *[Laughs]* That's just how I am. A friend hit it on the head when she said—I'm volunteering at the school that she and her friend work at, he's in charge of the program and was saying, "I want Sandy to work next year. Do you think she'll commit herself to a year?" My friend laughed and said,

"You couldn't get Sandy to sign a contract for anything. If there's not a way out, she won't do it." I think that's what it is. I have to have that backdoor open. I'll help with a class, but I don't think I'll commit to teaching one.

What about your own training? How much time and energy do you have for that?

I don't really spend that much time. Classes are here four days a week. On a good run I make it out to three, sometimes four classes, but I average about once a week, because work and kids make it kind of hard. Although I started twenty years ago, my practice hasn't been real consistent. I've been out of it a year, year and a half at a time, between kids. But I could do it when I was pregnant. I could do it a month after I gave birth. I could do it with a kid on my back. It was just I couldn't put as much time into it like Steve can. But it's never really left me. I can stay out of it for a couple of months and come back and it's still there for me.

Maybe that's because it is a woman's style. When some of the guys stay away, they come back saying, "I haven't worked out for two weeks now. I'm really rusty." It's hard for me to comprehend that, because I can stay out of it for two months and come back and it feels the same. Maybe being men, they have to reorient their bodies to doing it again. I've had women come in and take to it like that *[snaps her fingers]*. It's a natural style for women. With the Aikido or the other styles, I could do the movements, but I didn't know if they would work. I had a hard time making them work. I think with Wing Chun the application just kind of came. If you could do the form, I think you could make it work.

And how do you see it working in the larger context of your life?

I used to be very shy. I never liked approaching people. But because of the way we practice, which is very direct, one to one, very close, making eye contact—I find that's how I deal with life situations now. I don't back away from them. I don't avoid them.

I think I look at things a lot more straightforwardly now. Working out with somebody in Wing Chun is—it's a very straight line, and I think your thinking tends to become that way also, as far as seeing what's important and what's not. If something has to be taken care

Sandy Wong (right) and her husband, Steve, sparrring at the San Jose Wing Chun Club (San Jose, Calif., November 1994).

of—I'll go and do it. You may not know what'll work and what won't work, but you know that one thing will lead to another. If this doesn't work, you'll do this. You know that you can take care of whatever it is. It's not something I really thought about, but I notice when I think back that that's what's been happening.

I look at things now and they make so much more sense. It clarifies my own stand, but it's also increased my frustration, because I can't see why people can't see things clearly. *[Laughs]* Either that, or it's made me closed off to everything else. I think a lot of social issues and problems that

come up have to do with the lack of respect people have for each other, and their own sense of victimization. If you can feel good about yourself, know who you are, and what you're capable of doing, and you treat people with respect and expect to be treated with respect—I think that would eliminate a lot of problems. If taught right, Wing Chun will teach a lot of that. Any martial art will. But in the different schools, I see a lack of respect in the way that it's taught.

Another thing, I've noticed—before I did Wing Chun, because the people I used to know did a lot of basketball, I could look at somebody and kind of know about how tall they were, five-ten or five-eight, I could tell the difference. Now guys all seem the same size to me—eye level. *[Laughs]* They may be six feet, five-ten, six-two. They're eye level. I don't know how tall guys are any more! What used to be a fine line is very fuzzy now—on a physical level. I think maybe that translates to everybody being the same on some internal level, psychologically, emotionally.

And what about with you and Steve? Is Wing Chun something you do together or is it more that you're on parallel tracks in a similar direction?

More like that. Parallel, separate. I have a hard time with it; Steve not so much as me. I guess I have this streak in me that's real stubborn, real competitive. I don't like that, but it's there. I try to stay away from it, but it starts to surface when I work out with him. So I don't like to work out with him. Ben has told us, "You can't teach your family. You can't teach your kids. You can't teach your wife. Somebody else has to do it." So we leave it up to him to teach our kids, and I don't really work out with Steve that much.

And has it been like this all along? Or in the beginning did you train more together?

It was worse in the beginning! Now we can do a little bit more together. Like I said, it's mostly me. We're very different personality-wise. I don't like the way he teaches, and I don't like his tone of voice sometimes. I'm always getting on his case about that, but it's him, it's how he grew up. He's a bus driver and he deals with management and

nasty issues all day. I don't blame him for it, but I don't like it, and so if I don't have to listen to it, I'm not going to listen to it.

And we learn real differently. I think we both know that we're both very different, so we stay out of each other's way. In class I'll work out with different people, and he'll work out with different people. Just kind of keep our own separate thing going and it works out fine.

What about your children? What part did your martial arts play in raising them?

I see it as real good for them. They've always been around a very mixed crowd of people, new people coming in, this off-handed rowdiness and arrogance going on. I think they can deal pretty much with all kinds of people because of it. It's something that they, I think, take for granted. They haven't been very disciplined about coming out and practicing, and we haven't pushed them, although there've been times where Steve has tried to get them out there.

When my youngest one was in the fifth grade, he came home complaining one day because there was a group of girls that always picked on him and his friends. The girls would trip them or hit them, and the boys couldn't do anything back, because the teacher was always backing the girls— "You don't hit the girls." You know the way that they try to teach in school, try to give the girls more confidence, get them to be more assertive. Sometimes I think it goes a little too far. Even if the boys tried to explain, "They hit me first," the teacher wouldn't hear it. I told him, "You have enough Wing Chun. You just don't let anybody touch you." He didn't have to hit. He didn't have to fight back. "Just don't let anybody touch you."

And so he did that?

Well, I didn't hear any more after that. I said, "If the teachers have a problem with that, you tell them to call me." Because nobody should have that right to violate. You know. And you're not teaching the girls anything good anyway. It's just how to run over people and take advantage of people. And no respect. I think what I like best about our school is the respect. Ben has a lot of respect for everybody and that carries over. I think that's what's missing a lot everywhere. Respect and responsibility.

I think our kids have a level of confidence that a lot of their friends lack, and I think it's from being around this situation all the time, but it's hard to say, because we had no point of reference to compare them to had they not had it. For them it was practically from day one.

Do you see your martial arts as part of the cultural context of your living in Japantown?

It's a plus having the dojo in your backyard because it's woven into your life. You wake up and walk out the door, it's there. You come home at night and people come there and it's there. Living in Japantown was good because at the time my kids were little we still had a lot of the older community around, and because we were so far away from our own families they had a lot of surrogate grandparents. The uncles and aunts that weren't there were the store people. They knew who our kids were; they knew who our dog was. The dog could never get lost. She'd always get a ride home. Or we'd get a telephone call, "Your poor puppy is sitting out here waiting for you."

A lot of our friends who are Chinese or Japa-

nese or whatever moved out to the suburbs. They're very separate from this kind of lifestyle. Their kids get to a certain age and they say, "I want them to learn this or this, because I want them to learn some of the culture." But if you haven't had it in your home, it's not really going to be part of their culture. They're just learning another thing and it's still very separate from their life. I think for us the difference has been it was just there. It's been there all the time. Our friends bring it to them too. They wouldn't be so much a part of my kids' lives had we not had the school here, live where we live, and maintain these ties.

We were active with a lot of community things when the kids were little. A lot of the things that we did with the community were very grassroots, just getting organized, a lot of manpower involved, working in the trenches. Now this next generation has taken over, it's become very organized, and it's not fun any more. We've stopped doing a lot of it.

These days, I think you said, you've been investigating healing. I gather that isn't included in Wing Chun the way you've learned it, although some of the other Chinese martial arts have this tradition of ch'i and of healing going along with the martial art—using the energy both for healing and for fighting.

I've always had an interest in bodywork and picked up a few techniques here and there. A lot of friends I've known from before I did the Wing Chun do shiatsu and massage. Now I do Acu-Jenesas, which is related to Regenesis and Reiki. It involves using breath and ch'i to adjust corresponding points on the body that get out of alignment. A friend and I saw it in an adult ed class and started doing it. Two years down the line we start to see, "Well, this will work with this." "Hey, I learned this. You got something hurt here, I can—" I've been doing it three or four years now and it's really starting to come together. I didn't have a general plan, but with all these little bits, things start to look like they were part of a plan. I think I was lucky to be exposed to the right things at the right time and that's kind of made my thinking come around. I think a lot of that is opening yourself up.

Is it mostly injuries that you deal with, or illnesses too? It's the same principles either way?

Yeah, getting the body back to normal. What's good about the bodywork I've been learning is that it'll deal with illnesses. Viral things. Diseases. Working on the immune system. I found too that if people feel good—just physically feel better—then they're able to deal with things better, emotionally, psychologically, or whatever. One less thing to be dragging you down!

Also just practically, with four kids, and they're all into sports, I see them get hurt. Even with a little bit of knee pain or back pain or whatever, I found if you deal with it right away—and it's just a matter of an adjustment—it saves them a lot of pain and disability time later. It just makes sense.

In Wing Chun, somebody gets hurt and two months later they ask me about fixing this or that. I say, "How long have you been like that?" and

they go, "Well, a couple months now. It hasn't gone away." Of course it's not going to go away unless you take care of it! If they ask me right after it happens, we deal with it that next week. If you take care of it, it's not a problem any more.

The Eastern philosophy teaches that the body has a lot of potential, healing potential, and these amazing things that you can learn to do. It's the interplay of all these things that if you're lucky enough to look for the right things, if you're lucky enough to fall into these things at the right time, then you can integrate all that and things really start to make sense.

I think a lot of it is attitude. If you do martial arts with the right intent, I think it gives you a different perspective on life and how you look at life. If you really love the art, you try to carry through all the principles that you've picked up, incorporate whatever you can. A real martial artist is someone who loves the art—like Tanaka Sensei, who I've studied Naginata with. She's incredible—there's this gusto for everything. I've seen it in Ben and a lot of the T'ai Chi masters—they carry those principles with them all the time. I mean in everyday stuff. You want to work out, go work in the yard, do your gardening, pull the weeds, do whatever, and use your horse stance, use whatever it takes that you've learned in Wing Chun. On a very simplistic level it's like *The Karate Kid,* washing and wiping, but as ridiculous as that may seem, to some extent that's what you do. Carry it out on all aspects. I think a true martial artist isn't narrowly focused. That's what I strive for—to achieve that, be able to attain that higher level of development.

CHAPTER 11

The Difference for Me Is That I Am Myself

The transmission of the martial art of Ng Mui and Yim Wing Chun in the seventeenth century to Sandy Wong in the twentieth century without any intervening women that we know of is indicative of the obstacles to women's traditions in martial arts as in other fields. In every generation, it seems, women must rediscover or reinvent knowledge vital to the very preservation of our lives. Women's physical self-defense is an area that another twentieth-century woman, Midge Marino, has made her life's work.

Midge started with Judo, an art developed in the late nineteenth century in Japan by Jigoro Kano, who synthesized and rationalized the earlier Jujutsu fighting traditions, adding a component of ethical teaching. In 1882 Kano opened the Kodokan Institute in Tokyo, initially for men only. Later he taught Judo to women in his family, and after consulting medical practitioners and scientists, in 1923 opened the Women's Section at the Kodokan Institute. This was during the Progressive era in the United States—a time of reexamination and reforms based on scientific inquiry and a time of political action by and for women, such as the campaign to get the vote. These things were happening in other countries as well, and although the restrictions that Kano established for women may seem troubling or patronizing now, at the time it must have seemed a great advance that men scientifically looked into this and determined that at least some aspects of Judo were very appropriate for women. Certainly Midge, who started with Men's Judo, found Women's Judo rewarding when she later came to study it.

In 1969, teaching Judo to women, Midge realized that many women who needed to be able to defend themselves would never have the time or interest for a full course of study in a traditional martial art—they needed a method that could be learned quickly and used right away. She has been developing and teaching self-defense for women ever since, in addition to working full-time as a printer.

I found Midge, now in her fifties, to be the straightforward, no-nonsense sort of person she describes herself as, down to earth and easy to talk to. She was dressed rather formally in a suit and scarf, with her hair cut short and coifed in a stylish, swept-back manner, as befits what I think of as the business world. And indeed she does operate in the business world these days, expanding from the women's groups and college settings where she began teaching, to workshops for employees in private industry, government agencies, and other large institutions.

MIDGE MARINO

Judo and Women's Self-Defense

When I was in my senior year in high school in Vacaville, California, the school bus driver was also the man who ran the Boys Club. He was a real special kind of person, one of these guys that like kids and do everything for kids. He had boxing for the boys and weightlifting—he did a whole lot of stuff in this small Boys Club in Vacaville.

Travis Air Force Base of course is close, and the men there had a team—actually it was a nationwide team—in Judo. They had been stationed in Japan and learned Judo there and then continued doing it on their own. Burt, the bus driver, went out to the base and asked them if they would send instructors in for the Boys Club. He also asked a group of girls, about five of us that rode the bus, if we were interested in taking Judo, and of course I said, "Yeah, I am!" Not only because I was going with this young man who was going to the Boys Club and had told me about it, but also because I played sports a lot and I loved that kind of thing. So that's how I started Judo.

Did the other girls study Judo too? Or were you the only one?

There were about five of us that started. I was the only one that went on. This was 1956, and women just didn't do Judo in this country in 1956. There were a few, but very few, and most of them probably were the daughters of men who did Judo. I feel now that I learned the real Judo. I see martial arts in this country as being bastardized—you know, the *Karate Kid* thing.

Losing the philosophical and ethical context?

Yes, the true meaning of the martial art—I'm not saying everywhere, but over the years I have seen that happen. I feel very lucky to have studied proper Judo. One man in the air force had been in Japan, lived in Japan, was married to a Japanese woman, and he was a fourth-degree black belt. He was one of the first American men to achieve that rank, and he was very, very much into the way that it should be taught, and he brought that here. He made sure that the men that he taught had this, and he came and talked to us and gave us the philosophy and morality and the history of Jujutsu and then Judo and all of those things. Judo changed my life—because of those philosophies. I'm a different kind of person than I would have been, I think, had I not had that kind of training and the belief in the morality and—just the whole thing. I was also very lucky to have Burt, because he took me out to Travis Air Force Base and other places my parents were unable to. My father was a farmer and we didn't have a whole lot of money.

PHOTO COURTESY OF MIDGE MARINO

Midge Marino as a brown belt, executing a katagaruma *and throwing one of her Judo instructors from Travis Air Force Base (Vacaville, Calif., 1957 or 1958).*

But your parents weren't disapproving?

Oh, no, no, no.

It's just that they didn't have the resources?

Right. When the men weren't teaching at the Boys Club, Burt took me to Travis, and I was getting more practice, more practice, more practice. And then he found out there was a woman—Helen Carollo—in Oakland, who was one of the first Western women that studied at the Kodokan Judo Institute in Japan. She and her husband were in Japan, I guess in the service, and she had been able to study Judo. Burt took me down to their dojo—and she was appalled at my Judo.

The reason is because I did Men's Judo, which is what the men had taught me. They even put me in tournaments, and when I'd get to the tournament I was very embarrassed, because they said, "She's a girl. She can't compete." And the men said, "What do you mean she can't compete?" These guys in the air force had groomed me, and they had me going and all this kind of stuff. But I couldn't compete. Women did not compete in those years. Mrs. Carollo thought I was a good *judoka,* but she said, "Oh my god, you can't do that kind of throw!" That's when I started learning what they call Women's Judo, which is kata—prearranged form with partners.

The men hadn't taught you that?

No, I had been doing *randori,* or free play—sparring is what it amounts to. Actually, kata is, I think, a very good foundation, even though, for an active, competitive person like I was, who wants to get out and do the randori, it seems not only boring but pointless. But it isn't. It is showing you exact steps of how to apply the techniques. I personally feel that if you learn that, your skill improves in randori. Kano Sensei, who developed Judo, certainly did all the kata. He's the one that developed the kata in the first place. All of the old tenth-degree black belts of course had to do kata. They had to carry it on. But it would be rare for any man today to know any of the kata. Very rare. They just don't do it.

There're basic beginning kinds of techniques that they always teach—the men too. And they teach you to fall. I think that Judo when I started was much better in terms of learning the foundation even with men teaching. The reason, I think, is because they were learning the right kind of Judo in Japan. They were practicing the real, true Judo, and they brought it here firsthand from Japan. Over the years everything has been changing—you know, people want to do everything fast. The reason why the men do it faster—and did it faster then—was because that's the way they were promoted. Women were not promoted through randori, or *shiai—shiai* is the fighting, the actual contest. Because the men gain their belts that way, they immediately want to go into that kind of thing. As they go up through the ranks, they were supposed to learn kata, and a lot of them had to do it when they were in Japan and with the old sensei. In Japan, women had to perform kata to be promoted, because women were not allowed to shiai. *[Laughs]* It was okay to randori, but it was not okay to shiai.

I see. So you, somewhat reluctantly at the time, switched from Men's Judo to Women's Judo.

I studied with Mrs. Carollo in Oakland—she was teaching women's classes. Later I worked with young women at the Boys Club in Vacaville, helping teach them. There were about thirty young women in the dojo—high school students and some moms of the girls. We had one of the bigger women's groups in northern California. I became a brown belt—the men gave me that rank. Because the men here followed the Japanese rule that women could not shiai, there was no way of promoting women in this country at that time other than your teacher says, "Okay, you can have this belt, because you've reached that level in our eyes."

We also found out that there were more

women in the Bay Area that were studying Judo—daughters of men who were in Judo, like I said. We started going to San Francisco once a month. We'd all get together to study and do the kata. This was at the men's dojos—there were no women's dojos—and some of the men were helping teach the kata, some of the older sensei who knew the kata.

Do you know who Ben Campbell is? Ben Campbell is a congressman now, from Colorado. He studied Judo in Japan for quite a while. He was in the Olympic Games in 1964 and took a bronze medal. I worked out with him and the other guys that were going to the Olympics. He took over the Sacramento Judo Club, so I went and taught there.

Then I started teaching in the San Juan School District and recreation department with Ken Santiago. He introduced me to all of the older sensei in Sacramento—they were his sensei. They had been interned during World War II and were teaching Judo in the concentration camps, from what I understand. I began to learn Nage-no-kata from Ikimoto Sensei, and after I learned Nage-no-kata, the men said, "Okay, here's your black belt." That's how I got my first-degree black belt. It was in 1965. The men recommended certain women—because of your studying, because of how they watched you, because of your participation, because of your teaching. They looked at all of that kind of thing and then did the promoting of women, in those days.

We also formed a women's section in the Yudanshakai of Northern California, the Judo association. We began to seek out better ways of promotion for women—and to perfect the knowledge of Judo. What better way to do that than to bring an expert here? In 1965 we asked Miss Fukuda to come from the Kodokan Institute to teach, and she said she would. Miss Fukuda is the foremost woman judoka in the world today. At that time I think she was about third. She had traveled already, and she spoke a little English. We paid for her trip here and then she would go to each of the leaders, the instructors like myself. She went all over northern California to where women were teaching and had women's classes and gave us her knowledge of all of Judo. She spent a month with me, and every day she would have me out on the floor when I came home from work, doing kata. It was quite an experience! What a woman. She's incredible. She is the dearest lady—but a hard taskmaster, believe me.

She was our foundation of really learning Women's Judo. Based on things Miss Fukuda told us that they do at the Kodokan, we set up a way of promoting women that was not through competition, because the Kodokan did not recognize that and we were strictly Kodokan registration. Women had to learn kata and perform a certain amount for each rank in order to advance. We sat on the board and did the exam and they had to perform in front of us. I eventually became the chairperson of the Yudanshakai for Women, and then I became the coach, because what happened then was that nationally they were doing competition for women—in kata, performing kata, not free play, not randori, although on the East Coast women were doing randori and shiai and in Europe they were doing it, in England especially.

They had no restrictions—they were too far away from the Kodokan, evidently. We were very close on the West Coast, and all of the old sensei, the male sensei here, who were from Japan or were the second generation that had studied Judo, were very much Kodokan and wanted to keep this pure. Which—that's fine. In the long run, as far as I'm concerned now, when you learn kata you learn better Judo. When you only learn to compete, sometimes it's very sloppy and it's not based on the real principle of leverage and balance: It's based on muscle.

I read that there was one throw or move in particular in Men's Judo that was considered too dangerous for women—*makikomi-waza* I think it's called. I'm curious, what is that and why is it so dangerous?

Waza is throwing. Makikomi-waza is that you throw the person and go down on top of the person, so that their body is not only hitting with full force, but you're coming down on top of them. There are a number of throws like that. When I went to see Mrs. Carollo, I'd start doing a *kata-garuma,* for instance, which is I pick up this person *[stands up to demonstrate]* and they go right over my head like this up here and drop from here. They wouldn't let women do that. And there's some others—well, you can make any of them into something that can be real dangerous.

I think their idea is that it has something to do with women giving birth. The same crap that we've heard all along. I have known women—Myrtle, a Japanese woman down in the Bay Area, did Judo till she was five months' pregnant. On the mat. She was out there teaching and doing Judo. Now certainly, any other woman can't come in and do that, but when you're a judoka and you're doing this practice all the time, it's not going to be bad for you. She knew her body. She knew what she could do and what she couldn't do, and it didn't hurt the baby. Certainly you're not going to do anything outrageous, but she was still doing Judo.

Look at Miss Fukuda. She's over eighty years old and she's still doing Judo. And the woman's had a triple bypass! In July a few years ago—and she was back on the mat in October!

So I promoted Women's Judo, coached Women's Judo—did all of that. We were also then a part of the AAU, the Amateur Athletic Union. I was a voting member of the AAU as well as the national Yudanshakai as the chairperson from my particular Yudanshakai. I was not at that point a rebellious feminist. Yeah, sure, I wanted to go out and compete, and I was upset that I couldn't do that, but I just felt very lucky. In 1969 I went to Japan for the first time, and it was a dream come true for me.

I was teaching in the San Juan Judo Club and they paid my way to go to Japan. There were three male instructors, and they had all gone, they had all got the money to go, and they said, "It's your turn to go, we're not going to go." I would imagine that that's kind of unusual for them to do that at that time, but I was seen as very equal with the men when I was doing Judo. And I was quite good. I'm not bragging about that, but I was very good at the art. At that time I probably had thirty girls that were studying Judo under me.

They sent me to Japan for two weeks, and it was absolutely marvelous. They had what they called Summer Session at the Kodokan, and I met Noritomi Sensei and the other two older women sensei at the Kodokan. The women's section was separate, at least at that time. Only the high-ranking women were allowed to go into the main dojo and do Judo with men. The other women had to stay in their own dojo. I again learned kata, but I also went out there and started working out with the black belts, the women black belts. *[Laughs]* Did I learn something! I was looking up most of the time. They were incredible. They also practice five, six days a week, and they have the original people there.

Miss Fukuda had set it up so that I met the two women who spoke English. One of them was Kuniko Takeuchi. She had traveled to England and taught in England. She was one of the sensei, she was a third *dan* then, I think. She only weighed about ninety-six pounds. She was an absolutely incredible judoka. I had a great experience, it was wonderful, and I didn't want to leave, but I had to. Later Kuniko came here, and not only was Miss Fukuda here, but Kuniko was here, and Women's Judo was improving boom–boom–boom–boom. Kuniko and I had a school for three years—Judo and weightlifting and self-defense classes. It was a complete women's dojo. I got my second-degree black belt after I came back from Japan. I was again promoted by the older sensei—and Miss Fukuda. This time I did go through a test.

With a row of old men sitting in judgment?

Some men, but mostly women by then.

It sounds like Judo was a central—perhaps the central—focus in your life?

It was a main portion of my life. We would go to San Francisco once a month and do seminars, and the women's group was very active and very cohesive, keeping the women together and promoting and doing all that. As I'm sure in any other martial art, the higher rank you have, the more you should give back. That's what this is all about. The moral aspect is that it builds character, and of course you never use your art to harm someone unless it's absolutely your life or theirs—that kind of thing.

Do you think the Men's Judo, with more competition in it, ends up with the same ethic?

No, absolutely no. It's not that I don't think competition is good, because I do think that competition builds self-esteem in some ways. But I think it's been taken to a very, very bad place—for all sports today.

But I see Judo being a much better martial art than, for example, Karate. The reason why I say that is because there is a completion. In other words, you can actually throw somebody, and you know that your skill is better than theirs, because you've done it. Completely. In Karate you have to pull your punches, unless you go into full contact. But there aren't a whole lot of people that go to full contact.

Judo also taught me a great deal of control. Control in many, many ways in my life. It has also taught me tenacity, to strive, and to move forward, not to be a quitter.

Were these values in your family also? That you learned from your parents?

That's part of it for sure. All of those things were there, but also when I was younger, I used to beat the shit out of people—boys; I had to fight with boys all the time. Judo just—you already know you're better than somebody else and you don't display that. Only if it's absolutely necessary. I think it makes you a softer person, not a hard person, if you think about it in the right way. I can be a very dangerous person. I could do lots of things to you or to anybody because of my knowledge. But I don't think about that. I think about putting a stop to something before it gets to that place. I don't want to deal with it that way.

But I stopped doing Judo in the 1980s. I haven't done any Judo for years. Not because I don't want to! I don't have the time; I put it into the self-defense.

In 1969, after I came back from Japan, I had a lot of women coming into my Judo club and saying, "I'd like to learn how to defend myself." And I'd say, "Well, you can. You join the Judo club, and probably in five or six years you'll be able to do that." And of course they would leave. But like most martial artists, I felt that the only way women could learn how to defend themselves was to practice a martial art, to really practice it. Over and over and over—it's repetition.

What I was finding was that women were leaving Judo, because that was not what they wanted. And Judo's very hard, because you have to take falls, and a lot of people don't like that. That's why Karate also is much more, I think, impressive or—easier. That doesn't mean that they don't have hard practice, but when you get slammed on the floor all the time, that's very different. I was losing these women, so I decided that I should look into teaching an experimental kind of class in self-defense. I had seen a book on self-defense for women. I thought it was a joke, but there were some things in there, and I said, I'm going to do that. So in 1969 I did, through the Judo club. And it was rather fun and the women really enjoyed it.

This was before very many people—if any— were teaching self-defense? So you were pretty much on your own to figure out how to do this? You saw the need and just plunged in?

Yeah. And I was interested. I became involved in the women's movement and began to learn about rape and violence against women, which made me want even more to develop a system—something that would stop that kind of thing. Because I believed that women could stop it. I never was a person who believed otherwise. I guess it's because of the way I feel about myself. I always felt that women could stop it.

And of course, you had this background in Judo. From what I've seen, some of the kata seem to have been designed for very practical self-defense—isn't there one specifically for women where you carry and use a handbag?

Yes. Kata gave me the self-defense. It shows you how to take guns away from people, for instance, and that's how I learned all that. But they're not pure, the way I use them. The reason why they're not pure is because in kata you have to show exact, pure form, inch by inch, so they can see every stage of it. Naturally, when you're going to take a gun away from someone, or you're going to do something to someone, hit them or whatever— and certainly in Judo we don't do that, only in kata, only in the self-defense—there are certain stages of that that take too long, and you can take some of those out and make it more efficient for a person to use on the street.

And kata doesn't speak to modern-day violence against women in this country. Those are things that need to be a part of any kind of self-defense presentation, but the main principle of Judo—leverage and balance and using that person's strength and weight against them—that is absolutely key to all of the things that I teach. Never fight against it. The first thing that happens when somebody grabs hold of your arm is what? When they try to pull you by the arm, what do you do? You try to take it away. When you try to pull your arm away, you create a struggle. Struggle is not fighting back. Struggle can be overcome. Instead of you pulling away, you go with that person, using their weight and strength against them. That's the principle that is very, very important. Also to have focus and direction into any target. Not just hitting wildly, but thinking about it, looking, and focusing on it. Focusing all of your energy.

A lot of people say, "Just do anything to get away!" "Hit him and when he lets go you can run away!" No! That isn't what you do, because when you do that, you're going to have the person after you, and if you are only thinking of getting away, you don't put everything you've got into fighting back. What I say to the women is attack your attacker. There're only two ways that person should be when you're through with them—either incapacitated on the ground or running away from you. And until that time, you don't stop your attack. Period.

In 1971 the Women's Studies program started at Sacramento State. They asked me to teach a class in self-defense if they could get the units, and I said, "Yeah!" I was working in the print shop there already. They got the units, and I started teaching.

I also became involved in the newly formed Rape Crisis Center. I started doing workshops where they would do an hour talk and then I would come in and do two hours of self-defense. I didn't know anything about rape at that time, but I found out. What finally came out was that in order for women to be able to defend themselves, you first have to break down the socialization. You have to do this on a psychological level, on the mental level, before you can ever get them to do anything on the physical level. Because no matter what I did in terms of teaching them how to physically take care of themselves, they would never ever be able to use that without being mentally prepared to do it.

The more I learned, the more I looked at things differently in terms of why women—most of them—would not fight back if a man were trying to rape them. I was learning about myself and all of the things that I had seen all my life, and it all came together. I started looking at, wow, the reason why women can't really physically do something is not because they're not capable. It's because we've been told we can't. And because we have been brainwashed by society into believing that we were too weak and that we must be dependent upon males for our protection.

That's when I started realizing that I had to do an awful lot of deprogramming, if you will, and getting back to the basics of the human qualities and instincts that women could act on. And then to give them some very simple, but effective physical things that they can use. That's empowerment, the control that you take back over yourself, which is a combination of all of the positive elements of control, confidence, and individuality also. So I started teaching very differently, and talking about socialization as part of the classes.

Did your view of Judo change as you developed your self-defense teaching?

Not of Judo, no, because what I did was I put all of the principles of Judo, in terms of the physical techniques, into what I taught physically. In the early days I was teaching people much more technical kinds of things than I do now—that was a learning process, again. Running the experimental classes made me weed out some of the technical things of

Midge Marino demonstrating a hammer blow to the groin of an attacker for students in her self-defense class at California State University (Sacramento, November 1995).

Judo, making it much easier for women to do—yet still be effective.

And I continue to learn. Every year I learn more—I learn from my students how to make the class better. I never stop learning—that's one of the things of course that Judo teaches you, that you never stop learning. You start off with a white belt, you go through all the black belts, and you go right back to a white belt—that's the tenth degree. I think that's a very wonderful way of teaching. There's always something more. The nice thing

is that you learn it from the people you teach. I feel that, anyway. I *love* to teach. It's become my life. Part of that is probably because it's something that I developed, but I also believe in it, everything that I say. And it's not just me, it's women in general. I feel very fortunate that I'm able to do what I do.

How does this work on a practical level? What format do you use in your classes?

The classes as Sac State meet twice a week. I lecture in the first part—I talk and I have them talk and begin to feel as a group. After six to eight sessions I start with the foundation; I start with a body movement kind of drill, so that they can get used to using their body in certain ways. These are all drills that are in Judo. They come from a kata. I teach them the eight off-balance positions of the body, so that they can learn how to maintain and stabilize their body.

Then I move into the actual physical techniques. I don't teach them throwing or anything like that—that's too difficult. In my intermediate class I do teach them some of the wrist techniques that we learn in the kata to take knives away from people, and guns. Also some bone-locking techniques for the elbow and that type of thing. At that point they're advanced to a place where they can learn that very technical aspect.

I bring humor into it. I think that one of the ways of learning is to make it a little bit humorous. I make them laugh at ourselves as women. And so it's fun. There's a portion of it, when I start talking about all this stuff, it gets real depressing, but I haven't seen anyone except maybe someone who has not been able to deal with their own rape situation or molestation or something—

sometimes they will want to leave and say, "I just can't—" I say, "Really, if you'd stay, you'd be much better off." Well, not at this time. They may come back. But most of the people are there to stay. It's difficult to get in my classes at Sac State. They're filled to capacity, and I always have people on waiting lists.

The students keep a notebook during the semester, and at the end I have them write a summary about how they felt when they came into the class and how they feel about themselves at the end of the class. Those are the things that are very interesting to me. Many of them say, "This is the best class I've ever taken in my life. It's the most worthwhile class that I will ever take."

I see it as bringing women back to their natural state of personhood. Most people, when they say self-defense, they think of physical things, but I see it as stretching out in every aspect of your life. Because if you have your personhood, then you're going to say, "Wait a minute, excuse me, uh-uh, that's not going to happen to me. I'm not going to take that kind of stuff from you," in job relationships, in personal relationships, or anything. People are going to stand up and say no. So I see it as a much, much broader thing than only learning how to defend yourself against a rapist or a mugger.

I feel very strongly that you need to get back in touch with your natural instincts as an animal. When we are in touch with those instincts, we're more capable of stopping something from happening to us before it gets to that critical stage. Reading signs. Picking up on keys. Looking, really looking. Awareness is more than people think. Awareness is using all of those instincts, and certainly that instinct, that inner instinct, that tells you there's something wrong with something. Which most women don't pay attention to.

I feel that in myself—that I have actively been trained to distrust that instinct. And so it's a real struggle to—

—to listen to that! And to act on it! That's absolutely right. We're told we're paranoid. Women are constantly put down. Negative, negative, negative. Women have to give themselves permission to act in a way that is not a "pink" way of acting. They really have to do that. They have to make a decision, which they're not allowed to do most of the time.

I have tried to keep the classes at Sac State only for women—which is difficult sometimes. I've had men break in there. I would have to tell you that out of twenty-six to twenty-eight women in each class, I have had from one to six women who have been molested or raped. I want to keep a safe place for them, where they can come out and talk about this, and feel free—I think it's a bonding thing that happens between women too. Because this violence is so prevalent in our lives. It's a common thread for all of us, it's a common thing that we all feel, this kind of fear. And they're doing something that is so nontraditional for them. It's difficult if there's men in the room, because it's not ladylike behavior to rip somebody's eye out or to break their bones or that kind of thing. So to get them to that place, I feel it's important to keep men out. And it's a way of women getting away from all this crap and stigmatism of separation, you know, divide-and-conquer kind of thing.

You also teach outside Sac State? You do workshops?

I started off doing the workshops with the Rape Crisis Center, and then they of course lost their funding as all of these things have, but I continued to do the workshops. I have my own business, and I do workshops all over—state agencies, private industry. I just finished up a series of three for a radiology lab.

My feeling was that I was only reaching a certain amount of people at Sac State and if I go out and do this I can reach a lot more. When I had my school, that was okay, I could do a series of classes for a month or two months. When you have people off the job and paying for it, a three-hour workshop is okay. What I've tried to do is take a lot of the things that I do in my class and put it into this three-hour workshop. Which is difficult, but at least the people have something, and they do indeed go out with enough to take care of themselves.

Now I do a series of three-hour workshops—four separate ones. The people don't pay for it; it's the corporation or the business or the state agency that does. Sometimes it's difficult to get them to do that, but they're recognizing more and more that that's a part of—almost a part of a wellness program. That it would behoove them to do it in terms of litigation, if anybody would get hurt or whatever on the property.

You've had all this practice now, but you've also had a lot of exposure to how much danger there is, which a lot of women can avoid being aware of. How do you feel about yourself? Do you feel safer in the world? How do you feel about the situation at large?

You know, I've been doing this for all these years, and I thought it would get better. Instead it's gotten much worse. That is certainly depressing. It's sickening to me, to see our world, our civilization, whatever you want to call it, falling down in the way it is. The way that I keep my sanity is because I am doing something about it, I feel. I'm doing something real positive about it. And I feel very pleased to be able to do that. But yeah, it is certainly depressing to me, like it is to many, many other people. I personally feel that there's a whole lot of things that contribute to this, and I talk about that in my classes as well—the pink and the blue and the rules for gender roles.

Do *I* feel safer because of what I know? Yeah, absolutely. But you see, the difference for me, and one of the things that I think is the most important, is that I'm myself. I really am very comfortable with myself. I don't pretend anything. I don't like to play games. I'm straight up. You know. That's who I am.

There's a real peace, I think, that comes with that. A peace within yourself. You don't have to prove anything to anybody. You don't have to be mean. You don't have to—there's a whole lot of you-don't-have-tos, maybe. You can just be who you are. And feel free and—and just very peaceful.

Judo has given me that. A whole lot of other things that I've learned in my life along the way have helped. Certainly the women's movement had a profound effect on me. But Judo started leading me down that peaceful kind of path. Learning how to control myself. Learning that I could be confident. Because I was a very shy person. I still am in a lot of ways. There are people who would say that's a lot of crap, but I wouldn't stand up and speak in front of anyone for a long time. I was that shy, and I felt very awkward and inadequate, very inadequate. I think that Judo has given me a form not only on the physical level, but the mental.

It's what Kano Sensei wanted to teach! Really and truly. To develop a person's body and soul—to become a decent human being, to be a good citizen, to care about other people. That's what I learned and it became a part of me.

CHAPTER 12

Women Will
Transform the Martial Arts

Several years ago my simu, Janet Seaforth, told us that a group of women were establishing a martial arts monastery near Dos Rios in the far north of our county. We were both fascinated and puzzled. The conjunction of women, martial arts, and monasteries was too remote from our experience for us to understand what this could be. Every so often Janet would hear something more: A work day was scheduled or a celebration. These activities made sense to us. "We should go visit these women!" we said. But we didn't know them, we felt uncertain of our welcome, Dos Rios seemed a long way away, and we never quite organized the expedition. Then Michelle Dwyer told me, "There's a woman who lives up near you who you should interview," and I realized she must mean at the monastery. I called to ask if I could visit, and early on a summer morning I set out.

Dos Rios—where I had never been before—turned out to be a short row of houses at either end of a high bridge above the confluence of two major forks of the Eel River. A flock of wild turkeys walked along the edge of the roadway. A brown dog sleeping in the middle of the pavement twitched one ear but did not look up at my passage. No people were in sight. I turned off onto smaller and smaller roads, finally to a dirt road that climbed upward through a scrubby second-growth forest of oaks and conifers. Presently the ranch road forked to the left, toward the river, a narrow, steeply dropping dirt track hemmed in by close-growing trees and chaparral. The brush opened as I passed a meadow where a flock of deer bedded down in the dry grass. Their heads swiveled in unison, ears pricked, a dozen pairs of eyes watching me drive by. After another few curves through the trees, a larger clearing opened, and I arrived at a small settlement of sheds and outbuildings, a travel trailer and several other vehicles, and a white ranch house with a spectacular view south and east across the Eel River canyon.

Coleen Gragen and Saskia Kleinert, two of the founders of Young Forest Monastery, came to greet me and invite me to join them for an outdoor breakfast at a picnic table with a wide view of the property. A sleek weimaraner and several cats settled nearby. Coleen is a tall, well-muscled woman in her forties with a wild bush of curly brown hair. Saskia, in her early thirties, is small and slender, with black hair and blue-gray eyes in a striking combination. The third of the original partners, Verbana Ostrom, a second-degree black belt in Aikido, was away. Now in her sixties, Verbana is retired from a career with the U.S. Postal Service. She divides her time between the San Francisco Bay Area and Young Forest, where she maintains a studio for her work with stained glass.

The founding vision for the monastery, Coleen told me, was to promote harmony among martial artists of different styles, encourage excellence in training, unite martial arts study with love and protection of nature, build bridges of understanding between martial artists and other seekers of the Way, and extend the art to those who need it most. These goals are encapsulated in the name Young Forest, a translation of the Chinese *shaolin* and a reference to the Shaolin Temple in China. "I saw the Shaolin Temple as a cusp place for the martial arts," Coleen said, "with the process of the bringing of yoga and meditation and Buddhism from India into China and the blending with the Taoist influences and the way that gave rise to

the development of Kung Fu—not to say that this place will be that, but in honor of the fact that we want this place to be a home for that process of growth and development where the women's martial arts movement is impacting the course of development of the broader martial arts movement."

Coleen's livelihood derives from the martial arts school she runs in the San Francisco Bay Area, and Saskia also has work in the city. They often can spend no more than three days a week here, but in a few short years, with the help of land partners and volunteers, an enormous amount of work has been completed toward implementing their vision. At times the endless chores of country living—repeatedly repairing and replacing water lines, clearing fallen trees, cutting firewood, and maintaining roads—have seemed like obstacles to training. Those who stayed have had to find opportunities for practicing their fighting skills in digging, carpentry, fruit and vegetable harvesting, and animal care. There have also been more dramatic challenges calling for warriorlike resolve, including a late-night fire in the attic of the ranch house after a guest overstoked the woodstove. With the fire department an hour away, everyone present had to pitch in, chopping out walls and ceiling to get at the flames with a garden hose and buckets of water. And they saved the building. "You did well," the firefighters said when they arrived. "You went after it."

All in all, Young Forest encompasses more than a hundred acres of forest and meadows steeply sloping from the ridge-top road to the Eel River. From our breakfast table Coleen and Saskia pointed out the garden and orchard they have nourished and the various buildings and outbuildings they have constructed or remodeled. Hidden from view by the trees from where we sat, an old barn was in the process of being converted to a training hall.

Much work remains to be done, some of it

imposed by the elements, some by adverse pressures from the human world. In the early days encampments of visitors combined work with martial arts training. Then county officials prohibited such gatherings until the facilities under construction were actually finished and fully met building and health department standards. The accompanying expense scared off several land partners and has temporarily halted the program of occasional weekend or weeklong workshops. The property is zoned for this use, but improvements to the road, kitchens, bathrooms, and so forth remain to be completed.

The land requires restorative work as well, for a century of logging and sheep ranching has left the slopes eroded and unstable, invaded by star thistle. Coleen and Saskia described their vision for stewardship of this land by a community of individuals, some permanent and some shifting, but all, while they are here, living, training, working, and meditating with thought for enhancing the land in the process. It struck me as a powerful act in itself to seek such flexible occupation of the land, with a care for the relationships between people and wild country, domestic and native animals, domestic and native plants. The ecological diversity that is vital for a rich and healthy mix of plant and animal species seems likely to nourish a wider range of human experience as well. And that, I realized as I sat listening to Coleen and Saskia, was what a women's martial arts monastery was about.

Their vision includes fun as well. With the August sun pushing the thermometer toward the hundred-degree mark, it was time to go swimming. Trailing our gear, we traipsed downhill through the orchard, across a meadow, into a stretch of oak forest, a few hundred yards along the railroad tracks, and then down a steep bank into the tumbled rock, grown up with willows, of the river canyon. Beside a mountainous pile of boulders

offering smooth surfaces for sunning at any desired angle, a sandy beach curved beside a pool of clear, shining water that must have stretched a hundred feet to the opposite shore and several hundred feet up and down river to rocky narrows at each end.

We dove in, luxuriating in the cool, silky feel of the water now the day had grown hot. Another large pile of boulders jutting from the water near the far shore offered a resting place. I sat there for a while sunning with Coleen, and we talked lazily about my book. Work of any sort seemed remote from this idyllic spot, but again and again we came back to the vision of martial arts training as the discipline at the center of responsible individual and community life. Coleen also told me about the background of her own art, Kajukenbo, in which she holds a fifth-degree black belt.

In the years after World War II, Hawaii was filled with groups displaced from different Asian countries. Many of the young men among them had martial arts training from their homeland, and with little to occupy them and an uncertain and mostly discouraging future ahead, they turned more and more to fighting each other. Under these conditions of turmoil, five martial artists from different national and style backgrounds came together to synthesize their various arts, testing and honing their decisions in street fighting with the dual aim of creating an effective self-defense system and breaking down ethnic rivalries. The primary leadership came from the Filipino Adriano Emperado; the arts of China, Korea, Japan, and Okinawa, represented through the other cofounders, are also reflected in present-day Kajukenbo. The art includes just about everything, but the moves are executed in the style of Chinese Kung Fu, with low, powerful stances and long, expansive kicks and strikes.

A work project that weekend at Young Forest was to complete the fruit harvest. The cherries were long since finished. Plump Bartlett pears lay individually wrapped in newspaper in stacked cartons in a back room, together with boxes of apples, perfuming the air with a spicy aroma. Other apples remained on the trees to pick, and plums were just ripening. Saskia had already picked several buckets of plums. After returning from swimming we pulled chairs up to a table in the ranch house kitchen, talking nonstop as we pitted bowlful af-

ter bowlful of plums, which Saskia set in large kettles on the stove to cook. Then Coleen and I moved to the cool, tree-shaded living room with the tape recorder. Shadowy and indistinct in the dimness from the trees growing close outside the windows, Coleen sat in her overalls in a rocking chair, slowly rocking, speaking in her calm, even voice, which carries such conviction, I always feel I can see before me the things she talks about.

COLEEN GRAGEN

Kajukenbo

Timewise it was 1973, shortly after the Vietnam War and also the height of the radical feminist upsurge. I had just graduated from the State University of New York, but going on to graduate school was kind of out of the question. We were all very critical of the bourgeois nature of the educational system, things of that sort. I didn't know where I was going exactly. I was a philosophy major with an emphasis in comparative religion—I was very interested in Buddhism and Taoism—and I got a job teaching philosophy and religion in the all-girls' Catholic high school in New York where I had gone to high school myself.

I was living in lower Manhattan, and there was a street fair one weekend. I pushed my way through the crowd, and it opened onto this scene of about thirty women in black uniforms doing a synchronized Karate kata. They dedicated it to Yvonne Wanrow, who was a Native American woman who had been imprisoned for killing a man who had molested her two children—so there was this combination of Asian philosophy, political activism, feminism. I had never thought about

doing martial arts, but all these things aligned in me, and I said, "That's it." The next day I went down and signed up. For me martial arts was a coming home kind of thing. I felt like I had done it in a past life or something—I knew right from the beginning I would stick with this for the rest of my life. That was twenty-one, twenty-two years ago now.

It was Karate that you started with?

Goju-ryu Karate, yeah. I started practicing in a place called the Women's Karate School in Manhattan. Actually the group that I had seen was Brooklyn Women's Martial Arts, and I thought I was getting hooked up with them, and I ended up not and had to make some changes to get to the right place. But that didn't matter, because I knew that this was the path for me. I trained at the Women's Karate School and then at a school called the Temple for Spiritual and Physical Survival in Harlem, with a man named Gerald Orange. It was

Coleen Gragen (right) in the training hall at Young Forest, 1994.

a combination of radical feminists, lesbians, Puerto Rican street fighters, black youths, and this personality, this African-American man who was able to tie all of these groups together. It was a wonderful place. Gerald was the teacher of Annie Ellman and Nadia Telsey, who were the founders of Brooklyn Women's Martial Arts, and I would go there and train with them for extra classes.

Unfortunately I was forced to leave my teaching job. I was responsible in the religion classes for a family-values section, and the girls were asking questions about homosexuality, whether or not you would go to hell if you were queer and things of this nature. Being myself homosexual and having had a relationship with the nun who was the

principal of the school at the time, I had to answer that I didn't believe that I would. Of course I didn't tell them that personal information, but I spoke positively about homosexuality, and the parents of the girls came down very heavily on the principal. She panicked and told me that I had to recant. I left instead.

My life was thrown into turmoil because this was a place that was very special to me. I had been raised by these women and then I was rejected in this gut-level way. I wasn't out to my family, and there was no way that I felt I could make this struggle—I didn't have support. So I sold everything I had and got on my bicycle and rode out of New York City.

I rode my bicycle for three months across Canada—cried a lot and turned my back on that part of my life. I ran out of money in Eugene, Oregon, and moved in with a radical feminist country collective up there. But I missed my art. I found out there was a woman teaching some style of Kung Fu in Eugene, at an all-women's school called Amazon Kung Fu. It was Barbara Bones, who teaches Kajukenbo. She was different than the people I had worked with so far—very demanding, a very rigorous instructor, not so political and community oriented. But her technique was superb, and at that point that was important to me. Over the years I ended up being her senior student and the first person that she promoted to black belt, so we had a very long, intense relationship. It still exists. She lives in Palo Alto now.

How did Kajukenbo fit with your Karate?

Actually, I preferred it to what I had been doing, because what I saw in Kajukenbo was a blending of hard and soft that I hadn't seen in Karate, and it really spoke to me. Low stances, circular movement—and just a fierce fighting style. I was athletic, and I was drawn to external style and to the style that I thought was applicable for self-defense purposes for women. I had that focus very strongly. When I saw this system and saw my instructor and the way she moved, I thought, I want to move like that. So I felt I had come to the right place. She worked for probably two years to get some of the hardness of my former system out of me—she was respectful of what I was doing, but she felt that I had too much tension and too much emphasis on power.

I stayed with Barbara for seven or eight years. I moved to the Bay Area to do some political work shortly after I got my black belt and I started a class at the San Francisco Women's Building in 1980. In that same year I found a location in Oakland to open the school that I'm still at, Hand to Hand, so I've been there, it'll be fourteen years in November.

You were saying the community and political aspects of all this are important to you. How has that come out in your martial arts practice?

My martial arts has always been hooked up with my political process and development—political in a broad sense, my social thought. The early seventies was a point when women were awakening in a very, very strong way. We were going to take this art out of the hands of men and transform it and use it for the purposes of stopping violence against women. There were tons of women at that period who trained with men for a period of time and then broke away.

What was unique for me—and has really synthesized something in a different way for me—is that my instructor was a woman. A lot of the struggle women had in breaking away from male instructors and criticizing the tradition was eased for me by the fact that my instructor was a woman. She was not a political woman. She didn't have a problem with her male instructor. She was one of the guys. She loved being with them. But she translated the tradition through a woman's perspective.

The school in Eugene was run by a collective of students, because we wanted a dojo so we would have a place to practice more. Barbara didn't think she needed a dojo—she held our classes in an elementary school. So we took over the business of the school and hired her, and we got into a lot of difficulties because there were real limits on our power as a community and as a collective, because if she didn't like something, she would say, "Fine, but I'm not teaching any more."

I always felt it was true that it wasn't an equal relationship, that she had a very deep skill and a wisdom that we wanted and needed, and so I always had one foot on each side. I think that did a lot to form me as an instructor. I'm different from her from the point of view that I'm very concerned about the social process within my school. I do a lot to make sure that there's communication, that we talk openly. At the end of every class we have a feedback time. I really promote it, and what I think is different about that is that it makes a responsibility and an expectation for students to speak their mind about what's going on.

That's a major step. First, it's public—people can criticize me publicly and do it lovingly without feeling there's going to be a repercussion. It makes the power balance a little different and allows people—the women in particular—to let me lead, because there's room to criticize me.

For a long time it seemed like women didn't want any leadership, but I think it's unaccountable leadership that's the problem, leadership that's not open and changing and reflecting the rest of the group. So although I'm very much the leader of the school, the process in the school is not the traditional patriarchal process. There's a lot of communication, a lot of sharing, and a lot of openness. I feel I'm able to practice that model because I had an instructor who was a woman and who took it one step and then I was able to integrate something else.

Martial arts is not an intellectual game! If you're going to teach a fighting art to women in this day and age, you should teach them to fight well—because we really need it. The violence that women are experiencing is extreme. I've felt that and I moved toward the art for that in my own life. As women crawl up out of this imposed dependency on men, we're coming into conflict with them and there's a whole new level of effort to control our behaviors in the form of sexist violence. I wanted to be able to fight for real because I wanted the freedom to go about my life. I also wanted to get the wisdom of the tradition in terms of internal development.

That was my political stance. I wanted to teach Kajukenbo because it was effective. On the other hand, I wanted to teach it differently, from the point of view that in my personal training I had wanted to feel more loved by my teachers. I didn't want to be encouraged by negative criticism, I wanted to be encouraged by love, and I felt that in my own instructor that was kind of subtle—I did feel that she loved me, but her manner is very old style in the sense of push, push, push, push. I spent many years without getting much feedback, and that was how I knew I was doing well—you know what I mean? I wanted to be able to teach toughness in a loving process.

This would also be teaching the art across a broader spectrum of a student's life— integrating it into more aspects of life?

Absolutely. I have experienced people—women— at the women's training camps, who had come out of male schools and were extremely competent fighters, but my sense of them as human beings was of an extreme vulnerability, an emotional fragileness. In conversation I would feel, "This person's very mistrustful." And I know where it comes from. In certain kinds of patriarchally dominated martial arts environments, an individual woman who can tough it out can get an incredible amount of support for that part of herself, the ability to withstand and endure—but whether that instructor has the understanding to notice what's being lost or being shut down in order to withstand is questionable.

I'm thinking of a couple of examples, from schools that have almost like a ninja framework. There's one guy who got into teaching Special Forces, Marines Special Forces, and then he became the instructor of Somoza's National Guard in Nicaragua. He taught assassination techniques, this kind of stuff. There are a lot of different trends in the martial arts world, and there's one trend that is very violent and very survivalist. I think there are women affiliated with that trend who are getting a very narrow kind of a training but think that they're getting the very deepest kind of training because they're hooked up with these world-class assassin-type people. They think of themselves as the elite of the women's fighting corps. And that kind of scares me. They come out with critiques—I've seen them critique the camps that we have because they're all-women camps— "How can you learn to fight with all women?" "You guys are not tough enough." The place that criticism comes from is a scary place, because it leaves women in the hands of some of the most vicious, limited, small-minded men. There's no future for us there.

But part of me—because I'm always looking for that applicability too—part of me sees something that these women are seeing, because sometimes I have a concern, you know, Can this woman really protect herself? She loves this art so much, but can she protect herself or is she being so coddled in the community of a woman's school, for instance, that she's not really being challenged?

I've seen places where feminist process is so centralized that the technique that's coming through is—really bad. I've seen people practicing in self-defense groups in Europe, for instance, in self-taught groups, and they're wonderful people, wonderful process, and a lot of study going on, a lot of good political work, but the actual technique that they're working with is not very good, because they've distanced themselves from hierarchy and cut themselves off from old wisdom.

So they're having to start over from the beginning—

Totally coming from scratch, yeah. I think that process goes on for women in Buddhism and in lots of traditional fields. The process I find interesting is to make sure that we're growing as whole people. Not just the ability to endure and withstand, but also the ability to walk away and to heal and to laugh and to laugh at yourself and let yourself be vulnerable and open. That's what I think we're discovering and working on now that is so great, and ties in so much with a process that's going on on the planet, in terms of the feminization of power and understanding that comes from our nature as women—that power is life giving, not life extinguishing. In the martial arts, I see a whole generation of instructors, the many women who have been teaching—struggling and teaching—for fifteen, twenty years, maturing into human beings who I can respect on a broad range. What they're doing with their life broadly is harmonious, is integrated. I think that's a healthy sign of where we're going with the art.

I've also seen incredible technical improvements in the women's martial arts movement over the past ten years. When I first started going to camps, there used to be this horrible rumor that the Kajukenbo women were just—you had to stay away from them, they had no control, they were vicious fighters, and all this stuff. It was because we were used to practicing contact sparring. We would hit the body, we would touch the head, and a lot of the women's schools at that time—like women in Shotokan, for instance—were not being allowed to touch at all. So we got branded in this way.

At the time it was very difficult for us, because we made a big point of safety, but over the years that's all kind of mushed together. Now everyone's practicing controlled-contact sparring. There's been a lot of change and growth, and now we're just in there with everyone else and not branded in any way. There's a much higher level of practicality. The art has really developed. But when the movement first got strong, there was a big emphasis on just process—and politics.

Maybe it was a necessary stage?

It was. I think it was an important foundation. It used to be at PAWMA demonstrations, half the demonstrations would be very political in nature, and ours were always that way. We were always talking about political issues, and I think that was an important foundation for us to keep ourselves rooted.

Keep clear about which war it is that we're fighting . . .

Right, and I think we've realized the war is broader than we conceived of at that point. Violence against women is an important part of what we're fighting in the world and in ourselves, but we can see now that that's a reflection of the much broader struggle that's going on. For instance, in the opening of *Women Who Run with the Wolves,* Clarissa Pinkola Estés's book, she makes an analogy between the destruction of the environment, the killing off of wolves, and violence against women—that it is the same mentality that looks at wolves and old women as useless.

I think in ourselves too, starting from a focus on the violence that was directed against us, we have come to experience our commonality with the Earth and animals, the air, the environment. The way in which we're practicing now, with breathing exercises, Ch'i Kung, harmonizing our energy, is as important as learning an effective knee-to-the-groin because we realize that in resisting the violence turned against us, we can't make ourselves not whole.

There've been a lot of men doing this art traditionally who also realized in themselves the need for that balance. I started with the thought that this was a separate thing that women were doing, but I really don't feel that now. The presence of meditation and Ch'i Kung and internal exercises, along with the external training that was done historically in the monasteries in China, reflected an understanding of human nature, and I feel the way that we're practicing now is very traditional.

But you had to go through a number of stages to get to that. How does this work for your newer, younger students who come in now? Do you see them going through a quicker version of all these stages? Are some of them missing some of the stages? Or do you think they can start out with

where you are now and they don't each need to go through all the stages?

When I first started teaching, most of the women were coming from some kind of political interest. My students were all the same age as me and the same lifestyle for the most part. They liked the fact that our school had some political affiliations and awareness. But now I find that the women who come are inspired just to see this art on women's bodies, to see the art well done on women's bodies, and they want that. It's a similar motivation, but it's not sifting through politics so much.

We were so anarchistic and rebellious when we first started practicing—yes, it's important to have a teacher, but you have to be self-identified. Now it's, "I want to have a really good teacher." They want me to be a sifu. They want the rules to be laid out more clearly, the requirements for belts.

And you're older now and there must be more of an age difference between you and new students?

Yeah, people don't equalize me with them as much as they did. When I was teaching students all the same age as me, the same lifestyle, it was a setup for competition between me and them, them and me. I can see that people are starting to perceive me as the older teacher, and that's kind of curious, but it's helpful in the sense that it's a much more relaxed environment. There's not so much challenging. It's just they love me, they want to train with me. The other side of it is to make them realize that if I'm not here, life goes on, teaching goes on, practice goes on.

Are they working into the same political understanding eventually? Or are they doing something different?

We have a real active self-defense program, with a ten-week beginning-level class, and I would say twenty-five percent of the women who come into the martial arts program come from the self-defense program. In the last four or five years self-defense has—I mean, you don't have to promote it, women are really looking for self-defense, not from a political point of view, from an absolute need, terror, fear. In the last four self-defense classes that I've taught, one of the women in each of those classes has had a best friend, a coworker, someone else raped or murdered. Violence has been very close.

The course is called Healing from Fear, and the perspective that we take is that it's not just about preparing to defend yourself against some possible future attack. Most of us have already spent many years up against violence against women through actual assault or through that pervasive process of living in a culture that is so violent that taking a self-defense class is actually a recovery process, not just a preparation process. We take that seriously. We talk and try and look within ourselves to see, What ways have I internalized fear or disempowered myself in the way that I'm carrying myself, for instance, and what can I do to work back through that to retrieve some of that personal power that was lost from those experiences?

It's not just learning technique, though the thing that I realize is that physical technique is important, because what women report is that just getting up and hitting that target pad, doing a simple palm heel strike, shakes things up in them that sitting in a therapy session just does not do. It's like the memories, the feelings, and the emotions are stored in the tissue, and getting a chance to release anger—you know, universally the women, the first time we hit something it's, "Oh, god! That feels so good!" That's not coming from a violent place; it's just a chance to release some of that stored-up tension and anxiety.

There's this whole process of socialization and disempowerment that goes on. How we are treated and how our bodies are looked at and how we are judged by the way our bodies look. It takes power away from us and we can get it back really only by once again working with that body. One thing that women report in the classes is that they feel so good to be in an environment where they're working with their bodies but there isn't a judgment about how they look. It's very freeing, because women don't get a chance to experience that very much.

Essentially I'm a martial arts teacher, but I love and am fascinated by the process of teaching self-defense—it's an encounter with the average woman in relation to her body and her mind and her spirit and her confidence. I find it a very deep work, a work that brings together many different aspects of myself. And this is all that I do—I don't have any other work. I work with adults and kids—mainly adults these days, because one of my students has taken over the kids' program and is doing such a fantastic job that I'm not too involved in that any more. And most recently, I started to work with men also.

This is in the martial arts or self-defense?

We have men in our martial arts classes, but the self-defense classes are for women only. I teach self-defense on a one-to-one basis with several older men. I'm finding that an interesting complement now to the other work that I'm doing, because I'm starting to delve in and understand the pressures and fears and anxieties that they're up against. They're different, but there's so much commonality. It's fun for me to work with these guys—it opens up, broadens my compassion and my perspective to work with fifty-year-old men who want to learn how to defend themselves.

These two men that I'm working with—one's a psychiatrist and one is a real estate agent—both came in and they went, "I don't want any of the bullshit, I only want strict self-defense. Teach me how to fight if somebody attacks me." I said okay, because I realized that that's the point of entry for them. They have this intense fear, they feel very threatened, and the way they're understanding what they need is this. Now I've been working with them for about three years, and one guy says, "You know, I realize I'll probably never have to use this stuff and what I'm really interested in now is how to relax my shoulders more." *[Laughs]* And then he said, "I saw this movie"—he watches Kung Fu movies all the time—"and this guy was doing this thing"—it was a form, and he said, "And it was so beautiful. Why don't you teach me that kind of stuff?"

When the fear is lessened, then the broader, deeper parts of the self can emerge. The same thing with women. I've seen us go through this process when we learn the self-defense that we don't feel quite so anxious for our immediate survival and the deeper layers of personality come out and say, "Now teach me something that relates to this part of my psyche, not just that immediate fear."

It's great compassion work. I love doing it. The hard thing for me is that there's such a bad rep for the martial arts in a certain way. Every time someone says to me, "What do you do for a living?" and

I say, "I'm a Kung Fu teacher," I always get this same ignorant response—they put their hands up in kind of a Karate chop fashion and, "I better stay away from you! I better be careful around you!" It's just such a misunderstanding of the field. I talk with Wen Mei Yu and I see how she's taught at universities in China and it's a whole respected area of expertise in her country. I've dedicated all my emotional, intellectual, and physical energy to this field, and yet when I speak to someone about what my career is, it's just total ignorance. That's hard for me, and I feel it also influences that more people don't come in this direction. They think it's only for kids or, "I don't want to be breaking things"—stuff like that.

Yes, my mother didn't like it when I had a science fiction novel published with a naked woman on the cover, and then when I told her I'm doing a book on martial arts, she just stared at me. Why won't I ever do anything that she can talk to her friends about?

Talk to her friends about! Exactly! My parents have just started to go through a change in that—and martial arts have been it for me for twenty-one years! They had really high hopes. They thought I was going to get my Ph.D. and all this, and so they were very disappointed. They saw it as an extension of my extremism during the Vietnam War—which some of it was. About six years ago, Special Training—that's the annual training camp held by the National Women's Martial Arts Federation—was in northern New York. My parents live in Vermont, and I told them, "There's a demonstration on Saturday night, and you can come if you want." They've never expressed any interest,

and I was surprised when they said, "Yeah, we would like to come."

It was at a college and there were about four hundred women. I had been teaching at Special Training for a number of years and I was a pretty popular instructor, and so here this gymnasium is filled with women, and here's my parents, sitting in these front-row seats. I did the demonstration where I tell the history of the *nunchaku,* which is made of two sticks connected by rope. It's a tool used to thresh rice, which the Okinawans used as a weapon after they were disarmed by the Japanese, who colonized Okinawa. I use the nunchaku to act out this story about the Okinawans fighting back with their farm tools against the Japanese. At the end of the demonstration I got the most incredible standing ovation, and then the whole crowd—they knew that my parents were there, because I think they announced it or something—and the whole crowd turned toward my parents and were standing up and clapping toward my parents. They broke down sobbing.

All of a sudden they realized that I had actually done something that had meaning, and it hit them like a Zen flash. Afterward we went to the motel where they were staying, and my mother and father were just, "We just didn't understand, we didn't realize. We're sorry." It was a nice breakthrough, and ever since then they've made real efforts to try and ask me questions and figure out what it is that I'm doing, and they talk to people about it. My mother sends me any little thing in the newspaper that has to do with Karate. You know—"This is the up-and-coming thing, Col!" It's great, because finally, before they die, they've gotten a chance to realize that I didn't totally blow it. But it's been difficult, because that lack of understanding in the culture has been so close in my own family.

But do you think, given that you did get into this from that period of the Vietnam War and the women's movement and all, if it had been an institutionalized part of U.S. society that you would have been attracted in the same way?

I feel I might have found it anyway, because I had so much physical energy and no way to channel it that I could feel good about. When I saw that demonstration of martial arts in 1973, it coalesced the intellectualism and the philosophical interest that I had, but in the context of physical practice. I felt it saved my life in giving me a way for it to be okay for me to pull those parts of myself together and be myself. So I think I either would have come to it or would have gone down the tubes in some way, become a drug addict or something like that.

One thing I think is really incredible about the martial arts and women is people come up to me sometimes when they see us demonstrating and they say they can't believe that they're seeing this conjunction of power and beauty on a female body. There's something that points to the future in that. It's almost like it awakens a part of the brain to see that union of power and beauty, because it points to a way that we need to evolve as human beings. We love that part of ourselves, which is that animal nature, but we fear the violence of the way that it's been used. To see it on a female body conjoined with female energy is like, "Oh! We can do this! We can bring these sides of human nature together in a beautiful way."

My teacher, Janet Seaforth, talks about something like that. She holds most of our

T'ai Chi classes in a park rather than on her property partly because she thinks we should be doing this in public—that even when we're not involving the public, we are making a statement by being in a public place, claiming public space for ourselves as women and for an activity we think important. To me this points up that there's something deeper going on than exercise or sport—but I find it difficult to pin down the distinctions.

I think there are many people who practice sports seriously and with a lot of love and a lot of devotion, but the general way that sports are practiced I would say is very different than what the martial arts are about. To me the physical training isn't the primary thing, martial arts are really a tool for conditioning the mind and the spirit. I think there's a real different mental and emotional state that's required—a different ego state is required to prepare to face a tremendous fear and the potential loss of your life. That reality of confronting death is, I think, the root of martial arts training—and it's also something that's difficult for us to know how to put into our training today, since the actual reality of going out and fighting and living or dying is not there any more.

Perhaps in a way it is for women, given the violence directed against us?

It is, except that I think that we can distance ourselves from that. Individuals who were practicing the martial arts or choosing to put themselves into those situations were conditioning themselves emotionally, physically, and mentally to make that choice and to carry it out, to actually walk into danger like that. It required an ability to center yourself, I think, that was pretty extreme. I think about this a lot, and I taught a workshop once at Special Training, a self-defense workshop, in which the last exercise that I did I had the women in the class do a visualization about an assault situation where two assailants came into their home, and before they could really get up out of bed and do anything, they were wounded with a knife very badly and they were actually dying. The meditation was about trying to pull back from the ugliness of the situation they were in with these two assailants and take some moments to center themselves and to congratulate themselves on their lives. I took them through this meditation that was kind of like a preparing for death meditation.

I got letters for about six months afterward from women who took the class, a lot of black belts in particular. I remember one letter that was representative of the others. This woman said that she wanted to thank me for the workshop because she always felt somewhat like a phony because she had a horrible fear of death—she was a black belt and yet she knew that there was this area where she was afraid to look. She had gotten very upset in the class and cried a lot, but it had opened up to her the possibility of letting herself imagine this.

The other thing women wrote and said was, "It was important to me to do that exercise, because so often all we visualize in our training is success." We visualize positive endings to these gory situations—the man grabs you and then you do this, do this, and you kick him and he's down on the ground and you run away. You know what I'm saying? The reality is that might happen, but there's also the reality of you do the best you can and maybe it doesn't work out to be good enough in that situation and you are seriously injured. And then the training is to stay present with that real-

ity and to work with it and to not consider yourself a failure, for instance, if before you know it you're down on the ground and you've received a bad blow.

To have that kind of reality in our training is to realize that we are vulnerable—that we are *not* creating invulnerability, that we are creating *presence,* and in creating presence we are increasing our ability to cope with what comes. It's to not pretend that we are making ourselves into these superhuman beings and then be terribly disappointed if a door hits us when we weren't looking—"Oh my god, I hope no one saw that!" *[Laughs]* I think about that a lot, how to incorporate into our training coping with failure and not just imagining, or fantasizing, that we will not fail.

Do you find resistance to thinking this way? You were saying your students wanted more rules, more clarity. Would they also like to see things be simpler—more like a sport, say?

No, I don't see that. There's an incredible lack of intelligent ways to train the self in our culture, and I think people are extremely happy to find something where they really feel that it's more than just a little class they take for a few months or something like that. Even if they only take it for a few months, in that few months they're in some way being reflected back to themselves. Especially if your teacher's at all skilled and on the right path. There're so many ways that you have to look at your competitiveness, look at your fear, look at your self-hate, look at ways in which you're out of balance. Martial arts give a chance to break through these patterned ways of looking at ourselves that we get into in our culture and to really learn something. Most of the calls I get, people say, "Do you work on the philosophical elements of the training?" I say yes, and then they're interested. A lot of the people that I get are in their thirties or forties and they're not looking for competitive sport.

I have a theory about what's going on, which I call simultaneous awakening—that it isn't an issue of individuals necessarily achieving enlightenment one by one, but that somehow almost *because* of the things that we've done to hurt the planet, our brains—the brains of human beings around the world—are starting to put two and two together and take some leaps of understanding, realizing, "Oh my god! Now look, if we live this way, we're cutting our foundation out from under us, because we're destroying the very thing that we need to live, which is the planet Earth," and that's accelerating a process of awakening that all over the planet people are coming to similar conclusions on their own without any organized teaching.

If you look closely, what you need to grow to the next stage is in front of you. Unfortunately we live in such a daze that often we miss those connections when they appear, but it can make you very excited to look around and see who you're going to meet or what's going to come in the mail that's going to help you. For me it's who walks in the door of the dojo every night. My commitment to saying, "Whoever walks in this door, I will work with," has been an incredible experience because a lot of people have walked in that door that my sort of day-to-day self thinks, "No, god, please! No!" And yet I feel my responsibility as a teacher is a role that I take on that is bigger than me and it says, "Work with this person." So I try, and some of those people have ended up being people that I really loved and respected. I would never have opened to them without the assistance of that re-

sponsibility of being the sensei, the sifu. It's opened my heart. And it carries over to the martial arts, because to try and find a place to connect with even the person who's coming at you with extreme aggression is what it's all about, I think.

Another thing that I think is really special about the training communities that we're building is that in our culture it seems for a lot of people the average length of a relationship is two years—a friendship, a partnership, whatever. Or if you have longer relationships, you have them with maybe one person. But we've got this training community, for instance, in our school, where people have known each other—not necessarily as friends, but they've interacted with each other in a very intense way over a period of eight, nine, ten years. There's a certain quality that comes in when people know you over time like that. There are lessons you can learn from each other that are not available in a two-year-old relationship. Our culture is such a move away, move around, change up, new things culture, but we're creating these little environments in which there's this kind of long-term stability, and I think that's healthy.

Maybe that connects back to what you were saying about the development of consciousness—that it takes time and persistence. Staying with something. And maybe staying in one place too.

I've been teaching in the same facility, same room, same hall, now for fourteen years, and I feel literally that the walls and the floor reflect back the right effort and good energy of all those souls that have gone through there. I'm uplifted by that. I walk in and it really is a temple. It has an existence separate from my efforts to keep something going. It's a holy place, a sacred place, that I can receive energy from. I'm sure that park where you practice has that feeling to you.

Sometimes people say, "You need a bigger space," or "You should move to Berkeley, because you're in a bad neighborhood," and I think to myself, unless this building burns down or falls down in an earthquake, how can I leave this place? It's almost like my ancestors are buried there. That sense of place, sense of commitment to place—and it doesn't have to be the perfect place. Certainly, the reason that I got the dojo in the first place was because the rent was very low. It's in a neighborhood that some people would call bad. It was a junk shop; it didn't have any special, sacred energy. But it has been transformed.

That seems good, to take a place like that and transform it. If it's a pretty place to start with—it's like having this young, healthy student who can do anything without being taught.

Yeah! Things like that that come back to you through the art are really special. That's what I would like to do here at Young Forest too. I love that place in Oakland so much, but it is true that when we have morning meditations there, at seven o'clock in the morning, the buses are going zo-o-om, z-o-o-oom, zoo-o-o-m, and people are yelling and garbage trucks are pulling up. You would literally have to sit at four in the morning to have any kind of peace, and still you can feel the tension of the city coursing through your veins. I started to think about setting a rural location up in such a way that it would be really conducive. Good mats and a hot tub to jump into after practice. Places to run and little isolated spots to practice. Things that were really set up for our art. And to grow the food that we would eat for that and to know where the water's coming from—the complete picture. It's a very long-term goal. It might take me a lifetime, but that's the idea; that's the start we're trying to make here.

The reason that I named this place Young Forest is because I see women coming to the martial arts as a young movement, a young transformation, a new growth in the martial arts that will transform it forever in a very deep way. The martial arts will never be the same again for this influence, and that's been what my life has been about, sitting right on that cusp and watching that process and being engaged in that process.

CHAPTER 13

An Inner Sense of Freedom

Coleen brought the rocking chair to a halt and we sat silent in the shadowed room, which had grown warm as the afternoon advanced. It took several minutes for the plain, white walls, wooden floor, and simple furnishings of the living room to come into focus, so far had we wandered in our talk. Presently Coleen got to her feet. "Time to return to the plum wars!"

In the kitchen Saskia wielded a stirring spoon with the authority of a general over the pots of cooking plums and water boiling for sterilizing jars. One by one we filled the jars with rich red plum jam, sealed them, and set them aside to cool. As the sun rode low on the western ridges, we went out to forage in the garden for dinner. We found tomatoes and basil and onions, from which we made a sauce for pasta. As we ate at the table in the living room, periodically a metallic *ping* sounded from the direction of the kitchen. "Music to my ears," Saskia said. For it meant the jar lids had sealed properly.

It was late when I went out into the night the short distance to a little travel trailer that serves as guest quarters. The dome of the sky sparkled with myriad stars I never see in the city, but at ground level the darkness was thick. Every so often a vehicle passed on the Covelo Road, a mile away on the other side of the river, a distant, fleeting engine hum that only emphasized how silent the land was around me. But when I lay in my sleeping bag in the little travel trailer, the night seemed to come alive with chitterings and rustlings and the feel of bodied beings in movement.

From the earliest recorded times, martial artists have looked to animals both as models for physical capacities and as sources for metaphors and myths to explain human experience. At Young Forest I had already seen deer for myself, resting but watchful. The house cats too could make their way independently of people: The mother of the other two had lived here six years while the property stood vacant, and even when people took up residence and fed her, she kept her hunting skills honed, Coleen told me, by practicing leaps and strikes under a certain bush near the house for an hour at the same time every morning. Returning from our swim that morning, Coleen and Saskia had showed me a meadow where once they saw a mountain lion. Other times they have felt its presence, and they believe it lives in a cave nearby.

I lay awake, contemplating what I've read about mountain lions living harmoniously in proximity to humans, disdaining sheep and cattle and sustaining themselves on their traditional prey. Experts speculate that young lions learn from their mothers what to hunt as well as how to hunt. The recent upsurge in the number of conflicts between humans and lions may result from increasing human disruption of lion habitat. If lion mothers are too hard pressed to fully train young lions, each new generation of lions will be faced with figuring out for themselves how to survive. The situation pointed up for me the importance of the women's work at Young Forest—both to allow space for the resident lion and to build a context of enduring community for women in which our training can add up to more than developing isolated individuals.

I must have dropped off to sleep, for next I knew the moon shone brightly through a gap in the eastern mountains, lighting the trailer through the wide windows that face in that direction. All was still, and now that the noise and movement outdoors had ceased, I felt strongly the presence of the Earth itself, the great mass of the hills rising beneath me toward the east and south, the rugged terrain protectively surrounding the little settlement of buildings on three sides, the powerful river curling at the toe of the slope—these are, in dramatic form, the traditionally desired elements I have read about for *feng shui,* the Chinese study of landforms and building sites. Hills, considered to be alive, are often referred to as dragons, and this ground, with on a daily basis but surely were appropriate for the site of the intense learning expe-

Saskia Kleinert picking plums at Young Forest (near Dos Rios, Calif., August 1994).

riences the founders of Young forest envisioned.

When I awoke again, the sun was high and I went out to find only the small cats stirring. They washed themselves lazily, keeping an eye on my early T'ai Chi practice. Later that morning Coleen showed me the training hall under construction in the old sheep barn, a few hundred feet away in the woods. An enclosed loft at the far end offers dormitory space. Wide stairs or a deck will lead down to the ground, deeply shaded by live oaks and fir. Coleen spoke of planting ferns and other water-loving plants along a seasonal creek we could see from the unglazed window openings. The creek banks would make a pleasant setting for meditation. Beside the creek, too, could be the outdoor hot tub. As with all that Coleen plans for Young Forest, she described this so clearly and in such detail, I saw the finished result shimmering like an overlay upon the present, almost more real than what was actually before me.

After breakfast, at the outdoor picnic table, Saskia and I settled in to talk. Deer wandered into view on the hillside in front of us, a long line of them, with many fawns. They stopped to gaze at us, then moved on briskly at the roar of electric tools that started up in the workshop. Coleen was constructing a weapons rack for the city dojo, Saskia explained. She speaks with a very slight accent that sets off her only-too-accurate English— her second language—and gives her speech a refreshingly crisp quality, as if the words she uses are themselves newly minted.

SASKIA KLEINERT

Jujutsu and Kajukenbo

I grew up in Switzerland. The first time I was introduced to martial arts was when I was about thirteen. I wanted to do Judo, but my parents said that wasn't for girls—I could do yoga, but I wasn't interested in that. It wasn't serious enough for me to fight over it.

Then when I was nineteen, I moved to the city of Zurich and lived in what we call a living community of twelve people, a mixed group of men and women in the Swiss youth movement. During the early and mid-eighties there were radical youth movements everywhere in Europe, and the movement in Switzerland was pretty strong for a while. Unfortunately that provoked a lot of neo-Nazis and skinheads to organize against us. Because of that and our confrontations with police in the street we wanted to learn how to defend ourselves.

The youth movement wasn't nonviolent?

No, it was very confrontational; we had big-time riots. So we had this interest in self-defense, but we were not interested in going to a martial arts school, because we felt that hierarchy was not the right thing for us to place ourselves in. One of our women friends had been training in Karate for maybe two years. We were able to rent a space, and this woman taught us once or twice a week. I remember often she wasn't sure about the details of the techniques she was teaching us, so it wasn't a great way to learn.

At the time I lived really unhealthily. I was a cab driver and worked at night, and I didn't get up before noon because I didn't go to bed before four o'clock. It's a life where working out isn't exactly the kind of thing you're looking forward to doing! *[Laughs]* Plus, to go running or swimming were not cool things to do. I smoked about three packs of cigarettes a day. I have low blood pressure, and I can't really deal with things like smoking. I used to faint in the beginning of the class. Cl-a-b-o-o-m! I was out. *[Laughs]* Then I got back up and did the class, but it *was* rather disturbing.

That Karate class lasted for about half a year, but it became a dream for me to train in martial arts because I had this idea that it would give me strength in a different way. One of our neighbors at the time was a black belt in a Karate system, and I was in awe about the way he was. He was a very quiet person, very calm. I remember hearing things like, "When you are a black belt, your inner power and strength will reflect on the outside and you won't so easily get into confrontations you'd rather avoid." Simple ideas of what it could be fascinated me. A big part of my interest in the martial arts was fear of being attacked by men, but I kept that motivation to myself because I didn't feel that reason had much room in my community at that time, even though we all felt that we were feminists.

In 1983, when I was twenty-one, I found a school and started training. I trained a lot—three, four times a week, and then pretty soon it was five times a week. I stopped smoking. I would swim every day. My living situation changed as well. We had to move because the building was going to be torn down. Everybody moved out and I ended up being there by myself for about two months. It was the first time in my life that I lived by myself. I was involved still in mixed political groups, but pretty much at that time I started to become involved in women-only groups.

And this was still Karate you were studying?

That was when I started Jujutsu. It was a mixed school with a man teacher—Marco Torti—and maybe forty percent women, sixty percent men.

Did you find that a struggle, having a man teacher and a preponderance of men students?

For the first two to three years it was not a struggle for me at all. After I came out as a lesbian it was hard, because I didn't want to have that much physical contact with men. In Jujutsu, you're lying on top of each other a lot because a lot of the technique is ground fighting—it's like wrestling.

When I had been training for, I think, three years, I heard about FIST—Feminist International Summer Training—a women's camp in Holland. My best friend Bea had started at the Jujutsu school and she and I went to the camp together. It was an intense experience—incredible. It was the first time that I met women teachers. At that point there wasn't any woman teacher in Switzerland that I knew of. I met this woman who was a Jujutsu teacher, and I was thrilled.

The changes I went through after being at FIST that first time caused some friction between Marco, my Jujutsu sensei, and me. Now I think maybe it was that he was afraid he was going to lose me as a good student. He came around, but he made me wait for my next belt. In Jujutsu the belts are yellow, orange, green, blue, brown, black.

I was a green belt at the time. After green belt you're not allowed to ask, "Can I test?" because it's against the etiquette, but usually between green and blue it's about a year. Also you had to have a certain number of hours of training. I was way over that and I was way over the time. I really had to hang in there. After two years Marco finally said he wanted to test me, and that again turned something around, because after the test he said to me that he never had anybody do so well.

Being able to train with women at FIST, I had picked up an intensity that you don't usually encounter in a mixed school. It's a mind thing, an emotional thing, not a physical thing. I think it's hard for heterosexual women or women who are male identified to be out there and strong—they would have to question too much of the rest of their life. There were some women in the school who felt powerful, but it didn't feel as deep as the strength that came across at camp where so many of the one hundred and fifty or so women were woman identified in one way or another—their lovers or their politics. I felt unless I saw that strength in a woman as a role model it would be hard for me to be able to change that inside of myself.

When I went to FIST again, I heard about Coleen Gragen's school, Hand to Hand. Three of my friends were talking about going to San Francisco for vacation, and they were going to visit Hand to Hand, which made me decide to go on the trip with them, and when I came to Hand to Hand, I felt I found my school. Part of that was that there was a spiritual aspect to training, where my school in Switzerland wasn't like that. We did a short meditation, we bowed to get on the floor, we bowed in front of each other, but there wasn't any more than that. There was no spiritual or philosophical part, no history of the art that we had to study for our tests or anything like that. I started

to feel burnt out with just that sports aspect of the art.

I think the first thing that I noticed at Hand to Hand was that there was an altar. I remember one of the first times when I was training, candles were burning, and that felt really, really different. I felt touched in a different place inside. The same thing happened when I observed the belt tests for the first time—the way some questions were asked, how some things were explained, the metaphors that were used to explain certain ways of movement, like saying that you draw up your energy like you had the roots of a tree. It felt like a new aspect of the art opened for me. In the Jujutsu school, of course, we were told that we should be breathing on the *kiai* and so on, but we would never start a class standing in horse stance and pulling up energy and breathing out. Or even being told that you can pull up energy—that was quite mystical to me in the beginning.

And did it work? Could you feel the energy?

Yes! *[Laughs]*

So this was a big change? But you had been getting something from your Jujutsu training?

In the Jujutsu school what I mainly found was that when I went to class it was the only time in my life when I didn't think about anything else. I didn't worry or think about my relationships or my political work or anything. It was really clearing for me, always. I felt I could be just me and didn't have to have a certain kind of role that I felt I had to keep up where it was more about words. I think it fed—it still does feed—a lot into my personality. It strengthened me and made me a lot more open, because it made me feel more safe and secure within myself.

Just the plain fact that I had been doing something on such an intense basis for so long, that I was able to have that kind of continuity in something, meant a lot to me. I left school when I was seventeen and moved out of my parents' house. I didn't finish school and so I didn't have anything like that that I could hang on to. My work that I did for money was never work that I was committed to—it was always just to support my political work. So to have continuity in one place that was about me and not about anything on the outside strengthened me emotionally and spiritually in a way that nothing else strengthened me.

One of the main things that I feel now is that my training allows me to get closer to an inner sense of freedom. I feel most of human behavior is reactive because you're so much immersed in your own history and your own past and your own perception, which has so much to do with fears and worries and things that you think might happen. Because this has happened, so then that could happen out of this. If you say this word, then that—you know what I'm saying? I feel so often that we react in a way that isn't even the way we want to react!

Right. You find yourself doing things—

—and you're thinking, "Why am I doing this? This is not what I want to do!" It's like there's another layer that says something before you get a chance to say, "Wait a minute." The main thing that the martial arts have been giving me is I'm starting to be able to take a breath and think before I speak or react. I see this inner kind of freedom and I have an incredible desire for it.

One of the things I think that's so great about martial arts comes from the fact that you never are able to do it right. You think you know how to do it, and then you realize that, no, you don't know. You have to put up with that if you want to stick with it. It's different every time you do it. The partner you work with is different every time. And it's such small things that make things work or not work! I think just being in that environment where you're working with those facts starts to change your soul over time—if you're aware, if you're not just in there bulldozing over all the details and subtle aspects. I feel I'm confronted with the details because I'm not somebody who's incredibly talented in the sense that I walked onto the dojo floor and things came to me. What I gain is much more through the seriousness and practice than through a natural ability.

Had you been athletic when you were younger?

No. I wanted to be a gymnast as a child, but I was very inflexible—which is still something that is bothering me. *[Laughs]* But as a child, I wasn't able to do gymnastics. I climbed trees and we hiked up all the Swiss mountains. I played outside, I played badminton with my sister, I ran a lot. I beat everybody in the school when we had those short races, sixty meters and eighty meters. I loved to run and my teacher told me that I had a beautiful running style and if I was just taller they'd put me into the national team, and you know—shit, oh well, I wasn't. *[Laughs]* Those kind of experiences didn't exactly help.

Saskia Kleinert at Oberiberg, Switzerland, 1994.

You said your teacher in Switzerland taught both Judo and Jujutsu. Why did you choose Jujutsu? How did they seem different?

I liked Jujutsu better. I'm not sure I can remember why it appealed to me. It's more oriented to self-defense, and self-defense was my reason for studying a martial art. Judo seemed to me to be more sports and competition oriented, and I was more interested in the street aspects of the art. Jujutsu has no rules or competition. You can do whatever it takes to take the person out.

I've heard Judo and Aikido people—and others—talk about Jujutsu being sort of a barbaric precursor, something really nasty, that people later came along and—

Smoothed it out?

Yeah, brought it into the modern world. Civilized it. I wonder how you see that?

Jujutsu is geared toward breaking the bones and the joints. That's one of the main things that Jujutsu does. It works well for a small person, for one thing, because it works with leverage much more than with mass or weight. Doing a technique a little bit more this way or that way will make the difference. If you have the angle of the arm a little more to the right side than to the front, it might exactly make the difference for you to be able to break that bone.

As a small person, when you start the art, you are at a disadvantage, because if someone has a lot of mass, of course it's easier for them to break your bones, because they can just lean on you. You have to work very accurately to get it right. Later on in training, you get very much of an advantage from that. Someone who's big can work with their mass for a certain amount of time, but then at some point they start to need technique. I had to study very clearly what I was doing right from the start.

One aspect I like about Jujutsu in terms of self-defense is that I feel comfortable on the ground. Sifu Coleen always says one of the first things that a man will do to weaken a woman is to punch her in the face to knock her to the floor. I know how to move on the floor in a way that can be to my advantage. I wouldn't feel like it's all over. I would feel in certain aspects even more confident than standing up.

There're a lot of things that are really neat about Jujutsu, like the different choke holds, which don't require a lot of strength but just placing your hands in the right position. And it doesn't take long—half a minute and the person's out. There're little things—working with someone's finger joints. If somebody grabs you and you don't want to punch them out, but you want them to let go, you squeeze their fingers in a certain way that hurts them, and they'll have to let go. But it's not a defense that will necessarily escalate the situation. I

think that's a good aspect of this art, that you can have different levels of reacting to different kinds of attacks.

So in a way, the nastiness of it gives you more control over what you're doing and more choices of things to do?

Yeah, there're a lot of different ways to react with those kind of techniques. You can work your way up in terms of what the attack is like, what you're confronted with. I feel it's a great combination with Kajukenbo, because Kajukenbo teaches me more to fight in a distance, and Jujutsu is fighting close in. From a self-defense point of view, okay, I'm out in a distance fighting, but if something happens and all of a sudden I'm close in, I didn't lose my abilities. I have different things to draw from.

Then all the throwing and that stuff in Jujutsu—that's beautiful, but I don't think that's very self-defense oriented, unless you really know how to work with balance and are an incredible Judo fighter. Which I'm not. But it's beautiful. It's very beautiful to fall and to throw someone. And so easy. It is incredible to me, how smooth that can feel.

Also it can absolutely not work if you're in the wrong position. You can pull on that person and they feel like a rock. Then something changes, the timing, the momentum, something very small, and all of a sudden it's just this big ball you send flying through the air. *[Laughs]* It's very satisfying. The first time I threw a six-foot-tall guy—well, it was satisfying enough for me to still remember the exact moment. Rolling and falling is my absolute favorite thing to do. I think it's the only thing that I have a natural talent in. I totally love it. I had never even a second's worry. I was never afraid. To be thrown by someone who throws well—I think it comes the closest to flying that you can experience. It's a thrill.

And when you came to California and started studying at Hand to Hand, how was it, switching from Jujutsu to Kajukenbo?

What's nice is that both are eclectic systems. They both incorporate many different styles. Jujutsu historically was the basis for Judo and Aikido and Karate, and so all these styles are part of Jujutsu. I had a certain amount of experience in kicking and punching. It wasn't completely foreign to me, though that Karate aspect in our Jujutsu school was a little weak because my teacher is traditionally much more involved with Judo. There is Jujutsu-like stuff in what we call the punch attacks and the grab arts in Kajukenbo, techniques and combinations that I felt comfortable and at home with and helped me feel I didn't have to start completely from scratch.

Sparring was a big change and a challenge for me, because we didn't spar in Jujutsu. When I first had to spar, that scared the shit out of me. I was really afraid of getting hit, particularly in the face. With time I lost my fear, but for a long time sparring was something I really didn't enjoy. It's challenging when you have all these different things flying at you. I guess part of what makes you grow spiritually is that you go back into situations that are challenging, situations that you don't like— and you do it over and over. You think, "Oh my god, I hope we're not going to spar tonight!" You don't want to do it and on some level you do want to do it because you know the only way to lose that fear is by doing it. I think that in itself changes your personality—to keep on going with something that is hard.

There is a small Jujutsu class now at Hand to Hand. A woman who's a black belt, Lisa, and I are teaching twice a week. Every once in a while, because in the punch attacks in Kajukenbo you are supposed to be able to fall, Sifu Coleen has Lisa and me teach a falling class, which I really, really enjoy.

You mentioned that a year ago or so you went back to Switzerland to take your brown belt test in Jujutsu—what made you decide to do that?

Part was that I had been training for a long time and I wanted to be able to wear a different color belt, you know? *[Laughs]* Because I felt the color belt didn't show the time I had been putting into martial arts. One challenge for me with changing over to a new style—on some level challenging and on some level also a helpful lesson—is that I've been doing martial arts for eleven years and I'm not a black belt because I switched styles. I'm a brown belt in Jujutsu and a green belt in Kajukenbo, which is one level below brown—the belt colors are different in Kajukenbo. So I chose two styles where it takes a long time to get a black belt.

Also, by going, I think I was tying loose ends together. I felt I needed to get to this place where things would come together and I would be able to see my abilities and my strength. Brown belt is such a major test. At that point I knew I was going to stay here for a longer time, and I didn't want to leave that undone.

So I wrote to Marco and asked him if there would be a way in which I could take my brown belt test, which took me some courage to do, because as I said after green you're not supposed to ask whether you're allowed to test. He said that I would have to come for three months. I felt honored that he would let me do that. I decided that I needed to go for a little longer, so I went for four months and worked in Switzerland but mainly trained. I was totally focused on training.

There're set rules for belt tests of what you have to know in terms of your technical ability and the length of training, but with Marco, the way he approaches the brown belt test is that basically it's his final test with you. When you test for black belt, it's not him who's testing you, it's a board of different people from the Budo Federation, who are people from Judo and Jujutsu. He might be on the board but he might not—it depends on whether he's chosen for that particular testing date. I think that's a reason why he tests brown belt pretty hard. A lot of people who took their black belt tests said that the black belt wasn't as hard for them as the brown belt.

Brown belt is never just on one day, it's over a period of a week to two weeks—in my case, two weeks. Every time I'd go to class a portion could be test. It could be that I would be tested for an hour, it could be that I'd be tested for five minutes. I didn't know and that added a lot to the— the friction.

The job that I had was on night shift in a home for disabled people, so I wouldn't sleep a lot, and then I'd go to class and have challenging situations. One time I had to do part of the test in the beginning of a class and then the class went on at its regular pace and we did an exercise where he had us do this funny thing that he saw the night before in ballet, which was something where you would sort of roll over a person's back with your legs stretched out.

The woman who had me on top of her collapsed, and I fell straight on my head from the height of her shoulders. My neck bent under and it cracked and I saw stars and then my right arm went limp. It was really, really scary. I never had had an injury quite that serious. It hurt for a long time. So I was in the middle of that and I had to keep testing, because my plane to the States was at a certain time and I needed to be done with my test to be able to make it back here. So that was an added challenge to the situation.

Another thing was kata. You don't do kata in Jujutsu until brown belt level and then it's a partner kata that you do with somebody else. You have to practice both roles of the kata and it's specified in a very detailed way that is particular to the Japanese arts—each little step or the bending of your toes and everything is extremely precise. So it's a challenging kata. I remember coming from the night shift to a morning seminar with people from schools all around Zurich—all of them were brown and black belts. I was really tired. I said to Marco, "I just want to let you know I didn't sleep last night," and he said, "Oh, okay. Good." And the next thing he said was, "In this case, I will have you show this kata now." I thought I was going to die. *[Laughs]* But obviously I didn't.

There were a lot of situations like that in which I was really pushed. I think a certain amount of it was the relationship that we had. Other people said to me that he was testing me harder than they had seen him testing people prior to me having that test, but I hadn't been there in a long time, so it's hard for me to judge that. I think some of it was he was pushing to see how far I could go without losing it. I definitely felt that way. I felt I was being pushed in a lot of ways to limits that I just had to kind of sit with it and say, "Okay, I'll be fine." I remember going home from class and thinking, "This is just part of the test! Take it the way it is."

One time I thought I was supposed to be testing—it was a Friday night and I thought I was supposed to be having my main portion of my test and I was of course really nervous. Time went by and went by and nothing happened. About ten minutes before the end of training, I realized this isn't going to happen today. That was one of those points when I thought, "I'm going to lose it." Because nothing—nothing happened. And I don't know whether that happened by mistake or whether that happened to see what I would do. I really don't know.

But it wasn't—you know, I don't think it was something bad. It wasn't something that I feel, "Oh, he shouldn't have done this."

When it was over, did you think it was good to see that you could survive that?

Yeah, it gave me a good feeling about myself. And also, after I was done, Marco was full of praise, and he gave me the belt, which is something I had only seen him do once before. Usually you have to buy it. At my three final classes before I came back to the States, every time he said in front of the whole group what an incredible test I had been able to pull together—to the extent where I got embarrassed. I thought, "Oh, my god, they're all going to hate me!"

So then you came back to the Bay Area and began to study massage therapy? Does that fit in with your martial arts too?

I've always been drawn to healing. In my political community in Switzerland I was a person people came to to ask about herbs for different things. I had kind of my own tiny herbal pharmacy at home, to give stuff to people. My grandmother taught me about natural ways of healing. She had a lot of knowledge and believed in the power of herbs, crystals, healing baths, etcetera. I was always fascinated by that. I've been studying aromatherapy on my own off and on for many years. Now having become a massage therapist, it's great for me to integrate that knowledge. To bring that together with martial arts is a dream come true for me. For one thing, to me it's so much the other side of martial arts. It's so much of a balance. I think it becomes necessary sooner or later to have both of those things together if you want to be able to do the martial arts for a long time. You have to start to learn how to heal the body, because you learn too much of how to hurt it.

And healing work is another side of sparring, I suppose, in that you have to understand the other person to be able to do something useful for them?

You have to be intuitive about that other person; yeah, I feel that. On some level becoming a massage therapist is to me another aspect of training. It's something where I'm finally able to bring my money-making profession together with martial arts. There's never been anything in my life that I enjoyed doing as much as being in this place where I can work with people as a—"healer" is not the word you're supposed to say in massage, but I don't think there's anything wrong with that word. It's a long-term goal for me.

I don't think I would have been able to start my own massage practice if it weren't for my experiences in the martial arts. I was able to develop a trust in my abilities to do something that I really wanted to do. And to be grounded—it takes strength to be a good massage therapist because you have to be able to play many different roles. You have to be comforting and compassionate to the client coming in and make them feel that they're coming into a safe environment. Then you have to draw from your own energy to be able to be a good massage therapist at the time of the massage. When the massage is over you have to be a businesswoman. There's a lot that has to come together in a way that feels smooth and round for that person who comes to see you. It's a challenge! I don't think I would be able to do as well as I'm doing if it wasn't for having been in the martial arts so long—and having finally learned how to breathe! *[Laughs]* One of the main things that I've learned in martial arts is one must breathe! Continuously. It's okay—there's enough time to take a breath! And then things look different. It's interesting what that does to you.

What about your interest in political action? Is that satisfied living here in the United States?

No, it hasn't been satisfied. I think the way in which I would be most able and happy to bring it in is by teaching women self-defense—and I've assisted Sifu Coleen in classes. I think that's a great way of trying to have some kind of impact, even though it's on a very small scale of one to one. I used to do politics on a bigger scale, not so much working with one group but in a national or international way, trying to influence laws and so on. That's hard for me here. Things are so much more widespread that I don't know where to hook into it.

I miss that as part of my life. On the other hand, I did intense political work for ten years. I did not take care of myself very well in those years. I was always ready to stand up for everybody else, but I wasn't able to stand up for myself. Now I've been here for six years, and sometimes I think maybe I need another ten years working on myself as an individual and developing myself before I will be able to fully integrate both the external and the internal work in my life.

◆   ◆   ◆

Almost a year later Saskia called me to report an epiphany she experienced in her training shortly after taking her brown belt test in Kajukenbo. Leaving class one evening, she said, she suddenly noticed how good she felt. It occurred to her that Kajukenbo was like a new language that she was only now learning to feel as much at home in as she did with Jujutsu—Kajukenbo was now there for her "in her body" and no longer "just as a theoretical concept." It was like a buzzing all through her body, she said, "an excitement that goes into your bone structure. I don't know how the change happens," she mused, "other than just time and practice. Staying with something and practicing and going back and looking at yourself and making mistakes and learning again and making new mistakes and learning new things again—it's like it opens a window in your soul. Just from time and practice! You don't have to do anything difficult or anything you don't know how to do; you just have to practice!"

CHAPTER 14

Our Family Has Always Done Weapons

Sandy Wong mentioned to me that her ideal of women martial artists was embodied by the twin sisters Malyne Chiu and Alyne Hazard. Didi Goodman, when I later interviewed her, talked about training with Malyne in Naginata, the use of a traditional Japanese weapon consisting of a sword blade at the end of a staff. "She's great to practice with!" Didi exclaimed. "We're lined up there, facing each other, and she'll get this intense look on her face, like a samurai. She's looking at me like maybe she'll really cut me with her weapon if I happen to blink—a total intensity of focus and connection. You really get a sense of what it's about." When I met Malyne for myself and she told me about her background in martial arts, I realized that the qualities and understanding Saskia Kleinert spoke of discovering over years of training had been Malyne's almost by birthright.

Now in their forties, Malyne and Alyne hold advanced rank in both Kendo, Japanese sword fighting, and Naginata. I was fascinated by Naginata from the glimpses I had seen of women at practice and from Sandy's comment that in Japan it is a women's art. The naginata was originally a battlefield weapon, but after the advent of firearms in the 1600s in Japan, Naginata was practiced primarily by women of the warrior class—wives and daughters of samurai—both for self-defense and as a method of moral training. Beautifully decorated weapons became an important item in women's dowries. Malyne later told me several stories about Japanese women using these weapons in earnest. The last stand by the women of the Aizu clan was the most sensational of several incidents. It took place in 1868 after the Tokugawa shogun surrendered to the emperor. The Aizu clan held out. The men of the clan were killed or scattered, and the women made a last stand at a stronghold in northern Japan. They were defeated and exiled, but later received amnesty, and in the 1870s many of these women served in the police force.

Kendo also intrigued me. In Kendo the curved, single-edged steel blade of the samurai has been replaced by the bamboo *shinai*, and fighters are protected by padded head gear and coverings for the arms, chest, hips, and groin. Beyond these concessions to safety Kendo seems to retain much of the ferociousness of its origins in medieval Japanese warfare. Linda Atkinson, in her 1983 chronicle of early U.S. women martial artists, *Women in the Martial Arts: A New Spirit Rising*—now, sadly, out of print—quotes the kendoist Valerie Eads about her initial, formative visit to a Kendo dojo: "As soon as I heard their yells and saw them step in to attack, I knew this was for me. They were flying around the room, masked, padded, black pants billowing, bashing each other over the head and shrieking. I couldn't wait to try it."[1]

Malyne grew up in San Jose, California, where she now lives with her husband and son and works in the wholesale flower business. When I called her to ask for an interview, she sounded as interested in what I was doing with this book as I was in what she was doing with her martial arts practice. That sense about her of being totally involved in what's before her, even in a telephone conversation with a stranger, is, I think, an element of what Sandy and Didi were talking about. Malyne herself said that cultivating the quality of "pres-

ence" is what most interests her in her martial arts practice at this point. My teachers of T'ai Chi Ch'uan often urge us to bring our whole mind and body to each movement. I saw that lesson take flesh when I watched Malyne, a sturdy, muscular woman with short, curly black hair and ready laughter, practicing a Naginata form in class with her sensei, Miyako Tanaka. Dressed in white tunics and long-skirted black hakama, the two women used modern practice weapons made of an oak staff with a bamboo blade. They performed the now slow, now explosive movements with their seven-foot weapons with power and grace, the various turns and strikes and pauses that in themselves seem so mannered, fully imbued with purpose.

I found Tanaka Sensei's Naginata class intriguing in other respects as well. There was little ceremony, and the students shifted casually between chatting and practice—but practice they did, with a full measure of dedication and effort, but also with obvious joy in the activity and the company. Tanaka Sensei moved about the room with gently worded suggestions, integrating an open, calm manner with a wholehearted commitment to training. A baby was present the day I visited, an infant just starting to crawl. I never did figure out who the baby actually belonged to, because everyone there took turns carrying it about or playing with it on a blanket laid out on the floor at one end of the dojo. Tanaka Sensei herself carried the baby for much of the time, balancing it on one hip as she moved from pair to pair of students with critiques. Often she would hand over the baby to whoever she was talking to and take their weapon to illustrate some detail of technique. The baby, I might add, seemed happy with the arrangement. Never once did I hear it fuss or cry.

After class and lunch with the group at a nearby cafe, Malyne and I went off to talk. Malyne's

---

1. Linda Atkinson, *Women in the Martial Arts: A New Spirit Rising* (New York: Dodd, Mead, 1983), 123.

characteristic attentiveness to what is before her often makes conversation with her intense. She talks with an energy and immediacy unlike any I have encountered; a degree of formality in her speech that I imagine derives from her early immersion in dojo etiquette adds to this effect.

MALYNE CHIU

Kendo and Naginata

During the Korean War, my father, Benjamin Hazard, was in Tokyo, and he began studying Kendo. He is not Japanese, but ever since his teenage years in Los Angeles, he had been interested in Japanese and Chinese culture, and he spoke Japanese fluently. Traveling to Japan, he took on more of the Japanese culture for himself. It was far more comfortable for him, I believe—he was just not born for these times. He continued to make Asian culture a profession after the war, teaching Chinese and Japanese history at San Jose State University, where he is now a professor emeritus. So we grew up in San Jose.

My mother was Japanese—my parents met in Korea. Because she was going to live in the United States and her children were going to be American, she did her best to become an American—meaning she didn't speak Japanese to us and she was not particularly enamored of us studying Japanese culture. It was my father who kept these things alive. And fervently hoped that we would be sons. *[Laughs]* He had four daughters as it turned out. But we're dutiful daughters. I think we did well for him.

Our childhood was pervaded with Japanese culture, essentially from my father, who really worked to present it to us—mostly from the martial side, quite frankly, budo culture, Kendo culture. Our study of martial arts started in 1959 or 1960 when my twin sister and I were six.

Was it your choice to start training?

No, it wasn't our choice, but we didn't object. It didn't occur to us that there was anything else to be doing on a Friday night. In those years the dojo life was pretty strenuous. There wasn't much tolerance for fooling around and giddiness, though I think the actual honest training was maybe all of forty-five minutes out of a three-hour evening. The rest of the time we were expected to be obedient. Keep a low profile and be obedient. It was strict, but it gave us a chance to observe social behavior, the hierarchy, and develop a sense of separation from the kids' life.

We had, now I look back on it, a less playful feeling about Japanese culture than we migh have. We missed a lot of the fun stuff that is part of Girls' Day and festivals and that sort of thing. We didn't do Oshogatsu—the New Year's—the Dolls' Day, or other holiday observances. We didn't go to the Obon, the religious Buddhist observance of the Day of the Dead, or the other things that I found out later that Japanese social contact involved. We didn't go to any of these things until we were in college. My mother was not a practicing Buddhist, so all my childhood observances of Japanese culture were from the dojo.

My father would also take us to films, Japanese films, historical films, benefit movies maybe at a Buddhist church. We'd see *chanbara*—that's a slang term for Japanese shoot-'em-up movies, samurai films. I think it's an onomatopoeia—the sound of swords clashing. We would be curious about what we'd see. Was it real? Did it happen? On the way home my father would explain the historical background.

Kurosawa's *Chushingura* made a big impression on us—the tale of the forty-seven *ronin,* the forty-seven retainers. We must have been about ten when that came up. It's an epic four-hour film of the forty-seven retainers who avenged their lord when he had to commit ritual suicide. He was misinformed about protocol and embarrassed and goaded into drawing his sword on the palace grounds, which brought an automatic death sentence, and he had to commit suicide. His retainers

hit on a plan—a multiyear undertaking—to take the head of the man who caused the downfall of their lord and the clan.

To see these kinds of stories and people sacrificing themselves made a big impression on us as kids. The films had lots of pain and suffering. People giving up their lives. We thought this was the right thing to do—fighting to the point of giving up your own life. Of course we couldn't possibly grasp that, but it kind of worked for the dojo. You go to the tournaments and you fight for your teacher—it was that kind of romantic notion. Our heroes as children were in these film scenarios, and our play with our father—because he was the one we played with most of the time—was colored by these films we saw. Play for us was King of the

Malyne Chiu (right) in a Naginata match at the Cherry Blossom Festival (San Francisco, Spring 1995).

SHARP SPEAR, CRYSTAL MIRROR

Mountain, but with shinai, with the weapons.

Our family's always done weapons. It was never looked at as we grew up as something for self-defense, or there being a need for self-defense. It was a pursuit of a martial art that was handed down, keeping this tradition alive, preserving the culture. I think it wasn't until we experienced modern life for ourselves and the dangers of being a woman in modern life that it occurred to us that this could be used for self-defense. Because fighting in Kendo is real time—most of your practice is taken up in real attack, real-time fighting—you find that you have a sense of timing and an eye for things when you actually fight.

This must have been something you just had without even realizing where you got it from.

Yeah! And I think that's a little bit of a problem when you start from childhood. I appreciated it later because I stayed with it long enough to look back and say, "These are things that held me in good stead in these situations—this situation and this situation." When you come to it as a child, you do it out of—we did it out of a sense of duty. And there's plenty of distraction as you head into the teen years, to make you want to stop.

That's what I was thinking—there must have been a point when you and your sisters wanted to explore new directions on your own?

There's a lot of pull from school and the social world and the normal renting, tearing of trying to be an adult and having your own things that you want to do. All four of us started, and as it turns out only two of us stayed. My twin sister, Alyne, is still teaching Kendo—well, she's taking a hiatus now. Just this year she's going to take a break, but she's pretty much continued straight through teaching Kendo. She does some Naginata. She's *sandan,* third degree, in Naginata, and *godan,* fifth degree in Kendo. She's also a dancer. She's been doing the balancing act of work and family and martial arts and dance and it's hard, so she's going to take a break from dance as well as Kendo. My other sisters dropped out of it in junior high and high school.

I stayed with budo through college and even after I married and had children. I stopped Kendo about eight years ago, totally, because I took up Naginata—though I'm still on the board of directors of the Northern California Kendo Federation, because I owe my teachers. I am indebted to them and to my father.

When you're given teaching, at some point you have to give it back. If you recognize the goodness of the teaching, you can't turn your back on that responsibility. At what point you decide to take on the responsibility of teaching is up to you and your teacher, but if you don't feel that—that's unfortunate. For my teachers—and many of them are gone now—and my parents, who brought us this education, I stay with it.

But at some point this must have been something that you chose to do for yourself rather than out of childhood duty and just being told. Was that a transition that you remember?

I still look at that every now and then. Part of it is something that I recognized even in high school—practice is very satisfying in itself. There's nothing like a good fight! And we were fortunate that we were good at what we did. If I would stop for a while and not go, I would miss it. There's something very exhilarating about the life-and-death match. You can test yourself with every person, every practice. And you miss that.

And part of it is a socialization, because there's something beyond just the physical practice. It's part of the fabric of my family life. Also it's a place you go to that's separate. You step out of your workaday life. And this is something I recognized in high school—the dojo life gave me a sense of responsibility and community that wasn't evident for a lot of us in the teenage years. We were trying to find what niche we belong to—I'm not Japanese, I'm not American, I'm Eurasian, and I was starting to find there's a group of us like this, and how to relate to—how to talk to strangers, how to deal, move in the world.

Those were serious times. My college class was the last class that got drafted for the war in Vietnam. What we learned from Kendo supported our political interest and concern about the situation in Asia—and vice versa.

All in all, it sounds like Kendo may have been more an anchor for you than something that you rebelled against.

Right! It definitely is an anchor, and I think that's why we would come back. You could go away and come back and the community was always there. People who have committed their lives will be there. The sense of quiet and order is there—I go to practice for the peace and the quiet and the orderliness that I don't get on the freeway.

I look at everybody's face in the dojo and I know that everybody is having the same struggles in their personal lives or business lives or family lives. These are things that you don't speak of necessarily in the dojo. You pass through the door and you take on the character that you are in the dojo. I'd like to say that it's the same character as in the outer world, but sometimes it isn't. And it allows a dignity even for children that children don't get sometimes in class in school.

I see that in my own son, who went to the dojo with me as soon as I was able to practice, about seven months after the birth. He would be strapped on my back and I would work out. He's seven now and he does Naginata. We try to keep the training enjoyable—twenty-five minutes is fine—then he can go play with the guys. We keep that balance.

One incident with my son made a big impression on me. You know, in practice, you pair off and then you switch, pair off and switch. Two years ago, when my son was five, he was in line and for some reason my father didn't rotate him in. I was on the other teacher's side so I couldn't stop—I didn't stop—but I was watching what my father was doing. He stopped to rotate again and he didn't put my son in the line again. He didn't see my son or something, and left him out three times. There were these big tears rolling down my son's face. I had to point out to my father—"You cannot leave him out. He is part of this community. *We*"—my sisters and I—"had better instruction."

It made an impression on me—that a child at five also needs to be afforded this respect and this attention. This is what I got from my father and it was important to me as a child—that there's a place for us because of who we are and not necessarily who my father is. We're welcome, we're expected. And we have responsibilities.

Things can be scrambled in junior high school, but we came to this circle and it raised us up from being part of the rabble—but in a way that wasn't elitist. It was a way that says, "There are good men here, and we can be like this." I'd like to have said there were good women, but there weren't women practitioners. And this was kind of a curious thing for me, because looking at the older men I always wondered, "Hmm, I like the way this person is calm. The character of the person is very calm—will *we* be like this?"

Are we going to be old men when we grow up?

[Laughs] There was a little bit of that! But there was that sense that you can mature here. You're accepted as part of this circle of adults. It was an adult world that we got into at an early age, and that's pretty sobering.

As I got to be a young woman and a teacher, we could sit with the teachers at the luncheons at a tournament, which was very interesting for Alyne and me. These men had to work out their differences, because they lived together. This roomful of teachers teach together, we practice together once a month, we work together on the board. Yet if there's turmoil, it doesn't show. Your training doesn't permit you to deal with your problems that way. There's no dignity in direct conflict and scrapping. This is not the way for us.

And how do people manage problems? Because those certainly did come up. What I liked about the men, most of the men, was that they are very direct and very straightforward. Difficulties that should be brought before the board were brought before the board. People would stand up and say, "I know I'm always being blunt, but I've got to say this. I just don't like da-da-da."

That's my experience with teachers resolving problems. Sometimes it might have been done on the side. I don't know because I was not party to every resolution. I think a lot of things were done by the wives too, politically. *[Laughs]* I imagined the men were managing things, but maybe they were ignoring them. What I saw was that in the meetings of the Kendo Federation board, people would come forward, and I thought, "This is the best way to deal with it, be honest, and find the right forum for it."

It was a different approach to problem solving. I think Kendo, or any martial art, asks more of you than just to have a full-blown conflict. There's another way to resolve it. I thought, "I want this for my life." I wanted my life to be calm. And dignified.

And was an element of this that Kendo is Japanese and you are part Japanese?

It never occurred to me that it was Japanese. It was, "This is what we do." And many people were not Japanese. My father is not Japanese. But it made sense to me from childhood because my father's a historian. Our house was a historian's home. Our childhood excursions were to the Brundage Asian Art collection in San Francisco. Artifacts in the house are military artifacts. Military stories, myth—that was part of what growing up was like. A romantic sense of history and chivalry.

There's a whole lot of romance, now I think about it, with Kendo and our practice. Kendo is not self-defense. People sometimes ask me, "What's it good for?" Or Naginata. People say, "Why? Why do you do something that doesn't help you?" I think people come to Naginata and Kendo for different reasons. They're interested in Japanese culture. Or costuming. Or sport. Or they have a romantic

Malyne Chiu (right) and her sister Alyne Hazard after Kendo practice at their father's dojo (San Jose, Calif., 1990).

to practice with, we think about ourselves that way or remember different skills or the sound of someone's voice. With fighting for self-defense, I don't know if you get that.

When we got a little older, games, sports, didn't make as much sense as fighting. *[Laughs]* What is more than fighting for your life? This is it! I loved soccer. I enjoyed these things, but sports were not part of our upbringing. My father wasn't interested in football. I never understood basketball. But the whole idea of a match, the intensity of that, and recognizing the personal power in people that you square off with, and you're trying to maintain your personal power in the face of somebody that's more experienced or older or better at it than you—it's a *big* job, and very exciting. During the college years, it was those aspects of testing myself, trying

notion that it looks like fighting. It's play acting a little bit. When you fight, everybody has a style you can recognize, or you can hear their voice. It's a kind of role playing that you get to do as an adult. My father really enjoyed the position he had in the dojo, being head of his dojo. We were nothing less than his retainers.

Those kind of romantic notions persisted. That kept it enjoyable for a long time. We still look at each other and think about how we were fighting when we were young and fast and could do it. *[Laughs]* When we see old friends that we used

to make my skills better—those were our competition years, when Alyne and I were competitors in tournaments.

We had a period, maybe about twelve years, of really good quality Kendo. We've both been U.S. national and international women's champions. In 1973 I was first place and she was second place in the world championship women's division. I think Alyne was first the next time at the world championship in Paris, and I think I took third in Sapporo. The field was small then, to be sure.

I enjoyed competition. I also enjoyed the community. Again it's going back to, this is the way people should be treated. These are good people and this is the way the world should be everywhere in terms of respect. In the dojo people address each other, there's eye contact, even for kids, and there's the expectation that you'll do your best. There're all these good expectations.

The dojo experience is powerful for children—for women and for children, who sometimes feel powerless, because it gives the opportunity, which you need to experience somewhere and preferably early, of dignity afforded you. Early. Right away. No waiting on that one. I'm aware of batterers and abuse and I think that had people been given the kind of experience we had—and I imagine that it comes in other places, like organized sports—but budo is different—

Can you pin down what that difference is?

Because budo puts such a high premium on personal dignity and integrity. It's a big responsibility sometimes *not* to be yourself. *[Laughs]* They want you to be yourself, but they're expecting much more of you at an early age. It puts a premium on that dignity afforded to your teachers—and, actually, to the underlings. You never snub your nose at somebody below you, because you were there once. And it's not just that they're below you, but you're responsible for this person. That relationship is peculiar, I think, to Japanese martial arts. At it's best that's what people get from it. I think that's what we got.

As you got older were there more women in the Kendo?

No, there never were very many. Kendo is hard; physically it's hard. You need to develop pretty good upper-body strength, which women don't characteristically have. Not to say that there aren't excellent kendoists that are women, because there are.

There were no other people in our high school that did Kendo. We didn't have any peers that did what we did. It was unusual, low-profile—it wasn't something that you would invite your friends to come down and see. My older sister eventually dropped out. This was the seventies too, so there were a lot of interesting things going on politically, and Kendo was sort of archaic, feudalistic, possibly chauvinist—though I never viewed it like that. I never personally experienced chauvinism.

Was there any confusion in your mind or your twin sister's as to whether you belonged with the male sensei or somewhere else with women?

Nope. We decided we belong with the sensei. Because we were trained. When I saw women over there and the sensei over here, it didn't occur to me that it was chauvinism, but simply that the women weren't instructors. Sensei are here. If she'd been a sensei she'd be here too. It didn't occur to me that they were all women in the kitchen, for example. It's just that they were not sensei.

In tournaments, in the last twenty years, they have separated the sexes. There's usually a women's division. That started happening about when I was nineteen—we were not children, we were too old to be children, so they developed a women's division, for us, probably. At age nineteen my sister and I were the grandes dames of

Kendo, because nobody had stayed. In the women's divisions maybe there were eight or nine women at most, especially at our level. We could also compete with our level in a mixed group. You definitely would want to go for the women's division to support it—though a lot of women rebelled against that and said, "Why make this distinction? We want to compete at our level with everybody." Which is the way it is locally often—there's mixed men and women. If you're sandan, you go in with the sandan group. Most women do both. So you can see how your skills compete against a male.

So it's not that women are not allowed to compete with men?

No. Because the pool of men is so large and the chances of a woman successfully competing in that large pool are small I think is one of the reasons that they tried to encourage women by developing a women's division and giving them a place. Some women argued that it lowers the competition, because there's just so few. That's why they kept the ability to compete with the men also. Which most people enjoy. The other problem is women staying. Women—people—marry. You try to raise a family or your own business and culturally there's a lot more pull on women to leave martial arts forever or for those child-rearing years or the business years, so there're relatively fewer women.

There were no women teachers in Kendo when I was growing up. Since then two or three women have come from Japan to America on tour and—their style is a little bit different. Women don't have the upper-body strength, but there're some technical things that these women showed us that would help sustain us as we get older. That was

important to see, to meet other women. It's heartening to meet women who do this—to see that to do this is not so unusual. I can understand why women don't pursue training—life is hard as it is; it's easy to drop out. Women don't age the same way men age physically. Childbearing is hard. Coming back is hard. There were no female role models, so I didn't see a vision of it.

So these are all reasons why you ultimately switched over to Naginata?

If you're trying to put your effort into teaching and training, some people may be able to do two or three things, but I found out, just practically, I can only do one thing. And I found there're advantages to Naginata practicality-wise that would work for me in my advancing years.

Naginata does not rely on upper-body strength. In Kendo the weapon, the shinai, is this long *[illustrates about forty inches with her hands]* and the movement is linear, like fencing. It's on a straight line. Everything is done essentially with the arms, two handed—it's a two-handed sword. Power in the legs is needed for forward motion, for jumping forward or leaping forward. It's very physical, which I enjoy *[laughs]*, but sometimes you have full-body contact where people run up against each other like this *[claps her hands together hard]*. Well, that's fine. I can do that for the rest of my life too, but it makes sense to me as I become older that I'm moving to longer weapons and a bigger ma-ai. I will keep further away from my opponent and have a longer weapon. And it works—again, practicality. Naginata works. It doesn't require physical strength. The mechanics of the weapon and the way the body moves make it for me more suitable for women.

How was that shift after so many years of Kendo?

It was hard! It's awkward at first to learn to manipulate something that long—it's nearly seven feet long. You have to learn to make it work. The sword becomes an extension of your body, and the naginata is an extension also. It happens to be a good deal longer. Another thing about Kendo is that the body position is the same virtually all the time. In Naginata, because of the length of the weapon, to manipulate it, you have to be able to change the grip on it, which means that your body's going to be turning one-eighty on one side and maybe turning a whole one-eighty on the other side to manipulate this long weapon.

That opened up a whole new method of movement that my body had never had to deal with. I have to work to be strong on both sides. Everybody favors one side, but Naginata requires that you be proficient holding the weapon on the right-hand side or the left. That's a challenge all by itself. Naginata also opened up technical techniques that Kendo didn't have. Kendo has three head points that are legal to hit—the center and sides of the top of the head—and the thrust to the throat and either side of the torso and either wrist. Naginata adds the shins, the outside and inside of the shins.

That would be cutting the leg tendons in a real battle?

I think just taking the leg off. My father liked to describe the details of sinew and bone and how you really can't make multiple cuts because of the fat that would get on the blade.

And in Naginata all this was not just standing in one position. You could hit all those points from either the left-hand side or the right-hand side. That's a lot to train for and manage. From that standpoint it was more interesting.

The other thing was competition. I didn't know at the time how far women could go in Kendo. At age nineteen I had many good years ahead. Alyne and I were speedy, we were young, we were fast, we were doing well. But I was looking for the future, and there were no role models. At nineteen I had not met a woman older than me doing Kendo. Then I had a chance to see a demonstration of Tendo-ryu Naginata by Chiyoko Tokunaga Sensei and Miyoko Shiratori Sensei at a world Kendo championship. This is the first time in my life I'd ever heard a woman's voice, a mature woman's voice, or seen this kind of spiritual power in a mature woman.

I'd seen Naginata before. My father had some exposure in Japan with Sowata Sensei and he wanted to introduce us to Naginata. When I was sixteen I went to her dojo in Tokyo and had my first lesson. And then when we came back my father taught us from a book—which is very unusual. I'm accustomed to people saying, "You don't have the authority to teach or to rally a group, so I think it's unwise." People rarely say no, no, no, but they'll discourage it in some way. Naginata is the only martial art that I have been involved in where people didn't mind—"You practice on your own, and we'll come to you." And they send people! The All-Japan Naginata Federation actually sent people to the United States to come and train with us, without asking payment. There's an international Naginata federation set up to help people outside of Japan practice Naginata and you can petition them for assistance.

But we learned from my father for a number of years before we met other people who did Naginata in California. Which was an eye-opener.

My sister and I went down to Los Angeles and brazenly took a test. *[Laughs]* You know, we wanted to be part of it and we wanted to meet people who do this. We passed the test, but they were saying words and doing things that we'd never seen before—obviously book learning is different—and I'd never seen anything like this demonstration by Tokunaga Sensei and Shiratori Sensei. I'd never seen another woman doing weapons, let alone a woman who was fifty years old.

It wasn't shiai, it wasn't a match—it was kata. The thing that impressed me was not only that these women were powerful, and they were women doing this, but it raised my expectations about kata in general—what kata should be. These were heavy oak weapons they were using. The cuts were wholehearted. There's no doubt in my mind that the intent was there. The kiai, the voice, and the intent—these were clear even to someone as young as I was. The *kissaki*, the tip of the weapon, doesn't die. The cut is finished and you're moving back to center—and that tip, it has to be live. You never know what's going to happen. Someone will change their mind. It's not just hmm-hmm-hmm *[pantomimes lackadaisically walking backward]* that I see sometimes. We have kata demonstrations, mostly by younger people, and they don't play the life-and-death thing. This was the first time I'd seen it played out in kata—with all due respect to everybody that's gone before us. It also changed the way I did my kata in Kendo. I hope it changed a lot of the people who saw that in the way they did their kata.

So it was the two things—one, that they were women. I was saying, "Hmm, when I'm fifty, I want to be that strong. I can't see graying at the temples like my dad *[laughs]* and bellowing like my father, but this I can see. I see that there's a possibility for women to continue doing this." But also it changed my Kendo, which I continued to do for another fifteen years after that. When my sister and I got our godan, fifth degree, in Kendo, we were asked to do the kata. And it was with that demonstration in mind that we said we've got to make clear that the intensity is there. People came up to us afterward, very high-level teachers, who said, "I could not have done better." It influenced the way Alyne and I decided we would teach also. Kata are crystallized forms, and sometimes it gets relegated to a waltz. There should be no laxness. This is no different than a match, even though you know exactly what's going to happen.

At that point I began to study Naginata more seriously. Tanaka Sensei came with a group of women in 1973 and we had our bona fide teacher, though weekly practice was with my father. It was in tandem with the Kendo club. Everybody did Kendo and then some people had an interest in the Naginata also. Then I switched over completely about eight years ago. I was becoming more interested in form than competition, and the pursuit of my ideal, magic experience with Tokunaga Sensei and Shiratori Sensei. I saw them again this summer. They're in their mid-seventies now and they're even better. And there are many women in their fifties, sixties, seventies, eighties doing Naginata.

What does your practice consist of at this point? How much time do you spend?

About six hours a week. We have a practice on Wednesdays in San Jose and in Berkeley Friday nights. Once a month on Sundays. I have a dummy at home—and kata, you can practice that alone.

What I've been working on at my age and my level right now—godan, fifth degree—is developing a presence. Once you get over the hump of trying to make your body work and trying to learn things technically, there's an element also that you have to project in a fight. It shows when you look at somebody, but also you try to manage that aspect of your own skill. At what point do you move? At what point do you see that chance? If physically you're slow, then there's other ways you have to manage your fight. I'm trying different things technically in a fight, in my sparring, to assert that power. This is the fun part! And I still have to work on things technically. I have some habits I'll be working on forever, I think.

You were saying how much it means to you to have so many women to practice with now. What is it about that that matters to you?

Because women's struggles with business and life and families are similar. They understand. And there's instruction that men can't give you as a woman. If those women Kendo instructors had been there earlier, my life might have been different too. They would say, "Let me show you some things, a technical thing that if you just change this a little bit, you'll be able to survive a four-hour practice. Just change this form a little bit." Or, "This is a little bit speedier. I'm going to show you these things as another woman."

These are things that might occur to a teacher who trained with women and knew the special abilities of women—women have better balance. We can be just as fast. There're certain heavy-handed techniques that aren't really suitable for people who don't have upper-body strength, which are most of us women. Sometimes it was simple things like, "Let me show you how to tie your hakama differently." Hakama, you know, the clothes you wear, are pretty cumbersome—how do you go to the rest room? A man would not tell you that you don't have to unwrap yourself all the way. *[Laughs]* Simple things like that, practical matters. You and I are laughing about this, but—

It could make a big difference!

Yes! These are basic differences, and just that someone would recognize that and offer that information—but it doesn't come because culture, polite culture, doesn't allow that. Or they don't have the same physical circumstances so it doesn't occur to them. A good teacher will. There are teachers who are able to read a person's ability and say, "This is going to be to your advantage to do this." There are teachers who do that.

In Naginata there's a whole history of hundreds of thousands of women working through these things. Working through birth and crisis—when you have a baby, how long does it take to recover? My father couldn't tell me. When can I start practicing again? These are not little things. What steps should I take to practice after the birth of the baby? What sort of things can I do now? What is reasonable to do now? The obstetrician says, "When you feel like running, start running." *[Laughs]* Well, that wasn't good advice.

In Naginata there's a whole community that supports you. There is a history of women doing what I'm doing. I can ask these questions and there's some history to look back on. They say, "Well, some people say this, some people do this, I've had this experience." This is helpful. Also women will appreciate if you are in a household where there are other stresses that men don't have. I often used to say on the Kendo Federation board—"I wish I had a wife to manage my affairs so I could do this business." The men sensei looked at me like—"What?" Not that I expect women to make unfair allowances, but there is some sympathy and understanding of what it takes to get the job done and just knowing that makes a difference in how you work together. And not that women aren't competitive. We *are* competitive—I think that's pretty even, having worked with both men and women.

Another thing that I thought was interesting about Naginata is, it doesn't go any higher than godan, fifth degree. Which could take fifteen, twenty years. The thinking is that your proficiency goes so far. We expect you to be proficient. After that, as you get old, it's doubtful that you'll increase in power and speed, but we expect your character to improve. I thought, "This makes sense." We want women to continue, but this takes out that sense of beat out people, you know, beat out people, beat out people, beat out people. It took the edge off that for me. You participate in other ways in addition to practice. Serve on the board. Support these efforts. Try to change. Try to improve the community. Advance it. And enjoy it—meaning for instance that we go out together. Like we had lunch together today after practice. We take trips—that Amtrak trip we took together to see an art display at a gallery in Sacramento. It's partly because of Tanaka Sensei, because *her* culture from her teachers is that you share your life. Meaning socially. I think that is another thing that will sustain women.

I think that's what PAWMA is about too—because everybody has their own personal practice, their own personal school, and what PAWMA training camp does for us is it pulls us out of our schools to share an experience together, the practice, the problems, the politics. For four days I'm going to try some style I've never tried—try your body and try your experience with other people. That is sustaining. I think that's important. I wish that more women in Kendo would do that. Someone once said, "We should start a practice group for women." Because some things are different, and it's hard to stand up against the physical beating that happens sometimes. It's disheartening. Naginata, for me at least, my cultural experience of Naginata, addresses that and does that very skillfully—that there is something beyond just practice.

◆ ◆ ◆

It was time for Malyne and me to pick up Tanaka Sensei, who had wanted to shop near the cafe where we ate lunch. I worried that we might be late, but Malyne reassured me—"She is a formidable shopper—she has staying power. Talking. Shopping. Practice." But after reading the interview transcript, Malyne commented, "I didn't give Tanaka Sensei her due. That experience"—of seeing the two women demonstrate Naginata kata—"cemented it, but she's the reason that I persist. She's incredible. She has never turned down a practice, no matter where it is or how late—in a parking lot, if it was just one of us. Even if she's sick she shows up."

Malyne spoke further about the sense of community she finds in Naginata. "Tanaka Sensei has worked hard to build a community," Malyne said. "I came into a community that already existed. That energy came from Sensei. She built it from scratch—that's the sense I get."

On another occasion Malyne mentioned how Tanaka Sensei explicitly set out, in a new dojo in the United States, to build a community among her students—that she spoke of building a new community as a multiyear project and, to the point indeed of rather scandalizing Malyne, relaxed the strictures of traditional dojo etiquette to make students comfortable. "The students don't call her Sensei," Malyne said. "They call her by her first name!" But there is no scanting on the rigors of training.

This was the culture of teaching, I remembered Malyne saying, that Tanaka Sensei had learned from her teachers in Japan, who were also women. Here, I realized, was a living strand of the women's martial arts lineage and tradition that I and others regretted the absence—or suppression—of in our own arts.

CHAPTER 15

What I Create Teaches Me

A supportive community—but for the purpose of rigorous training: This is a goal of many of the women I interviewed. In addition to communities they form in their schools, many of the women participate in two national associations of women martial artists, the Pacific Association of Women Martial Artists (PAWMA) and the National Women's Martial Arts Federation (NWMAF). Both founded in the mid-1970s, these organizations grew out of weekend camps women set up to train with other women at a time when almost all women martial artists were a minority in schools and dojos heavily dominated by sometimes hostile men. At the early women's training camps the small number of women in any one art made cross training a necessity. Today the number of women in many arts is substantial and there are many women-only and women-friendly schools around the United States; but interest in the perspectives of different arts and an ethic of joint training among women of diverse backgrounds remains strong.

In 1994 the annual three-day PAWMA training camp was held over Labor Day weekend at a camp facility in the Santa Monica Mountains. Rumbling onto a dirt road after a long day's drive from Northern California, I arrived into an unpaved parking lot overseen by several women dressed in skimpy shorts and tank tops but exhibiting a strong air of command. Laden with gear—clothes and bedding, sword and staff—I made my way on foot to check in. Now there were women everywhere, women of every conceivable age and size, all moving with a bold air of competence and self-possession. I quickly regained the heady feeling I remembered from my first camp the year before of several hundred powerful, physically active women gathered in one place. Along dusty trails shaded by dust-covered oaks, everyone greeted each other, whether we were acquainted from before or only potentially.

On the slope of a narrow arroyo I found my assigned cabin perched on stilts among the oaks. Bunk beds stood in rows between the two long walls curtained with loose screening. I chose a bottom bunk on the outside with a view of the hillside, manzanita bushes framing the smoothed rock of a dry waterfall. The weather was balmy, but everything was dry and dusty so deep into the long Southern California dry season.

More women arrived, full of bustle and excitement. I forgot my idea of a nap. With formal training and events scheduled from before breakfast until late in the evening—to say nothing of impromptu training encounters and simply visiting, making new friends, and catching up with old ones—there would be little rest for any of us for the three days and nights of the camp. Already it was time for an early dinner before the opening training session.

First we must move the tables and benches out of the dining hall—we needed the floor space for training and we could just as well eat outdoors under the canopy of oaks. As evening settled over the hills the camp staff brought out food and set up a buffet on battered formica tables. The line of campers moved briskly. My plate full, I looked around for a seat. Here were women I knew. One of them slid over to make room for me between herself and a tall, pale-haired woman in her thirties. From the next table someone leaned over to speak to this woman, addressing her as Janet. Suddenly I realized why she seemed familiar. "You're Janet Aalfs!" I exclaimed.

Janet E. Aalfs is a poet with a Master's of Fine Arts degree from Sarah Lawrence College. She is also head instructor of Valley Women's Martial Arts in western Massachusetts. I first encountered her as the writer of an extraordinarily original and intriguing story, "A Chicken's Tale in Three Voices," in which she told a story about chickens from the point of view of people who keep them for slaughter, the tree stump on which they are killed, and a chicken who flew the coop and lived to old age in freedom. Theresa Corrigan and I published the story in 1990 in our anthology on relationships between women and animals, *And a Deer's Ear, Eagle's Song and Bear's Grace,* and I became acquainted with Janet through correspondence with regard to that book. Only later did I learn she was a martial artist—and then I hoped for her participation in this book as well. I had looked forward to meeting her in person, and now that I had found her, I quite forgot my hunger and plunged into an explanation of my interest in her take on combining writing and martial arts. It was a personal quest, I told her, for me to learn the stories of those like her who had gone before me. "Why else do a book?" Janet asked, smiling. "Good books get written because you want to know something!" She pulled out her camp book with the schedule of classes and we searched out a block of time we would both be free to sit down and talk.

On the following evening came the demonstration by women representing the different arts at the camp. It was already dark when Janet climbed the steps to the stage of the small outdoor amphitheater. She wore the black and white gi of her style, the severity of the cut and color of her garments softened with wear. The woven black belt knotted at her waist had faded and frayed—I saw a measure of pride in this silent display of her years of dedication and discipline. Tall, long-necked, long-limbed, she moved lightly and easily. Against the darkness of the night and her clothing, with her pale hair and coloring, she seemed a creature more of light than substance. Yet for all the grace of her movements, she was not, I thought, what one would conventionally call graceful. Rather, in all she did, she very sparely, clearly, precisely expressed her own particular being. What she was demonstrating for us, I thought, was that phenomenon more often spoken of than actually seen in the martial arts—inner energies and realities manifesting on the outside.

Later Janet told me that written spiritual interpretations accompany both the forms she demonstrated. *Gopei sho*—Advanced Tearing Peacock form—was traditional to Shuri-ryu, the Okinawan style of Karate she studies. For a section where the peacock spreads its wings preparing to defend itself, the interpretation reads: "Through my fingertips I receive streams of energy that I will direct deep into my lower stomach, and which must flow uninterrupted throughout my entire body." She believes that every move has this kind of spiritual interpretation as well as self-defense applications, though not all have been written down and preserved.

The crane form *Tsuru no kata* is one that Janet created. Again, the moves have self-defense applications as well as words. The form opens with breaking a choke hold, followed by strikes with the edges of the hands—wings—to the sides of the opponent's neck, and then with the fingertips—wing tips—to the eyes. Or in words:

> *Palms open to night*
> *lifting, I circle*
> *the moon, drawing*
> *her light and shadow*
> *into my outspread wings.*

"I have been feeling more and more in my movement like a large wading bird such as a crane," Janet told me. "I wanted a way to practice crane moves, so I made this form in which the moves emerged from what I knew about such birds, how they protect, expand, and enjoy themselves in the world. As I explore this form more, I will probably identify other spiritual interpretations—that's how it goes. I create something, a form or a poem, and it in turn teaches me more."

This process, the relationship between physical movement and the flow of words, I told her the next day over lunch beside a dry creek bed, was precisely what I wanted to talk with her about. Janet laughed. "I will tell you how I combine martial arts with writing," she said in the storyteller's ritual tone of beginning.

JANET E. AALFS

Shuri-ryu Karate and Modern Arnis

I do an Okinawan style of Karate called Shuri-ryu—the name means "beautiful and graceful." One of the really important things about the style and why I love it is that it came from Okinawa, which is a place where women have been responsible for passing on the spiritual teachings and practices of the culture. It's clear to me that women have had a lot to do with various different martial arts, both creating them initially and developing them over time. It's very clear in

Janet Aalfs performing three movements from the Shuri-ryu Karate crane form Tsuru no kata at PAWMA

Shuri-ryu, and it becomes more clear the more I practice the forms, with the solid stances with power in the hips and lower parts of the body, which means a low center of gravity and a deep connection to the Earth. And the concentration on speed, flow, and power rather than mere brute force to defend against attackers, as well as strategy and cunning, agility and pliability, the harmony of soft and hard. I get a feeling, a physical, spiritual, mental feeling, when I do the forms—I can *feel* the women who went before me in these movements—and that feeling has become stronger over time.

Did you have an idea about this before you started, or is it something that unfolded along the way?

I probably knew about it on some level, because I was initially attracted—well, I have to back up a little. When I was fourteen I went to a self-defense class for several weeks which was taught by a man in New Bedford, Massachusetts. I kind of forgot that I had taken that course until I saw the woman who was to become one of my teachers, Wendi Dragonfire, do a performance with a few of her students. She had just started a school in North-

training camp (Olympia, Wash., August 1995).

to know change was possible.

On the other hand, I was really shy as a kid, and I still was when I started training in Karate. That whole process was a big step in finding a literal voice. I had been writing a lot from when I was a little kid—I found writing a way both to figure out what I knew and to experience myself as a presence in the world. I put words on paper and at most maybe my mother would read them or maybe I would show them to a friend. Having a literal, physical voice in the world, the bigger world, became more of a possibility when I started training in martial arts. The connection was clear to me right from the start of my training—which was in 1978, when I was twenty-one—partly because of the fact that we did these yells and I had this squeak of a sound. I always knew, just like I know now, there's something else there, something deeper, something to pay attention to—and there came a point when I finally came out with a really big sound.

It was not just about yelling, or making animal sounds, which we were also doing, but also about articulating the process of discovering the power of my voice. Knowing more about what was possible for me, I got a much stronger idea of what was possible for other people, especially women. And children. I had the feeling of wanting to be involved—in whatever way; but my skills, as they've developed, are in writing and martial arts. My work now is to use these skills to make spaces for people to be more who they are.

That's the basic, basic thing—to be more who we are. That's what I keep feeling in my own life. The beauty of the art, and the excitement, the joy when I write a poem or do a form or spar or whatever—that's making it clear to me that I am becoming more who I really am. Whatever parts are there or not there—I'm getting more of an insight into what those are.

ampton, Massachusetts. I looked at those women and thought, "They are intense! I want to do that!" And then *bing!* I remembered that I had taken that self-defense course seven years earlier.

Clearly there was something there for a long time. Some of it was seeing the violence in my family. My father was abusive, physically, mentally, emotionally—especially to my mother, but also to us kids, and I was a witness. Even though most of the people around me were totally denying the situation, as is typical, I was getting enough from my mother and from other people of, "There's something to be done here and you could do it," for me

At the point in my life where I became one of the head instructors of the school, I don't know whether I would have had the nerve to say, "I'm going to do this; I'm going to start it myself." But something said, "This needs to happen, and you're here, and you could do it. So do it." I thought, "I'm scared. How can I make this commitment? What's it going to mean in the rest of my life?" It's still scary—how do I balance the incredible amount of energy it takes to deal with people and teach here and teach there and all the organizational work and blah-blah-blah and still make the space that is required to write?

Yeah! I know I need a lot of time that's free—time that's not even threatened—and then I spend a lot of it looking like I'm not even doing much . . .

Oh my god, yeah, that's a major challenge! It's partly taking my own advice. I'm always telling people, "You gotta make space for yourself," and if *they're* going to do it, and figure out how to do it, well—it's a constant process. The more I am challenged in my life, the more difficult it is to take that space. But at the same time, the reason I take it is because I *am* being challenged by something and I want to find out more about it. I go to my writing or I go practice, and that gives me more information about what I need to do.

Do you use writing and martial arts practice for the same purposes or do you find different categories of things that you answer through one or the other?

That's an interesting question. They're both arts. And they're both information-sharing vehicles. But

there are many differences, too, and I have to be careful not to force crossovers. And they're always in different points of development in me. I try to create a balance, and it shifts. I used to think that writing had to be an internal thing—but that's shifting into martial arts, which was initially a way for me to be more external. I'm coming around to this other point of, "Where does that external come from?"

It's a back-and-forth. For instance, I do all this organizational work for the school—and then I have to ask myself, am I putting that kind of energy into sending out my writing, dealing with the publishing aspect, the business aspect? And how is writing a physical act? What do I learn about paying attention to details from movement? From language?

I'd been writing for years and years, and living very much in my head, before I started doing T'ai Chi, and then for a while I turned away from my writing. With this book I'm coming back to it, seeing that it is important for me to see the world not only from within my body and in whatever space I'm in, but also through making it into words, particularly written words. Writing has been an organization and a discipline for me, similar, I think, at least in some ways, to martial arts. But it is interesting that an early response to T'ai Chi was to not even want to deal with writing for a while. And it's still very difficult for me— sometimes words and physical movements just seem so utterly irreconcilable.

That balancing effect again. I did a workshop here yesterday—Return to the Source—where I combined martial movement exercises with segments of writing to explore sources of power and creativity and the connections between breath, spine, and voice. One of the things I was talking about is that writing is a physical activity and that a lot of times we get away from that part of it—academia really focuses *[she gestures with a slice of her hand across her throat]* on cutting off the head. We've been taught that the mind is something separate and off in the airways somewhere.

That's one thing I think that I've been conscious of since I was a kid—I was six or seven and I already knew I wanted to be a writer. But I also liked to be outside and was active physically, and I had this dilemma, which was, how am I going to sit still long enough to write? *[Laughs]* I remembered that recently, and I was laughing to myself, "Well, I fixed that!" Sometimes I fix a little too much!

It's a challenge to acknowledge how physical writing is and how important it is that the senses are engaged and that you know where you are in space—that whole thing about women taking up space, how important it is to be able to put even one word on a page. If you don't think you can take up any space, those words are going to be stuck somewhere. The physicality of writing is something I learned about from doing martial arts.

The second martial art that I do is Modern Arnis, and that's based on figure-eight movements, the symbol of infinity. It brings into the Karate more of the circular movements that are at the roots of Shuri-ryu. The weaving motion of the Arnis sticks brings in another element of connecting. Arnis is a whole system, a discipline, an art in itself. We teach it in combination with Shuri-ryu at Valley Women's Martial Arts.

I started studying Arnis because I met Remy Presas, the grand master, in 1981 or 1982. He was on the West Coast and we brought him to the school to do a seminar. When I saw what he did, I thought, "That is really cool, I'm going to do that."

I tell you, my process is totally *[Laughs]*—I see something and, "Oh!" That's how things happen. I'm not the kind of person who follows a prearranged plan.

So you weren't looking for something to fill a gap—you were happy with what you were doing and Arnis just appeared?

Just appeared, yeah. Which has happened a lot. Mostly I appreciate it, even though sometimes I might want to have more control, because it feels like, "Okay, I must be doing what I'm supposed to be doing because there's something here that just appeared." Where did it come from? I don't know, but it must have come from me or I wouldn't be noticing it.

The other thing I want to underscore is self-defense—the practical self-defense applications for women and children. And how that is a real educational tool, a political tool. We do workshops all over the place, with all different organizations, who probably wouldn't come anywhere near anything that said "feminist" or the kind of basically radical concepts that are in women's self-defense as it has developed. So to go to these places and be working this stuff with people and see them soak it in and put it back out!

It starts with, "I don't feel safe walking in the street at night," and then we get into, "The greatest percentage of violence happens in the home, with men assaulting women they know," and then it's, "Well, why is this?" and "What's the situation we're in here?" I'm happy doing this work because I feel like I have a lot to share. I've also learned an incredible amount from people who don't have any formal self-defense training, but their survival skills are incredible. I've heard the most amazing stories. And that of course feeds my own sense of what's possible. Then I go around and share what I've learned to some other group, and they say, "Oh, really?" Sometimes I think, "Well, of course. It's common sense." But it's not "of course." It's taken all these years for me to learn what I know, and it's going to take a lot more years to learn something more.

So the self-defense gives you a sense of the martial art being larger or more serious— it's not just a sport or an individual inquiry into whatever you're personally interested in, but grounded in this immediacy of practical survival?

Yeah. It also gets across the concept of prevention. That word is almost a negative word—horrible things happen and then you try to prevent them. Maybe there's another word that would be better—creating, creating a space, creating an imagination, creating a desire for something to be different than it is. Self-defense and martial arts are different, self-defense being more short term and martial arts more of an ongoing study; but I feel that by not separating them it's possible to practice in a way that creates more imagination, to believe, "Oh, I could live in a world where I could be a whole person!"

What a radical concept! And it is constantly reinforced in this work. We make these different categories, but when you connect them, what comes through for me is that it's possible to be a whole being. It's also *im*possible in this culture and in this world right now, so I'm faced with this very big paradox of doing something that I know on the one hand is impossible, but that I totally believe with my whole being is possible. *[Laughs]* You know? At times I feel *boom!* I could do anything! Of course I have to come back to the prac-

tical aspects, and there are limitations on the physical body. But I have a constant sense that there *is* a larger picture, though so many people get stuck, get isolated.

Women are incredibly isolated. The media isolates us. It makes us think if you get attacked you're going to get killed or you're going to be seriously maimed—that's all we hear in the reports, right? But it's not true. It's to keep us living in fear. You start spreading around stories that say women can do this, we can protect ourselves, we *do* do this, and you get a whole different sense of what's possible. Sharing this kind of information—it has to happen. It has to! That gets back to the writing again. In my poetry I include this information, it's all part of it—this is my life, this is what I know, this is what I've been given, and so—here. Here.

I feel it's the least I can do to give back something to this world. I have difficulties, but I feel I've been given a lot. Sometimes I'm doing a form outside just by myself, by the trees or whatever, and I have such a strong sense of, "Here, I'm giving this back to you. You gave it to me, I'm giving it back."

I feel it with my students, too—appreciation that they could take the risks to do something that's very, very difficult. I received a lot in my training, and I continue to. Like I said, I feel lucky to have that chance, to have a place to do it and to be creating that place, as in the school. And we do a lot of networking in the area with battered women's shelters, women's centers, schools, and other community organizations. Over time the network's grown and more people know that martial arts isn't just this thing that happens in some little corner store somewhere, you know, sign hung out on the front, "Oh, yeah, people go there and take classes, but it's not really anything." There's more of a sense of, "If we could do more of this then maybe we would have less women to have to patch up in the battered women's shelters."

It's now been—what, more than fifteen years that you've been doing all this? And in the same place? The school where you teach is also where you studied?

It's changed a lot, it's moved to different places, but it's the school that my teacher, Wendi Dragonfire, started in 1977. She moved to open another school and Beth Holt and I, who were new black belts at the time, took it on.

You often talk and write about the generations of women that you have at your school and that lineage.

That lineage, yeah, that's something! I started my training with a woman, I went through the whole process to black belt and beyond with this woman, I had—have—the chance to be in a position of promoting students to black belt, and then I have these black belt students who have their own students. I get this great perspective of what I went through in my training and how it's different now for students and how it's different for even newer students.

I can't say, "I had to do this when I was training so you have to do it too." I can't get into that one. I ask how is it different for me to have had the opportunity to train with a woman than it was for my teacher, who was in a male environment and had a lot of problems from that? How is it different for students of mine? What are the challenges for them now? What do they need more of?

I'll tell you what I do see is we're getting away from that concept of "pain is gain," and getting at that it's possible to go for joy, go for caring about each other. It's something that these women's train-ing camps have generated and encouraged—compassion. That's a strength women have, why not keep building it? Here we are, we care about each other, we respect each other, let's figure out how we can help each other grow.

I see real progress in that. It's no longer, "These men squash me down, and now I'm going to prove that I'm as good as they are." It's getting far beyond that, not for everybody, but for a lot of women. Now it's, "I don't have to prove myself, but I can feel challenged and feel that I'm being taken seriously."

Perhaps there's now enough women, and enough generations, that we can afford more space for individual variation? Maybe it doesn't even matter what the varieties are but just that there get to *be* varieties and we get to work with them and they develop and do whatever they do and go off here and there? That seems to me a luxury the early generations of women who did this may not have had.

I think that's true. There's more confidence in general and not feeling so pressed all the time to be some one thing that a martial artist is, that is, a male martial artist. *[Laughs]* What a concept—"I could be myself!"

And not just *a* female martial artist—now we have ten thousand female martial artists. Just look at language in general— men often write about "the martial artist" or whatever, in the singular. Whereas feminist writers in all fields use the plural. We're not having just one mold the way

there was this one male mold—or it seemed like that to women. Maybe men thought there were differences.

And of course there are. But I'll tell you—before I came to camp, I was talking with some male martial artists who were saying, "How come *we* don't have a training camp like you women have?" They talked about going to martial arts conferences and men are like killing each other. Political battles all the time. They're all at each other's throats. And I'm saying, "It's not like there're not problems among women." But there is this basic level of respect. When there's a problem, there's a possibility for it to get worked through. This guy was saying, "You totally have it over the men. These men can't handle somebody else being good." That little ego thing. It's a big snag! *[Laughs]*

You don't teach men at all in your school?

We have special events sometimes, workshops. There're a couple of other schools in the area that are mixed that have come to our school. I go to Arnis training conferences, which are mixed—way more men than women. At this point I have not so much tolerance for some of this stuff that goes on, but it also helps to keep giving me a perspective. I see some progress with men. There are plenty of them that still can't handle anybody else being good, but there are those who are trying to get it, really trying to understand what it is like for women—not that I enjoy getting into that much of an explanation, but I appreciate when some man at least makes an effort to want to know what it's like.

But you think it's important to keep a women's space for training?

I think it's extremely important. This issue comes up a lot, not just in martial arts, but also, for instance, in universities and colleges—you know, this move to make all of them co-ed. I live in a town that has two women's colleges, two of the very few that are left, and I get messages from here and there about why those places are so important and how women have been able to excel, really excel, in an environment with other women. So I don't have any question about the merit of that. When someone says, "How can you be any good if you train with women?" I think, "I guess that about says it" *[laughs]* "what you think of women. We have no more to discuss."

One woman I talked to teaches some women-only classes, but her school is co-ed, and it's more men than women, because there just are more men than women that have money and time and whatnot. She thinks it's important for the women to be able to train in the mixed classes because she thinks they need to learn to deal with men's energy—that if they stay out of that situation out of fear, they're missing something that they could learn.

That may be progress for women who are in a situation where they don't have any other idea of how something could be than that it's mixed, and not only mixed, but that there's more men. I will tell you that over time, over years and years, women who train at our school—and I know this is true at other women's schools also—who then go to events where there are men, do really well. The biggest problem is, "I can't believe these guys aren't taking me seriously." To me that's progress—to be shocked that someone would not take you seriously.

What happens a lot in mixed situations is that certain women can excel and they can be the exception. That's what happened to my teacher: She did really well, she was highly skilled and they recognized it, but she was the exception, and in the end she was more or less ousted. Also for being a lesbian—they could not handle that at all. I think a lot of that attitude toward women's environments is homophobia.

It is also fear of women's power in general, basically saying, "Oh my god, maybe women don't really need us, who-a-a, scary-y-y," right? Which isn't true. This world is not going to go anywhere if we don't work together. It's not like this is a totally separate thing. It's saying, These are places for us to recognize who we are underneath the lies we've been told, places where we can challenge each other to become more whole. I believe that in a women's space our strengths come through in a way that they won't when we're constantly having to question our worth and ask, "Am I responding to this person because he's a man?"

But let's face it, women are all different ways, *all* different ways. Some women and children participate in our programs and enjoy them and learn from them. For others it's not the right thing. So it's a women's thing, but it's also something about the respect and compassion and ability to be open that women tend to have more right now in the world—I do believe that that's what's being developed and it is women who are developing it. There are men who are developing compassion, but not enough at this point—especially not in martial arts. It's a power issue, and the power needs to shift a lot before we have anything close to egalitarian.

But just seeing that it's possible! A woman comes into a women's school and sees all these women who've been training for years and has no question that it's possible. And now there's

PAWMA and NWMAF and all the other women's organizations that are springing up here and there, or have been going forever, but we're starting to hear about each other—and women who've been training and teaching for thirty, forty, fifty, sixty, however many years. That's worth writing about! *[Laughs]* To bring in the writing again.

And we better write about it!

We better is right! The more that's written down, the more women are going to be able to find out, "This happened and this was possible." Like when I stumbled on a book about women in Okinawa, the *noros,* shamanic women who were responsible for making the ties for their people between the human and spirit worlds. Their power instruments were the bow, spear, sword, bamboo wand, and branch—that says a lot right there!

We get plenty of information about this master who's a man and that master who's a man. We have this big book, the *Pinnacle of Karate,* written by Robert A. Trias, the grand master of our style, who died a few years ago. In the original version there was *nothing* about these women in Okinawa. That's not even where I heard about it first. Now in the new edition there's a small paragraph—I'm not kidding—maybe ten lines about these women. I thought, "It's a miracle that there's even that much," and then, "Wait a second! Where is all the rest of it?"

Have you been trying to research that further?

It's an ongoing project. I'm in the process of collecting more information to put in a book. It'll be about my own experience and about how women have contributed to the development of martial arts. I don't know what shape it's going to take, but it's in there somewhere.

That certainly extends your lineage way beyond your school! Some of the other women I've talked with, who trained with men and then became teachers, talked about how they had to renegotiate what they learned in order to teach—that there were aspects of what they learned that they found they couldn't comfortably teach and perpetuate. It was a struggle for them in a way that I've never heard any men say they had to struggle. With your lineage, did you avoid that whole question?

Actually, I believe it's necessary to translate no matter what. I think when women have had to translate in order to learn from men, it's been more of a survival thing: "I will not be able to go on if I don't translate this." But to me that should already be part of the process, that should be encouraged—that it's not only possible to translate, but it's essential to translate, because every person is different, has a different body, has a different way of learning, a different way of perceiving things. So instead of looking at it as something that I *have* to do, I look at it as, "Oh, of course." It's a given that part of my training is learning how to translate—it's a gift even. I think that's something that I've learned from women—that it's important for a teacher to say, "I'm telling you this, this is my way of seeing it, this is my way of knowing it, you're going to find your own way."

What is *your* way? How much of your own practice is with other women, or other people—students, teachers, partners—and how much by yourself?

I think I wouldn't be happy with something that was totally one way or the other. To me it's important to have a balance, to have parts that I can practice on my own, that are about a kind of meditation or personal development, and then parts that have to do with working with other people—teaching, learning from other people, the social aspect.

There is also the aspect of how my ability to be anywhere has opened up. That's an individual thing too. I can be somewhere now and see more. That comes from practicing martial arts and from being a poet. It's something that I experience in myself, though it extends to the rest of the world. Part of the reason that I feel that connection is because of the exchange with other people and learning more and more how to be open as well as to protect myself.

You know, the more I know how to protect myself, the more I know when to be open or when to pull back. That's a skill, a survival skill, that I use every single day, every single moment, that has clearly come from training in martial arts and self-defense. People typically ask, "Have you ever had to use any of this stuff?" and I say, "Every day." They of course picture something like *[demonstrates a punch]*, and then I explain that I wouldn't be doing anything I'm doing now if I wasn't training. I'd be doing something, but I truly believe that I would not have the sense of fullness that I have, fullness and openness.

And do animals as well as other people enter into this? I'm thinking of your story,

"A Chicken's Tale in Three Voices," that Theresa and I included in our anthology on relationships between animals and women. Does your martial arts practice influence your relationships with other species?

Oh, yeah! Friday night, when we were doing the Lian gong exercises with Wen Mei Yu, I was opening my arms out like this, and an owl flew by. I said, "Hi!" *[Laughs]* Things like that of course could happen any time. I didn't have to have my arms out like that for the owl to fly by—but it did happen just at that moment and that made it a special connection.

I have developed a greater sense that I *am* an animal. I have that sense of the other, which is me, and I am the other—with people, with animals, with trees. I can feel myself in that other being's place. It's about imagination. All of this is about imagining oneself in other places.

It's not like these capacities wouldn't be there necessarily, but I feel they're more developed and I have more of a sense of what the connections are and what the power is that it's possible to exchange between all different kinds of beings. So again, connection, how important it is to feel connection—for this world to survive! Besides it's fun! I have a blast doing different kinds of animal forms, and learning animal forms from other martial arts. The movements are beautiful. It's inspiring. . . .

◆ ◆ ◆

We paused, each taking breath seemingly for the first time in what must have been more than an hour. "Well," I said, "I'll just take a look at my list of questions." Janet laughed. "See where we've been flying here." It *was* like flying. But now we had landed. A group of women crossed the clearing behind us, striding proudly, laughing and calling in high, strong voices. Awareness of the rest-less energy of two hundred and forty women glorying in our physical prowess flooded over me anew—and over Janet too, I think. "Good questions," Janet was saying, "Really good questions. And I'm very, very excited that you're doing this project." She leaned over to hug me. "I think I'm going to go check out the sparring scene and see what's happening down there. . . ."

"Yes, of course," I said, hugging her back. Make a note, I told myself, this is important too, that one moment her attention can run passionately and lucidly upon analyzing political implications of her martial arts practice and teaching and the next moment she is flushed with eagerness and excitement to get away into action—that a grown woman can feel the freedom to find play in fighting, even as she dedicates herself to fighting in earnest, or as she herself has put it, doing all that she does full open.

Full Open

Survival has a body
big as the sun.
She shatters
the smoke blue shell
of twilight, wanting me
to remember first
sound of wind,
bird, shadow of tree
on snow, to speak
the way they speak
interrupting. Her voice
explodes inside me, gold
needles from every pore.
And though it hurts
to breathe full
open in her light,
bold is the way
she chooses me.
                    —Janet E. Aalfs

CHAPTER 16

A Chinese Master

Michelle Dwyer initially inspired my interest in sword practice, but I received my first formative instruction at the 1993 PAWMA training camp from Wen Mei Yu, a Chinese master of Taijiquan and Qigong (she prefers the pinyin romanizations to the older "T'ai Chi Ch'uan" and "Ch'i Kung" that remain widespread in U.S. martial arts writing).[1] I looked forward to studying with her again at the 1994 camp. Indeed, her teaching has come to permeate my practice, and she is a model and mentor to quite a few of the women I have talked to. A story Karlon Kepcke told me is typical of their responses.

Several years ago Karlon attended an all-women martial arts tournament in Los Angeles, bringing a group of capoeiristas to perform at a benefit the night before. "We had never been to a tournament, and so it was very interesting watching the different events," Karlon said. "It was in a conference room in a hotel, so it didn't look like a gymnasium, but maybe about that size, with a funny carpet. I saw this woman stand up and start to walk across the room—she must have been one of the judges. I remember looking at her and going, 'Wow!' You know, being really taken by just her standing up and walking across the room. She had a whistle around her neck and was dressed in—oh, tennis shoes and sweatpants and a shirt or something.

---

1. See *Note on spelling names and terms* in the Glossary.

"'There's something there'—that's what clicked in my mind. 'This is a master.' I felt inspired by the presence of all of that just in her walking across the floor—that she had all that with her at every moment, with no fragmentation."

The woman was Wen Mei Yu. Karlon encountered her again when both of them were in British Columbia to teach at the Women's Festival of Martial Arts. "That Friday night, we talked about our classes and also did a short demonstration," Karlon said. "Master Yu started to demonstrate one of the forms she was going to teach, and what's interesting is—well, the energy in this room was a bunch of women seeing each other for the first time since last year—very chatty, very excited. We had just watched a woman do this wrestling with a live blade—really exciting. It wasn't a context of we're going to watch a demonstration and get all quiet and settled and ready for the next thing. Then Master Yu starts to do her form.

"In one breath, she centered the whole room, because she was centering herself. Everybody was transformed. It went from totally chatty girl talk, kissing each other happy energy, to completely centered and focused like we were all doing the form. She did about three moves of the form and then said, 'Thank you' and 'I hope to see you in class,' and it was like we all got a healing. Did she get this just from practice? I thought. Or what's this esoteric thing? And then I thought, well, of course, it's practice. *But—*"

But what? That was, in essence, my question if I got a chance to talk to Wen Mei Yu at camp. Given the tight schedule of classes and other activities, it seemed an imposition to ask her to make time for an interview, but she was willing to sit down with me immediately. Then she recollected other commitments she had already made. Yet she wanted to accommodate me as well. "Perhaps tonight?" she said. "After the shiai?" "Oh, yes!" I

said. "Thank you!"

The shiai, or tournament, was an innovation introduced by that year's camp organizers. It was to include competition in forms, with separate divisions for internal and external styles, and sparring. Wen Mei Yu, together with Michelle Dwyer and several other women with many years' experience, served as judges for the internal-style forms division. As I walked into the hall where the competition was held—it was the former dining hall from which we had removed the tables—Karlon Kepcke stood at one end of the row of judges with a stopwatch in one hand, waiting for the next contestant to signal she was ready.

One of Sandy Wong's fellow Wing Chun practitioners stood in the ring outlined with colored tape on the linoleum floor. She performed a training form in the pigeon-toed horse stance of her style—feet wide, toes turned in, knees only a fist's width apart. With her back inclining slightly backward she seemed to look down her nose at the hand movements she made with machinelike precision, extending an open palm along the centerline from her chest, turning the wrist, coiling the fingers to a fist, pulling back to the waist. She moved her body to this side or that by sliding her feet in the pattern of parallelograms that is so effective at getting into a new position with one's feet firmly beneath one. She came to an end and bowed to the judges, who held a brief discussion among themselves and then called out numerical scores one by one. The numbers were recorded and averaged and the result announced while the contestant waited at attention. After receiving her score she bowed again and made way for the next contestant.

A student of Michelle's performed a sword form. Other women performed fast, flashy Kung Fu sets, with and without weapons. My friend Margy Emerson performed a portion of her Wu-style T'ai Chi Ch'uan; even at a pace faster than normal practice speed, her performance was a pool of calm on our side of the room. Across the room the crowd intensified around a second ring, where the external-style forms competition was under way.

Master Yu and the other judges rose to award prizes for the internal styles, medals embossed with the Women Warriors Reclaiming Strength motto and logo of the camp and hung on violet ribbons. Then the quiet formality of the internal-style competition was swept away on a flood of sparring contestants taking over the space in their bright-colored protective gear, helmets and mouth guards and padding for chest, shins, hands, and feet. Throwing mock punches and kicks, they shouted challenges at each other. Across the room Master Yu waved to me—she would be with me in a moment.

And so she was. We briefly conferred. The noise and energy of several hundred feverishly excited women coiled around us, reflected and intensified by the low ceiling of the room. There would be no talking here! We agreed to try the administration building—there was a sitting room there.

As we passed the open-air eating area, the ranks of empty tables deeply shadowed in the darkness under silent oak trees, the noise of the shiai dwindled behind us, but the air still seemed to pulse with unusual energy. I felt myself uncentered by the driving energy and physicality of the camp, rising now to a crescendo with the shiai. I told myself to breathe, to relax. I was whatever I was—if I was nervous and uncentered, so be it. My method of interviewing did not depend on the quickness or cleverness of particular questions but rather the open, questioning self that I brought to listen to the women I talked to. *I* was the question I asked them to respond to. If on this occasion I felt stripped of familiar contexts and supports, perhaps, for interviewing the woman walking softly and calmly at my side, my condition was appropriate.

In the administration building I pushed open the door of the sitting room and discovered a woman lying on a couch. A pair of crutches leaned against the end of the couch near her head. "Oh!" I stopped short. "It's all right," Master Yu said. "We won't be that noisy." She crossed to an armchair on the other side of the room, her lithe, graceful movements and bearing belying her nearly sixty years. Every time I have seen her, she has had a bloom of health, set off by her direct gaze and a charming smile. "I'll give you a magazine that has the story about my background," she told me.[2] "Many things I already have repeated and repeated—the information is all there."

Wen Mei Yu—she puts her family name last in the Western manner—was born in Shanghai in 1936, on the eve of the Japanese occupation and World War II. During her school years she was interested in Western-style sports like basketball and Ping-Pong as well as dance. She recalls thinking Taiji was too slow—that it was "hard to concentrate" on something so slow. But already in her early teens she was beset by the health problems that eventually led her to Taiji practice. At age seventeen she was diagnosed with a bleeding ulcer. "My stomach was in constant pain," she reports.[3] When medical treatment proved ineffective, her family and friends urged her to try the healing exercise of Qigong. She learned some of the simpler movements and relaxation techniques

2. Gareth Smith, "A Tai Chi Master Among Tai Chi Masters," *Masters of Kung Fu* (December 1993, Vol. 1, No. 7), 70–76.

3. Wen Mei Yu and G. A. Sharp, "Master Yu's Healing Journey of Personal Power," *Women Warriors Reclaiming Strength* (Camp book, Pacific Association of Women Martial Artists 17th Annual Women's Training Weekend, September 2–5, 1994), 28.

and after three months' practice felt much better. "However, I didn't continue, and my problems returned. I lost much weight, had stomach pain constantly, high blood pressure, my pulse was fast, and I was very uncomfortable—I was in a lot of trouble," she concludes. In fact, she was close to death, and Western medicines that she took at this point only made her more ill.

"That is when I made the personal commitment to practice daily," she says now. "Making up your mind to overcome your personal obstacles and commit to healing yourself and taking control of your own life requires that you believe in yourself and believe that no matter what, you will succeed—whether you stand alone or with others. Standing alone is never easy," she adds—but she found she could do it.

For a while she trained in a local park with the people who practiced there. At nineteen she began systematic study of Qigong and Taiji at the Shanghai Wushu Association, learning old and new open hands Taiji forms as well as weapons forms with both the curved, single-edged saber, which the Chinese call a knife, and the double-edged straight sword. After a year or so she was asked to serve as a coach for the Shanghai Physical Culture Association for the Elderly. Although she did not believe she had yet learned the material well enough to teach it, at that time—the late 1950s—there was a great demand for teachers of the Twenty-Four Taiji form, developed in 1956 as a synthesis of older, longer systems. She agreed to teach, training ever harder herself as well as reading books to prepare herself. During the years of the Cultural Revolution (1966–1974) it was forbidden to maintain contact with any martial or cultural arts association, but later she resumed her connection with the Shanghai Physical Culture Association for the Elderly, serving as secretary until she left China in 1987.

About the Cultural Revolution she has written, "The Red Guard occupied my house one time for a nine-day period. During that time they took everything of value from me, including my silverware and my personal jewelry. Most people say they would fight or rebel to the death under such circumstances, and believe me, there were people who did just that. However, I practiced remaining calm as I had learned in my Taiji and Qigong training. I practiced standing meditation when soldiers forced me to stand by my own dinner table after my twelve-hour workday to wait on their every whim. At all times I remained calm, not smiling nor frowning on the outside, but smiling on the inside and remaining strong inside. Otherwise it is hard to imagine what would have happened to me under those circumstances in those times. Taijiquan and Qigong practice were forbidden in any public places, including the parks. However, no one can stop you from practicing within yourself, and it was in those times I learned real in-depth internal training."[4]

After the Cultural Revolution she resumed studies of three of the major styles of Taiji—the Yang, Wu, and Chen styles—working with grand masters, both women and men, who had themselves studied with the famed nineteenth-century originators of the modern forms of these styles. She also pursued advanced studies in Qigong and other healing methods, including *tui na,* traditional Chinese massage and acupressure. Later she learned Lian gong, the health exercises Janet Aalfs and others have mentioned. Lian gong is a modern synthesis of traditional Chinese exercise

---

4. Wen Mei Yu and G. A. Sharp, "Wen Mei Yu's Power of Grace," *Women Warriors Reclaiming Strength* (Camp book, Pacific Association of Women Martial Artists 17th Annual Women's Training Weekend, September 2–5, 1994), 28.

therapies, consisting of a series of thirty-six exercises for relieving stress and strengthening the joints, ligaments, connective tissue, and internal organs. Wen Mei Yu taught Lian gong widely in China, as she also does now in the United States. When I studied with her, she urged the class to perform the movements in unison, holding up to us as example a group of many thousands she had led in China for a demonstration film—all the thousands of people performing the exercise sequence as one person. I have made these exercises part of my morning routine before I sit down at my desk to work, and I credit them with freeing me of the back and shoulder pain and stiffness I used to experience from long hours of desk work.

In China, throughout the late 1970s and the 1980s, Wen Mei Yu continued to teach Taiji and also competed, placing first in most of the tournaments she entered. In 1983 she was named the top Taiji teacher in China. The following year she was appointed professor of Qigong at the Jin Wu Athletic College in northern Shanghai, the oldest public Kung Fu institution in China. She also served as a Taijiquan and Qigong coach at the college, and students came to her for coaching from all over the world.

In 1987 she came to the United States, where she settled in the Los Angeles area. Besides teaching Taiji and Qigong, she works tirelessly to publicize the history, study, and benefits of Chinese martial arts. She has published many interviews with Chinese masters in U.S. magazines and arranged exchange visits between the United States and China. In 1993 she received the National Women's Martial Arts Federation's Award of Excellence and she has twice been named to *Inside Kung Fu* magazine's Hall of Fame.

When I first met and studied with Wen Mei Yu, I remember feeling as if I learned from her without effort. In her Taiji sword workshop, in-

PHOTO COURTESY WEN MEI YU

Wen Mei Yu demostrating Taiji sword.

stead of the two or three moves I might ordinarily have taken in at a single session, my companions and I grasped at least the rudiments of some twenty-four movements—nearly half the form. We practiced the moves on our own in free moments in camp and stopped several times on our drive home to go over what we knew, flourishing our shining new chrome-bladed, betasseled Chinese practice swords to the bemusement of other travelers—and the delight of several small boys—at highway rest stops.

All in all, I was extraordinarily inspired in my sword practice. Initially I supposed it was the fascination of the weapon itself—and certainly, the long blade glinting in sunlight draws me powerfully—but I came to see I was influenced above all by Master Yu herself. At the 1994 training camp I noted more carefully the clarity and fluidity of her movements when she demonstrated the forms, the preciseness of her spoken instruction, her way of talking and listening, even her manner of walking. It is not calmness, exactly, although she is calming to be around. Rather, in all she does, Wen Mei Yu seems to reflect the pool of her own special being, contained and unassertive, yet open and overflowing in gentle, generous ways toward others.

"Something like calmness . . . contained but overflowing." As I search for words I realize the qualities I am trying to describe are precisely those the Taiji classics talk about—nothing you can put your finger on or attach a word to, yet you feel it as clearly as wind or water flowing. *This* is what martial arts mastery consists in. It is not about physical domination or indeed in any way imposing oneself upon anyone else but rather about inspiring others to follow—as an attacker is sucked into an irresistible defense or a student seeks to incorporate such qualities in her own being.

WEN MEI YU

Taijiquan and Qigong

How did you decide to leave China and come here?

Several reasons. One is I got an award in 1983—I was recognized as the top Taiji master in China. The government told us, "You'll get a chance to go to another country to visit or to teach." I was very excited. I got one chance, but it fell through. Two times this happened, and I still did not go anywhere. That made me feel very upset.

So I said, "I will try to find some chance just by myself to go somewhere." It just happened to be the United States. The president of an international Kung Fu federation invited me to come to the United States, and he wanted me to stay to teach.

Later he used me—I would teach and not get any pay. He would say I shouldn't go anywhere, just stay with him and he would give me food and a place to stay. Some friends told me, "You have to find a real job. If you find a job, you can live

fine. If you stay here, there's no future, and also you don't have any money."

So that's why I found another job. I took care of an older woman who had had a stroke. She had difficulty moving her foot. I did some massage, some exercise, and tried to help her. On the weekends I practiced in the park. Some people walking by said, "Hey, your form is really good. Do you teach?" I said, "Yeah, I teach." I taught them for free. So I had little money. Later, at the encouragement of my close students, I charged money for lessons. Then I quit the job and now I just teach—since 1988, teach, teach, teach, all the time.

And you're happy with this?

Yeah! I get a lot of students. *[Laughs]* The same thing happened in China, when I walk in the street, many people say "Hi!" but I cannot remember their names; there's too many. At first I stayed in the

Los Angeles area, but now I teach workshops all over, all across the country. So I meet more people, more and more people. Also at the women's camps, I meet a lot of different people every year.

I joined PAWMA in 1992. In 1993, I taught at Special Training—the National Women's Martial Arts Federation in Long Island. Then in Canada at the women's martial arts festival—this was the second year. So I went to Canada twice, Special Training, twice, and PAWMA, this is the third year. Also this year I went to Holland, the FIST, the international women's training camp. I went there to teach. I also give a lot of workshops—more and more people want to arrange workshops.

Mostly it's Taiji and Qigong. They're getting more popular—people understand more about what they are now. In the beginning they asked what it is. Now nobody asks this question. People know. They just don't know how—some know how to practice, but some are not really practicing well because they don't have good teachers. My opinion is, if you want to develop very good Chinese martial arts in the United States—or different kinds of martial arts, but mostly I focus on the internal martial arts—I think you need to follow the principles of good teaching. Just step-by-step and teach people solid, consistent basics.

What do you include as the basics?

Strong basics are solid and consistent stances, movements, and hand positions. Also harmonizing hands and feet, wrists and ankles, elbows and knees, eyes and spirit, mind with will, internal with external energy, upper portion of the body with lower. The waist masters all the limbs. Tightness in any joint or limb is let go in order that the spine, waist, and hips can move the limbs with precision and power.

If you get strong basics, every style is learnable. My focus in my teaching is to spread one or two forms, like now I try to spread Lian gong, because it's really helped people get benefits. If anyone wants a workshop, I suggest Lian gong. If in one workshop we cannot finish the Lian gong Series One and Series Two, I just teach Series One. Then next time, if I go there, I teach Series Two. Or Wu-style Taijiquan—in one workshop maybe finish Sections One and Two and the next time finish Three, Four, and a third time finish Five, Six. Divide it into a few workshops and finish the whole set. People like this kind of workshop because there's a lot of follow-up. So it's going well.

How do you feel about these Chinese arts being translated into the U.S. context? Without a background in Chinese culture, how well do you think Americans are learning?

I feel some Americans learn very well. Some not very well, but their heart is pure. Some people do not really understand very well, but they already teach. I don't think this is responsible. Because my opinion is if you want to teach students, first of all you have to understand the form and basics very well. If you're still studying and you teach other people—it's not right. If you teach the form wrong, or teach the basics of a system wrong, then the student's practicing the wrong way, and that's very hard to change or correct.

For me—I don't say any person, just for me— if a form is not one hundred percent clear in my mind, and if I don't fully understand it, I never teach people. I feel I have a lot of responsibility for the students.

Concerning the need to understand Chinese

culture, there is some truth in it, but mostly it's a language thing. If I were interviewing you, and you were speaking broken Chinese, like I am in English, I would try my best to understand you and speak the essence of your language in the best Chinese that would better help Chinese people understand what you were saying. Many people in America feel natural is as things are and appear, but there is a lot beneath the surface which language—language of the heart—can reach honestly, truthfully, and deeply. So there is a language barrier that separates people, but a language of the heart that moves beyond the barriers. This takes time to learn. However, as an interviewer and writer in both English and Chinese, I feel I have the responsibility to help the person express herself or himself. For students, language of the heart is important to understand. Listening in the beginning is the best way to start learning.

The students here mostly are very good, and their study is good, but they come and go. It's not like people in China, who continue and are dedicated. I have a lot of students—I cannot count them all. But those who stay are not really very many. Some come, some go away. Some come again, some stay away. I think it is maybe the job changes or the home moves—things happen more rapidly and continuously here in America.

And are you happy here? Do you miss China? It must be a big change.

I'm happy. From my heart I sometimes want to go back to see my older students more, but I feel I have not yet done enough here. I want to work more and let more people enjoy Taiji and Qigong to get good health and long life. So I think my work is still not done here. What I do now is some-times take students to China for training. When I go back to China, I don't teach, because I don't have time. I just take care of the students and visit my teachers, family, and friends.

This year, 1994, in April and May in China there were two big events. One was the Yang-style Yongnian Association—they celebrated their fiftieth anniversary. And the second big event was the Second World Wushu Festival. I brought nine people, and they demonstrated and competed, and we won eight gold medals, three silver medals, and two bronze medals. So they were happy! This made them feel good, because they worked hard, they practiced hard, and they got results. I don't know if they got all they wanted. Unfortunately people who go to China for the first time make extreme demands. China's ways are very different from America's ways. However, I feel they got what they needed.

How do you feel about competition in the United States?

I think now in the United States the competition is fine. The problem is not having good judging. Because if you're judging the internal martial arts, you have to have experience in them. But sometimes in the tournaments, some of the judges are practitioners of external arts. I don't know how they can judge internal. They just look at whether you kick high or have the lowest posture, and give you the high score. But in internal martial arts you have to follow the principles, the internal principles. Yeah, you kick high or you have low posture, they give you good score, that's fine, but if you go against the internal principle and you get the high score, that's not right. You are fooling yourself. What you are practicing is a dance at best, not a martial art or an art that will really build up your health.

So I think for judging in the United States there are not yet enough good judges. Also now a lot of people are interested in internal arts. It's coming more into fashion. Everybody is looking for an internal teacher. So some external teachers just teach the internal. I'm not saying they are bad. It's what I said before—if you don't exactly understand what you teach, you teach the student the wrong way. That's my opinion.

What about the Push Hands competitions?

Push Hands is the same—just this afternoon we were talking about Push Hands in class, Push Hands and wrestling—push–push–push! It's not right! Everybody knows it's not right, but still it happens. Maybe it will take time. There are some good Push Hands; I saw some from New York— really good Push Hands, very soft, really using the Taiji tactic. It was very good.

How is it in China?

In China sometimes competitions have this kind of wrestling. But better than here. Better than here because of the many years of experience culturally and socially.[5]

How do you feel Push Hands interrelates with forms—do you do the Push Hands to help the form? Or do you do the form to help the Push Hands?

Both. If you push hands without studying forms, you don't understand and you cannot push hands very well. If you only practice forms, and no Push Hands, your form has no use. So you have to have Push Hands and the form combined together. Push Hands can help your form, and form can help your Push Hands. So both, I think.

Have you studied other martial arts?

No. Focusing my energy on Taiji I think is enough, enough, enough for me. I teach several different styles of Taiji and many different Qigong methods. Also I have the health exercise, the healing exercise, so it's about twenty-five internal forms, including weapons. That's something.

It is! With all of this, do you have time for your own practice?

It's my feeling that teaching and practicing are totally different. Your practice builds up your health. Teaching is spending your energy. Some people think teaching is the exercise. I don't think that's right. Teaching, you have to spend a lot of energy, because you talk a lot, and you repeat and

---

5. Elsewhere Wen Mei Yu has written that in China people practice Taiji for health rather than fighting. In China, she says, the thinking is, "If I can get healthy, I can get everything" instead of "If I can beat you I am great." She herself practiced some Push Hands in China, but until recently women did not practice self-defense with men—men didn't want to teach women fighting techniques, although they would teach them forms, and women generally could practice Push Hands only with other women. Wen Mei Yu, "Basic Points Build Health and Internal Energy," *T'ai Chi* (April 1992, Vol. 16, No. 2), 2–5.

repeat and repeat. You might think through teaching to get more energy. It doesn't happen, in my experience. I teach to teach. I practice to practice, separately.

Mornings I always leave free, no class in the early morning. I get up very early, about five-thirty, six o'clock at the latest, and I practice for an hour, sometimes an hour and fifteen minutes. Then sometimes in the evening, if there's no class, I relax a while and I practice another half hour, something like that. This is to get my energy back. Otherwise I always spend energy to teach, I never get energy back and cannot build up my health, and later maybe I will die *[laughs]*—because of too many classes.

Usually I have private classes all the time: eight o'clock to ten, one class; and one to three; and three to five; and seven to nine. Four classes—eight hours teaching. And sometimes no time to eat lunch or dinner—I eat very fast, eat fast food. This cannot help build up health. It's difficult—sometimes I think, too much teaching, maybe need to cut some.

When you go back to China, do you visit your teachers? Do you still study with them?

Yes! In 1987 I came to the United States, and 1990 was my first time back to China. I visited all my teachers. Since that year, almost every year I visit them once a year at least. Sometimes twice a year. Because I never can forget my teachers. If they hadn't taught me, how could I teach my students? Always I need to remember where it is I drink the first water. Another thing is all my teachers now are getting older. My oldest teacher, Ma Yueh Liang, is the son-in-law of the creator of the Wu-style slow set, Wu Jian Quan. Did you see the TV series "Healing and the Mind" [Bill Moyers's PBS series]? The old master who talked about being ninety years old—that is my teacher for the Wu style, Master Ma. He says, "It takes ten years to find out how to feel the qi, and thirty years to learn how to use the qi." He is ninety-four years old. And another teacher, Wu Jian Quan's daughter, Wu Ying Hua, is eighty-nine. Fu Zhong Wen is eighty-seven. I feel you must go back and practice, let them check on you, get some corrections.

After all these years?

Yeah, always, get more corrections. Also some forms I practiced before, but then I didn't practice for a long time, and I forget. And some forms I just pick up, so practice again. Too many forms. One day I practice, da-da-da-da, one, two, three, four. The next day practice four, five, six, seven, like that, in turn. *[Laughs]* Otherwise I will forget—and how will I teach students or develop myself?

Now I focus mostly on the Wu style. I still teach the Yang-style form, but mostly, if there's a demo, or when I practice, I choose Wu style.

You like that better now? Why is that?

I love the Wu style. It's many reasons, so it's difficult to say. Maybe the smallness—the small frame. The movements are small and slight. Your limbs never travel outside the perimeter of your shoulders—at least not often! As I was saying in class today, all the different styles have their special points, so if you learn many styles, you get more experience. And then look at all the different forms—the principle stays the same. Even the Wu

Wen Mei Yu demonstrating Retreat Step to Beat Tiger from Wu-style Taijiquan at a photo session for Inside Kung Fu *magazine (Los Angeles, Calif., Fall 1994).*

style, where you lean the body forward, but still the spine stays straight. We talked about keeping your body straight, keeping the line.

Are you still looking for new things to learn?

I really want to learn some Sun style. I learned a little bit, but I think, this year if I have the chance to go back to China, and also to Beijing, I will try to visit Sun Jian Yua. She's Sun Lu Tang's daugh-ter, the Sun-style creator's daughter, and eighty-one years old this year. She's still very healthy. I will try to visit her and learn more Sun style from her. Next year, for the PAWMA camp, I will try to bring her to the United States. I'm trying to arrange that.

I like to help the women's camps. I think women's camps are great. Not a lot of ego, all peaceful, and everybody looks like one big family. Very warm. I have a very good feeling here—any women's camp, I always get a very good feeling, Special Training and PAWMA. I love the women's events.

This year, just last month, is the first time I went to Europe, to Holland, to teach at FIST, the international training. They liked my teaching, and they said, "Come to the Netherlands next year, come again." So I said, "Good, I would like to." Sometimes traveling, you are very tired, really tired, on the plane a long time, but if your feeling is good, you don't feel really tired. And even if you're not really tired, if you have a bad feeling, you feel tired— have you had this experience?

Right! That's very true!

I think at the women's camps, just since 1992 Taiji has developed. You know, in 1992, it wasn't really popular. My class was not really big—1993, getting more. Now it's bigger still. Some people tell me after they learn some Taiji, it helps them in other martial arts. I have seen the same thing happen in China. I think all the martial arts have things to teach each other, because every martial art has a special point. Even like Karate or Judo. Jujutsu. And Aikido—Aikido looks very much like Taiji. Some martial arts are very similar. I think they need to learn from each other and put this together.

It can be helpful. Some people, after they took the Taiji class or the Qigong class, told me, "I feel much better now. I feel more relaxed." And if they do kicking—"I feel more strong." Or punching—more strong. So that's true. Because if you cannot relax, you cannot punch very well. You have to release first, then your punch will have the power. Otherwise you use force and the punch has no power. Do you believe that?

Yeah.

[Laughs] Yeah, it's true. Some of my teachers have disagreed with my openness in learning different types of internal arts. I believe you should be wider. Don't be narrow. I used to have some masters who were mad at me for learning other styles or systems or for studying with other teachers. Now they're nice to me. They know that I respect them. I visit them. I bring them gifts—they like that. Some masters still look cold at me, but I don't care—they are all my teachers.

I think I'm right to be open to other styles. I tell students to go ahead, learn from others. I get benefits from different teachers. Some masters are very great but can't explain techniques clearly. I explain clearly, partly from having a lot of experience and partly from my formal Taiji teacher's training. In my experience I made a big circle to get to the bottle. Now I give my students direct instructions in how to get there—just straight, get it. I am not perfect. I still make many mistakes. If the student is higher level over me, that's good. I'm happy. I say, "Good, pass me." Anyone can learn the form but to get in the door of Taiji is difficult. Maybe I'm still not in the door. I don't pretend to know it all. It's like the bottle—if you're full, you can't put anything else in.[6]

So you like teaching? You like having students and passing your knowledge on?

The one problem is I don't make a lot of money teaching martial arts and I don't have another job—I just teach. It's getting better. Some sponsors really support me and are very honest. Like in Michigan, I was just telling this story: We had a contract where I take twenty percent of the income and they pay for the air fare and the lodging and the food.

After the workshop the sponsor told me, "I give you the bad news, I give you the good news." I said, "What's the bad news?" They said, "We're going to break the contract, we want to give you more money." I said, "Wow, this is the best bad news in the world." Right? I think I met honest people. I'm happy, because they showed me on paper exactly how much income there was. They said, "We cannot take all the money we make on you. You need to make money, and you need to improve your school." I say, "I don't have a big school," and they say, "You need to start a big school!" So I feel very, very excited, because people treat me very, very good and honestly. But you know, I cannot start a school yet, but I think in the future maybe one day I will start my own school.

Actually, I do have a school, Jian Mei Internal Martial Arts—*jian* means "healthy," and *mei* means "beautiful." Also Jian is the Chinese name of my senior student, Gerald Sharp, and I am Mei. Together we formed the Jian Mei Association in

---

6. These two paragraphs are from an interview by Janet Aalfs, "Master Wen Mei Yu: Teacher and Healer," *Women in the Martial Arts* (newsletter of the National Women's Martial Arts Federation, Fall 1993, Vol. 11, No. 3), with Wen Mei Yu's revisions, January 1995.

1990. But I don't have a large studio. The students come and we practice together. My students treat me very well, very good.

You treat us well!

I try. Like today, Terry was doing massage, so I got some food to send to her. I'm not exactly, "Oh, I'm the master, you need to respect me all the time." I just think about everybody being equal. In the classroom I'm the master, the teacher, and you are the student. After the teaching everybody is equal, like brothers, sisters, like one family. That's very, very warm. If you're always serious—"Oh, you are the master"—the students will not get close to you. They will not learn real mastery. Like my teacher Ma Yueh Liang—when you visit Master Ma in Shanghai he pours tea for everyone. You can't stop him. So I stay natural, not too serious. I think both student and teacher need to learn something. The student needs to learn how to respect the teacher, and the teacher needs to learn how to love the student. If you love your student and the student does not respect you, no, it will not be right. The old tradition in China, the custom, is that students have very, very formal respect for the teacher.

And you think that should change?

This is something I'm still uncertain about. I think if we keep the tradition, sometimes it is not right. I've seen some masters here in the United States—they have students do everything: "My house has something happen, come to my house—help me do this, help me do that." Like labor. I don't think this is right. And some students don't respect teachers—that happens too. I think there should be a balance—don't be too traditional but don't be too open. Because you have to respect your teacher, of course. The teacher is teaching you something. If you have no respect, I think this is wrong. But if you're the teacher, you cannot use your students all the time to work for your personal things. I don't think that's right. They need to be taught how to give by giving to them, like the example of Master Ma and the tea. Do you understand what I mean?

Yes, that seems very clear.

How many years have you come to the camp?

Two years.

Last year at Two Rivers? You were there?

I took your workshop, the sword workshop. Janet and I—Janet Seaforth is my teacher—and she and I were so excited about the sword form that when we got home we still remembered up to Horse Leaps over the Ravine. You had given us a paper with the names of all the moves and I found several videotapes of Yang-style sword and a book that had some of those same moves—and I figured out all the rest of the moves.

Wow, that's great. Next year, I will continue to teach the sword. Teach the sword, review the knife.

That'd be great! Today I bought your new videotape too, so now I can practice all of it.

Yeah, I think the tape is very, very good, with different angles. From the tape you really can learn this. I have a very good relationship with *Inside Kung Fu* magazine—Unique Publications. They help me to shoot a lot of videotapes, seven forms already. Five on the market—Forty-Eight, Wu style, Lian gong, Yang knife, Yang sword. And we're just now editing the Da Yan Qigong—Wild Goose Qigong. We'll finish the editing, then give it to them, and they edit it again, add the voiceover, make copies. After this will be Wu-style fast set. More people want the Qigong now, so Qigong maybe in the future will be more popular than Taiji.

How do you see the Qigong interrelating with Taiji?

I think Taiji is Qigong too. Taiji is like very-high-level Qigong. I think with Qigong it is easier to feel the qi, because for Taiji you need very good coordination of your upper and lower body. Your mind is thinking about the movements so it's harder to feel the qi. Also, in the Taiji movement, if you are not relaxed, the qi still cannot move. So it's harder to feel the qi. With Qigong you can feel the qi very directly. My experience is that to learn Taiji, you have to learn some Qigong. If you learn the internal aspects of Qigong, you improve your Taiji. If you practice Qigong well, your qi flows, and you can be more relaxed and put that in the Taiji form and feel the qi. So if you can learn both, that's very, very good.

In the future I think more people will see the benefits of Qigong and Taiji and do more research on how to improve further. Then it will advance. I believe without research it will stop. You have to keep learning. The creator of Lian gong, Zhuan Yuan Ming, took the old traditions and put the movements in order, from the shoulder, neck, to

the low back, to the hips, knees, ankles. I think that is right, because the world goes on and everything else has to keep going too. You cannot stop at any one spot. To keep the old tradition is good, but to not research and develop is not right.

But you have to use some judgment about what you're doing—

Yeah! You have to know the tradition, but develop new things. Keep that combined together. Otherwise the world changes and the martial arts don't change. If more people can keep going, learn some Taiji or Qigong, it really can help build up their health. Now a lot of people believe that. There's no longer any question. Before, some people didn't believe it. We say if you want to know whether the pear is sour or sweet, you have to taste it. You have to learn something—then you know whether it helps or not.

◆ ◆ ◆

The tape hissed to an end and the machine turned itself off with a click. It was nearly midnight. Across the room the injured woman tossed and moaned in restless sleep. In the ordinary but unfamiliar room, the windows showing only the moonless night filled with the persisting pulse of the shiai, I felt myself and my companion to be somewhere apart, in a loop of time and space cut off from everything else I knew.

Wen Mei Yu came from a past I could scarcely grasp, the turbulent decades of modern Chinese history with civil war, the Japanese occupation, the Maoist regime, the Cultural Revolution, the present modernization. Through her teachers, born when empresses and emperors still ruled in her country, she seemed to me to have a foothold in the ancient, mythic China of dragons and phoenixes and wise

Wen Mei Yu with Chinese spear.

immortals of Taoist lore. Yet here she was, telling me quite simply about her everyday thoughts and practice.

Listening to the soft flow of her voice, her speech somehow made more vivid by her often-Chinese phrasing of English words, I gained a sense of how she worked step by step, little by little, to spread and share her great and wonderful knowledge. Her life seemed to me to exemplify Taijiquan method in her use of what came to hand of time, opportunities, students. I felt an enduring strength in her—a deeper and truer reality underlying the hardships of her life in China and the loneliness and difficulties she must have encountered in the United States. For mastery does not relieve one of discomfort or discouragement, I suspect. One just gains the wherewithal to go ahead anyway.

She leaned forward in her chair, lifting her hands to show them to me. "My hands are not really good," she said. "This is from the Cultural Revolution. I was an engineer in a factory, but I was sent to work in the workshop, over twelve hours daily. I had to put my hands in cold oil to wash machine parts without gloves or hand protection. It was too cold and hurt the joints."

She laughed, this time with no amusement, a hard, grating sound that was so different from her usual clear voice as to seem to come from some other person. Unable to speak, I watched her flex her fingers. "I exercised them so they did not get worse," she said. "Without exercise I would not be able to bend my fingers." All I could think was how I had never noticed any deformity but only how flawlessly fluid and sure her hands always looked when she moved them in Taijiquan.

CHAPTER 17

The More You Do the More Things Come Together

Late though it was, after talking to Wen Mei Yu I returned to the shiai, which was still far from over. Watching from the sidelines, I felt myself brought up against my ambivalence about fighting with an immediacy that I hadn't found in conversation with the women I had interviewed. The roiling, shouting crowd and the feeling of group intoxication disturbed me, but at the same time the excitement was enticing. Wanting to understand what it might feel like to participate, I searched the contestants' faces for clues. But I was put off by their anonymity in their close-fitting helmets and glossy plastic safety gear. They all looked alike, interchangeable and lacking individuality, faces reduced to stock sets of eyes, nose, mouth.

Everyone was so charged up, the contestants could hardly stand still for the brief moment when the referee drew them in pairs into position before giving the signal to fight. The actual encounters lasted but seconds—a flurry of kicks and punches and the referee stepped in blowing her whistle to separate the fighters. The judges at the four corners of the ring, solemn in the black or white gi of their particular style, signaled the award of points with formal gestures of their arms. For all the contestants' restless twitching and flexing, much of the time was spent in formalities: contestants bowing to each other, to the referee, to the judges; the judges considering rules and points; the referee consulting with judges, timekeeper, scorekeeper. Then, after so many points or minutes, the match was over.

We women are well advised to know how to fight for our lives in the United

States, as elsewhere, but this contest seemed almost to mock that need. The militaristic dress, the ranks of watching sensei, the hierarchy, the retinue of support personnel, the deference to arbitrary rules—all seemed to glorify fighting for its own sake, the sort of fighting that has been turned against women. If these had been men, I would have dismissed them summarily.

But they weren't men. They were women, many of them women I knew and respected. I could not reject them out of hand and so I had to question my own reactions. Perhaps I did not fully understand what was going on—perhaps they were not simply reenacting men's rituals of domination and display but undertaking something different. Or perhaps there was a more complex intermixture at work that neither I nor any of them could easily untangle, a searching for appropriate and fruitful avenues to express their energy and hone their skills within the male conventions of competition that was the only model they had.

Perhaps it was only that this was something I didn't know how to do, and if I learned I would feel differently. Perhaps, too, the participants, or some of them, were simply trying this out because the opportunity arose. Doubtless the reactions of the different women there spanned the full range of possibilities. I stayed through match after match, trying to immerse myself in the event, but finally, in some frustration, headed for my bed.

Stopping in the communal bathroom to brush my teeth, I overheard two women talking on the other side of the bank of mirrors that partly divided the room. The voice of one of them caught my attention, more for her hard, feverish tone than her actual words. The other woman murmured sympathetically, not really saying anything one way or the other, just hanging in, being there.

As I walked off into the darkness toward my cabin, that driven voice echoed in my mind. The judges had unfairly denied her points and she had lost her match. But she was glad she had made the effort—she came back to this more than once. She called it a success that she hadn't backed out of the tournament altogether. I would not deny her any satisfaction or accomplishment. But was this the only or best means to that end? And where did *I* fit in with my meditative practice of T'ai Chi Ch'uan, with trees more often than humans for companions? The slow, graceful movements of T'ai Chi Ch'uan are fighting moves, and deadlier ones than the controlled, rule-bound punches and kicks I had seen at the shiai. Wouldn't I use them if I were attacked? And how well would I do in case of need without more realistic practice of the fighting applications? Not that tournament matches bear much relation to the desperate, all-out necessities of self-defense, but they do provide experience in handling stress and adrenaline in a physical encounter.

At home again I ran into a friend, Mary Buckley, who had recently enrolled in a T'ai Chi Ch'uan class that turned out to include the sparring exercise of Push Hands as well as the healing Ch'i Kung she was more interested in. Only a few months after she joined the class, a number of the students—including her—entered a large, regional competition in Push Hands. I asked about her experience and a few days later she sent me several pages she said my questions had motivated her to write:

> My first Taiji teacher was very yin, very meditative and gentle. He didn't teach this push-each-other-over sparring called Push Hands at all. He called it Join Hands and taught it as an extremely gentle practice of sensitivity to another's touch and energy. So it was a bit shocking to me to see and eventually learn this form of what

originally struck me as macho pushing and shoving—but it was part of the class I wanted to take, so I went along with it.

I came to appreciate the sensitive aspects of Push Hands—how powerful and fascinating a lesson it is in paying attention to the other person's center of gravity, point of balance, quality and direction of energy, and so on. It is also a great exercise in split-second attentiveness and resilience, in maintaining your own form and equanimity in an adversarial situation. It is definitely more challenging to develop technique and mindfulness while someone is trying to push you off balance!

Originally, of course, Taiji was as martial an art as any—you needed to be prepared to fight for your life. But my attraction to it had more to do with inner energy work. I wanted to bring meditation, movement, energy awareness, energy power, and healing into my life, into my health practice, my dance experiences, my spiritual awareness. Well, if it integrates into all these aspects of life, why not also into a competitive tournament situation? I had to find out for myself. I felt I had to participate in the competition if only because of my own resistance to the idea.

What is the real value of competition? Do we need it to bring out the best in our practice? Even if that's true, competition also brings out some of the worst in us. Is that inevitable? Is it useful, in the Buddhist sense, in allowing the karmic emotional muck to surface and allowing it to evaporate by observing it with equanimity?

And what if competition is successful? At the tournament I had to deal with my own ego response to winning a silver

Mary Buckley (left) and the author, Stephanie Hoppe, practicing a sparring exercise at a workshop (Ukiah, Calif., June 1994).

medal, even though, with only a few women competing, the odds made receiving the medal practically meaningless. It helped to have made friends with my opponents beforehand, to share notes and jokes, get acquainted a little, forgive each other implicitly, beforehand, for whatever ego affronts we might inflict. I saw the men doing this, but not as much. It's easy to say, "That's because that's how women are; men wouldn't connect that way," but I'm not sure that's true. There were over five times as many men as women, and I did see camaraderie among men who were strangers.

What spiritual benefit I derived from being in the competition was more from my own insistence at the attempt than from anything intrinsic to the tournament process. The technical benefit of being challenged may have been something, but the masters have traditionally assigned that to discipline rather than display motivations. Is this our modern get-it-in-a-hurry way of bypassing pure discipline? If so, is it an appropriate adaptation for modern times? From another angle, does arousing competitive hormones constitute its own kind of meditative practice—in transcending them? And is that possible? Wise? I still have more questions than answers!

I had no answers for Mary—rather I added her questions to my own. I remembered Wendy Palmer and Michelle Dwyer commenting that without working with partners I would miss an important component of practice. My simu, Janet Seaforth, rarely included partner exercises in her classes. Occasionally I encountered other opportunities for Push Hands or other partner practice and forced myself to participate. Sometimes I was successful in keeping from being pushed off balance or in pushing my partner. More often than not in such cases, I didn't understand what I had done or why it worked. The interchange seemed a pointless exercise in being invaded and invading another. I didn't enjoy it or feel any of the benefits I heard others talk about.

Then I started to learn a form of the two-person T'ai Chi Ch'uan Michelle Dwyer spoke of. Practicing the slow, choreographed progression of attack, block, and counterattack with the men who were teaching me, I saw how an attacking move arose as a defense against a previous attack and in turn created the potential for the opponent's block and counterattack. If my partner struck at my left side, slipping my left side back to allow the attack to pass by brought my right side forward, and the spiraling extension through my right arm of that turning movement served both to block the all-but dissipated attack and to strike at a point on his body that was opened by his attack.

This interested me. I found an elegance and efficiency in these interlocking movements that appealed to me. I looked forward to practice sessions as I never had to Push Hands. I liked figuring out how and why the interchanges worked, and working at performing them more smoothly and sparely. And when I returned to my solitary form, I noticed my balance was more certain and my movements felt better defined, crisper, and sharper. But I did not notice much difference in my Push Hands—moving faster, and without the choreography that told me what to do, I felt almost as much at a loss as ever.

And I seemed as far as ever from appreciating, or even understanding, the shiai. A number of the women I had interviewed participated in competition, but the issue had remained tangential to our conversations. Now I sought out women in the harder styles of martial arts in which sparring, competition, and fighting seemed to be more central. What did these activities amount to in practice for particular women? What drew them to these things? What larger, long-term context and meaning did their overall lives provide for these aspects of martial arts?

Karate seemed like an appropriate starting point. It is often held up as the epitome of hard-style martial arts. Many people use the word as a term for martial arts in general. My impression, confirmed by others with more experience though there seem to be no firm statistics, is that Karate is the most common martial art practiced among women or men in the United States (Judo, Aikido, and T'ai Chi Ch'uan also enroll large numbers of women). Several of the women I have talked to studied Karate at one time or another. Lloyda French is one who stayed with Karate. Her Karate experience includes competing and judging in tournaments and teaching—this in a life of political interest in women's community, empowerment, and self-defense that has led her into teaching self-defense for women, founding an all-women's dojo, and serving as board member and president of PAWMA, the Pacific Women Martial Artists Association. She agreed to talk to me and invited me to come early to observe a sparring class she teaches.

A sunny autumn Sunday morning found me driving through a seedy-looking commercial neighborhood south of Market Street in San Francisco. The area is becoming trendy, bustling at night with the traffic at bars and clubs, but in daylight it looked abandoned, the two- and three-story industrial and commercial buildings shuttered and silent. At one of these I pressed a doorbell beside a small, neatly printed label—Ronin Dojo. *Ronin*, I had read, means "masterless samurai." Lloyda had told me the school was founded by herself and six other black belt women who had left their previous school and wanted a place to train together. The door buzzed for me to enter. On the second floor I found an airy, sunlit room that extended the width of the building to the bank of open windows in the front through which I had heard scuffling sounds, grunts, women's voices, and laughter as I waited below. A dozen women faced off in pairs, all ages and sizes and dressed in everything from crisp white gi to tattered sweat pants and T-shirts or tank tops printed with martial arts logos or political slogans. Some wore helmets or shin guards of glossy, bright-red plastic. Lloyda, a sturdily built woman in her forties with red hair cropped short and a direct gaze and manner of speaking, was one of those dressed formally in a gi, with a whistle on a cord around her neck.

"Change partners," she called as I entered. For a moment the women milled about, some of them coming to fetch a drink or deposit an unwanted layer of clothing in the corner where several young children played and I set down my gear. The women had already been at it for an hour or more, and their faces were bright with exertion, wisps of hair plastered to damp skin on necks and foreheads. Lloyda explained the next drill: As the attacker punched, the defender was to step "off the line" of the attack, either to the left or the right—she illustrated the difference in footwork—and punch to the back of the attacker's head. The women paired up with new partners, bowed, and began. Lloyda circled the room, correcting this one's balance, that one's aim, waiting while the woman tried again, making further suggestions or moving on with a nod. She took more time with one young, very willowy woman who seemed scarcely to be attached to the ground. When it was this woman's turn to punch, the gesture of the jab she made in her partner's direction caused her to drift backward herself. "Hit her like you mean it!" Lloyda urged. "Use your whole body!" Lloyda talked her through the drill, explaining it in different ways, searching for words that would enable the student to feel the moves concretely in her body. The young woman nodded, listening attentively. I could see the difficulty lay not in any lack of desire but in a connection as yet unforged between her will and her body. I empathized with her even as I admired the more proficient women who planted themselves in strong stances, their faces intent with purpose, their punches landing firm and true.

Lloyda blew her whistle and reviewed the techniques they had practiced. "Now we'll put them together in three-minute rounds. Remember to tell your partner about any injuries you have where you don't want to be hit. And agree in advance how hard you're both going to hit." She checked that everyone was ready and punched a stopwatch. "Time!"

All of the women had put on mouth guards now, and more of them had added other protective gear. They looked to me to need it, given the blows they traded. This was different from my solitary practice of T'ai Chi Ch'uan forms! And different too, from the to and fro of the Push Hands I had seen, in which the movements are generally smooth and continuous, the partners remaining in contact. Soft style, hard style . . . This looked hard, yes, punches, kicks, and blocks backed by grunts of effort. Here was not the level of excitement I witnessed at the shiai, but I saw equal, if more sober, determination. I also saw connections fostered more expressly than often seems to occur in Push Hands, in the way a woman would exclaim, "Good!" when her partner landed a particularly solid punch, the pride each took in her partner's accomplishment, the close attention with which partners coached each other, the brief discussions about preexisting injuries and training goals with each new partner, and the hugs after bowing when the whistle blew for the end of a round. I felt a flow throughout the room of care and concern. Precisely because of their care, I thought, these women offered each other the hardest challenge they could.

The class ended with a circle and discussion about the day's practice. Then Lloyda directed everyone to turn in the same direction and give the person now in front of her a back rub. Here was a practice I could to take home to my school! Leaving behind a bustle of catching up on each other's news and planning future get-togethers, changing clothes and packing gear, Lloyda and I went to fetch a takeout lunch. As we waited in the restaurant she remarked that two of the women in the class that morning were not regular students but visiting from a nearby town. "There's less and less for women only," she said. "That's why those two women came today. They're in a mixed school. I met them last weekend and it was—'There's a women's martial arts organization? There's a women's school? We can come and just spar?'—'Would you like to do that?'—'Yeah!'"

The availability and survival of schools for women was a question she would return to. During the past two years she had served as president of PAWMA and had hoped to get around to the different schools where women train to build more connections and community and foster mutual support. "I haven't been able to do that," she said regretfully. "No time."

"I can see the need for it," I told her. "When I talked to Sandy Wong in San Jose she mentioned the Wing Chun classes for women they had for a while in her school. But there were never more than three or four women in the class. She was saying they needed to get out more publicity and put on demonstrations to show women how useful this training is. But it was all very daunting to her."

"It's daunting to me!" Lloyda exclaimed. "This school runs on a shoestring mainly because all of us have full-time jobs—I make my living as a student adviser at a medical school. I know what you have to do to keep a martial arts school going. You have to go out. You have to demo. You have to make contact. It's an enormous undertaking— and I don't have time."

We carried our food back to the dojo and sat down to eat on the sunlit floor beneath the open windows. I turned on the tape recorder.

LLOYDA FRENCH

Kenpo Karate

I gather there are a number of different styles of Karate. I'm curious about what differentiates them.

My original style was American Goju, which is an adapted version of traditional Goju that started in Japan, probably before that in Okinawa. Traditional Goju is a hard style like Shotokan. Closed hands. Hard blocks. Very focused, powerful kicks. A lot of linear movement. American Goju incorporated some soft stuff, a little more circular.

When I moved here to San Francisco I couldn't find American Goju. I could only find traditional Goju, and the school that was teaching it was notoriously awful to its women students. I had no interest in supporting that. I looked at a number of schools and saw American Kenpo. It was an all-women's school. It had a lot of good energy, which was mostly what I was interested in, and it seemed a compatible style from where I came. So I transitioned into American Kenpo and went through the ranks, and I am at this point primarily a Kenpo stylist.

American Kenpo is an eclectic blend of styles. It has hard blocking. It also has soft blocking, circular movements. It has some grappling—it's a lot like Kajukenbo, like Coleen Gragen's description of Kajukenbo. We're a little more stand-up, where-as they have the Kung Fu element, longer and lower stances, as in Michelle Dwyer's wonderful example of a Chinese martial artist. As you saw from my class today, we have much more upright stances, and while we move in circles and get around, we don't quite get as low as they do. It's not quite as internal looking—although it's all internal.

And Shuri-ryu, which Janet Aalfs does, is softer and more circular than Kenpo?

Shuri-ryu is actually more like the American Goju, leaning more toward the harder style, I would say from what I've seen of it. Janet is an interesting blend. I know her teacher, Wendi Dragonfire—the style has evolved as Wendi and Janet have integrated other influences into it. It seems a little more Chinese to me than when I first saw it.

The differences between styles are primarily influences—Where did the teachers who founded the style get their influences? All these American styles are blends of styles. A lot of them came from soldiers who learned one style on their tour of duty here and then another style there and came back and started blending styles. Kajukenbo is an example of that, and Ed Parker, who founded American Kenpo, is certainly. He was a soldier and then a scientist and developed Kenpo as a "scientific" martial art. I have quibbles with that—it gets very abstract; you're all in your mind all the time, and I do Karate to be in my body.

The two arts I studied were founded by men who took them from Asian arts. They were changed—they're really Americanized. I've never been particularly attracted to traditional Asian styles. I don't know why—chemistry, I guess. Down the line I may yet do it. I think in some ways their translation suited me, made it more responsive. It also allowed the cynic in me—I didn't idolize them. I didn't think, "Oh these are just incredibly great masters." Nope! These were American men who decided they didn't want to do it the old way, so they declared themselves tenth degrees and made the art. And so I feel free to change the art. In that way it's freed me. I like the Asian influence, particularly the Chinese styles. They give a lot of spirituality to the practice that I like. It was interesting today to have these two women come—we virtually had the same kata. That is very unusual.

They do still another different style?

They do Kenpo too, but I've had people come from Kenpo schools and have different names for kata, a different numbering system. And it looks different. They even have different spellings of "Kenpo." People change and adapt. It keeps martial arts living.

I think you find what you like. What matches your body. I studied Kajukenbo and I never could develop that flexibility. I didn't like the pacing, the timing. It didn't suit me. My body doesn't like to get that low and be that long. When I watch Kajukenbo, I think it's incredibly beautiful and powerful and inspiring. But it didn't suit me. And that was a lesson.

I think the concept that sometimes our bodies like certain styles over other styles is not often talked about. Why do people choose their school? Sometimes it's the political environment. A lot of times it's because of the class schedule and the location, and for a certain percentage accidentally it's the right thing in their body. For other people it's not. They either leave the martial arts or they find another school. Or they go to a camp and— "Oh, that's beautiful! I need to do that." I always tell people who call me, "Come to class. This may not be for you. I'm happy to give you other schools and other styles." People don't even know—What is Aikido?—that they have an option to roll on the floor.

How did you get started?

I started martial arts around 1972. I was in my early twenties. I was living in New York and teaching in the South Bronx, which at that time was only marginally better than it is today. I was teaching English in a public junior high school—which was fine—but I was traveling long distances and I was also out at night a lot. I wanted to be able to defend myself. I was also coming out as a lesbian, and I met and was dating someone who was a student in a women's Karate school, and that was like, "Wow! I get to learn how to defend myself *and* be with all those women learning to be strong?" I went and watched her class and then I joined. I couldn't wait to begin. And I'm not— I've never been an "athlete." I didn't do team sports. I went to Catholic schools, which didn't have even a gym requirement. I was more in my head than in my body. Karate from day one was in my body. They would show it to me, and I'd have it. I don't know where that came from or why, but it made it fun for me.

I bet it would! But was it work still? In that you were stiff and not in shape?

I'm sure that I was. I don't remember that. It was wonderful. I would go Thursday, Saturday, Sunday. It was nice when the woman who owned the school added a couple more classes, and suddenly I could come on Tuesday. The more I did it and the more in shape I got, the better it got. I don't remember being sore. I do remember lots of little injuries and bruisings, stuff like that. I didn't care. It certainly didn't bother me—whether I have this sort of jock mentality or what. Karate continued to be wonderful. The Karate school didn't continue to be wonderful, but I stayed for a while. Coleen and Anne Moon joined within that first year, and we became close friends.

Eventually we left the school, going to a place with a teacher named Gerald Orange, the Temple for Spiritual and Physical Survival. There were two women there, Nadia Telsey and Annie Ellman, who had Brooklyn Women's Martial Arts and trained in both places. I eventually taught at Brooklyn. It was much more politically aligned with me, with a collective sense and empowering women. That kept me interested. And having Anne and Coleen and Nadia and Annie was inspiring.

We were truly into it! We would train all the time. We would hang out together, we would talk about what worked, what didn't work—twenty hours out of twenty-four were somehow involved with martial arts. We went to our jobs, but our main life was martial arts. That was what the first three or four years were like. Full of injuries, as I said, jammed toes, no equipment. Sparring against men—that was terrifying. *[Laughs]* I studied in other schools at the same time—our teacher gave us freedom. I give my students the same now: "Somebody else has a school, you want to go try Shotokan—please go! It's fine!" I did that.

It took me about five years to get to black belt. I visited a number of other schools, but once I joined Gerald's, I kind of stayed. Anne and Coleen

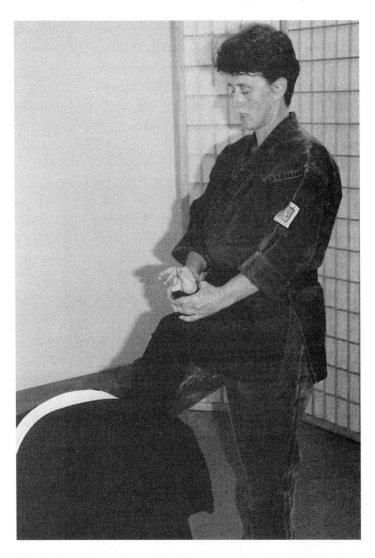

Lloyda French sparring with a Karate student (Ronin Dojo, San Francisco, December 1995).

moved on to Oregon and started Kajukenbo. That's how we split our styles—originally we were together. But we're all still doing martial arts, however many years later. It's amazing, because you know that the dropout rate is just incredible.

I had the same luck in a little bit larger number when I joined the Kenpo school here in San

Francisco, it must be ten years ago. A great group of women, really into it, really into training. We've gone through all the ranks together. I was the first to get the black belt in Kenpo, but they followed within a year, and we're all still training. It's very remarkable, knowing what I know about how people drop out.

That was at the beginning of the women's movement when you started, and everybody had a lot of energy for things like that. There've been some ups and downs since then in the women's movement. I wonder how that has played out in the martial arts that you've been involved in?

The first school was an all-women's school and the teacher was an example of someone basically who was not as qualified as I would have liked for her to be and I think endangered us. We were naïve, so we didn't know it. Then going to a much better school—which seemed at the time a much better school—everybody was so highly skilled in the school in my estimation that I felt a lot safer. It was. And Brooklyn was just incredibly clean and clear about the politics and has continued to be a real model of anti–violence-against-women. That's been my motivation. Where that occurs, I'm fine.

Over the years unfortunately I've seen a lot of women's schools not succeed, the women teachers not respect their students—not being any better at it than the men. I think it's really discouraging. When women talk about being abused by male teachers, I have to say that most of the worst cases of abuse I know of are by women teachers.

Are these women who start out with feminist ideals?

Not necessarily. These are kind of jocks—they were very good athletically, good in martial arts, and they thought they'd start a school. And they had ego problems. The reason we started this school was our woman teacher suddenly decided that she wanted to be a commercial school. She wanted contracts—you pay a year in advance. If you could pay a year in advance you got the lowest fees. If you had to pay month by month, because you didn't have that kind of money, you got the highest fees, which is a really regressive. The poorest women wind up paying the most.

That was anathema to me; I just couldn't stay. Nor could most of the other black belts. Some of them for other reasons. There are many fewer schools where feminist politics really are operating, even if you're a women's school, and there are fewer women's schools.

Fewer than there were ten years ago? Five years ago?

Even two years ago! Ronin Dojo is the only all-women's Karate school in San Francisco—which has a huge women and lesbian population. There's an all-women's Judo school, which has been around for ages—Fukuda Sensei's school at Twenty-sixth and Castro. There're more in the East Bay. Seven Star up in Seattle has done very well. It's an all-women's school. Really successful at this point.

It's difficult both to attract women into the martial arts and to keep women. Because we have a sliding scale and we're month to month, we don't pay any of our teachers. Nobody gets paid to do this. Teachers pay dues, in fact. I wonder if we'll last.

We were very fortunate to get a grant from Bay Area Career Women's A Fund of Our Own, which is a lesbian-funded group. There's a lot of resistance to funding women's martial arts. That was a one-year grant. Our part was to offer a series of free self-defense seminars, and then a subsidy for people who wanted to start Karate, but the dues got in the way. The seminars were fun to do and a very nice service to provide, and we had a lot of women come through the dojo as a result of being able to offer that.

We managed to get this grant largely because one of our students—she's a grant writer—was willing to do it. I'd love to do more. The problem is time. Both for writing the grant and then making the time to implement parts of the grant. Right now time's the biggest constraint. We're all too busy.

I get phone calls, "Can you recommend—?" Women would like there to be more all-women schools. And, "Why isn't there an all-women's class at least?" I think women could ask for those things, but there have to be enough women in the school.

Do you think that the schools that aren't all-women's schools are failing to carry through with the politics?

I think it depends on the teacher. With Coleen, for example, politics have always underlaid her martial arts. You don't join that school unless you share that. I think that's true of some other schools and not true of some. We're a lot less political certainly than Coleen's school. My political bent on the martial arts is that we need to be available and we need to have space for women to feel safe to train. We need to offer self-defense as part our training, and we need to be quality martial artists, because women *can* be quality martial artists.

Those two women visiting today were totally surprised to hear that there's a women's martial arts organization. So there's still a lot of outreach to go. When camps were first held about twenty years ago, there were hardly any women black belts. Now there're so many women black belts, so many quality martial artists—women are getting trained and teaching other women and demanding quality instruction from their teachers.

At the same time, I know of many women whose male teachers are not serving their interests. Women don't spar. Women don't get the same treatment. Women don't get promoted in the same way. Women aren't encouraged to stay in the dojo in the same way. The men have a different agenda. A lot of the leading men's schools don't respond to women's needs. My big argument when men talk about self-defense is it's not my self-defense. They talk about getting grabbed in the street and off the bars, and I'm, "That doesn't happen to me. I don't hang out in bars and get into bar fights. Sorry—that's a male experience. How about the partner abuse? That's a female experience." I question a lot of Kenpo techniques because they're based on the male experience of self-defense, which is different.

Do you think that your training has also developed your social and political views—furthered your awareness in that sense?

Yes. Yes, I do. I was somebody who had some anyway, and I was supported in my views. I came in with a self-defense interest and was exposed to women who were into an antiviolence movement and then trained with people with a lot of political sensitivity in a politically explosive time, in the late sixties, early seventies. But somebody who's coming into it for sport—I don't know how much they are impacted. In fact I think some might never be impacted.

It can become just sort of a personal journey. I can think of a couple martial artists I know who were never very politically aware. Self-defense isn't very high on their list of things. They like the feeling of their body in space, being able to do forms and techniques, the social atmosphere the dojo becomes, and they're good at it. It hasn't changed them at all politically. Even self-defense—they avoid it. *[Laughs]* I can see that martial arts need not have an impact. But for me it did.

The martial arts and the self-defense pushed me to look at, How does violence against women happen in the society? It's not the stranger down the street; it's in your home. I started teaching self-defense against gay bashing and looking at issues of partner abuse in gay and lesbian couples. Getting that kind of awareness. Understanding how violence happens between people who care about each other. That came out of martial arts. Putting those things together, using my training for that, I had to also think that it couldn't be an individual solution. It isn't every single woman's responsibility that she learn a martial art and how to defend herself. It's forced me to look at what should be the community and global responses to violence against women and violence against individuals. That's been very empowering to just know that I can tell women, "You can hold your community responsible. We can keep each other safe. We can keep our kids safe."

How do we go about doing that? For some it's been getting involved with places like Community United Against Violence. Becoming an advocate. Or being in the women's shelter movement. We've had a couple of people come through

and do that. Other people have become more involved with organizations like the Women's Building. We've had people on the board from that.

This is unfortunately a new concept—America was built on individualism—and I don't think there are that many of us who say, "There can be a community response." There're safe houses and safe neighborhoods, and some of those things have come out of these movements too. That's helpful. In self-defense, and sometimes in Karate, I look at how do you fight *together?* It's empowering to people to have the sense that they have someone at their back supporting them. That's opened a new psychic level too.

It's taken different effects. Some of the more satisfying self-defense success stories to me were not, "I fought off an attacker," but I'd get a note saying, "I'm not afraid to go out at night, and by the way, you know that boss who was harassing me? I told him to get off my back." Just the sense I got of women taking power back in their lives on a daily basis—talking to other women, joining unions. Those are great stories. That for me is the essence of self-defense and Karate. I don't worry too much about the stranger. That's a terrible experience, we never want to go through it, and not many of us will, but all of us every day deal with some form of sexism.

I think every woman martial artist is changed by her martial art and is a powerful woman in the society.

How do you see tournaments and competition fitting into this?

I long ago stopped competing. We trained the month preceding this year's PAWMA camp because I knew there would be a tournament. I do a little more reffing than I used to do. Several of my students are very into it and the other woman who shares Sunday teaching does a lot of tournaments, and so she's bringing in tournament-style drills for people, and hopefully we'll have a balance.

Going to a tournament, you put yourself under pressure, you put yourself on that edge, you have total strangers looking at you, judging you. I think it's a valuable learning lesson. Winning makes you feel terrific. It was incredible for one of my shy, shy, shy students, who loved to spar, to go and in her first tournament come back with a trophy. That did it for her! That clicked in. At some point it's probably not as productive.

Tournament-type sparring is very different than the kind of sparring that you saw today. The kind of sparring that you have to do, you have to be quick and clean and score your point, and as soon as the referee yells point, you have to stop. So there's a lot of stop, start, stop, start. There're a few exchanges. Sometimes it goes on because nothing clean is being thrown, but in general, you get to a good target with a good shot, they're going to call point, three points it's over.

The disadvantage—which the visitors got today—is that people don't always stop even after they've been hit. When you come into this school and spar for a two- to three-minute round, somebody may keep forward-pressuring you, no matter how much you throw. You may score a point on me, but I'm not going to stop. I may take one of your blows low and come in with five high—it can startle a tournament sparrer. You're going to have to learn that sometimes you have to really throw for someone to respect a hit, and just the idea that there's such a thing as taking a sacrifice hit—it becomes a different kind of sparring.

For women, I think, if you're looking at defending yourself, you need to know that the fight doesn't end because you've been hit and maybe injured. You can fight through. You can stick in there, and you're going to have to throw probably a lot more than you think. So that's the value of training in the way we do—endurance and self-knowledge. I'm sure other people have remarked that the hardest thing about the sparring, for women, is hitting, not being hit. It's important that women learn how to throw and hit a strong hit.

Both types of sparring, you have to respond, or hit clean and with contact. So the sparring does help women who weren't natural jocks learn to hit. I keep working with one student—she finally is making contact. It's very light! *[Laughs]* It's reassuring somebody that, yes, we can take a hit. A lot of times in a women's school you'll hear, "I'm sorry! Did I hurt you? Did I hurt you?" You're not doing them any service. Hit strongly! They can take a lot!

What about your own experience? Why did you do competitions and why did you stop?

I did it because I was in my twenties. I was new to Karate. It was a challenge. I wanted to know how my Karate stacked up in the larger world of tournament fighting. I think that's a lot of the curiosity for people initially going out. I was in a school that was very good and we did very well. It was fun. It's fun to win. And it was interesting.

Then at a certain point it was true, at least in the New York area in that time, that a lot of tournaments favored certain schools or certain styles or who you got to judge. The politics of tournaments became more clear the more I was around them. And that wasn't really where I wanted to spend my time. I was starting to do more teaching for Brooklyn Women's Martial Arts, a completely unranked school, and I just wasn't that interested and challenged any more by going off and doing tournaments. To be a really good tournament sparrer, I think you need to spend a lot of time on that, and that was not where I was willing to spend my time any more. I had a good time doing it and then I lost that urge. I didn't want to be involved in the competitive side that that seemed to provoke. That's just a path I took. I'm supportive of my own students doing it. I'm happy to sit and judge.

What about the shiai at the camp at Los Angeles—would you say that was typical?

It had elements that were pretty typical. It was meant to be a safe place for people to experiment with tournament-like things. An outside tournament would have been a lot more pressure filled, a lot of people you didn't know. Often the men from a school or the male teachers sit in the stands telling the refs they don't know their business. There wasn't any of that. Anybody who got up and did a kata didn't feel like even if they blew it totally they were an idiot. I think that that was a good look at tournaments—in their most positive form. It was a very long night though.

It was. I didn't stay for the whole thing.

That's too bad, because the black belt sparring was exciting. Very seldom do I get to see in tournaments really good women's black belt fighting, and it was very good.

But we got very mixed results in terms of feedback. A lot of people hated it. Hated that it was so much like a tournament, thought it was way too rigid. A lot of people didn't want to have it. And a lot of people had a really good time.

There aren't very many women's tournaments. Maria Doest's done one in Los Angeles and talks about doing another. There were some in the Northwest, but basically there're mixed tournaments and there's not a large showing of women. Women and men don't normally fight each other. I know a number of women who would like to fight across gender, by age and weight class. It makes a certain amount of sense.

You mentioned about the two women visiting in class today—that when you worked with them you could tell they spar with men. What is the difference?

They tend to hit much harder because of being in an environment where the men are not afraid to hit hard. They learn to block and hit hard because otherwise the men don't react—the men just don't pay attention to anything else. Generally when I'm sparring with somebody like that, I know from the quality of their hits and sometimes their reaction to a woman who actually does spar pretty hard. And their aggression! Much more aggressive. They are just in people's faces. One woman did tournaments too. She had that, "I'm going to get my hit in *right now.*"

They tend to be a little wilder and more out of control. They're used to hitting more out of control because the men just slough it off whereas women react more. And we're also all really afraid of hurting other women. I still remember big men coming to teach us and it was like, "Wow! We can hit them really hard!" And I remember the men saying they would go home covered with bruises. Our perception was just because they were big and thick it didn't hurt, but it did.

Do you think there's a risk of women training with women learning not to hit hard enough?

Yeah. I think women teachers and all-women schools need to pay attention to that issue. Not hitting hard enough is certainly a problem that runs through here. And hitting out of control or hitting too hard all the time and intimidating students—having a sense of what that is.

But what about hitting full strength? You can't really do that, can you, without too much risk of injuring each other?

People hit pretty hard! We don't call it full contact, but it feels like full contact some of the time. That's part of a learning process, to learn what contact is. We put the bags up. You can hit full contact into the bags. I usually allow people to adjust their contact as they spar, and I encourage people that at least one of their rounds at a sparring class should be medium-to-heavy contact. You know at what point it's enough—"If you hit me one more time, I'm going to burst into tears or rip you apart." Then it's time to lighten up. But try to get used to being hit a little bit harder.

People are pretty good about it. For the younger belts, control is certainly an issue—what they think is light is not light at all! I've had this conversation with many teachers, men and women—as a teacher I'm in much more danger than I ever was as a student. I've gotten hit a lot. I'm careful now who I demo with.

One of the women I talked to used to practice and teach Judo, and she was saying one thing she liked about Judo was that it had a completion to it. You went through a whole process of taking your opponent down and immobilizing them. She thought in Karate you couldn't really do that, it was too dangerous to do the techniques in earnest, and so you'd spend a certain amount of time training *not* doing what you were really ultimately trying to learn to do.

I don't see us out on the street doing full-contact Judo. My body can't handle full-contact Karate, and the techniques we do, like putting your fingers in someone's eyes and ripping them out—we can't do that! That's true. We're training our bodies to have a response. When I teach women's self-defense and I describe the technique, what we're actually doing in the technique they have never imagined doing to another human being. The act of visualizing that is part of the self-defense training.

With my Karate students, I can go much more graphically. Their visualizations of what they can and would do. *[Laughs]* Kenpo's known for overkill, so they get into it. Much like men get into it. If you're in a big seminar with lots of men and there's somebody teaching a technique which involves a takedown, stomp to the knee, neck break, rip down, pull out the eyes, the men go, "YEAH-H-H-H!" And Karate women eventually go, "Yeah."

I think it is important to train your body to have an automatic reaction so that you're not thinking about your response should you need it on the street. You're not going to be trapped—your body's going to let go. Actually, you'll be a lot calmer. You *will* think. But you set yourself up automatically. And to have the visualizations.

Understand what you're doing to somebody. And what the intention is behind it. I think it's important to talk about intention, whether you're intending to maim, injure, or kill.

You get the response programmed in your body from training, and you make the judgment at the time as to how seriously you are doing this?

Right—and actually, what you're hoping to train for is never to use it, right? *[Laughs]* And you're training your awareness and shedding those victim mentalities and you're not putting yourself out on the street as a target any more. It's not going to be easy to attack these women. They *are* going to fight back. And they're going to be more effective, fighting back. I think your Judo teacher is absolutely right. On the other hand, I can't do Judo—I mean, my body wouldn't be able to do Judo. And their bodies give out. And Jujutsu too—the Jujutsu stuff I do, I mean, there's just so much my throat can be choked. They choke each other out regularly. That's part of their training. And recovery from that.

The bad thing is sometimes you do that Judo throw and the attacker gets up. And the same thing with Karate. You think you've done a real good technique, but the attacker continues. So I think it's important to know that these are not necessarily the end of the sentence. I don't feel the need to have to actually take everything through to the ultimate. We don't do that in all of our lives. We kind of rehearse things through.

Men have mentioned a similar point to me, but maybe to some extent what they're talking about are the kinds of fights men would get into, which, you were saying, are different than the kinds women get into.

Women don't go into bars and get caught up in a bar brawl. Even like Scott's—yeah, women pick up the pool cues and bash them on each other's heads. I mean, let's get real! In the bars in New York, women pulled knives. Men are basically the big boys in the schoolyard *[demonstrates big, swinging punches]*. Women don't get into this swing out. Women carry knives! "Hey, I've got a knife."—"I'm outta here. You win fight." Women give up more easily. Or they pull each other's hair. I've seen that too. But overall, it's not nearly as common an experience for women. When I talk to men, it's just more common for them.

At the other end of the spectrum, it seems that important aspects of many of the internal arts are spirituality and healing. Do you also find these in your art?

I'm not sure Kenpo talks about healing. As I said, it's overkill—that's spirituality: You will see the light! That's when I say Karate is a little more external. When I'm really focusing—people call it the flow, or being in the zone, and I have been that way in Karate—you and your partner are yin and yang, really the opposite of each other. You're one. That's a wonderful state. It doesn't happen every single time. It happens more as you practice.

I think every reputable martial artist and art has a spiritual side. The spirituality's very—vague for me. There's certainly ki and I certainly have a connection to my ki. I have a feeling that everybody will find it, and it's not for me to say that this is the path. This is my path, but there're a lot of paths. I've gotten that from martial artists—from martial artists in other styles, actually. It's been helpful.

There's an ethical component to Kenpo. Parker has written about that. He has a whole series—as you progress you also make an increasingly more serious commitment, starting out from basically learning to take care of yourself to nurturing your students, not harming your students, not talking about them in derogatory ways. We don't always talk about that. I have to remind myself to overtly weave it in as I teach.

I found it necessary to go out of my art and learn healing stuff, maybe *because* of all the visualization, knowing about all the violence against women, and battering on my body, battering on other bodies—I wanted to know how to heal as much as I wanted to know how to break a bone. I took acupressure classes and massage classes. I spent a couple years in classes and then training with other practitioners. It has been incredibly helpful in encouraging my students to breathe and relax, in including massage and touch in closure of classes, so you can feel like you got some nourishment as well, and in immediately treating injuries. I'm not freaked out when one of my students drops from having her diaphragm collapse. I know what to do. And there's a lot of exchange around that.

We have a requirement—it just reminded me I was supposed to go do this: For black belt you have to be CPR and first aid certified. I made that requirement in the school. I think by black belt it's very important that you have looked at how do you heal. Because if you've injured—have you ever injured another person?

No more than a scratch—

It is incredible—I have dropped people. And I have been the cause of someone not being able to train for a couple months because of an out-of-control strike. To do that—to be on that end of things is probably more internally painful than the actual injury. I would much rather be injured than cause an injury to someone else! I'll heal! But to know, for example, that I blew somebody's knee out—I never blew anybody's knee out, but I do know of people who have, and it was accidental. It was truly accidental. You feel so awful, you have to have something. You have to know how to give back! You know, it's inevitable in this kind of contact that you're going to injure someone. If you know that you can provide some kind of compassionate care, maybe not at that moment, but for others, then I think there's a balance that happens. That's what I'm after.

That's kind of the learning I want now—more of how do you heal. How do we get our bodies stronger, more flexible? I spend a lot of time on body mechanics. The thing that's interesting—you're going around finding this—is the more you do, the more you train, the more experience and years you put in, the more things come together. When I go to a weightlifting class—"Those are the muscles I need for that punch!" Everything starts to feed my martial art. That's my primary area, and other things support it.

CHAPTER 18

There's More to Fighting Than Smashing Things

Like Lloyda French, Didi Goodman came up with thoughtful and thorough answers to my evolving questions about hard-style martial arts, fighting, and competition. Also like Lloyda, Didi has long experience in the women martial artists' community. She also has served as a PAWMA board member and president, and she was one of the organizers of the first PAWMA training camp I attended, in 1993 at Two Rivers Camp in the Sierra Nevada. She has made her living as a writer in the past but currently pursues martial arts full-time, teaching at the school she founded in Oakland, California, Cuong Nhu Redwood Dojo, and at her teacher's school in neighboring Berkeley.

Cuong Nhu, an eclectic art sometimes referred to as a style of Karate, is the style Didi has come to consider hers, but she started her martial arts training with Tae Kwon Do, a Korean hard style known particularly for kicking—Didi told me that the name means "The Way of the Foot and Fist." She has also studied both Karate and Aikido. We met one afternoon at her home high in the hills in Oakland, California. From the back of the living room a grand piano that seemed to me to be unusually large loomed over us, but the rich autumn sunshine pouring in through the front windows held it at bay, warming us and an elderly cat who dozed through our conversation. Road work under way in the street below the house gave me some concern about tape recording, but I needn't have worried. A small woman in her late thirties with dark hair and eyes, Didi has a larger presence than her slight build suggests, and her voice, though pleasantly low and soft sounding, came through on the tape with definition and clarity.

DIDI GOODMAN

Tae Kwon Do and Cuong Nhu

I started Tae Kwon Do when I was in college—this was in 1976, when I was eighteen or nineteen—just because one day I saw some friends of mine practicing kicks. They had taken a class the year before and gotten together to see if they remembered their stuff. I was drawn to it for completely inexplicable reasons: "What are you doing?—I have to do this." I started training, and I just loved it, learning these kicks.

The modern dance program was big at my college, and everybody would take modern dance to get some of the PE credits we had to have to graduate. I would see them doing these silly exercises, and no way was I going to do that. I was too embarrassed and shy and inhibited. But I guess I have a dancer trapped inside me, and the Tae Kwon Do class was perfect—this is in retrospect—because the discipline and structure of it, the militaristic structure, takes away your opportunity to be embarrassed. The guy says, "Do this," and you do it. Because of the structure you don't have the opportunity to worry about having to do things in front of people. It's also more like work. You're working to do something difficult with your body and you're not thinking of it as self-expression.

Did you have a background in athletics?

I was an athletic child, but then I repudiated all that right about the age girls are supposed to. I went the "I'm an intellectual" route. "Sports are stupid. Competition is stupid." The only tolerable way I had found to do my PE credit was to swim laps.

But I wasn't even doing very well at that, because you had to actually get around to going and then get someone to sign the paper. I've been shy all my life and I still am, although people don't believe me any more. Getting the lifeguard to sign the paper for me was almost too much sometimes. When I found this Tae Kwon Do class with my friends, I went every day, I was so into it. If there wasn't class, we worked out. I worked out so hard, and having been out of shape for all those years and never using those kicking muscles, I got really sore. I could hardly walk a lot of the time.

I had a background fighting with my brother too—a little bit of sports, but also violence. I wasn't a nonviolent person or timid really. I'm a shy person and a combative person in the same body, so that's got to be why this was so perfect for me. It was discovering something that completely fit my nature.

The guy who taught the Tae Kwon Do class was a sophomore in college. He had grown up in Thailand, where he'd studied the martial arts and gotten his black belt. Now I realize how inexperienced he was. He had only had his black belt for a couple of months. And then he discovered college life and quit teaching. My friend and I practiced together for a while, and then that wasn't enough. She started going to a school—this was in Portland, Oregon—called Karate for Women.

I eventually followed her there and took classes for a while. The woman who started the school, Pauline Short, was awesome. I think hers was the first women's school in the country. It was founded in 1965. To go through all the bullshit that women had to go through before people like her started schools—she got to where she was by beating men and forcing them to let her compete in tournaments. But I'm sure she would have hated to be called a feminist. She was from a different background.

She saw that women didn't get proper training from men because men didn't respect them, so she started a school where women would respect each other and train each other as hard as the men did with each other. Karate for Women used to turn out hordes of tournament-winning women, and they were sometimes resented by other schools, especially mixed schools, who would send women to tournaments; but since they didn't train them very well, the women would get clobbered. Clobbered by this macho gang of women who didn't even train with real men! This is how it was back in the old days. A lot has changed over the years. There're lots of women's schools now, and lots of women role models in mixed schools.

How did the Karate compare to the Tae Kwon Do that you'd been doing?

It was very similar. One difference was that Pauline was a very competition-oriented teacher, and we trained for sparring. A lot more partner drills, really intense kicking, blocking, kicking, blocking kind of stuff. More hand techniques than we were doing in Tae Kwon Do—that's sort of the defining thing about Tae Kwon Do, that it's kicking. Tae Kwon Do kicks might tend to be a little bigger and there're more jumping kicks so the kicks will just look—I don't know, bigger. There are some stylistic differences, like whether your knee goes forward or around on a certain kick, which in the Tae Kwon Do kick makes the kick bigger. But we also, in Tae Kwon Do, did the shorter version. We regarded it as the shorter version, sneaking in and sparring as opposed to doing the big powerful one. In some styles you learn it the short way and you never do the big way. Pauline's style had strong kicking, all the same kicks, but a lot of hand fighting also. And there was more intensity in terms of partner work and sparring in Pauline's school.

That was her personal emphasis?

It was her style actually—they called it Wu Ying Mun. My understanding is that she and the man she trained with and was partners with for a while developed this style for top-level competition sparring, taking what they regarded as the best fighting techniques for that type of training and competition. So it's really an American style; they just gave it a Chinese name. I don't know whether people call it that any more. People who studied with them teach what they call American Freestyle Karate, which is, I think, pretty much in the same spirit.

I was lucky to take classes from Pauline, though it was only for a short time. It was just a couple of years before she retired from teaching. The school still exists. Some friends of mine ran it for a long time, actually, including the same friend I started training with in college.

My senior year of college I convinced myself I didn't have time to do anything except worry about school. Then I moved to Berkeley to go to graduate school. So there were two, two and a half years where I did absolutely nothing physical whatsoever. I remember going back to Portland to visit my friend, and we went to the dojo, because she had continued training there. Pauline walked in, and she was *teeny*. I had remembered her as if she were ten feet tall, and she's like five-one. I thought, "My god, I'm bigger than she is!" I'm five-four. But that's the kind of impression that someone like that makes. I think martial artists who have trained and achieved a certain level of skill—or *presence*—are big, and it doesn't matter how small their bodies are. She was just this tiny little woman, and how she went through all those years of training with obnoxious men in the early sixties must have been amazing.

I spent a couple of years in graduate school at UC Berkeley—basically hated graduate school, wasn't very happy. They had a Tae Kwon Do club and I kept thinking of going, but not going, because I was too shy to walk into the room. I finally did just march in and take it up again, just flat out started going every day and got really sore—got really sick—but I never stopped again after that.

At UC Berkeley Tae Kwon Do, I trained with all these huge guys—they were huge because they were just starting to do full-contact tournaments at that time and working toward getting into the Olympics, and gradually littler guys and women would get sick of getting bashed to death and would quit. I remember looking at a videotape of, I don't know, maybe it was my brown belt test, and it was like this *[traces a silhouette with her finger in the air]*, one guy, another guy, another guy, *me [a sharp dip down and then back up]*, another guy, another guy. They were training gladiators basically. There were a few women and we were the same size, so whenever they'd say, "Pair up by size," the four women would end up sparring with each other over and over again and the seventy-five men would have lots of people to train with. There was a lot to put up with there.

My mother—I was never raised with any doubt that I should do whatever the hell I wanted. I was at least as good as men. I always looked at all the attitudes in the world as being kind of surprising. I still have that kind of outlook even though I know better—"People don't really think that, do they?" They do, of course, and I've been angry and frustrated and all of that, and yet I still think, "People don't really think that, do they?"

But in this case the training was worth it?

I loved it! I liked a lot of the guys, too, even though many of them were sexist jerks. There's something about training in martial arts, because of the nature of it, the ritual and formality, and the hard work and striving and shared ordeals, the baring of what it is to be human, that brings together people who are vastly different from one another and who wouldn't ordinarily get along together. I am constantly amazed at how many great people I have come to know through martial arts, and how many of them are people I would never have had anything to do with before martial arts gave me this different perspective on people.

Mr. Min, the head of the martial arts program—he's great. He taught the PE classes and oversaw the evening club program, which was mostly taught by his black belts. I fault him in a way for all the sexism, but really the problem is attitudes that are too big for some head of a university program to cure, I guess, unless he sets himself out to do just that one thing. He was always wanting to have more women—he wanted to have a women's team because there were some other colleges that had women who were always beating us. Competition was the big thing there, and I wasn't interested in competition.

When we sparred in class, I was competitive. I wanted to do my best. I wanted to score points and beat them. But when you make it into a tournament, with medals and trophies, people change. Suddenly this person will do anything to bash you and get the judges to call a point. My response to that is if this person cares that intensely about winning the match, then let them have it. I just don't care that much. But you can't have an attitude like that and compete. I would go to tournaments and get bashed and lose sometimes to people who were obviously not very good.

Didi Goodman demonstrating a kick, Redwood Dojo (Oakland, Calif., 1995 or 1996).

What was it exactly that did interest you? Can you pin that down?

Training. Working out. Seeking excellence. Practicing forms. And sparring—not for tournaments but for training. Trying to master difficult things, jumps or spinning back kicks—things that one doesn't think one can ever do. I did a lot of that there. Those were my formative years, where I put in a chunk of years in a row.

The fact that it's very physical and exhausting is exhilarating. You work hard, and you sweat, and you're trying to master something really difficult. You're striving. And with all these other people— even though it's a very individual thing, all these other people are there working toward the same thing. You're sore all the time. It feels great! It makes you realize you're a living, physical thing. What's appealing about martial arts practice to me is reaching an understanding of what it is to be a mental and a physical thing at once.

And you could just train at the UC program. Mr. Min appreciated people who were interested in martial arts even though the system wasn't appreciating them very much. But he didn't have a clue as to why the women kept quitting. He thought, "Women don't like it. They don't like to get bruised."

So many of the guys were completely disrespectful of women. People don't understand how it wears on you to have to put up with that. You can grab them by the throat and make a few of them see it, but—you know, young, educated American liberal guys are the ones who perpetuate all the sexism, and they don't have a clue. They can't put themselves in your place. There were people who would treat women partners with total disrespect and then wonder why all the women quit. The only women who did well were the ones who were as big as the guys, so they could bash on them and get bashed on and not get demoralized, and people like me, who could get all bashed up and limp around and not be demoralized by it.

A certain number of women did seem to fit the stereotype that they wanted to do the pretty parts, they wanted it to be like ballet, and they didn't want to fight, or they found it too unpleasant if they had to really do sparring and actually hit people. A lot of those same women, if they were given the right sort of training and attitudes, would see that it was something they could do and that it was valuable to do. I have seen lots of women who start out being timid about it and not liking it, adjusting.

I didn't have to overcome anything like that. [Laughs] I was perfectly comfortable with fighting and violence and kicking people. It just stands to reason that you're going to get bruised if you train hard. I guess it maybe is the same thing that other kinds of athletes have—the ones who excel are the ones who are willing to suffer pain and injury and keep going. I just happen to be one of the people who is willing to do that, I guess. In martial arts. I was never willing to do it in anything else. I found the thing I loved doing. I wanted to do it and part of what it involved was this kind of violent physicality.

There was a problem in that there was way too much bashing. At that time bashing was just

about what it was about, and training for tournaments. So maybe there wasn't enough time spent on the other sides of it that would have shown people what was worth pursuing about it. What got to me finally was that I realized I was hurting people on purpose to make them respect me, and I didn't want to do that. I would pair up with a guy and he would look around, hoping to find some other guy or find a woman and make me go pair up with her. I was constantly having to say, "No. I won't do that. You're going to work with me." I would hit them really hard so that they would stop acting like I couldn't do anything. I did that so many times, I finally nailed a perfectly nice guy who didn't need to be nailed, and he said, "Ow! Could you not hit me that hard?"

I started thinking about it. I thought, I've turned into this monster because of this attitude, and that's not what I want out of this. A friend of mine who had also trained at Cal answered an ad for an all-women's Tae Kwon Do school, and we went there together. For about four years I trained at both places. Eventually I got my black belt and faded out of the UC club—where graduate students are considered old people, and by then I had quit graduate school and—and gotten even older. [Laughs] Mr. Min would refer to me and some of the others as "Old Man" and "Old Woman." Affectionately, of course, but I was—How old was I? In my early twenties. Got to be maybe twenty-five. I guess at the time I thought that was pretty old too.

So I kind of faded out of the UC club and was going to this other place, an all-women's school. Which had a lot of problems. It served a good purpose for me while I was also training at Cal and then stopped serving that purpose, I guess. It couldn't stand on its own.

It was a little pressure cooker, an intense,

closed social group with an us versus them attitude—and you were expected to like it that way. If you knew there was a world outside that had a lot in it that was of value, that could actually enhance what you were doing, then you weren't welcome or you were beaten out of your attitude or you were eventually driven out.

The school didn't have any interaction even with women outside of the school?

No, none at all. The fact that I did was always kind of, I think, grating on people there. Although I chose to be ignorant of it in the same way I was talking about earlier—"You can't really think that!" That's kind of been my problem. Maybe it's a blessing, but it's also a problem.

It could be a good defensive position at times. . . .

Yeah. When the instructor would say completely irrational things, I would say, "She didn't really mean that. She must have meant—" You know. I didn't realize what sort of thing I was in, I guess. The stuff about dysfunctional families only came into vogue later, and I didn't come from a dysfunctional family, so I didn't know what they looked like. Now I see what was going on there. I think part of it was there wasn't any real politics behind its being an all-women school—nothing about the quality of training or feminism. Those of us who had political beliefs were really just pretending they applied to the school, because they should have, but the school as such had no relevant ethic. It was more a girls-only social group.

Anyway, there was a woman in the school who found out about PAWMA. She went to PAWMA camp and talked about it, and the following year, I got another friend of mine to go with me. We were black belts, Tae Kwon Do black belts, just about the only ones there. There weren't too many Tae Kwon Do people for a few years there. We saw all this great stuff and all these awesome instructors and went back trying to share some of this at this little paranoid school, but it didn't go over that well. There was a lot of resistance to outside ideas. But now the two of us knew about PAWMA camp. We went again the following year, when Mary Davis, a Cuong Nhu sixth-degree black belt, taught some classes. I found out also that my cousin, who had been a Tae Kwon Do black belt at Cal when I was just coming up through the ranks, was studying Cuong Nhu, and I started getting interested in that. Also that first year at PAWMA camp I saw an Aikido demonstration and something about it captivated me—although Tae Kwon Do people hate falling down. We have to be standing up and kicking. We don't mind knocking other people down, but we don't want to fall down. I thought, that's awesome, and that instructor in particular—this was Jamie Zimron—you can just see the power in it. For about two years it was kind of percolating in my mind. The next PAWMA camp I took some of her classes, and some months after that I woke up one day and said, "I have to go to Aikido classes." I found Jamie's phone number and called her up and started to go.

This precipitated my falling out with the Tae Kwon Do instructor. It started out as a discussion of money, because Aikido classes were expensive. I was doing a lot of teaching at the Tae Kwon Do school, and we had had an arrangement where teachers didn't pay dues, but that had gone away because we hadn't had any new students in a long

Didi Goodman demonstrating Cuong Nhu techniques at the opening ceremony for Redwood Heights Community Center (Oakland, Calif., December 1991).

PHOTO COURTESY OF DIDI GOODMAN

I think you said Cuong Nhu is a Vietnamese art?

Its founder, Sensei Ngo Dong, is Vietnamese. It's an eclectic art based on several styles. *Cuong nhu* means "hard, soft." Shotokan Karate is the hard-style foundation of it, and we practice Shotokan forms, but they've mutated a bit. We learn Wing Chun forms as well, starting at green belt level, and Aikido techniques, Judo techniques, and principles from T'ai Chi and from *vovinam,* Vietnamese martial arts. More and more as we advance through the ranks, we incorporate the spirit of soft style—yielding, flexible, defensive rather than offensive, blending rather than clashing with an attack.

Those are things that aren't in Karate or Tae Kwon Do?

I think they are, though perhaps not overtly. Not at first. The purpose—if you want to look at superficial purposes—the purpose of starting with hard style is to develop your sense of power and ability to break things *[laughs]* and strength—muscle strength. Get conditioning. Start from nothing and get a sense of how strong you are. The soft-style arts we see as going in the direction of getting more subtle about how you use your strength, how you use your body, and avoiding clashing, because clashing only goes so far. In Cuong Nhu, after black belt level, one of the ways you can get points toward promotion is to earn a black belt in another style, usually a soft style like Judo or Aikido.

time. I brought up the subject with her and that precipitated this whole discussion about why we didn't have any new students. But I was doing Aikido at the time, which was nice, because when I got thrown out of the Tae Kwon Do school, I had a dojo to go to! Then my cousin told me to go talk to her Cuong Nhu teacher, and I ended up going there. It was perfect—Cuong Nhu was like Tae Kwon Do plus Aikido. I wouldn't say that all the trouble I went through before was something that should have happened, but it did end up sending me where I belonged.

There's More to Fighting Than Smashing Things

That seems like a switch! A lot of the women I've talked to do seem open to other influences, but traditionally didn't most of the arts emphasize keeping to themselves?

Chauvinism and purity, yeah. In Cuong Nhu we are actively encouraged to study other styles. Sensei Dong—who is still alive and active—started Cuong Nhu officially in 1965 in Vietnam. He came to the United States to get his Ph.D., in 1971, I think, and started a school in Florida. I guess he put a pretty solid foundation into his core students there. He went back to Vietnam and got in political trouble. He was an intellectual, the president of a college. He's a very interesting person. Very hyper, very philosophical. Active. I'm sure he would never keep his mouth closed about anything. So he got in trouble with the government and had to flee. His students in Florida thought he was dead.

Eventually he did escape and some day hopefully he'll write a book about it. The people who thought he was dead found out he was alive and brought him back to the United States. Now I think most practitioners of Cuong Nhu are in the United States. I've met and trained with Sensei Dong many times. There's a national camp every year, and I've been going to that every year since I started. He gives the black belt tests and dan tests, and he gives seminars. He's quite a character.

What do you find the status of women to be in Cuong Nhu?

There are five sixth-degree black belts in the style, the first ones to be promoted to that rank, and one of the them is a woman, Mary Davis, the woman I took classes from at PAWMA camp. Mary is awesome, and I am sure a lot of women have looked up to her. I don't think, looking at Mary, that anybody could have ever doubted that women should do the training in every way. When my teacher talks about the old days, it sounds like Mary has the reputation of being the toughest, meanest teacher. To some degree, that's how it was for women in the early days. You had to be the toughest, meanest one. I think she's great. She has a big school in Atlanta with lots of women in her school.

The national Cuong Nhu camp is the closest thing that I can imagine to being like PAWMA camp with men. The style has so many styles within it, you're going to seminars from lots of different perspectives. It's very open. There's way more than a token number of women, and there're a lot of women black belts.

Cuong Nhu has been my art now for over six years—since 1988—which isn't really that long. I've been doing martial arts for sixteen or so years. In some ways I still feel that I'm a newcomer in Cuong Nhu, even though I have a school and lots of students, but I guess I can be in that position because of all those other years I have behind me. I did Aikido with Jamie for three or four years. I only stopped when I started my own dojo—didn't have time to commute. Not long after that she moved out of town. Sometime I'll find a class that I can go to, but right now, I can't fit it in my schedule. I do a lot of teaching, and I still work out with my Cuong Nhu teacher in Berkeley.

I wonder to what extent you can puzzle out what about these arts, this progression of arts, attracted you—whether it was the new range of techniques or movements, like the

Aikido rolling and falling, or the different teachers and the attitudes of people in the style? Or internal aspects—as you got older perhaps you got more interested in that?

I—hmmm. When I saw Jamie doing the demo at the first PAWMA camp, I sometimes tell people it looked like she had light sabers, you know, from *Star Wars.* She was doing practically nothing and yet obviously completely controlling her uke. I felt that I could see that she had command of some kind of *force,* and I wanted to find out what it was. I did not want to do rolling and falling, and I hated it. I injured my back almost right away. I'm a lot better at it now. I wanted to learn what—what the art was.

The funny thing is when I first started Tae Kwon Do in college, I didn't know anything about martial arts, and I picked up the way people talk about this style and that style and what they read in Kung Fu magazines. The black belt from Thailand who was teaching talked about Aikido as the supreme martial art. You had to study it for decades, but if you did, you would be in command of incredible powers. You would never have to strike anyone and you'd be able to defeat all opponents. It was also spiritual. It was superior to what we were doing but required too much investment. *[Laughs]* We wanted immediate returns.

So I had that notion about Aikido, and it seemed to fit. I thought going into it, this is really better than what I've been doing. The idea that you don't hit people. That fighting is messy and nasty and morally inferior. But also that Aikido is really, really difficult. It requires years and years of training to be effective. And patience and precision. It's too hard for most purposes. I feel that that's true, and yet with the foundation I had, a dozen years or so, I was ready to be a beginner.

I wouldn't have liked it initially, because you don't get immediate results—not if you have a sense of the quality of what you want. I know that beginners who haven't done other arts find all kinds of things in Aikido and probably do find immediate results in different ways, but martially, what you get immediately is—well, you don't get it immediately. You get other things. You begin working toward it, but you don't get the same kind of gratification as from kicking and punching and getting really sore and sweating a whole lot. I'm happy to admit that the inferior pleasure is what I wanted or needed.

As I understand Aikido, it's like T'ai Chi in that you use the other person's energy, not your own. My sense of Tae Kwon Do and other hard styles is that that's not part of them, but perhaps it is and I just don't see it?

That's an interesting question. Technique-wise, put simply, you're learning how to develop your power and smash things with it. Fighting is a different matter. Fighting is more subtle than smashing things. There are a lot of elements to it, including protecting yourself, and as you get more sophisticated you have to incorporate more concepts of using your opponent's movement, using less of your own energy—conserving energy. So those principles are there in the hard-style practice, but they come later on.

How close to fighting is the training that you do?

We wear protective equipment in Cuong Nhu, but

it's to protect against accidents—it's not sufficient to hit people *really* hard. We practice kicking targets and breaking boards. Kicking targets and bags gives you chances to learn how to hit as hard as you possibly can. Sparring teaches you different things. The things in sparring that are relevant to a real fight and to a real self-defense situation have mostly to do with being familiar with what a fight is going to look like. Being used to the idea of being hit—and you can get hit pretty hard—and to know that you'll survive it. And to know strategically how to deal with it. Not to be completely thrown off by someone charging at you.

It would be foolish to think sparring is like a real fight. I tell people to look at it as a game. I think it's important that people should know the difference, but at the same time, the things you learn by getting punched in the face and discovering that it wasn't that bad are important. In Tae Kwon Do we used to wear body armor and you were supposed to hit full power—you got a point by making the person stagger so that they'd know you really hit them. That was maybe good training in a way. Every school I've been in since has told me I hit too hard. In Tae Kwon Do there were other things that pointed to the fact that it was a sport and not a fight. You couldn't punch to the face, for instance, and that's the first thing that'll happen in a real fight. Again, though, self-defense is a whole different thing. Maybe the only way you can practice that is in one of those padded attacker things—and those guys actually get hurt all the time. You can't practice hurting people in class.

It does all fit together in the end. *[Draws a circle in the air between us]* If Aikido's up here, basic hard style is down here, and they move toward each other. They're all part of one whole picture, but they start out from completely different places and they emphasize different things and they look different. A lot of the people who start out down here aren't interested in what's up here and don't ever get there. Then they look at what they've done and think to themselves that the two aren't connected. But they are. Cuong Nhu acknowledges that as a style, and Sensei Dong—he wants all of it basically. If you discover a new art somewhere and tell him about it, it will become a requirement next year. He wants people to become more like aikidoists as they go up through the black belt ranks.

You were telling me that Cuong Nhu included Chinese concepts, too, of ch'i and so on. Does it get into that expressly, and is that something that is also underlying, say, Tae Kwon Do as well and it's just not expressed?

That's exactly what I think. I think those principles are present in all the arts. The arts that give you a lot of visible concrete techniques and tournaments and other things that can draw your interest down here *[again sketches a circle in the air]* cause a lot of people to think the rest of it isn't there. It permits people to overlook that part. But I don't think anyone who studies for years and years and years misses it. After a while you can't keep missing it. It really is all in there.

One of the best things I've gotten out of studying Aikido and various things I've encountered at PAWMA camp, some of which I'm pursuing, is the perspective on my own art. I still think I have my art, which now is Cuong Nhu, but I could say more generically hard style or Karate, and I take up Aikido and that teaches me things about what was already there in my own art. Not everyone sees it that way. The reason I've thought about it so much is because I would be in Aikido class and people would say, "In Karate, you don't do da-da-

da-da-da. In Aikido we do this." Or if I was having trouble with something, it would be because Karate is this way. No-o-o! It's because this is hard. I don't know what I'm doing!

A lot of Karate people do some Aikido. They're interested in techniques and they say, "There are a lot of good, powerful, nasty techniques that you can learn, but all that ki stuff—" Really what's going on is that they're misrepresenting what Karate is about. They're wrong. In Karate we do use ki flow, and you can't have excellent technique and make the most of your power unless you're doing that. Punching *isn't* about arm muscles. If it were, the only people who would be good at it would be big guys, and it's not true. Nobody thinks that's true.

Do you think these misconceptions come from the process of translating these Asian arts into the U.S. context? Are people just learning the physical parts? Do we need more of the cultural background and the philosophical background than we're getting?

My angle on this is as follows: The physical part, the technique part, doesn't make it martial art, in that for it to be martial art it has to embody an underlying philosophy. And it's the cultural background that ties the practice to the underlying philosophy. But you don't have to know anything about the culture or the underlying philosophy. I think the cultural rituals having to do with respect and reverence and making you treat what you're doing as if it's special bring you benefits whether you pay attention to them or not, whether you understand the cultural origins or not.

At the same time, in a superficial way, I think a lot of the rules and traditions don't fit very well

with American culture, and this causes problems all over the place. Now we're getting back to that women's Tae Kwon Do school! Because these things come from a culture where respect and hierarchy and power relationships are fixed and ordered and they're part of the deal and everyone understands them. Not to say that they aren't abused probably just as often in Asian countries, but people understand them. In their proper cultural context, people have a basis for telling what's abuse and what isn't.

So there's a potential for trouble in the United States when you get a teacher who can't draw the line in a culturally appropriate way. You get people who take the rules and traditions and misuse them for their own purposes. They mix personal and martial freely and they mix friendship and training freely, and then the things that go wrong over here get mixed in with the power relationships over there, and they use the power in ways that are personally satisfying that are inappropriate.

Martial arts attract people who like power. I guess all of us do in a way, and a lot of people who like power like it for abusive reasons—the same reasons, I guess, people in other positions of authority end up abusing their authority. There's a real invitation to it in martial arts, which are *about* power, really. I think people need to understand that aspect of it. There's a Japanese instructor in a school I know who runs the school in a way that must be how he was raised. Plus he's an abusive guy. And the school is full of Americans who are just dying to be injured by him in training and clean his house and do his laundry and he just—I don't know. Are we making these students into better people by appealing to something in their nature that is a little off? It's off because they were raised here in America and they need to be asking themselves why they want to act that way. Here what makes you a better person and one who's better able to function in society is a whole different thing, I would guess—I'm certainly no expert on Asian cultures, but from general impressions. There's a lot we can get out of the—the remnants of the culture that come with the art that is beneficial to us. It's the kind of universally beneficial stuff that makes a person react better and function better and be more calm, and that calls attention to the ideas of respect and honor and mindfulness. But we shouldn't accidentally take on things that really don't fit in our culture, like unthinking servitude.

I'm taking up Naginata now. I take Sensei Tanaka's workshop at PAWMA camp every year she gives it—I joke with her, "I'm here for my once-a-year practice session."

Now there's something with a lot of formality and ceremonialness about it—like where the partners slowly kneel with one knee facing each other and they each move one hand from their weapon to their thigh and slide the hand down the front of the leg facing the opponent—

I surmise that you're signaling your trust of the person you're practicing with by going on your knee and taking your hand off of your weapon to bow. But you don't take your hand very far from your weapon! I see the reason they do it so formally and as such a central part of the practice coming from the recognition that it's a matter of life and death. A sword against a naginata—you're practicing something that's meant to kill people. So you can't be casual about it. Even with an oak weapon, if you're swinging down at the person and they're not there with their sword, you crack them over the head. So imagine what it would be

like if it were a real blade. That's how I see that formality. It embodies the seriousness of it, the life-and-death part of it, I think.

You can't be sloppy with a huge sharp blade! We can be so sloppy with our fists and our feet that we get completely lazy, and most people never get beyond brawling really. Though it can be skillful, pretty brawling. I heard myself say in class—I never know what I'm going to say when I go teach—if my hand were a blade, if it were a sword—and Aikido sword practice is the same way—you wouldn't act the way you act when you're sparring. You would act a completely different way. You would know that your life was on the line. That's how we should be training all the time, but we don't. We forget and we get caught up in the particulars of our techniques.

Other arts are constantly teaching me about my art. I almost thought I keep going to new arts for new stuff to do, and that's part of what it is, but not all of it. I guess I would get bored of them pretty quickly except that it keeps feeding back in to what I'm really doing—I'm pretty much just doing martial arts right now. I have made my living as a writer, but I spent the last year or so taking less work and doing more teaching and building up my school.

It seems that just about everybody, by the time they've done this for some number of years, gets into teaching. They talk about how much they learn through teaching and through working with students—it's like students form a new medium that you do your art in. I'm beginning to wonder if teaching is perhaps the *only* way to advance after a certain point. How would you keep

developing and learning if you didn't have students?

Teaching has been a formal part of every art I've been in, in that you were supposed to start teaching. There's a bit of self-interest in that, because the instructors need assistants. Tae Kwon Do is very imperialistic. They want to spread it everywhere, so they need to make lots of black belts and make them go start their schools. Mr. Min was like that toward his older black belts—raise them up to a certain point and then he wanted to kick them out and make them start a school.

I suspect that what you said is really the case, that you can go only so far without teaching. Maybe it has to do with techniques versus the real meaning of the art, because you can get your techniques without teaching, although you do gain a lot of insight into them by analyzing them. Without teaching, you don't start thinking about other people. If martial arts are supposed to make you a better person, make you a better part of the world, you have to at some point start thinking about other people. And teaching makes you do that.

It's a technique for doing that maybe? Built into the system for that purpose?

That's what I was thinking. There used to be guys at Cal who didn't want to teach. They just wanted to do tournaments, but Mr. Min would make them teach. These guys were good at competing, but they were kind of—you know, I worried a bit what it was going to be like when they were teaching class. I'd think, "This guy's not very thoughtful, not very analytical." But they were forced to teach the class, and I'd see a guy who wasn't particularly thoughtful have to start thinking about what

he was going to teach and thinking about what the students were doing—and start to be interested in students and to do a good job. Pulling through. I don't know what it was like for him, but from my perspective he became much more human than he was previously. I had just thought of him as some guy who's good at beating people up in tournaments and not particularly interesting as a human being. Being forced to teach, he became an interesting human being. I think maybe that is what it's about.

Sensei Dong is an entomologist by training. He likes to categorize things. His philosophy is always the five this, the five that. He has the Five Loves of a Sensei: martial arts, teaching, sharing, students, and growth. Sensei have to love sharing, they have to love people—students—and they have to love growing, or learning from what they're doing. I was thinking he's describing something that's true—if you're going to teach, you have to go through these stages if you aren't inclined that way already. You do have to end up caring about people, because you have to learn about them and want to find ways to give things to them. You have to want to give them something. If you don't care about people, you can't teach them. A lot of people probably don't think of themselves as being interested in doing that and then find it by being made to do it. So it is a trick that way.

With the teaching you do, do you get enough time for your own practice?

I have to make a big effort. I would spend the same number of hours practicing probably, but—well, I don't know, you've got to find the hours. I still go to Cuong Nhu classes in Berkeley. The problem is I

I should be working out more on my own, but one thing I guess I haven't really learned is self-discipline. *[Laughs]* Martial arts is supposed to teach you self-discipline and it's supposed to spread to every aspect of your life. Of course, it doesn't. I've been wondering whether that might be true for kids though. Maybe if you get them at a critical period, some of these things we say might actually come true. The parents of some of the kids I teach say, "Oh, little so-and-so concentrates better and he's doing better in school"—all these things that we *say* will happen.

Didi Goodman teaching Cuong Nhu at Redwood Dojo (Oakland, Calif., Fall 1995).

You don't find that your concentration has improved, for example?

I feel that I always had good concentration and that this appealed to me because of that, but training hasn't cured my procrastination. I was thinking that if I had done martial arts when I was a kid maybe I would have practiced the piano more, because now I have this piano and I'm thinking after all these years of not playing how like practicing forms it is. Now I know how to practice forms, so I know how to practice pieces of music, how to get through the hard parts and be patient and all that, which I didn't know when I was a kid and I never practiced—all those wasted years! Some of these kids

also teach there, and you reach a certain point where the classes that are being offered aren't exactly what you need. I can do a certain amount of basic workout, and it's always good, but my perspective on that workout now is to be finding things that help students get better and apply them to my teaching, so that isn't so much applicable to my practice any more. It's hard for me to find workouts other than by myself that are what I need right now. I miss Aikido because of that.

that are my students are taking piano and maybe this is going to make a difference in their lives. We'll never really know.

I teach adults as well, but I have a huge kids' program. I teach in a recreation center that has a lot of kids' programs, so I get lots of kids. It's about fifty–fifty women and men in the adult class. The kids are mostly boys. I encourage the girls. Maybe I have more girls than I would otherwise, because I'm a woman—I think that's true of younger girls, anyway. When they get to a certain age, a lot of them seem to want male instructors, I've noticed. They think they're cuter.

But just to get them to the idea that it is a suitable activity for girls, having a woman instructor might matter.

And sometimes for their parents to think so. But it's still mostly boys, and the girls and boys don't like to train with each other. "Pair up." Girls—fwtt! Boys—fwtt! All the things that I thought were supposed to have been fixed haven't been fixed yet! The girls are timid and criticize themselves and think they don't know anything and think they're wrong even when they're right. The boys are pushy and think they know everything when they don't and—there it is!

I had a funny experience in Tae Kwon Do. Mr. Min had me putting out his magazine for a couple of years, the *Tae Kwon Do Journal.* That's the magazine of the U.S. Tae Kwon Do Union. I was sent, and a friend of mine went with me, to interview a general who was living in Emeryville, a guy who I'd heard was the commander of the Korean forces in Vietnam. At the end of a nothing interview, not finding out anything very interesting, he said he thought it was very nice that we were studying Tae Kwon Do, so that we could become better housewives and mothers. I thought, "You have to pick which people you decide to argue with. The commander of the Korean forces in Vietnam—no, today isn't the day I'm going to take this up with him." Women can do martial arts, but it's so they'll be better at what they're supposed to be. Which depends on where you're from. Unfortunately it hasn't made me a better housewife.

Have you changed in other ways?

When I think of the things that I thought I could never learn how to do when I first started out—I can vividly remember certain things as a beginner, thinking physically I would never be able to do. Now I can do them easily. And I see students learning them. It can't help but change your idea of your ability to overcome obstacles or accomplish the seemingly impossible.

I've changed in my feeling of powerfulness—it's kind of hard to define. As I said, I fought as a kid. I never thought of myself as not being powerful, but you get a completely different sense of your powerfulness if you study martial arts for a long time. Just a feeling of walking around knowing I'm someone who is physically competent. It does change how you feel.

There are still things that shyness gets in the way of, but now I just do them anyway—I'm a shy person doing stuff rather than a shy person doing nothing. I wouldn't say my shyness went away. It's too much part of what I am. Maybe it isn't even something that people should think of curing, just taming or something. Sometimes I say, "I'm a black belt. I should be able to do this." And a couple times I've had to say, "I'm a black belt, I can decide *not* to do this."

CHAPTER 19

Sixty Years on the Mat

Midge Marino talked in her interview about how the Judo sensei Keiko Fukuda came to California from the Kodokan Judo Institute in Japan in the 1960s to teach Women's Judo and eventually settled in San Francisco. "She was our foundation," Midge said, "of really learning Women's Judo." At Eighth Dan, with now sixty years' experience, Fukuda Sensei is the highest-ranked woman in the world in Judo—or probably any other martial art. In her eighties, she continues to teach at the dojo she founded in San Francisco and to travel all over the world to teach and promote Women's Judo.

The aikidoist Gayle Fillman has also studied with Fukuda Sensei. The physical training of Judo was not Gayle's primary interest in seeking to become Fukuda Sensei's student, although Gayle earned a brown belt in that art. Rather it was Fukuda Sensei herself, her character and experience and wisdom, that Gayle wanted to learn about. Like Kendo for Malyne Chiu, Aikido had afforded Gayle no experienced women as models, and much of Gayle's formative study of Aikido was in an entirely male environment. Gayle told me it meant a great deal to her when she found in Fukuda Sensei a woman of great skill and experience in martial arts practice and philosophy—for Fukuda Sensei had studied the philosophy and spirit on which Judo was founded in addition to her physical training at the Kodokan Institute. To this day Fukuda Sensei remains a mentor for Gayle and an adviser to Gayle's Aikido dojo in

Keiko Fukuda (right) and a student demonstrating Judo at the Cherry Blossom Festival (San Francisco, Spring 1995).

matters ranging from Japanese etiquette to budo politics to martial arts philosophy to day-to-day details of running a dojo. Fukuda Sensei's example has informed Gayle's work of community building over the twenty years of running her own dojo. Over the years the two women have formed a close working relationship and deep friendship on the basis of respect and support for each other's art—evidence of their dedication to a deeper spirit that all these arts share.

When I began work on this book Gayle invited me to accompany her to the annual celebra-tion of the Japanese New Year at Fukuda Sensei's dojo, the Soko Joshi Judo Club—San Francisco Women's Judo Club. As unofficial "daughter" dojo, Gayle's Aikido dojo traditionally supplies the mats for this event. I helped her transport them, and our effort was well rewarded with a program that included demonstrations by students, speeches and awards, and a feast of Japanese food. Fukuda Sensei herself also gave a demonstration, that year performing *Itutsu-no-kata* (Forms of Five), a part-ner form like all Judo kata, with Kuniko Takeuchi. Meeting Fukuda Sensei, a short, stocky woman with lively dark eyes and black hair, no one would guess the full span of her years. When she steps onto the mat, all who are present realize they are about to witness something out of the ordinary. Certainly we did that day.

Itutsu-no-kata is quite short, consisting of the five interchanges for which it is named. In fact the kata is unfinished and the name apparently was originally provisional, though both have endured as they are for more than half a century. I was told that this was the last kata that Jigoro Kano, the founder of Judo, developed, and he was still working on it at the time of his death in 1938. I found the kata very beautiful—and fascinating to watch. Unlike the other Judo kata, which even an outsider can see are based very directly on fighting and self-defense tactics, Itutsu-no-kata derives from the movements—or rather, the energetic interplay—of the elemental forces of wind and water. The uke—in this case Kuniko Takeuchi—attacks in long, sweeping runs that bring her up against *tori*—here, Fukuda Sensei—only to recoil from what seems more like a discharge of spiritual energy than any merely physical movement. I was put in mind of the curling explosion of storm waves in Japanese prints, and I saw an unusually clear illustration of the principles of T'ai Chi Ch'uan in tori's imperceptible but obviously effective reshaping and reversal of uke's attacking energy.

Early on in my work on this book, Fukuda Sensei agreed to be interviewed, but her busy schedule of teaching and traveling necessitated several postponements. Then I learned that she would be visiting Ukiah to attend a benefit performance of Japanese music and dance that Gayle had organized. In the early dusk of a stormy November afternoon I met with Fukuda Sensei in her motel room for the first of several opportunities I have had to talk with her. As on other occasions, Machiko Shimada, a Japanese-born Aikido student of Gayle's who has assisted me greatly with advice and explanation about things Japanese, was present as translator—and indeed collaborator in the interview—as the three of us talked in a combination of English and Japanese.

KEIKO FUKUDA

Judo

We heard that a few years ago, in 1990, you, Sensei, were declared a National Living Treasure in Japan, as part of a Japanese program that honors masters in different arts and activities. Certainly you are also a treasure for women with the example you set for us!

Thank you very much. I have been given many awards and prizes.

And you've just heard now that you've been awarded the Eighth Dan—eighth-degree black belt—in Judo by the American Judo Federation and also the Kodokan Judo Institute in Japan?

Yes. I am very happy. Yet this news also makes me sad, because another teacher, Noritomi Sensei, spent so many years as Sixth Dan when they would not award higher degrees to women. She died ten years ago.

Your grandfather was also a martial artist? Did that influence your interest in Judo?

When I was a baby, as was the custom, I was sent to live in the country with a farmer's family. Each child in my family went to a different family. When I came back to my family in Tokyo, I was five or six years old. Several years later my father died. My grandfather, Hachinosuke Fukuda, who had been a head teacher of Jujutsu during the Tokugawa Shogunate, died thirty-four years before I was born, but my grandmother told stories about him. She had studied Naginata, as was common for samurai wives. I was only a little girl while my grandmother was alive, but I grew up knowing that my grandfather was Jigoro Kano's first Jujutsu teacher. As you know, Jigoro Kano founded Judo in 1882.

◆ ◆ ◆

In her book, *Born for the Mat*,[1] Sensei reports that she began studying Judo in 1934 when she was twenty-one years old. The year before, her family received from Professor Kano an invitation to the fiftieth anniversary celebration of the Kodokan Institute for Judo. The celebration included a memorial ceremony for Professor Kano's three teachers, including Sensei's grandfather. Sensei's brother and mother attended the ceremony and told her about the three *sakaki* trees—ceremonial trees symbolizing the three dead instructors—arranged at the front of the new dojo. Professor Kano walked up to the tree that symbolized Hachinosuke Fukuda and spoke respectfully, as if to his teacher, about his memories of his early studies.

As a young man Professor Kano had learned Jujutsu from Sensei's grandfather, primarily for

_____

1. Keiko Fukuda, *Born for the Mat: A Kodokan Kata Textbook for Women* (1973).

self-defense. He combined what he learned from his different teachers with his own studies to develop modern Judo, which literally means "The Gentle Way." He also called it the "Way of the Human Being" and spoke of the need to develop not only a strong and healthy body but also a loving nature. "The purpose of the study of Judo is to become a good citizen to help society," Fukuda Sensei told us. The martial aspects of Judo were also honed, however, for Professor Kano and his students were challenged in combat by Jujutsu specialists, who at that time were seeing their livelihood and way of life disappear with the modernization that accompanied the opening of Japan to trade with the outside world in the late nineteenth century.

Shortly after the fiftieth anniversary celebration Professor Kano came to visit Sensei's family at their home. He was the head of the greatly respected Kodokan Institute, but he gave Sensei the impression of being a gentle old man. He invited her to come study in the *Joshi-Bu,* the Women's Section. He said it would improve her physical condition and she could acquire a healthy body. She had lived a very sedentary life up until then, attending a girls' high school and afterward studying the *shamisen* (the Japanese three-stringed lute), flower arranging, brush writing, tea ceremony, and cooking and sewing, as middle-class young women in Japan did in those days to prepare for marriage.

With her mother Sensei visited the Kodokan. She was impressed by the physical activity of the women—there were about twenty women students but only one woman instructor, Noritomi Sensei. The other instructors in the Women's Section were high-ranking men. Later most of the women students who were ahead of her dropped out, whereas Fukuda Sensei continued practicing, as she does to this day. In her book Sensei noted that early in her study she suffered from pain in her hips, but the pain gradually disappeared as she continued to practice, and she no longer became easily fatigued. "I firmly believe," she added, "Judo changed my physical constitution."[2] She studied at the Kodokan six days a week, from three to six o'clock every day but Sunday. She continued her weekly studies in the shamisen, flower arranging, and brush writing but never once missed a Judo class.

Sensei's uncle (on her mother's side) objected to her training because she was a woman, but her mother and brother both supported her decision. Their intention was that she might marry a judoka one day and carry on the Fukuda name as the granddaughter of Hachinosuke Fukuda. Judo soon became the most important part of her life.

Did you study directly with Professor Kano?

No. He was no longer teaching by then, but he would come to the dojo and watch sometimes. Before the war the women who were at the Kodokan were upper-class women like the Kano family. The Women's Section started with Professor Kano teaching his wife and daughters and then granddaughters. My family was more average. The other women spoke a different Japanese, an upper-class Japanese. I had to learn that to be like them. It was not very difficult, although it was very different. The women's teaching was very strict. All the moves had to be done very gently, without force.

Manners were emphasized in the Women's Section. When we threw our partners, we would immediately make a formal apology. Sometimes I went with the other women to men's competitions and we performed public demonstrations. Spectators would be very curious and point their fingers at us and stare and say, "Oh, that's a woman, but Judo is for men." Because of this sort of behavior I learned to be especially well mannered and bow politely.

◆　◆　◆

Before he died in 1938, Professor Kano told Sensei he hoped to spread Women's Judo throughout the world as widely as Men's Judo. "Miss Fukuda," she remembers him saying, "You must pursue the study of Judo with this in mind." "Naturally," says Sensei, "those words of the founder of Judo strongly impressed my young mind and still live vividly."[3]

In the 1930s the Women's Section adopted the men's custom of holding two hard training periods each year, in the hottest part of summer and the coldest month of winter, with the purpose of disciplining mind over matter. "It is not an easy matter to continually attend this training," Sensei has written about the winter training, which is held daily from five to seven in the morning throughout the month of January:

> One must wake up at dawn and travel to the cold *Dojo*. I will never forget the pain I felt when I received a misplaced footsweep on my numb toes, but, after a few throws were exchanged, everyone would get warmed up and start to perspire, and by the time the session was finished, the bright sun would be shining through the windows. Everyone would feel fine, the workout making the day worthwhile and delightful. We used to sign our name on the daily attendance record and place our

---

2. Ibid., 20.

3. Ibid., 10.

Randori partners' names underneath; we were proud to show the amount of people we practiced with that morning.[4]

Sensei continued training and teaching through the years of World War II, although the school was much reduced and often food was scarce. After morning training she and the one other Women's Judo instructor still teaching would make vegetable soup, adding what little rice they could find.[5] After World War II the social class restrictions were ended at the Kodokan and the fees were lowered, but still not a lot of women came. "The main thing to motivate people to study Judo," Sensei said, "is that they *want* to." Outside of samurai families Japanese customs and traditions do not support women's training in martial arts. Attitudes have changed greatly in recent years, but still Sensei speculates that Women's Judo might propagate more quickly and with less difficulty in other countries.[6]

When did you first come to the United States?

I traveled in the United States in the early 1950s to teach and promote Judo. Americans are heavier and bigger people than Japanese. I am very short in my body. My hands got sore in the demonstrations with Americans, from pulling them off balance, which requires twisting the fingers and hands in the lapels of an opponent's gi. I had to tape and bandage my hands.

***

4. Ibid., 17–18.
5. Ibid., 18.
6. Ibid., 11.

In your book, you wrote, "The higher the degree of techniques I learned, the more difficulty I found in trying to harmonize them spiritually." Can you tell us how you dealt with that?

This is a very important question. I came to the United States again in 1966 and spent a year teaching in different places in California, six months in northern California, three months in the south, three months in central California. A student asked me to do a brush writing, and I wrote the character for "love," because from this concentrated period of teaching I realized that you have to love your students and have a true concern for their welfare to be able to teach them effectively. It is very different to teach Japanese and American students, because they have different cultural backgrounds and expectations and behavior. And it is difficult, because of the language difference, for me to communicate with American students in words. I had to learn to communicate with students directly from the heart.

Your motto—which is also the official motto for Women's Judo—relates to this point also?

In English it is, "Be strong, be gentle, be beautiful." If I say this in Japanese, it is *Tsuyoku, yasashiku, utsukushiku.* This is what I learned from Judo. These are my three treasures.

"Be strong" means to achieve a healthy, strong body and at the same time to form confidence in your heart [she used the word *kokoro,* which means both heart and mind, in contrast to another word that is equivalent to the English word "mind"]. This is something you can't achieve in only a year or two. In the beginning you can't do

Brush writing by Keiko Fukuda: Tsuyoku, yasashiku, utsukushiku—Be strong, be gentle, be beautiful—is the motto Keiko Fukuda devised for herself and for Women's Judo.

anything at all and you feel weak. After three or four years of training the techniques start to take effect and you feel, "I can do this" or "I can do this much." Strength is forming in your heart.

As one continues studying [she used the word *shūgyō*, which is not the ordinary term for "training" but implies much more, including the pursuit of knowledge, with connotations of religious study, self-discipline, dedication, and continuity], one will develop a strong enough mind and heart to overcome even those hardships and obstacles that rush toward you like a strong wave and be

able to go on with your life.

"This is important," I tell my students. Only people who have worked hard can achieve such a state of mind and heart. If you take a lesson today but not tomorrow, if you are lax in your practice, you won't achieve that.

Next, "Be gentle," is *jū* from *Jūdō*. If I translate it, it means soft, but also one needs a gentle, meek, and humble heart. [Here she used the word *sunao*, which literally means simple, straight, truthful. The connotations are of being open and receptive to whatever comes, in the sense of having a beginner's mind, and of being obedient from one's inner nature rather than from imposed discipline. This is a word, Machiko noted, used most often in reference to well-behaved children and women.]

There are people with strong ego, but they have to give that up. If one's ego is strong, one cannot make good friends—one usually pushes one's opinions through and then will not listen to others' opinions at all. People who say, "What I'm saying is right," even when they are wrong—if one becomes like that, one has a strong ego, with a heart to push one's will through no matter what. To become gentle and humble is *jū*.

Jū is a fascinating word. It is like the flow of water. But water is strong, isn't it? Water drops trickling down can bore a hole even in rock. Water can go as fast as the current. It becomes round when it is placed in a round container. It becomes square when it is placed in a square container. This is water's nature. It is gentle and yielding and it has strength that penetrates even rocks. This is *jū*, and Judo therefore is something that is soft and gentle, but the core is strong.

Last, "Be beautiful," is to have a beautiful heart as well as to be beautiful outside. Because one wants to be good looking on the outside, one puts on pretty clothes and makeup and has one's hair done. I think a beautiful heart is more important. Even though you dress simply, if your heart is beautiful, it is as if you are dressed in fine brocade. My grandmother told me this. To be gentle to others, to help others, and to be kind to others—someone who does these things for others, not thinking only about oneself, is a person with a very beautiful heart, I think. Anybody can be beautiful outside, but to be a person who has a beautiful heart is rare. Few become the owner of such a heart, a beautiful heart.

Someone who does Judo must be gentle, strong, and give up ego. The purpose of Judo, the ultimate purpose of Judo, is to achieve higher humanity, to improve one's character and become someone who can serve others and be useful in society. I tell my students we must continue our study for this purpose. I don't want them to forget.

Does one learn purely from doing the techniques accurately and the physical training, or does one need instruction in the philosophy also to obtain the social and spiritual discipline?

One learns through the physical training, but it takes long and hard training. From hard training one learns to have a strong mind—that is what enables one to deal with hardships in life. Kindness comes from working with partners and learning that in order to work with them one must think about other people. From training with a partner, one learns a lot about oneself and also about the other person, how to observe and then empathize with other people. *Jū* is key to how the techniques work. By giving way to an opponent, one puts the opponent in a vulnerable position.

This is *Jū no riai,* the Theory of Jū—that it manifests in the movement. When I move, there is meaning in this. That's why it's been changed to *Jūdō* from *Jūjutsu*. It still has *jū,* although *jutsu* [art, technique] has been changed to *dō* [the way]. *Jū* is the gentle heart that is always in movement.

If an opponent thrusts at my head, I turn ninety degrees *[she illustrates]* and your hand will just fall away *[she points where the strike would have missed]*. As your hand falls, I dodge to avoid it, then pull your arm a little bit, like this *[she shows how]*. Your body will start to fall. If I pull more, you will stumble and fall down.

This is achieving the effect by small effort. Your hand becomes like this after you strike *[she shows how the arm misses the opponent and drops]* as I turn aside. Well, then, how far shall I turn? Just enough to avoid your hand. If I turn any more than that, I end up spending that much extra energy. In Judo, when you're pushed, then pull. When you're pulled, then push. This is the principle of Judo. My mind is always working to decide which technique to use. If the opponent tries to come this way *[demonstrating]* and then moves sideways, I might pull sideways and throw you.

You take control of the situation with your mind. You unbalance your opponent so that you can throw him or her. I don't move wastefully—my movement has Jū no riai. Making the least effort work the most—this is Jū no riai. This is the secret, most important thing.

You also tell your students not to move too much without reading the opponent's move and not to resist too much.

It's about not moving and not resisting. Judo techniques must be jū. You must move lightly to avoid attack.

Keiko Fukuda (right) demonstrating Judo self-defense technique in front of a photograph of Jigoro Kano at her dojo (San Francisco, 1996).

MARY ROSE SPRINGER

In response to an attack, learn to escape using minimal strength on your part, then subdue your opponents by turning their strength against them. I learned an important lesson of life from this rule of never meeting brute force with force—there is great merit in cultivating a gentle and compliant nature. If I may relate an incident from my own past: I used to be such a stubborn little girl that I once broke my rice bowl, but I just couldn't make myself say, "I'm sorry," to my mother. As I reflect on it now, I am so grateful for my Judo training, for I believe that it helped me to become a much more amiable, well-adjusted person.

◆ ◆ ◆

Sensei notes that Judo is also a sport and "it is natural that competition exists,"[7] but she emphasizes again and again that what matters most about Judo is that it includes a moral aspect. It is not "a mere fighting technique" or a sport; "its ultimate goal is to constantly develop a harmonious body and to train a sound mind."[8] In her book she wrote about Judo practice:

There is always an opponent; therefore, when practicing, any observant person will learn many things through encountering different circumstances. Sometimes, it may be something directly concerned with yourself, and at other times, something which can be learned from personal relationship with others. At the beginning by scientifically studying a technique which appeals to us, we will comprehend the movements of the human body, and obtain the habit of thinking of the other's mentality. As the techniques improve, so does our way of thinking, and realizing how important it is to practice diligently. This also cultivates patience and courage that is necessary in everyday life.

The correct techniques are reflections of our state of mind. We must strive to keep our thoughts pure even when we are not in the *Dojo*. One should respect the instructors and senior members who are always kind and helpful to us. Thoughtfulness and self-examination are related with humbleness, which is most impor-

---

7. Ibid., 10.
8. Ibid., 6.

tant in Judo training. As we continue our Judo training, we attain adaptability unconsciously. In this world of material civilization, it is a most precious gift.

In such a manner, as we practice Judo positively, we unconsciously obtain composure, and are able to make swift decisions in case of emergency. We must realize that a great deal of mental discipline is obtained along with physical training.[9]

As to the differences between Women's and Men's Judo, Sensei stresses that Judo itself is the same, with the same techniques and the same rules for competition. "In the beginning," she said, "Women's Judo was much softer and gentler than men's, emphasizing *Tai-sabaki*—body movements stressing speed—and *ukemi,* or falling. Professor Kano himself was said to have often said to men, 'If you really want to know true Judo, take a look at the methods they use at the Kodokan Joshi-Bu,' the Women's Section. After World War II Women's Judo became more like men's practice. This is because of changes in lifestyle and mind, with American and modern women being stronger and more forceful and not being content with the original Women's Judo."

MARY ROSE SPRINGER

Keiko Fukuda (left) demonstrating Judo technique against a knife attack at her dojo (San Francisco, 1996).

Men and women train and compete separately. And ranking is separated too. Could you explain why, please?

Other sports are the same way, aren't they? Many sports are played separately. Football players are all men. Women play volleyball among themselves. Women play basketball now, but women play with women.

Men and women are different physically. Men's bones are thicker. And then girls start menstruation at age of twelve or thirteen already, while boys start to grow beards. Their bodies grow differently. Men have men's bodies and women have women's bodies, and women become able to bear children. Since men and women are physiologically different, it's dangerous to have a match on equal terms.

But because there's no need for force to do

9. Ibid., 21.

Judo, shouldn't that make things more equal?

It's not necessary for men and women to train together. I think it's dangerous to do this together. It's natural for women to work with women, because they are the same.

How do you feel about competition?

I think this win–win–win attitude in competition is bad. The quality of technique is more important. I think people should do Judo for health and self-development.

[Later Gayle told me about the first Judo competition she entered, when she had been studying Judo for only a few months, although she had already been studying Aikido for years. She won third place, but Sensei told the judges to keep the trophy, because Gayle's techniques had not been clearly executed and were not deserving of reward. "Trophies don't matter," Sensei told Gayle. "Doing the techniques properly is what matters."]

How do you feel about the future for Judo?

I would like to see Judo spread more in the United States. Children and older people and women should do it for health, not just competition, because Judo is very good exercise for physical health and mental alertness, completely aside from competition. More Judo teachers are needed to teach in middle and high schools, not just universities.

I have taught in France, and people have very large dojos there—several hundred students at a time. Judo is more popular in France than in the United States. Dojos here are smaller, but I hope they will grow and develop in the years to come.

Do you yourself continue to learn new things from Judo?

Yes!

Different things after, say, fifty years, than after forty years?

Yes, because I learn new things about myself. I know all the techniques now, but I find new implications in watching other people do them and in continuing to do them myself.

◆ ◆ ◆

In talking to Machiko and me, Sensei several times mentioned ceremony and respect—that a dojo is not a gymnasium but a place where one behaves with respect, bowing when one comes in. She got up from her chair and demonstrated improper, lax bows, with head and rear thrust in opposite directions, and a proper bow, with the back straight, bending from the hips, and bending the head as well. She described a photo she has of her mother and her aunt kneeling on the floor in a Japanese room and bowing to each other, as was the custom even among family members on meeting, both of them wearing the full hairstyles of that day—she indicated wings of hair with her hand at the side of her head—and formal kimonos. She likes to look at the photo. "That is very nice," she said. "Those manners are beautiful. I like that much better than 'Hi!'"

In Women's Judo, Sensei is very much a pioneer. Indeed, for all women martial artists today she is the living embodiment of the title sensei, in its literal meaning of "one who goes before." In other aspects of her life, such as customs, manners, and spiritual matters, she is fiercely loyal to traditional ways—embodying here, as in all she says and does, the strong-mindedness that comes from her lifelong hard training.

CHAPTER 20

Talking to the Future

When I tell people I am working on a book about how women's practice of martial arts for many years affects their lives, I am often asked, "Well, how *does* it affect their lives?" The question seems reasonable, even inevitable, but I am hard put to give a short answer, for the truth lies in the details of the individual women's different stories, which have taken all the pages of this book to set forth.

There *are* commonalities among these women. They seem, on the whole, to have acquired the qualities of patience, persistence, self-assurance, and respect for others that are often held out as the goals of martial arts training. More basic, I think, is that martial arts training provides, for those who find it suits them, a method of working on themselves. Without exception, the women I talked to said they are better people because of their practice.

For myself, after eight years of practicing T'ai Chi Ch'uan, I feel not just in my flesh but in all my being a honing away of superfluity. My body and limbs feel longer, lighter, and leaner as well as more muscled, and my mind and spirit feel that way too. The connections and resonances between my physical practice, my mental attitudes, and my spiritual awareness seem deeper, stronger, clearer. I feel more open, more flexible, better able to deal with a wider variety of people and situations. I often think, these days, how *good* it feels to be in this body of mine, and I like the feeling I have of moving about the world more skillfully, not just with my body but also with my energy and spirit. This process that I feel at work in myself, I see as more advanced in women with more experience—they seem above all to be more distinctly themselves, whatever they may be, more conscious of what they are and freer of un-thought-through habits and attitudes.

I began my study of T'ai Chi Ch'uan at age forty. Most of the women I interviewed started their training in their late teens or twenties. Malyne Chiu's experience stands out in that she began studying Kendo at age six. I was intrigued to see a recent news story reporting that violinists who achieve world-class proficiency started their study before age thirteen. At least for violin playing there seems to be a period of physiological maturation that if passed without being taken advantage of closes the door on reaching the highest level of skill. As I got to know Malyne better, it seemed to me that she, who began her studies long before age thirteen, may indeed have incorporated such characteristic martial arts qualities as openness, present-mindedness, flexibility, integrity, and respect for self and others in a deeper, more physical and fundamental way than may be possible for those of us who start as adults. But Malyne is now in her forties, with the perspective of that age on her childhood experience. What would girls or young women say who are still close to the experience of such early training?

Coleen Gragen told me about the children's and youth classes she taught at Hand to Hand Community Arts Center, her Kajukenbo Kung Fu school in Oakland, California. Some years ago she expanded her Saturday morning classes for children to include a violence prevention program, Project DESTINY (De-Escalation Skills Training Inspiring Non-violence in Youth) in a Berkeley public school, working intensively after school several days a week with youth considered at risk for violence, teaching them martial arts. "This great turnaround takes place," Coleen said. "Their grades go up, their attendance improves—all this stuff. At first nobody wanted to let the program in, because it was martial arts—'What are you, crazy? These kids are already acting out; you're going to teach them to punch and kick better?' But it doesn't work that way, and that's finally becoming clear."

In 1988, Coleen turned the entire youth program over to the energetic and able direction of Kate Hobbs, a student of hers who holds a second-degree black belt in Kajukenbo. Kate has added dance training to the Project DESTINY curriculum and integrated the skills emphasized in Project DESTINY in the martial arts classes for children and youth at the Hand to Hand training center, now separately organized as the Destiny Arts Center. Kate and her fellow instructors, Sarah Crowell, a dancer, and Anthony Daniels, who holds black belts in Wu Chien Pai Kung Fu and Judo, offer affordable training in martial arts, self-defense, de-escalation of violence, dance, and movement arts to children and youth aged three to eighteen. They also teach this integrated curriculum in workshops for youth and adults who work with youth throughout the Bay Area. "For all children, exercises that build knowledge of calmness and stillness within their bodies and exercises that teach explosive power are the bedrock of my teaching," Kate has written. "Stillness and explosion, self-control and release, awareness and response—coupled with games and exercises that teach attentive listening, cooperation, respect for self and others, love and care for our world, and responsibility for our own actions."[1]

The Destiny Arts Center program reaches beyond classroom teaching to integrate lessons with

---

1. Carol A. Wiley, *Martial Arts Teachers on Teaching* (Berkeley, CA: Frog, 1995), 77–78.

SHARP SPEAR, CRYSTAL MIRROR

students' lives through a performance company in which the students create performances based on their own experience, weekend and summer outdoor and wilderness outings, and academic support for teens through volunteer tutors. The capstone of the project is a youth leadership training program, in which teens gain experience as leaders and teachers (receiving stipends for their work) and the community gains a pool of trained young people to teach violence prevention programs to their peers in school and community groups.

Students come from diverse racial and economic backgrounds. Project DESTINY participants are chosen from children deemed at risk for violence in their school. At the Destiny Arts Center, a few scholarship students have found their own way to the school, and their parents, if any, have no contact with the school; but most of the students have parents who support and encourage—and often initiated—their participation. Kate told me that a quarter to a third of the students, although they have stable, supportive families, live in very-low-income neighborhoods where violence is the everyday background of their lives. Kate believes the self-control and self-discipline that are integral to martial arts are crucial skills for children living in stressful and violent situations: "I can see on some children's faces the unspoken appreciation for the clarity and calm within the discipline, the etiquette, and the repetitive format."[2] And with the skills they learn, she believes, children can prevent sexual abuse and violence.

As I met more people connected with women's martial arts in the Bay Area, I heard more and more praise for the students at Destiny Arts Center. I attended several of their performances and felt inspired in my own training by the energy,

commitment, skill, and grace of the performers. I called Kate to ask whether I might interview one or two of the young women for this book.

Despite a workload that I only later realized has no end, Kate greeted my request with enthusiasm. "I'll put together a group for you to talk to," she said. "The other interviews I've done are all with single individuals," I told her, "but perhaps these young women would feel more at ease if there were two of them together?" "Three," Kate said firmly, "or perhaps four." She went on to say it would be good experience for the young women to explain what they were doing. In fact, it would fit into her plans for them for the upcoming summer's leadership training. She asked me to write up a proposal she could send to the parents to obtain their permission and promised to schedule interview time before or after classes at the center. Then she laughed. "You'll have to figure out what to do with it all," she said. "Yes," I agreed and mustered a wry laugh at myself and the anxiety I felt about deciphering a tape recording with many different persons talking. I need not have worried, however, for when the time came and I explained the importance of only one person speaking at a time, the young women observed that rule with a discipline I was hard put to match.

I arrived early for the Saturday afternoon interview so that I could watch the children's martial arts class—girls and boys aged seven and up. These were not the young people I would be talking with, but I thought they might afford me a glimpse of how the older students had started out. I found Kate and several teenage assistants standing tall in a restless, ever-moving sea of small bodies in black gi or Destiny Arts T-shirts. Kate divided the children into groups for different activities—sparring, kata, practicing Judo throws on a mat, kicking or punching hand-held target pads—rotating them frequently both to keep up

---

2. Ibid., 76.

the students' interest and to avoid their overdoing any one activity, for children's soft bones can be damaged by overstrenuous repetitive motions.

I noticed three small boys, each in a black gi, with purple belts trailing to their knees even after having been wrapped twice around their slender bodies, preparing for sparring practice. They pulled on helmets and other protective gear and went at each other with great seriousness, each in turn serving as referee while the other two sparred. From time to time the referee awarded a point, bringing the proceedings to a halt for heated discussion.

Presently Kate swept up the boys and reallocated them into separate groups. She spent a few minutes with one of them, whose temper had flared over the awarding of points—she seemed to have noticed this from across the room with her back turned. She sparred with the boy herself and at the same time, I suspected, schooled him on attitude and respect for others.

Class ended for the youngest children. In another training hall Michelle Dwyer was finishing the monthly class she teaches the teens in Kung Fu staff and saber. I caught just a glimpse of their practice—and the respectful attention they gave to both Michelle and the weapons. After Michelle gathered up extra swords and staffs then left, a dozen teens remained for a meeting of the youth leadership group. The group overall is about half male and half female, but this day there were mostly young women present, and the most challenging of the upcoming summer activities were for them: Some of them would teach workshops at the PAWMA women's training camp in August and three of them would accompany a group of women martial artists traveling to the NGO forum at the UN Fourth World Conference on Women in Beijing in September to teach self-defense workshops.

Kate announced they would spend a few minutes discussing what leadership is—a step in her campaign for the summer to get the teens to take more responsibility for the younger students and the wilderness outings. They went around the circle several times, listing role models each had learned from, qualities they had learned about, qualities they wanted to acquire. All spoke up readily, hesitating only to search for words or pin down elusive ideas; it was clear that they were used to expressing their thoughts and being listened to with attention, and for the most part they accorded each other that courtesy as well. But they were also healthy young people overflowing with energy even after, for some of them at least, several hours' training. They couldn't but interrupt each other when suddenly an idea struck. At other times they dissolved in giggles, one or another of them noticing or remembering something amusing and imparting it to the others almost without speech, so close knit were they as a group, with a long shared history among them.

As the meeting wore on, more and more of them stretched out full length, pillowing their heads companionably on each other's knees and shoulders. After a while Kate and I were the only persons in the room sitting upright. Some of the young people had been strenuously training for several hours and might well be tired, but there was something more here, I thought—an ease and presence in their bodies that I too once had but now realized I had lost somewhere over the years.

A latecomer joined the group to an excited welcome—a former student, Arlean Harris, who had just returned for the summer from her first year of college. "Give that woman a hug!" Kate roared, even as everybody already was. Arlean had taught workshops similar to those under discussion and Kate asked her if she had any advice for the beginners on what it was like to teach adults.

"You have to be clear in explaining things," Arlean began, "because they paid a lot of money and they want to learn. They ask questions. Lots of questions. Personal questions and questions about the program." With a start, I realized that the "they" Arlean spoke of included me. I had wondered how I would deal with this group of young women that I had yet to actually meet— would I see them primarily as echoes of my own youth or alternatives I might now wish I had been offered? Would I be able to see them like the other women I had talked to as whole and independent persons grounded in their own circumstances and lives? It occurred to me now to also wonder how they would deal with me. I had already noticed the gap in age between us, and now I added up the years I realized it was much greater than between me and Wen Mei Yu—about the same as between me and Keiko Fukuda—and in this case I was on the other end.

Kate summed up the work there would be for those participating in the summer youth leadership program. "How many of you want to sign up?" Kate asked. All of them did, and she divided them into groups to get started. "LaShonda, Emma, Dzifa"—Kate called out the names of those she had arranged for me to interview and sent us off to a separate room for the first of several sessions. That day Arlean Harris also sat in with us. At a later session Janine Bruno also joined us.

As with the older women I had talked to, we started with how and why each one had started training in martial arts. LaShonda Wilson, fifteen going on sixteen, is the most senior of the group in training, with eight years' experience. She is a sturdily built young woman with an open, expressive face and quick laughter—engagingly outgoing and friendly. The youth meeting had been con-siderably enlivened by her side comments and laughter. She holds brown belt rank in the eclectic Kung Fu system taught in the Destiny Arts, which the students refer to interchangeably as Karate and Kung Fu. She expects to earn her black belt this summer and will be Kate and Anthony's first student to achieve black belt rank. "I started when I was seven," she said. This was before Kate's directorship and the full Destiny Arts program began, when Coleen was just teaching Saturday morning children's classes in Kung Fu. "I think one of my preschool teachers was telling my father about it, LaShonda went on, "because she trained at Hand to Hand. And I brought my family and friends with me"—she gestured at others in the group.

"I started because of LaShonda," Arlean said. She turned to LaShonda with a grin, teasing but also serious: "Thanks, LaShonda!" Nineteen, she is shorter but sturdier than LaShonda, similarly open and friendly, but with a more developed presence and self-assurance. Kate told me Arlean plans a career in law and wants to be a judge, and after spending some time with her I could easily envision her presiding over a roomful of people and sifting disputes with thoroughness and fairness. Like LaShonda, Arlean holds brown belt rank, but is about ready for her black belt test, according to Kate. After training since sixth grade, she has been away for the past year at college but plans to train hard for the summer. "LaShonda's mother and my mother knew each other because we were in previous classes together, dance class and drill team," Arlean said. "Her mother was like, 'Oh, LaShonda's in martial arts, so why don't you try?' Me and my brother came and tried and liked it. It was motivating too. It made me set goals. Because LaShonda was here—I don't know how long she was here before I was, but she was in another class. I came as a white belt, and I wanted to reach that class so bad—they were doing interesting things; they weren't just doing the basics!"

Emma Alegria Wildflower Neumann, a tall, slender, soft-spoken sixteen-year-old looking forward to soon earning her brown belt, had been training almost as long as LaShonda and Arlean. "I started when I was nine and a half," she said. "I had gone to a few different schools. I went to Tae Kwon Do, but it was all boys, and discipline was really strict. Everyone was doing push-ups when they did a little tiny thing wrong. It was not the format that I wanted, but I was still interested in learning how to protect myself. I was small, so I was worried about that—I was scared! I came here and I really liked it."

Fifteen-year-old Dzifa E. Dugba, tall and rangy in build, had a more serious, even grave, air about her. She spoke rarely and softly, but as someone in the youth meeting had commented, when Dzifa spoke, people listened, because what she said was well thought out and to the point. The others had assigned her the role of recordkeeper "because she was going to be a writer." Dzifa started martial arts training at eleven and had recently earned her green belt, one rank below brown. "LaShonda was coming here—she's my cousin," Dzifa said. "I started with my sister, and a lot of my friends brought their families down here."

Dzifa's sister, Janine Dalon Bruno, twelve years old and also a fairly recent green belt, is tall and long limbed like her sister but readier to speech. "I was maybe seven," Janine said. "I started with my sister and two cousins. Basically because she"— LaShonda—"was going and my other cousin was going and our friend Arlean was going. We kept going because we liked it."

"So it was pretty much your parents' decision that you start martial arts?" I asked.

"I don't think I cared," LaShonda said. "I was in so much stuff—gymnastics and dance and drill team. It was, 'Hey, something new, yeah, I'll try it.'"

"It was so long ago," Janine said. "I think I just turned around, and they were like, 'You're going to Karate.'"

"But you stuck with it because you liked it? That was your choice?" I asked, and all of them agreed. They outgrew other activities or dropped them for lack of time, but kept training.

"I got to know a lot of people and learned how to protect myself," Dzifa said. "That's what I liked at first. Now it's more it feels like a comfortable place to be."

"Was that unusual for your parents to be encouraging girls to study martial arts?" I wondered, casting back to my own 1950s childhood, when if martial arts teaching had even been available, I couldn't imagine my parents considering it. "Are your parents different in this regard from your friends' parents?"

"No!" "Not at all!" "They want you to!"

"The parents are worried about their kids!" Emma explained. "They know that that's going to help them."

"And did you feel it helped you?" I asked.

"I'm not so concerned about protecting myself," Emma answered, "because I haven't had any encounters where I've had to use it."

Arlean spoke feelingly of learning to be strong, to be her own person, to be independent and not depend on other people. It seemed to me there were some life lessons mixed in with what she attributed to martial arts, but I also got the sense that her life experiences were illuminating and fleshing out her martial arts lessons, and she was finding a valuable framework in her training as she now went out into the world on her own.

Arlean Harris demonstrating Kung Fu forward stance at Destiny Arts Center (Oakland, Calif., 1993).

get into a physical fight—an eventuality she seemed to think unlikely—she would use ordinary street smarts, not Kung Fu techniques.

The others listened to Arlean's story approvingly, and I was reminded of Coleen telling me, "When the fear is lessened, then the broader, deeper parts of the self can emerge. I've seen us go through this process when we learn the self-defense that we don't feel quite so anxious for our immediate survival and the deeper layers of personality come out and say, 'Now teach me something that relates to this part of my psyche, not just that immediate fear.'"

LaShonda, Arlean, and Emma had started with just martial arts classes, like the little kids' session I had watched Kate conducting that morning, and as the Destiny Arts program grew up around them, they added dance and the performance company. Sarah Crowell, who also performs with the Dance Brigade, a dance/theater company based in Oakland, teaches a blend of basic ballet and modern dance with jazz and street dance in preteen and teen classes, emphasizing, as she puts it, dance technique and performance used as an instrument to explore social issues.

"It's dance theater," Dzifa explained for my benefit. "A little bit of Karate. Not really Karate Karate—like sports dance."

"When we got here," Janine said of herself and her sister Dzifa, "all three of these teachers were already here and we just signed up for everything."

All of them also participate in teaching and leadership training. As ruefully as many adults I know, they bemoaned their crowded schedules, which generally include martial arts and dance classes two evenings a week plus regular practice sessions for the performance company. I asked the group if they practice on their own, outside of classes.

She told us about a college roommate—the two didn't get along with each other, but Arlean said she had found that she could hear her roommate out with self-control. In one argument, the roommate had said, "And now you'll use your Kung Fu on me!" But it would never cross her mind to do so, Arlean said. Kung Fu is dangerous—it could kill people. She concluded that the purpose of her training wasn't for fighting, but for self-development, and added that if she did

"We are supposed to," Janine said.

Dzifa said, "When you learn a new kata, sometimes you'll practice, but once you know them . . ." Her voice trailed away.

LaShonda said, "I think when you're younger and you first learn kata, it's so interesting—'Oh, let me go home and show my mother!'"

Michelle Dwyer had commented to me about how quickly these students learned compared to her adult students: "Go through it once or twice, and they have it! They're ready to go on to something new." When I had watched them at practice, I had been impressed with the ease and naturalness of their movement. Not that they were more skilled than adults of comparable rank, but it seemed to me they had perhaps more deeply incorporated martial arts movement into their being. They agreed.

"It's like it's part of me," LaShonda said.

Emma added, "Even if we're not always practicing, it'll still be there. It's just in us."

As Dzifa had mentioned earlier, the school itself was also special to them. "Our mother tried to get us to go to another school closer to home," Janine said. "Because it's too hard getting back and forth. But we didn't want to."

"You can probably go anywhere to get martial arts training," LaShonda said, "but you can't get the same—I mean, most instructors don't care as much."

"At other schools," Emma said, "they rush you through your belts because they know people aren't going to stay."

At Destiny Arts, Janine said, "The instructors really actually are interested in you learning. They get to know you."

"It is like a big family," Arlean said. "We get along, but if there is a problem, we handle it. We learn a lot of skills that are useful in life. Destiny Arts Center has helped me to overcome a lot of fears and push myself to do things that I normally couldn't do."

"And what about what you bring to the process?" I asked. "Do you think you had qualities and strengths that you brought to your training?"

Emma said she found she had strength within her she could draw on, but her training was what first gave her awareness of that strength. She described the process: "When I first came, I was really quiet, but when I was sparring, I'd get really aggressive."

"You sure did!" one of the others exclaimed, with feeling, but also laughing.

"I didn't even realize that I was doing that," Emma went on. "I'd be hitting really hard"—again the others chimed in with agreement—"and that surprised me, because that hadn't come out in any other part of my life. I've been loud, but I didn't have confidence in my physical strength because I was so small. But a lot of this aggression did come out."

"Did you learn a way to use your aggressiveness?" I asked.

Emma answered that she thought the sparring was a productive use in itself. "And it is productive to use it in my life. I'm not angry. It's not like repressed anger. It's my own power, which isn't really encouraged in any other place."

I asked if they thought of themselves as martial artists. "Is that a major part of your self-identity? Or is it just one piece?"

They murmured among themselves, considering the question. Twelve-year-old Janine spoke up first: "I think we're artists in all kinds of different ways." She spoke in such a somber, thoughtful tone that we all simply regarded her in silence for a moment. Then the others broke out laughing. "Don't ask me what that meant!" Janine exclaimed defensively.

"I understand!" LaShonda said quickly. "I'm laughing because we're silent." This was a characteristic I had noticed in the youth meeting also: how quick all of these young people were to make an accounting of their intention whenever misunderstandings arose. And Janine sat back, content.

Emma returned to my question: "I think I will continue with martial arts, but it's like even if we don't use it, you have this strong foundation of knowing that you have really been committed to something. You really succeeded in something." She concluded rather primly, "That's it for me," and again laughter swept over the group. But I was getting used to that by now, and presently it passed, and I asked what questions they would ask each other if they were in my place.

"What do you guys get out of taking martial arts?" Janine asked.

"Self-confidence!" LaShonda said promptly.

"And discipline," Dzifa added.

Janine said, "I've become more powerful, it seems to me—I can answer my own question! I think I've become more powerful and my coordination has gotten better."

"It's like an inner sense of power that you don't need to like show off," Emma said.

"You know you have it," LaShonda agreed. "You know it's there. People know it's there. You don't have to show it off."

Emma began, "That's so much weaker if you have to always be like—"

"'I can do this,'" LaShonda interrupted. "'I can do that.' 'Let me show you.' If people know that you're taking martial arts, they're always going to say, 'Show me this kick. I want to see you do a jump spinning crescent—' you know, something like that. But you don't have to show them right then and there. You know you can do it. You

know if you can't—you just say, 'I can't do that.' It's not a big deal. But you know you have that inside of you."

Janine said, "I think we all become more self-confident, and I think people can tell by talking to us that we're confident about ourselves. Like our shows—people think we're good."

"We are good!" Emma said.

"Graceful too!" LaShonda added. "Especially the girls. We walk down the street with our head up high. And it's like you have a feeling about yourself like, 'Oh I'm great, I can do this, I can do that. I teach, I take Karate, I take dance. I'm good in school.' All this kind of stuff, it just all comes together and you can tell that you have that—that feeling about yourself. Proud and tall."

"I think we become more open too," Dzifa said in her quiet way. "We start to talk more. I know all of us were kind of quiet when we first started, and when we started teaching and all that kind of stuff, we were able to talk more. In front of big groups and all."

The ability to talk and express themselves was a point they returned to. Both LaShonda and Dzifa mentioned that they used to be penalized in school for not talking, for being unable to answer questions and participate in discussions, even though they studied and knew the material. LaShonda said martial arts—and Arlean's help—had given her the self-confidence to speak up for herself. Dzifa said in her measured way that she had "learned to talk when I need to." Throughout our conversations, she spoke more sparingly than the others, but always thoughtfully and to the point. More than once, I found myself looking to her when I felt the group was wandering too far afield, relying on her to get us back on track. Emma remarked that she had learned to talk more sparingly—people listened more if you didn't talk all the time.

Did they see themselves as different from others their age who did not study martial arts?

"Oh, yeah!" "Of course!" "Yes!"

"They don't know *anything!*" Emma exclaimed. Everyone laughed.

Janine leaned forward eagerly. "One thing, we understand what it's about more than they do. If somebody finds out that I take martial arts, 'Oh, you take Karate? You scared of somebody or what you need to learn how to fight?' And it's not about that. I try to tell them that, but no, no, no, it just—ugh—people just—" She searched for words. "I don't know—what's the word?"

"Ignorance?" her sister Dzifa supplied.

"There we go!" Janine said.

Emma took a stab at the question: "I don't know if this has anything to do with it, but a lot of people our age are sort of just annoying, sort of fake—"

"Flaky!" the others chorused.

"Superficial," Emma added.

"They're conceited," LaShonda said firmly. "And they don't even do anything. They think they're great and all that." She started to recon-

Dzifa Dugba (top left), LaShonda Wilson (top right), Emma Neumann (middle), and Janine Bruno (seated) with Kung Fu weapons at a Destiny Arts Center performance (Oakland, Calif., 1995).

sider even as she continued speaking. "I mean, you are—you always are—"

"Everyone is special!" Emma reminded her, obviously quoting what she had been taught—but meaning what she said and unwilling to let

LaShonda's comment go unchallenged.

"They are special," La-Shonda agreed. "I'm not saying that." She struggled to reconcile a principle she clearly believed in with the evidence of her own experience. "It's in a different way. They don't do anything, but they're always ready to talk down to someone that's doing something for themselves." Now Emma nodded agreement. LaShonda continued, "Like if I'm getting a grade, somebody who's getting really bad grades will talk down to me, 'Oh, you study; you don't have a life.' You know. That's what people our age are all about. 'All I want to do is party and have fun.' They don't have their priorities straight. I have a lot of things to do, but I have fun. I have a life."

I thought of Didi Goodman's comment about the children in her Cuong Nhu classes separating along gender lines. In the Destiny Arts classes I had observed, girls and boys seemed to pair up readily with whoever was at hand. I asked the group what their experience had been. Over the years, they told me, their classes had varied in the proportion of boys and girls, although at present it was fairly even. The boys—young men by now—participated equally in martial arts, dance, and the performance company.

One of the group pointed out that skill level and experience also made significant divisions among students. A beginners' class for teens had recently been started, but they had little interaction with these students. Janine, the twelve-year-old, found boys her age mostly "crazy and immature," but the boys she had grown up with were different. "We're like brothers and sisters," she said. "We're just all together. We don't like the girls more than the boys or whatever. We're just all together."

"They're our family," LaShonda said. "We're always together."

In her thoughtful way, Dzifa returned to my question: "In the younger kids' class, though, it's kind of like that. A lot of boys are friends, so they'll work with their friends. But they'll still work with the girls, so it's kind of mixed."

"Boys at that age are—feisty," LaShonda observed. "They try to beat each other up when they're at this young age, and for most girls, sparring—I know for me, it was kind of hard to spar. I didn't like sparring when I was younger. I hated it, actually. When I spar with some of the little girls here, they're scared to spar. The boys try to beat you up and knock you down, so that's why the girls don't partner up with them as much. I didn't partner up with boys back then, because I was always, 'This boy's going to beat me up!' I'd partner up with girls. I think that's why boys and girls don't partner up with each other. But now we're all at the same level. Now we love sparring!"

"How did that change happen?" I asked. "Do you remember how you got over being afraid to spar?"

"I was in a tournament," LaShonda said. We were sitting on the floor in the office at that point, and she had crawled into the cubbyhole under a desk, but now she sat up to tell this story: "It was my first tournament. I hated sparring. I said to the girl they partnered me with, 'How hard do you hit?' And she hit me—"

"You asked her?" Emma interrupted.

"Yeah!"

"LaShonda!" Dzifa began in a reproving tone.

"I couldn't do it!" LaShonda said with some heat. "I said, 'How hard do you hit?' She hit me. I said, 'Okay, that's good.'"

"She hit you to show you?" Emma asked, still unbelieving.

"You thought she was really going to hit you that soft in that fight?" Janine asked.

"She did!" LaShonda said.

"That's nice!" Emma exclaimed. "That's sweet!"

"It was," LaShonda said. "I mean, I was all scared. After that, I was, 'Okay, it's not that bad.' And so I started sparring more here and everything. I got better."

"I always liked it," Emma said. "Remember, I would only do my punches in the beginning. They called me a bulldozer."

"Yes, she was!" LaShonda affirmed. "You were the exception among us, Emma. I used to hate sparring with Emma."

"It was because I was so little—" Emma began.

The others chimed in, laughing and teasing. "She hit me in my eye!" "She hurt my knee!"

"That's because I was so little!" Emma insisted. "That's why I had to do that."

"I was little, too!" LaShonda exclaimed. "But I didn't kick people in the head."

"And what about you, Dzifa?" I asked. "You said that you learned to like sparring, too."

"I had to," Dzifa answered. "Because Sifu Anthony, he always wanted me to spar. I was always on, so if I didn't like it—it was the only thing ever I didn't like, so I just learned to like it."

Janine spoke up gloomily: "I don't think anybody would spar in tournaments if they didn't hold your belt against you. Like the people who've never been to the tournament, me and Coco, we don't want to spar, but they say we're not going to get our belt until we spar. So we have to. Me and Coco, we really do not want to spar. But they're going to make us." She added doubtfully, "I guess we have to try new things."

"What is it you don't like about it?" I asked.

"Sparring?" Janine said. "It's the new people. You don't know their techniques, you don't know

anything about them. Sparring with people here in the program is like—you know, if somewhere's hurting, they're going to go easy on you. They feel sympathy for you. People—you don't know them. They don't know you, they don't care about you."

"So it's tournaments you don't like?" I asked. "You don't mind sparring in classes?"

Janine agreed, and Emma also.

"That's how I am," Emma said. "I love sparring, and I always hate tournaments."

"I don't like competition," LaShonda said. "I don't understand the point of competing against somebody who has a whole different style than you. Because they don't care who's style it is in sparring."

"And it's like you're in there for two seconds and that determines whether or not you get a trophy," Emma said.

"If I'm sparring against Emma and I have never sparred against her, you never know," LaShonda explained. "I could have bad luck or something—"

"That's exactly it!" Emma agreed. "It doesn't really test if you're a good fighter."

"Why would you want to do that anyway?" Janine asked. "It don't make no sense to find out who's the best fighter and who's this, who's that."

"And it's *not* the best fighter!" LaShonda said.

"You really are in there for only a few seconds," Emma said. "It's like one point, two points, three points—"

"You win, you sit down," LaShonda broke in. "Somebody else wins—it's not really fair to me, because if I spar with Emma first and I lose, I sit down. I don't get a chance to go spar any more. That's my last chance, and there'll be like five other people that I know I could beat. But I didn't have a chance. The only person I spar with is Emma."

"And then you leave," Emma said, "either feeling completely happy or just really sad."

"And maybe she wins after three points," Janine added. "If you let us go five points, maybe I win. I don't know. You don't know. So it just don't make no sense."

"Do you think there's some point in doing the tournaments?" I asked. "Do you learn something?"

"You get a chance to spar with other people that you're not used to sparring with," Dzifa said.

"Yeah, expand out of your little school," Emma agreed. "And some people like competition."

They liked forms competition better than sparring.

"You get to see other people's form," Janine explained. "Forms are easier for me."

Emma said, "You can prepare and know whether you're going to do good or not."

"You're there by yourself," LaShonda said. "I like forms, actually."

In both forms and sparring competition they had observed favoritism in judging, especially where judges were the teachers of contestants. This was not supposed to happen, they said, but they believed it had and felt the injustice strongly. Janine mentioned a particular instance involving LaShonda.

"He won!" LaShonda said indignantly. "He did the worst form and he beat me!"

Janine thought the judging for sparring might be fairer. "With the sparring sometimes you really have no choice, even if you are trying to play favoritism with somebody. If the point is there, the point is there—"

"It's sort of obvious," Emma agreed.

"But when you spar sometimes," LaShonda objected, "some people want to win so bad, that if you hit them they'll say they have to sit down and you get that point taken away."

"You're called for too-hard contact," Janine

explained to me.

"They all exaggerate," LaShonda concluded.

"It's a game," Emma said. "It's not really a test of your skill."

"We need to learn how to do it though," Janine pointed out.

Tournaments are at the martial end of the spectrum of their activities. Dance and the performance company were other activities to which this group devoted considerable time. I asked what interaction they saw between the martial arts and the dance. "Dance and martial arts are mixed," LaShonda suggested. If you're a dancer, you "flow and make really nice kicks." And did martial arts training have an effect on her dance? "It does," she said. Her voice slowed and grew uncertain. "I really don't know *how* it does . . ."

"More the other way around," one of the others suggested.

Arlean was there at this point. She is older and had had a year away to gain perspective. "It's helpful," she said decidedly. "How martial arts helps dance, to me it seems, is the discipline. I didn't do the theater part, but theater I think helps—and the dance also—because you're envisioning something else, as in martial arts. The martial arts helps the dance because to stay focused is easier. Because in dance how they say, 'Don't look at the audience, look above the audience. Look out.' That's like the martial arts—they teach you how to be focused and look out. Don't look at one particular thing, but just look."

Janine saw a two-way connection in that each activity "kept her energy up" for the other. "I'm more flexible because of dance," she added. "If I wasn't a dancer, I don't think I'd be really flexible, and I think I would pull a muscle or something."

Dzifa thought dance "improves your body, your stance. It's a lot more graceful."

They distinguished dance from the performance company—about which their feelings were mixed.

Emma likes performing. "I like the group. It's good for my confidence. It gives me a chance to express myself."

LaShonda loves dancing, but theater she termed only "interesting"—"It's not my favorite." Yet she thought it was beneficial. "If you're doing a form, you have to be some kind of animal, it helps you get into that—transform to that way of thinking."

Teaching was another and increasingly large aspect of their practice. The substance of what they taught—self-defense and violence awareness and prevention strategies—had been laced through their study over the years as a result of their teachers' orientation toward martial arts. Kate described the leadership training as including skills training in presentation of basic self-defense and de-escalation concepts, demonstration of role plays, public speaking, answering questions raised during workshops, and how to open and close a workshop session or series of classes. She told me she planned to formalize this curriculum with more organized trainings in the future, but for this first generation of students, their teaching experience began with assisting adults in workshops in the community; the curriculum and an apprenticeship arrangement simply grew with the increased demand for workshops. For these young women, the teaching seemed to have unfolded of itself and they could not easily explain how it came about.

"Kate just brought up, 'Do you want to do this?'" Arlean said. "And I was like, 'Okay.' So ever since then, I just started learning more of how to teach self-defense, and then it got to where basically that's all I was learning, was self-defense and about teaching self-defense."

"I didn't know anything about it," LaShonda said. "I had never been to any class like that—when me and Arlean started teaching, that's when we started learning too. It was a whole learning and teaching experience going on. I still haven't like went to a self-defense class!" she added—except, of course, as self-defense had been a part of all her martial arts classes.

"I learned by watching," Janine said. "Like when they get ready to go teach a class, LaShonda and Arlean, and LaShonda and Dzifa, I learn from watching them, because I watch them almost every time they practice."

Later, watching the group prepare for the workshops they were scheduled to teach that summer, I could see that they knew more than they could explain to me. Kate needed only to tell them the intended audience—teens, or adults who work with teens—and they were ready with ideas for exercises or role plays to get this or that point across.

Arlean and LaShonda had taught workshops at the 1993 NWMAF women's training camp in New York and LaShonda and Dzifa had taught at the 1994 PAWMA women's training camp. "The people who are going to these things know martial arts, know self-defense," LaShonda said. "They're wanting to learn how to teach teenagers. We have a script, like a book, what we're supposed to tell them. We don't have to write down all the moves like we would have to if we were teaching teenagers who didn't know any of this. We basically tell them what they would do."

They also teach groups of teens, mostly girls but some mixed groups of girls and boys, including pregnant and parenting teens in the schools, foster teens in a county program, and low-income teens in a church-run neighborhood discussion group. "And we did Girl Scouts," Dzifa added. These are workshops lasting two to three hours, or a series of hour-long classes once or twice a week for several weeks.

This summer would be twelve-year-old Janine's first experience of teaching adults: "I have only taught people my age or younger than me. I'm scared because I'm going to be teaching adults. I never done it before, and I really don't know what—I'm just—"

"It's not going to be as bad as you think it is," her older sister Dzifa told her.

"I think sometimes it's more comfortable teaching adults," Emma said. "They're overly respectful—they feel so much respect for you because you're young *and* you know all this stuff that they're trying to learn. With kids, sometimes it's frustrating. Like the Girl Scouts—they are pretty clueless. They don't know what's going on, so you're starting from scratch. You can't expect them to be good at anything, you just want them to be assertive, you know, get that little at least."

Dzifa said, "It's not that scary for me, because whenever I go teach, I'm with one of my friends from here. I've never been the only teenager there, working with other teenagers. We have fun together, so then the other teenagers have fun, too."

"When I first started teaching," LaShonda said, "I started with Arlean. It was teenage mothers and she could understand kind of what they were going through because they were around the same age, but I'm sitting there, a twelve-year-old, teaching sixteen- or seventeen-year-olds. I was scared about that, but it was because I was young. When I started teaching with people my own age I felt better."

Janine said, "I think the most important thing is you don't go around teaching people unless you have fun, because if you don't have fun, they're not going to have fun. Every time I've taught, I've had fun and I have people who come up to me and say, 'We not only had fun—you're a good teacher!' If I didn't have fun, I wouldn't really be into it, and I don't think they would get all that they could out of it."

"It's something very new for them to learn self-defense," LaShonda said. "I'm scared when I go and teach, because I don't know the people, and I'm the only teenager there maybe, and they're all looking at you—but if you're cool about it they'll loosen up too. They'll get into it. What she says is very, very true. You have to get in there with them. If you say, 'Do this' or 'Do that,' you should do it with them, so they can feel more comfortable doing it."

As in the other areas of the program, young men participate as fully as the young women in teaching assignments, performing valuable service in after-school programs and outreach programs in at-risk neighborhoods, teaching self-discipline and conflict resolution skills to their peers. Kate noted that the young men do not get as much recognition for their teaching—given the level of violence against women and girls, greater funding and recognition goes to women's self-defense activities.

Kate had mentioned to me her plan for the summer of getting the older students more into leadership roles, taking more responsibility for the younger students. I asked the group for their view of what the upcoming summer held and discovered that for them the abstract qualities Kate summarized as "leadership" translated into concrete details. For example, at one youth group meeting, they discussed food for a backpacking trip, and Emma explained the reason for their involvement: "There's been a food problem."

"That's what the youth group does," LaShonda said. "We get to plan, because the adults try to plan stuff for us, which is really hard, because they don't really know what we want to do. Now for the trips this summer, we get to buy the food. They're leaving it up to us so we can't get mad at them if we don't have something we want. They're going to—" she broke off when Emma said something in a wistful inaudible voice. "Hunh?"

"I like tofu," Emma repeated in a tiny voice. "I want tofu."

"We can get tofu," LaShonda and Dzifa assured her. "We get to go shopping," LaShonda continued, "and we get to plan the activities."

Dzifa added, "We get to help say who's in which tent, who's in which car. That's what people got upset over before. They got put in a tent with anybody or in a group with people they didn't know—if you don't know them, you're not going to talk to them a lot. You don't have anything to say to them."

"They try to make these getting-to-know-people groups," Janine said disapprovingly. "They try to push you together, and it's like—"

"But it's a good idea," LaShonda objected.

"No, not really," Janine said. "They can't force that upon us. If we want to meet other people, we will—"

"But they do have to try," LaShonda persisted.

"We will!" Janine asserted.

"No, I'm saying, *they* have to try," As I had seen her and the others do on similar occasions, LaShonda spoke quickly to forestall a misunderstanding.

A major focus for the summer was, of course, the trip to Beijing.

"It's going to be huge," LaShonda said. "thirty thousand people are going—"

"They'll have to do it on microphones!" Emma exclaimed, apparently envisioning herself teaching all thirty thousand in a single session—and the prospect clearly intrigued her.

"We have like four classes," LaShonda said.

"But I think it's going to be a lot of people—that'll make it just more fun for me. I don't like teaching to a really small group. That's what happened to me and Dzifa"—she cast back to the previous year's PAWMA camp—"The first night we had a lot of people. It was crowded. The second night we had less and less, and then the last class we had like five people—"

"Actually," Dzifa said, "We were scared there wasn't going to be a lot of people at first on the first night. They started coming in a few people at a time so it was like we was just going to have like fifteen people. And then like a whole lot more came."

"At first, I was like, 'Oh, I don't want a lot of people, I don't want a lot of people,'" LaShonda remembered. "And then when I got them, it was like, yeah, yeah—it was pumping me up."

As to teaching in Beijing, Emma said, "It's more difficult. It's more of a challenge to go to China and see if we could do it." But she and LaShonda agreed, "It will be fun. It will be exciting!"

"I just hope lots of people come!" LaShonda added.

Kate had stuck her head through the door a few minutes before; still ahead on the schedule for the day were trainings and preparations for teaching at PAWMA camp and in China, designing warmups for use in teaching martial arts and a second set of warm-ups and introductory awareness exercises to illustrate to adults how to teach self-defense to teens. I thanked the group for talking with me. "Thank you, thank you," they chorused back with the courtesy that seemed to have become a part of them with so much else I admired: self-possession, competence, and openness to new experiences.

"If only I had been exposed to this when I was young!" "If only all our daughters learned this as a matter of course!" How many times have I heard women thus exclaim upon discovering some aspect of our own power revealed through martial arts or self-defense training. For myself, I have often felt that I spent the first twenty years of my life being broken down and disempowered, so that it took me another twenty years to reassemble myself constructively and only in my forties could I even begin to be able to take my place in the world. From childhood these young women had grown up with the training and role models so many of us have felt the lack of—and the results, it seemed to me, were very rewarding to see.

Kate spoke of having "an expansive interpretation of the teaching that falls within 'martial arts,'" emphasizing violence prevention skills, which she sees as including "meditation, listening skills, learning to set and reach goals, leadership training, and self-expression."[3] Certainly her students' grasp of the training went well beyond their physical skills, as I could see for myself in talking with them, taking one of the classes they taught that summer at PAWMA camp, and observing them teach others.

Dzifa had talked of what a comfortable place the school was for her, and Janine mentioned how she and Dzifa resisted their mother's attempts to move them to a school closer to home: "It wouldn't be the same at all!" Arlean had taken classes at a martial arts school near her college, but that wasn't the same either. The teaching was not supportive and inspiring in the way she was used to. School-work also required her attention, and so she stopped going, though she spoke wistfully of looking for another school in the future. It seemed clear to me that Kate Hobbs and her staff are what make the Destiny Arts programs so effective. But I also believe the strong component of martial arts in the program is indispensable. Respect for the very seriousness of the fighting skills these young people acquired seemed to be a thread that pulled the other elements into a coherent whole.

These young women are not superwomen, but very real teenagers, with foibles, distractions, frustrations, and difficulties—and charm—typical of their age. The five of them are very different from each other, and each has made something different of their joint experience. All this only strengthens the argument about the effectiveness of the Destiny Arts approach—the range of students who can benefit is wide, and they need not bring any extraordinary capacity to their training, but only what they are.

Nor has these young women's training made small or trivial the hard challenges that surely lie ahead of them. LaShonda is planning a career in medicine. Arlean, as I mentioned, aspires to be a judge. Dzifa wants to be a writer. Janine later wrote to me that she would "like to become a well-known poetess" and sent me a promising sample of her work. Emma is less certain of an actual profession. She wants to do some kind of social work where she can counsel and empower people.

These young women's place in the world may be more openly acknowledged than has been the case for women of previous generations, but it is not likely to be any freer of violence, discrimination, and exploitation. Yet, as Karlon Kepcke said about herself when I talked to her about her Capoeira training, LaShonda, Arlean, Emma, Dzifa, and Janine have "a zillion more resources" than they otherwise might have.

---

3. Ibid., 73.

Reflections in the Mirror of My Practice

The Dragon Tiger Mountain form of T'ai Chi Ch'uan that I practice concludes with kicks to the eight directions of the *I Ching*—heel kicks to the cardinal directions alternate with crescent kicks to the corners. These kicks are the most difficult part of the form for me to perform well. They are high but slow, not a throwing forth of the leg and foot but a controlled raising and extension. I keep working on them.

After the eighth and final kick to the northeast we come around again to face north, the direction of the unknown, where we began. In China, north is the direction of cold, drying winds from the interior, but in California the life-giving winter rains come from the north. Thus traditions encompass new realities; changes bring new richness.

◆　◆　◆

I began this book to learn about other women's sustained practice of martial arts. I found a wealth of women—women of all ages, backgrounds, interests, situations, and styles of martial arts, women with skill and experience and power. One book cannot encompass all that women have achieved in and through the martial arts, but this book does, I believe, represent the variability of and possibilities for women in the martial arts.

That these are women, that there are so many of them, and that their expertise and authority are substantial was enormously important to me. I *knew* women could

MICHELLE DWYER

Stephanie Hoppe performing the closing movement of the Dragon Tiger Mountain Yang-Style Family Set T'ai Chi Ch'uan for Janet Seaforth at the White Cloud Women's T'ai Chi School (Philo, Calif., June 1995).

do and be all these things, but I had not *seen* it; and the reality turned out to be larger than my imaginings. The sheer numbers of women martial artists I met along the way, at women's training camps and women's schools, also had a powerful impact on me. Here was not just a case of a handful of isolated if inspiring stellar women in a man's field, but hundreds of women at all different levels in what is clearly a women's field. Observing other women's struggles as well as their achievements validated my own in a way that men's expe-

rience had never done.

I have spent most of my adult life in situations where men have dominated in numbers, experience, and skill, even aside from their higher social status on account of their gender. Men's ways have been the norm, and like so many women I learned early to limit my speech, my thoughts, my emotional responses—my very self—to fit the model men set. Not until I saw women in large numbers, women in all their diversity, skilled and powerful women, going about the disciplined training of martial arts did I fully realize the extent to which I censor myself. It is a truism that a physical discipline like martial arts must be done in one's own body, with all that entails of capacities or limits. It took me an extra step to see that my *female* body is an aspect of my training that I must be aware of and take responsibility for—a step that only women could show me how to navigate.

Another lesson that women taught me that I perhaps could never fully accept from men, given how it touches on some of the most difficult issues that arise between women and men, is how much fighting matters. A number of the women I talked to stressed their belief that the fighting aspect of their art is more a matter of social and energetic contact and interaction than of strikes and kicks. But for them too, I came to see, the *physical* capacities that one draws on in actual fighting underlie their practice in ways that may not be altogether distinguishable.

An animal instinct of self-preservation may be the wellspring we tap to fully engage our being for any endeavor. We may never punch anyone in the face—but we may need to value ourselves as worth physically fighting for and obtain the mental and bodily wherewithal to actually do so, if we are to avoid the doing without diminishing or abandoning ourselves in important ways. I have come to this conclusion from seeing and talking to women who know how to do these things and from observing how *I* feel and act now that I have seriously begun studying partner practice.

This book motivated me to undertake a number of intermediate activities I might never have done on my own. I went to training camps and workshops primarily to observe what women did; but once I was there I tried out the activities for myself, if only to better understand what I was observing. The interviews also had an effect through the discipline they entailed of calling up strangers, asking them for their time, meeting and interviewing them, and following up on incomplete answers or new ideas—the emotional stresses and strains in such nonphysical encounters are comparable to those in the physical interaction of training with a partner.

The choreographed two-person T'ai Chi Ch'uan formed another important step. I continue to work at it and find new lessons in it now I have begun freestyle Push Hands as well. Partner practice has by no means supplanted my solitary forms practice. I seem to need the hours and repetitions of sheer physical movement to maintain my sense of my bodied being as the center from which I act. In a sense, though, even when I practice without a human partner, I am never alone, but always in physical and spiritual interaction with Earth, air, trees, and the myriad small beings that inhabit even city landscapes, and these are relations that nourish me deeply. When I do not get enough of this practice, it shows up in my encounters with training partners and others in a loss of center, groundedness, and focus.

I confess, however, to finding a certain satisfaction and sense of accomplishment in partner practice that is different and more outwardly oriented than what I feel in individual practice. "There's nothing like a good fight!" Malyne Chiu's words, edged with pleasure that is contagious,

often sound in my mind. The close trial of body and being in sparring does indeed engage one's energies and interest like nothing else; dancing, for example, now pales by comparison for me. Some days I can almost imagine myself participating in a Push Hands tournament.

Have I then come to terms with the questions about fighting that so beset me when I began this book? Certainly my understanding of fighting has changed. Now that I have more experience training and sparring with partners, I see why the heady physical release I felt in my response to the model mugger's attack in the self-defense course I took from Gayle Fillman dredged up the memory as a child of my own attack on my young brother. In that interaction with the model mugger I *was* behaving very similarly to when I attacked my brother so many years before: In both instances I lashed out with similar lack of control. That the first instance was unjustified and the second was desired did not affect the quality of the energy involved.

I begin to grasp how different a fighting art is from just lashing out. What I am learning has to do with developing conscious access to more and more of my being. From that seems to follow a clearer perception of others, a better understanding of them—and more empathy for them. Not long ago, practicing Push Hands with one of my regular partners, I suddenly had a palpable sense of the energy field that he maintained about him. Extending perhaps a foot or two beyond his physical body, it shifted and cracked as his focus changed or faltered. Except that I was utterly taken up with my observations and lost all thought of taking any action, I could unerringly and effortlessly have entered through the breaks in his field and he would have been unable to resist my attack. This is what the martial arts classics talk about—how one can see what someone is going to do before they do it and have all the time in the world to avoid or change their action. It's nothing magical, but rather a refinement of ordinary bodily perception, like seeing my hand in front of my face.

Such abilities come from training for them. It seems clear to me now that at least part of my old resistance to fighting was simply that I did not know how to do it and did not believe that I could learn—I still don't know very much, and what I do know is not reliably accessible to me. But I no longer feel there is no way for me to move beyond my ignorance or inability. I often remember Saskia Kleinert's words in this regard: "You don't have to do anything difficult or anything you don't know how to do; you just have to practice!"

For some women, martial arts and self-defense are not necessarily connected. But I continue to feel tension between my love and desire for the sheer movements of what I now accept as the fighting art of T'ai Chi Ch'uan and my awareness of how women live under constant threat of psychological and physical attack by men, not for anything we do individually but simply for being women. This situation, it seems to me, makes the physical integrity and safety of our bodies a political pursuit for women without which legal, social, and economic reforms will be ineffective. At the same time women need to go beyond reacting to what men do to creating ourselves and the world as we want and need the world and ourselves to be. For all of these purposes, truly inhabiting our bodies looks to be an indispensable first step. I see martial arts training, especially as taught in the developing women's traditions practiced by many of the women in this book, as offering a powerful tool for achieving the feminist aims of reclaiming especially women's bodies and accessing body knowledge lost through the Western exaltation of mind/spirit/male and devaluation of body/Earth/female.

And what of my principled concern for non-violence? Has that fallen away as an idea without substance in the light of my new appreciation of bodied being, self-defense, and physical empowerment? On the contrary, as martial arts emerge for me as methods for avoiding and defusing violence between individuals, my commitment to nonviolent social action has gained substance. At its best, martial arts training is about devising tactics that accord with the situation and available resources as well as being present and responsible. For achieving social and political change, these characteristics strike me as translating very directly into what has traditionally been called nonviolent action. And as my sense of my own bodied self strengthens, I see ever more clearly what power there might be in massed bodied beings.

"Civilian-based defense" is an overall technical term I learned for the many varieties of "passive" resistance that, throughout history, groups of people have engaged in to withstand tyranny and injustice. As examples of people persisting in their beliefs, their institutions, their way of life, despite threatened and actual loss of homes, belongings, family, and life, we can point to the Dutch resistance to Spanish invaders in the sixteenth century, the Indian resistance against the British in the 1930s and 1940s, the Hungarian revolution of 1956–1957, the South Vietnamese Buddhist undermining of the Ngo Dinh Diem regime in 1963, and the U.S. civil rights movement. In many different ways attackers' violence can be turned against them in the international arena, before their home audience, and in individual encounters. Theorists note that these strategies have been used more often than generally recognized—but always improvised on the spur of the moment, without the resources of planning, strategy, training, organization, and materiel that military action has traditionally been afforded. At a fraction of the social and economic cost of maintaining armies and navies, whole populations could be trained and prepared to ensure our collective security—with multiple desirable spinoffs of individual responsibility and empowerment.[1] All this sounds to me very like a large-scale application of martial arts training, and I have seen it referred to expressly as "political Jujutsu."[2]

The application of martial arts techniques and fighting situations in everyday life also can be systematically trained for, as Wendy Palmer's Conscious Embodiment training illustrates. An exercise she used in a class I attended affords an example: Students stand before her as she raises a wooden sword; she brings the sword down and they step to one side and then behind her to avoid it. Their task is to identify and, through breathing and centering themselves, manage the feelings and energies at work in them. Class discussion made clear to me that the students do find they can then draw on this training to deal with life situations in which similar feelings are evoked.

The promise such training holds, particularly for women, is underscored in the story told to me by Juanita Pat Ricc, an arts professor now in her fifties. For years, she told me, her sense of herself as economically and politically independent—even radical—did not extend to her physical self-defense. She was raped—twice—in her twenties and characterized her young adult life as full of terror. At age thirty-nine she took a self-defense course for women. It changed everything. She became, as she put it, a "buster—feeling wonderful about the power to defend myself. But it was intensely aggressive, and it affected my personal-

ity so that I became a puncher and kicker psychologically too." She was never assaulted again—"never even close," she said. "Crazies, once in a while, in my face. I would just sort of lean in, like, 'Touch me. Push me. I wish you would. I wish you would. Come on! Come on!' And they never would." But finding herself behaving in this aggressive way in her personal and professional relationships made her feel ambivalent about this new power.

A decade later, at the urging of a friend, Juanita took a weekend workshop for women in Aikido "off the mat" at Centerfield Aikido in Graton, California, taught by the Aikido sensei Sylvia Marie and Mary McLean. The workshop, entitled "Love and Power," used Aikido principles to explore nonaggressive self-defense. In one exercise the students tried to stop a partner from intruding on their personal space. Juanita described how it felt to be unable to convince her partner to stay back: "This was a friend I didn't want to hurt, so I was helpless. The physical feeling associated with that emotion of helplessness is that you vacate your body. You don't live there any more. There's nobody home. You're made of sand, and you crumble. It is a psychological equivalent of physical flight. No wonder you feel abandoned and helpless—you're not there!"

She tried anger. The problem with that, she reported, is that you also abandon yourself when you're hostile and angry: "You run forward out of your space psychologically. You're out there fighting, but you're not defending anything. You've lost your ground. You've abandoned your space. The aftermath of being aggressive, physically or emotionally, for me, is the same emptiness as being a helpless victim. Which is physical proof fight and flight, rage and terror, are flip sides of the same coin. Now, the truth is that violent abandonment of yourself to rage is a better defense against a physical intruder than collapse, but it still leaves

---

1. Gene Sharp, *Making Europe Unconquerable: The Potential of Civilian-Based Deterrence and Defense* (Cambridge, MA: Ballinger, 1985).

2. Ibid., 205.

you reactive."

The workshop leaders taught a third alternative, based on Aikido: "Don't leave your center and throw yourself into a fight, and don't shrink into your center. Fill up, expand, extend your energy. You have psychological space around you that you want to defend—fill it! Extend your energy out to the perimeter, encounter threat there, keeping yourself at the center of it. Neither abandon your space to attack, nor withdraw inward and hope the perimeter will hold. It will not hold. You must extend yourself, but you can't abandon yourself."

Juanita described the results: "It's not that hard! When your partners came close and you tried to stop them, you could feel the difference in energy. You could feel that the answer was not that you got hostile or responded with aggression. None of those were as powerful as just extending your energy." As attacker she also felt a difference: "You could feel that it was real. Nobody was pretending to have been stopped. So it was true that you could defend yourself without abandonment, without terrible adrenalin, without getting decentered, uncentered. And the aggression coming toward you wasn't heightened by this resistance, but diminished, because it was just a stop. It's peaceful resistance, but it is effective resistance!"

In the seven years since that weekend workshop Juanita has intermittently studied Aikido and T'ai Chi Ch'uan with a more standard martial arts approach. She has not found a school that satisfies her interests in physical training, but she believes the principles of these martial arts have become central to her self-identity. "I am not only physically safe, but more emotionally safe—from my own rage and terror as well as from attack—than at any time since adolescence," she told me. "I don't lash out any more, I've stopped being a puncher and kicker. I'm at peace with my ability to keep myself safe." And she finds constant application of her knowledge in teaching students, in her own artistic work, and in dealing with colleagues.

Juanita's words have on a number of occasions come to my assistance in my own life and practice, as have many of the comments told me by the women I interviewed. All these words . . . I remember how at the PAWMA training camp in 1994, when I interviewed Janet Aalfs and Wen Mei Yu, I acutely felt the "mere" words of our conversation lacked substance, body, reality compared to the intense physical immediacy of the camp experience. Yet writing draws me with an allure perhaps no less physical than T'ai Chi Ch'uan. Writing this book has been a repeated exercise in connecting words and the body as the experiences I hear about crop up in my physical practice, and through my practice surface the words that now appear on these pages. I have become a living counterpart of the book, listening to women's stories, telling these stories to other women I meet, and extending the reach of each woman's individual experience. The words you now read are not separable from my bodily being, but important modes by which I perceive and act in the world.

◆ ◆ ◆

Completing the interviews took me most of 1994 and 1995. By the end of 1995 only a few loose ends remained in the interviews, together with a few missing photographs. To photograph Midge Marino I visited her self-defense classes at California State University at Sacramento. The young women in her advanced class, who had studied with Midge for several semesters and developed an obviously warm relationship with her that spoke well for her methods, invited me to train with them. They were pleased to instruct me in techniques they had learned. In contrast to the time now years before when I first studied self-defense with Gayle Fillman I found I was able to kick, punch, and even kiai with a will and among strangers. More wryly I noted my continuing tendency to abandon my center and rush into something to get it over with rather than work through it fully present.

Back home I had occasion to talk to Karlon Kepcke on the telephone. After a year away from Capoeira because of the back injury she spoke of in her interview she was happy and excited to be training again. I asked whether she found a difference in her practice. Yes, she said. She feels a new empathy for others—and for herself. After such a long break she in a sense had to start over in her training from the beginning. Of course her progress was much more rapid than the first time around, but repeating the process gave her a new appreciation of what others went through. She feels her commitment to Capoeira to be deeper: "I want to do Capoeira forever! Until I'm ninety! People don't think that's possible, but there's one master I know who's seventy-three. . . ."

A few weeks later I attended the annual Christmas demonstration at the Destiny Arts Center. The full complement of children and teens performed a variety of martial arts and self-defense skits for an audience of parents and community members. The smallest children were of course enchanting, but I was most interested to watch the older ones whom I had talked to. One piece featured these young women and the young men in their class demonstrating the different techniques learned with increasing rank. After showing what was done at a given rank, those at that belt level dropped out, leaving finally the handful of brown and black belt students. These performed a gravity-defying sequence in which they leapt what looked to me fully shoulder height off the ground and at that elevation lashed out with front and rear kicks. Then the brown belts stepped to the side of the room amid tumultuous applause, leaving alone in the center of the stage Destiny's first black belt,

LaShonda Wilson. When I had interviewed her she had been looking forward to taking her black belt test and now she had successfully completed it. As the applause went on LaShonda looked at first a little uncertain but then grinned, relaxing and accepting the homage she had certainly earned. Presently Sifu Anthony Daniels stepped out beside her. "This isn't part of the program we planned," he announced, "but would you like to see LaShonda spar?" The audience response left him in no doubt. In comparison to Anthony's massive, nearly three-hundred-pound frame, LaShonda looked small and slender—but supple and resilient. And as the audience applauded wildly, she gave a good account of herself in an exchange of strikes and kicks.

I visited Lloyda French at Ronin Dojo in San Francisco to take photographs. Watching her beginners' Karate class reminded me of the work that is involved in pursuing a martial art, the long hours required to stretch and condition muscles and limbs and pattern appropriate responses in mind and body. I thought of my own ups and downs, occasional insights and periods of frustration and uncertainty, times when I feel inspired and other times when I am dull, tired, hurt—all the different moments of my accumulated daily practice, the tens, hundreds, thousands of times I have done this stretch, this strike, this turn. I thought too of Karlon's more severe injury, happily now healed. There is power in our trained bodies but also fragility. So much can change or be lost in an instant. And yet, from changes and losses too, practice deepens and grows richer. These are bodily arts, but they can be done by people who are missing limbs, are paralyzed, have any manner of physical disability.

One afternoon I visited Karina Epperlein and found her looking radiant. Just that week she had finished her work on the documentary film about

LaShonda Wilson (left) and Anthony Daniels at the Destiny Arts Center (Oakland, Calif., 1995).

the women in the Federal Correctional Institution, Dublin, *Voices from Inside.* We spent an hour comparing notes about her work on the film and mine on this book that had proceeded in parallel over several years, with many intersections. She brought out photos from her prison workshops and the-

ater performances, and we picked several out to include in the book.

Janet Aalfs wrote to me from Massachusetts that her book *KIAI: A Woman Shouts—Poetry, Martial Arts, and Self Defense* was taking shape. An associateship at the Women's Studies Research

Center, operated by the five women's colleges located near where she lives, gave her a boost in providing a physical work setting and a community of women who honor her undertaking. Jane Golden, who had spoken with contagious enthusiasm about her experience with T'ai Chi Ch'uan fan, reported that she was reaching outside the forms handed down to her by others to design a double fan set. Saskia Kleinert told me she planned to take her black belt test in Kajukenbo in the spring, and she invited me to attend. This was to be a five-hour demonstration before her peers and an examining board of what she knows of open hands and weapons forms, sparring and self-defense techniques, and the philosophy and history of the art, culminating in an hour of free sparring with a series of fifteen or twenty fresh partners; she would pass with praise from the examiners for her preparation, knowledge, skill, stamina, poise, and grace.

My last visit was to San Jose, at the far south end of San Francisco Bay, to see Sandy Wong and Malyne Chiu. They knew each other from the early seventies when they both attended San Jose State University and were involved in Asian American studies and Malyne's father's dojo. In recent years the day-to-day necessities of children and jobs have limited their social encounters, so this meeting was an opportunity for the two of them to catch up on each other's news and lives as well as answer some questions I had.

Malyne had brought with her a Japanese magazine with photos from a Naginata tournament in Japan in which she had recently competed. Leafing through the magazine while the three of us talked, Sandy spotted a photo of Malyne. Malyne glanced at the page. "My last and losing match," she commented. Then she added, "The woman who beat me took first." Her words made me think how for all the reminiscing I had just heard about the training in their youthful college years, now in their forties both Malyne and Sandy still actively practice martial arts and likely neither of them has reached what they would look back on as their peak.

The afternoon wound on. Malyne remembered household tasks awaiting her. I took Sandy to meet her family at a basketball game in which one of her sons was playing and started on my long drive home, mulling over in my mind all that I had talked about with one woman or another. Again and again I came back to the idea of how martial arts training seems to tap into some basic level of human physiology and spiritual existence deeper than culture. Indeed, martial arts themselves are perhaps in a sense only a superficial manifestation of how we can work with these capabilities of our being. I don't doubt that, say, flamenco dancing and belly dancing, among other physical arts, are rooted in similar possibilities. The notion fascinates and delights me with a sense of the freedom we may after all have to reach beyond the limitations of language, nation, and all the other categories that separate us to realize the goal of living peaceably and appropriately with all other beings on this Earth.

Glossary

Note on spelling names and terms: The martial artists I encountered most commonly used the Wade–Giles system for rendering Chinese characters in English. I have followed that usage except for a few variants used by an overwhelming majority in the community (for example, Shaolin rather than Shao-lin) and those terms derived from Cantonese pronunciation (for example, *sifu*). I also respected the wishes of individual women who expressed a preference for some other system (chapter 16, for example, is spelled according to the *pinyin* system). Where two spellings are given in the glossary, the first is according to the Wade–Giles system, unless otherwise noted, the second, pinyin.

Names are alphabetized by family name in the glossary. Treatment of Chinese and Japanese names in the chapters follows the Chinese and Japanese custom of giving the family name first, except where the speaker, or the person in question, expressed a preference for the Western custom of putting the family name last.

Aikido (Japanese, "the way of harmonious energy") a martial art developed in Japan in the 1930s and 1940s by Ueshiba Morihei; generally considered a soft, or internal, style.

berimbau (Brazilian) a single-stringed musical instrument made from a gourd with a long stick attached to form the neck; played by the *mestre* who presides over a Capoeria match, or game.

bokken (Japanese) wooden practice sword.

bow stance basic posture for T'ai Chi Ch'uan: starting with feet parallel and shoulder width apart, step forward with one foot and turn out the rear foot at an angle of 45 to 60 degrees.

budo (Japanese, "the way of stopping the spear") Japanese ethic of martial arts emphasizing self-discipline, self-control, and avoiding contributing to conflict; also a collective term for Japanese martial arts.

Capoeira (Brazilian) martial art developed by Africans brought to Brazil as slaves during the Portuguese colonization.

Chang San-feng (China, ca. Sung dynasty, 960–1279, according to some sources or several centuries later according to others) Taoist monk credited with developing T'ai Chi Ch'uan.

Chen style (Chinese) a style of T'ai Chi Ch'uan developed by the Chen family in the Wen district of Honan province in China in the mid-seventeenth century.

Chen Wang-ting (China, ca. 1597–1664) Ming dynasty official credited with developing T'ai Chi Ch'uan.

Cheng Man-ch'ing (China, 1900–1975) master of T'ai Chi Ch'uan who taught in the United States for a number of years. The shortened Yang-style form that he developed in the 1930s is perhaps the most commonly practiced T'ai Chi Ch'uan in the United States.

ch'i, qi (Chinese, "life energy") the vital energy that according to Chinese philosophy and medicine animates all life; Chinese martial arts cultivate and focus this energy for martial use.

Ch'i Kung, Qigong (Chinese, "skill with *ch'i*") a variety of health and breathing exercises for developing and channeling *ch'i;* also healing techniques employed by highly trained and specialized medical practitioners.

Cuong Nhu (Vietnamese, "hard, soft") an eclectic style of martial arts developed by Ngo Dong in Vietnam in the 1960s.

dan (Japanese) rank or degree above black belt in Japanese martial arts; generally proceeds from first to tenth.

do (Japanese, from Chinese *tao*) the Way.

dojo (Japanese) a place where one studies a *do,* or Way; martial arts training hall.

empty hands (syn. open hands) weaponless martial arts.

external (syn. hard style) martial arts with an emphasis on the external muscles of the body and techniques.

form (syn. set, sequence) a choreographed set of movements. In T'ai Chi Ch'uan long forms traditionally contain one hundred and eight moves; short forms are of varying lengths.

gi (Japanese) traditional dress for Japanese martial artists, generally consisting of black or white cotton drawstring trousers and a thick cotton or quilted jacket tied with a belt, the color of which may indicate the wearer's rank.

Goju-ryu (Japanese) a style of Karate.

hakama (Japanese) a traditional floor-length garment sometimes with split skirts. Black or dark blue *hakama* are often worn over a *gi* in Japanese martial arts; in some arts the *hakama* is worn only by persons with black belt rank.

Hapkido (Korean) a hard-style martial art.

hara (Japanese) physical or metaphysical center or point of balance of the body; seat of *ki;* corresponds to the second chakra or *tan t'ien* in the lower abdomen.

hard style (syn. external) martial arts with an emphasis on muscle conditioning and training specific technqiues of kicking, punching, and blocking.

horse stance basic Kung Fu stance with feet parallel, knees and hips bent so thighs are parallel to the ground, but spine remains vertical; in

Wing Chun the toes are turned in and the knees brought to within one fist's width of each other.

Hsing Yi (Chinese) internal martial art emphasizing linear movement; said to have originated in exercises for marching troops.

internal (syn. soft style) martial arts in which practitioners seek to develop internal energies and perceptions.

irimi (Japanese, "entering with or into the body") a term that appears in the name of numerous Aikido moves that involve entering into an attack; also the concept of moving toward rather than away from or around an attack or a threatening or challenging situation.

jo (Japanese) short staff or walking stick.

Judo (Japanese, "the gentle way") martial art developed in the 1880s from earlier Jujutsu by Kano Jigoro; emphasizes character development and moral conduct as well as effective technique.

judoka (Japanese) a person who practices Judo.

Jujutsu (Japanese, "gentle technique") a variety of traditional Japanese techniques for unarmed combat based on grappling, using the momentum of an attack to unbalance and throw the attacker, and joint locks.

Kajukenbo (from *Ka*rate, *Ju*jutsu and *Ju*do, *Ke*npo, and Chinese *Bo*xing) an eclectic martial art developed after World War II in Hawaii by martial artists from different Asian countries.

Kano Jigoro (Japan, 1859–1938) Japanese educator and senator who founded Judo.

Karate (Japanese, perhaps originally "Chinese hands," but now more often represented by a character meaning "empty hands" or "receptive hands") a term used for a variety of hard-style systems of empty hands fighting.

kata (Japanese, "model" or "pattern"; syn. form, set, sequence) in martial arts, a choreographed training exercise.

Kendo (Japanese, "the way of the sword") modern Japanese art of sword fighting.

Kenpo Karate a style of Karate.

ki (Japanese, from Chinese *ch'i*) life energy.

kiai (Japanese) outpouring of *ki* often physically manifested as a piercing shout; to yell or shout with *ki*.

kiatsu (Japanese, "ki pressure"; a parallel formation to *shiatsu*, "finger pressure") healing technique developed by the Aikido sensei Tohei Koichi.

Kodokan Judo Institute (Tokyo, Japan) Institute founded by Kano Jigoro in 1882 for the study of Judo; the Joshi-Bu, or Women's Section, was opened in 1923.

kuan (Chinese) staff.

Kuan Yin (China, "she who hears") Chinese goddess or bodhisattva of mercy and compassion.

kuantao (Chinese) a long weapon consisting of a staff with a saber blade attached (this is larger and heavier than the Japanese *naginata*).

Kung Fu (Chinese, "art or skill acquired by great effort") term used in the United States for hard-style Chinese martial arts, which are called by various names in Chinese, including Shaolin boxing. In Chinese the term *kung fu* is used with reference to not only martial arts but also all other arts and skills.

Kyudo (Japanese) the art of archery.

Lian gong (Chinese) a collection of 36 health and stretching exercises, developed in China in 1974 by Dr. Zhuang Yuanming, based on the physiological principles that also underlie Chinese martial arts.

ma-ai (Japanese, "harmony of space") distance in space or time; in Aikido the appropriate distance separating training partners, which depends on height, size, stance, and flow of ki of the partners, whether they carry weapons, and external situations such as light.

mestre (Portuguese) a Capoeira master.

Modern Arnis (Filipino) martial art featuring weapons and empty hands techniques based on figure-eight movements, the symbol of infinity.

nage (Japanese, "thrower") the partner in Aikido who receives the attack and executes the technique to throw the attacker, or *uke*.

naginata (Japanese) weapon consisting of a spear with a blade attached, altogether about seven feet long; Naginata, the art of using the weapon.

Ng Mui (China, 17th century) Buddhist nun at the Shaolin Temple who developed the martial art of Wing Chun.

noros (Okinawan) shamanic women or priestesses responsible for ties between the human and spirit world; their power instruments traditionally included a variety of weapons, and they were skilled in their use.

nunchaku (Okinawan) a tool used to thresh rice; made from a pair of hardwood sticks connected by a short length of rawhide, chain, or rope; used by Okinawans as a weapon after they were disarmed by the Japanese who colonized Okinawa.

open hands (syn., empty hands) weaponless martial arts.

Push Hands patterned and freestyle sparring exercises in T'ai Chi Ch'uan.

randori (Japanese) in Aikido, attack by multiple persons; in Judo, freestyle sparring between two partners.

Roll Back one of the eight "intrinsic energies" included in the thirteen postures, or methods, basic to T'ai Chi Ch'uan.

ryu (Japanese) martial tradition.

seiza (Japanese, "to sit in a correct, calm, or polite manner") seated posture with legs folded under and spine vertical; traditional for meditation and martial arts.

sensei (Japanese, "one who goes before") respect-

ful title for a teacher.

Shaolin Temple (Honan province, China; also Sil Lum) Buddhist temple founded during the Later Wei dynasty (ca. 386–534), long known for martial arts training; origin of Shaolin Ch'uan or boxing, now including Northern and Southern Shaolin Kung Fu.

shen (Chinese, "spiritual energy") a refinement of ch'i one achieves through Taoist practice.

shiai (Japanese, "match, game, contest") martial arts tournament.

shinai (Japanese) bamboo sword about forty inches long used in Kendo.

shomen (Japanese, "front") in martial arts, the front of a training hall where an altar with photographs of the founder of the art, flowers, and other symbols of respect and celebration are often placed; upon entering the hall or the mat, students bow to the *shomen*.

Shotokan a style of Karate.

Shuri-ryu a style of Karate.

sifu, simu (Cantonese Chinese; often translated as "teacher–father" and "teacher–mother") respectful title for martial arts teachers. *Sifu*, used for teachers of both sexes, is represented by two different characters in Chinese, only one of which refers to father, with the other being gender neutral; nonetheless *simu* is preferred by some women teachers.

slow set a T'ai Chi Ch'uan form or sequence that is generally performed slowly; there are also specific "fast forms" intended to be performed quickly.

soft style (syn. internal) martial arts emphasizing internal energy and awareness of an opponent rather than muscle strength and conditioning.

Tae Kwon Do (Korean, "the way of the foot and fist") hard-style martial art emphasizing kicking.

T'ai Chi Ch'uan, Taijiquan (Chinese, "supreme ultimate fist") an internal, soft-style martial art.

tan t'ien, dantian (Chinese, "cinnabar field," referring to the use of mercury in alchemical transformation) metaphorical name for energy center in lower abdomen, an inch or so below navel, where *ch'i* is stored; corresponds to the second chakra and the *hara.*

tao (Chinese, "the Way") basis of Chinese Taoist philosophy; corresponds to Japanese *do;* also the Chinese single-edged curved sword, which is variously referred to as a broadsword, saber, or knife.

tori (Japanese, "to take down") the partner in Judo who receives the attack and executes the technique to take down the attacker, or *uke;* equivalent to *nage* in Aikido.

two step an Aikido technique for turning one hundred and eighty degrees with a step and pivot, starting and ending in *hamni* stance; also used as a warm-up exercise.

Ueshiba Morihei (Japan, 1887–1969) Japanese soldier, teacher, and philosopher who developed the martial art Aikido in the 1930s and 1940s; often called O-Sensei, or Great Teacher.

uke (Japanese, "receiver") the partner in Aikido or Judo who initiates the attack and receives the technique executed by *nage* or *tori* and is thrown.

Ward Off one of the eight "intrinsic energies" included in the thirteen postures, or methods, basic to T'ai Chi Ch'uan.

Wing Chun (Chinese, "eternal spring") a martial art emphasizing close-range punches and kicks developed by the Buddhist nun Ng Mui in the seventeenth century and named after her student Yim Wing Chun.

Wu style several different modern variants of T'ai Chi Ch'uan developed in the late nineteenth century from Chen- or Yang-style Tai Chi Chuan by persons surnamed Wu.

Yang Ch'eng-fu (China, 1883–1936) grandson of Yang Lu-ch'an; formalized the currently widespread Yang-style T'ai Chi Ch'uan.

Yang style a modern variant of T'ai Chi Ch'uan developed in the early nineteenth century from Chen-style T'ai Chi Ch'uan by Yang Lu-ch'an.

yin–yang symbol (Chinese) symbol of the ceaseless change that is the basic condition of the universe, drawn as a circle half black and half white, each half with a spot of the opposite color, and each color moving into the other half of the circle; also called the *t'ai chi* in Chinese, or "ultimate principle of existence."

Resources

I. INSTRUCTION, BOOKS, VIDEOTAPES, AND SERVICES AVAILABLE FROM THE WOMEN INTERVIEWED

Janet F. Aalfs is a third-degree black belt in Shuri-ryu Okinawan Karate and in Modern Arnis. She helped to found the National Women's Martial Arts Federation and has been head instructor of Valley Women's Martial Arts in Easthampton, MA, since 1982. Valley Women's Martial Arts offers beginning and ongoing classes for women in Karate, self-defense and assertiveness training, and Modern Arnis (Filipino stick fighting), as well as classes, workshops, lectures, and demonstrations for special groups on request. For information call (413) 527-0101. Janet's poetry, fiction, and essays have appeared in numerous journals and anthologies. Collections of her poems include *Of Angels and Survivors* (Two Herons Press, 1992) and *Full Open* (Orogeny Press, 1996).

Malyne Chiu is a fifth-degree black belt in Kendo and in Naginata. She practices and teaches at the San Jose State University Kendo and Naginata Club in San Jose, CA, and with the Northern California Naginata Federation under Miyako Tanaka Sensei in the East Bay. For information about Kendo classes call Rich Penny (408) 255-4196. For information about Naginata classes call Malyne Chiu (408) 281-7382 or Miyako Tanaka (510) 236-2651.

Destiny Arts Center in Oakland, CA, with Kate Hobbs, program director, offers classes in self-defense, martial arts (Kajukenbo Kung Fu and Wu Chien Pai Kung

Fu), dance, and leadership skills for children and youth ages three through eighteen, as well as self-defense and de-escalation of violence workshops for youth. **LaShonda Wilson, Emma Neumann, Dzifa Dugba,** and **Janine Bruno** assist with teaching workshops for youth and for adults teaching youth. For information call (510) 597-1619.

Michelle Dwyer has been practicing Chinese martial arts since 1974. She teaches T'ai Chi Ch'uan (Dragon Tiger Mountain Yang-Style Family Set), Northern Shaolin Kung Fu, Hsing Yi, weapons, Push Hands, and meditation at Holy Names College, Oakland, CA; Napa Valley College, Napa, CA; and Silver Cloud School, Berkeley, CA, which she founded. In 1995 she published *T'ai Chi Ch'uan: Dragon Tiger Mountain Yang Style Family Set,* with move-by-move instruction in the form she teaches. For information call (510) 526-7387.

Karina Epperlein, a filmmaker, theater artist, and teacher, has practiced T'ai Chi Ch'uan since 1982. She teaches ongoing classes in Yang-style T'ai Chi Ch'uan (Cheng Man-ch'ing's short form) in Berkeley, CA, as well as private lessons that integrate breath–sound–voice. In 1996 she completed her one-hour documentary film, *Voices from Inside,* about women in prison, which has screened at international film festivals and universities around the United States. She continues to offer her workshop "River of Breath" to colleges, prisons, drug rehabilitation facilities, and community organizations. For information about classes or the film, call (510) 559-8892.

Gayle Fillman, a fifth-degree black belt in Aikido, is chief instructor of Ukiah Aikido, the dojo she founded in 1975 in Ukiah, CA, and Willits Aikido Dojo, in Willits, CA. She teaches Aikido and numerous practical applications she sees as flowing from Aikido, including gymnastics; team and individual sports coaching; self-defense for men, women, teens, children, and victims of violence; and nonviolent intervention alternatives for safety, harmony, and productivity in the workplace. For information call (707) 462-5141.

Lloyda French, a first-degree black belt in American Goju-ryu Karate and a fourth-degree black belt in American Kenpo Karate, has been training since 1972. She cofounded Ronin Dojo in San Francisco, and now teaches privately in the San Francisco Bay Area. In 1996 she was named Martial Artist of the Year by the Pacific Association of Women Martial Artists.

Keiko Fukuda, Eighth Dan, the highest-ranked woman in Judo in the world, began studying Judo in 1934. She teaches workshops in Judo throughout the world, as well as ongoing classes at her dojo, Soko Joshi Judo Club, in San Francisco. Her book *Born for the Mat: A Kodokan Kata Textbook for Women* was published in 1973. For information call (415) 821-0303.

Jane Golden began studying T'ai Chi Ch'uan in 1974. She teaches ongoing classes in Yang-style T'ai Chi Ch'uan forms, Push Hands, weapons, and Ch'i Kung at several locations in Sonoma County, CA. She also teaches workshops and camps at locations throughout the United States and Europe. For information call (707) 874-2042.

Didi Goodman has been practicing martial arts since 1976. She is a third-degree black belt in Cuong Nhu and a first-degree black belt in Tae Kwon Do. She teaches ongoing classes in Cuong Nhu for adults and children at the school she founded in 1992, Cuong Nhu Redwood Dojo in Oakland, CA. She is also an instructor at Berkeley Cuong Nhu Karate under her teacher, sixth-degree black belt John Burns. For information call (510) 531-1428.

Coleen Gragen is a fifth-degree black belt in Kajukenbo. She is chief instructor and teaches ongoing classes and private lessons in Kajukenbo and self-defense at Hand to Hand Kajukenbo Self Defense Center, the school she founded in 1981, and at Mills College, both in Oakland, CA. For information call (510) 428-0502.

Karlon Kepcke has been studying Capoeira since 1984 and holds the teaching rank of *professora*. She trains and teaches with Capoeira Mandinga in the San Francisco Bay Area under the direction of Mestre Marcelo Pereira. For information call (510) 655-8207. She also teaches on her own in Marin County, CA. For information call (415) 488-1988.

Saskia Kleinert is a first-degree black belt in Kajukenbo and a brown belt in Jujutsu. She trains and teaches at Hand to Hand Kajukenbo Self Defense Center in Oakland, CA. She also has a practice in massage therapy and aromatherapy in Oakland. For information call (510) 653-8263.

Midge Marino is a second-degree black belt in Judo. She has been teaching self-defense for women since 1969 and currently teaches at California State University Sacramento and Loretto High School in Sacramento, CA. Through her consulting firm Trade Your Fear For Anger she teaches seminars and workshops on personal safety and rape prevention in businesses, government agencies, and other groups. For information call (916) 927-5651.

Wendy Palmer is a fourth-degree black belt in Aikido. She teaches Aikido at the dojo she co-founded in 1976, Aikido of Tamalpais in Mill Valley, CA. For information call (415) 383-9474. She also teaches classes in Conscious Embodiment, the study of boundaries and relationships,

at the dojo in Mill Valley, through the Center for Investigation and Training of Intuition in Berkeley, CA, and in workshops throughout the United States. She is director of the Prison Integrated Health Program at the Federal Correctional Institution, Dublin, where she teaches conflict resolution, stress reduction, meditation, and yoga. For information call (415) 472-1619. Her book *The Intuitive Body: Aikido as a Clairsentient Practice* (Berkeley, CA: North Atlantic Books) was published in 1994. A seventy-minute videotape by the same name is available from the same publisher.

Kathy Park is a second-degree black belt in Aikido and a sculptor, quiltmaker, and basket weaver. She reports that she is not presently training or teaching any formal Aikido, but "it infuses and informs how I see the world and how I approach my art." Her artwork may be seen at the Taos Art Association in Taos, NM, and her baskets at the Firedworks Gallery in Alamosa, CO. For information write P.O. Box 45, Jaroso, CO, 81138.

Janet Seaforth began studying T'ai Chi Ch'uan in 1976. She teaches T'ai Chi Ch'uan (Dragon Tiger Mountain Yang-Style Family Set) at the school she founded, White Cloud Women's T'ai Chi School, in Philo, CA, and at other locations in Mendocino and Sonoma counties. Her sculpture can be seen at the Handworks Gallery in Yountville and Sonoma, Two Sisters Bookshop in Menlo Park, Castro and Company in Napa, the Moonlight Framer in Ukiah, and Rookie To in Boonville, CA. For information call (707) 895-2649.

Sandy Wong began studying Wing Chun in 1974. She is a senior student at Sifu Ben Der's school, the San Jose Wing Chun Club, in San Jose, CA. For information call (408) 293-3644.

Wasentha Young has been studying T'ai Chi Ch'uan since 1969. She teaches Yang-style T'ai

Chi Ch'uan (Cheng Man-ch'ing's short form), Push Hands, and weapons at the Peaceful Dragon School of T'ai Chi Ch'uan in Ann Arbor, MI, and at workshops and retreats at different locations in the United States. For information call (313) 741-0695.

Wen Mei Yu began studying Qigong and Taijiquan in China in 1954. She was named China's top master instructor in 1983. She came to the United States in 1987 and teaches ongoing classes in Los Angeles through Jian Mei Internal Martial Arts, which she founded. She also teaches workshops throughout the United States in Qigong, Lian gong, and several styles of Taijiquan, including forms and weapons, and coaches several national and international champions in these arts. For information call (818) 563-1878. She frequently writes about Chinese martial arts in *Inside Kung Fu*. Her videotapes on Taiji sword, Taiji knife, Wu-style Taijiquan, the forty-eight-move Combined-style Taijiquan, Wild Goose Qigong, and Lian gong are available from Unique Publications Video (1-800-332-3330).

II. WOMEN'S MARTIAL ARTS ORGANIZATIONS

Feminist International Summer Training (FIST), Postbox 16696, #1001 RD Amsterdam, The Netherlands. Holds an annual training camp in the Netherlands.

National Women's Martial Arts Federation (NWMAF), c/o Dara Masi, P.O. Box 820, Kings Park, NY 11754-0820. Holds an annual three-day training camp each summer at various locations around the United States, as well as regional trainings in martial arts and women's self-defense. Newsletter published four times per year.

Pacific Association of Women Martial Artists (PAWMA), P. O. Box 12861, Berkeley, CA 94712. Holds an annual three-day training camp each summer in the western United States, as well as regional camps and demonstrations. Newsletter published four times per year.

Women's Festival of Martial Arts, 600 Harrison Avenue, Coquitiam, B.C., Canada V3J 3Z5. Holds an annual three-day training camp each spring in British Columbia.

III. BOOKS BY AND ABOUT WOMEN MARTIAL ARTISTS

Aalfs, Janet E. *Of Angels and Survivors.* Two Herons Press, 1992. Poems.

Aalfs, Janet E. *Full Open.* Orogeny Press, 1996. Poems.

Atkinson, Linda. *Women in the Martial Arts: A New Spirit Rising.* New York: Dodd, Mead, 1983. Profiles early U.S. women.

Delza, Sophia. *T'ai Chi Ch'uan: Body and Mind in Harmony.* Albany: State University of New York Press, 1985. New edition of a classic work by one of the first Westerners to study T'ai Chi Ch'uan in China.

Dobson, Terry. *It's a Lot Like Dancing: An Aikido Journey.* Berkeley, CA: Frog, Ltd.,

1993. Edited by Riki Moss. Photographs by Jan E. Watson. Text by an early U.S. Aikido practitioner set off by dramatic black and white photographs, including some of Wendy Palmer and Kathy Park.

Dwyer, Michelle. *T'ai Chi Ch'uan: Dragon Tiger Mountain Yang Style Family Set.* Albany, CA: Michelle Dwyer, 1995. Form instruction.

Emerson, Margaret. *A Potter's Notes on Tai Chi Chuan.* Ferndale, CA: Artichoke Press, 1988 (distributed by North Atlantic Books). Meditations on the intersections between practicing T'ai Chi Ch'uan and making art.

Emerson, Margaret. *Breathing Underwater: The Inner Life of T'ai Chi Ch'uan.* Berkeley, CA: North Atlantic Books, 1993. Essays about the practice and teaching of T'ai Chi Ch'uan.

Fukuda, Keiko. *Born for the Mat: A Kodokan Kata Textbook for Women.* 1973. Includes short historical and autobiographical sections, as well as Kata instruction.

Hallander, Jane. *The Complete Guide to Kung-Fu Fighting Styles.* Burbank, CA: Unique Publications, 1985.

Kuo, Simmone. *Long Life, Good Health Through Tai-Chi Chuan.* Berkeley, CA: North Atlantic Books, 1991. Instruction in a sixty-four-move T'ai Chi Ch'uan form by the widow and student of Kuo Lien-ying, an early teacher of T'ai Chi Ch'uan in the United States.

Leung, Debbie. *The Womanly Art of Self-Care, Intuition, and Choice.* Tacoma, WA: R & M Press, 1991. By a Northern Shaolin Kung Fu practitioner who has developed, taught, written about, and promoted women's self-defense since 1979.

Palmer, Wendy. *The Intuitive Body: Aikido as a Clairsentient Practice.* Berkeley, CA: North Atlantic Books, 1994. Discussion about and exercises for Conscious Embodiment training.

Rafkin, Louise. *Street Smarts: A Personal Safety Guide for Women.* San Francisco: HarperCollins, 1995. By a practitioner of the Indonesian martial art Poekoelan Tjiminde Tulen, who has taught women's self-defense since 1989.

Rafkin, Louise. *The Tiger's Eye, the Bird's Fist: A Beginner's Guide to Martial Arts.* Little, Brown, 1997. An overview of martial arts.

Siegel, Andrea. *Women in Aikido.* Photographs by Jan E. Watson. Berkeley, CA: North Atlantic Books, 1993. A collection of interviews, including one with Kathy Park.

Stone, John, and Ron Meyer. *Aikido in America.* Berkeley, CA: North Atlantic Books, 1995. Interviews with longtime U.S. Aikido practitioners and teachers, including Wendy Palmer.

Wiley, Carol A., ed. *Martial Arts Teachers on Teaching.* Berkeley, CA: North Atlantic Books, 1995. A collection of essays, including pieces by Janet E. Aalfs, Michelle Dwyer, Didi Goodman, and Kate Hobbs.

Wiley, Carol A., ed. *Women in the Martial Arts.* Berkeley, CA: North Atlantic Books, 1992. A collection of essays, including pieces by Janet E. Aalfs, Michelle Dwyer, and Wendy Palmer.